Jewish Times

Jewish Times

Voices of the American Jewish Experience

Howard Simons

ANCHOR BOOKS
DOUBLEDAY
NEW YORK LONDON TORONTO SYDNEY AUCKLAND

An Anchor Book

PUBLISHED BY DOUBLEDAY

a division of Bantam Doubleday Dell Publishing Group, Inc.
666 Fifth Avenue, New York, New York 10103

Anchor Books, Doubleday, and the portrayal of an anchor
are trademarks of Doubleday, a division of Bantam Doubleday
Dell Publishing Group, Inc.

Jewish Times was originally published in hardcover by Houghton
Mifflin in 1988. The Anchor Books edition is
published by arrangement with Houghton Mifflin.

Library of Congress Cataloging-in-Publication Data

Simons, Howard.
Jewish times: voices of the American
Jewish experience/Howard Simons—
1st Anchor Books ed.
p. cm.
1. Jews—United States—Interviews.
2. United States—Ethnic
relations   I. Title.
[E184.J5S544   1990]   89-18186
973'.04924—dc20   CIP

ISBN 0-385-26697-9

To all those who came and those still to come

Author's Note

This is a book of memory with all the flaws that wonderful instrument can play upon its possessor. Some memories are possibly inaccurate because the memories are inaccurate. But the remembrance is real. And the telling is real.

Contents

Jewish Times

I

In the Beginning

MY PATERNAL GRANDFATHER, in whose brownstone I lived my formative years, came to the United States from Ciechanów, Poland, at the turn of the twentieth century, a poor, untutored cobbler who spoke no English on his arrival and subsequently learned but little. None of his children went to college, but all five of his grandchildren did. When I was young, this to me was the essence of the Jewish experience in the United States, a unique experience, perhaps as extraordinary an experience as the Jewish people have enjoyed in their long, rich, and burdened history. Only when I was older did I come to realize that for many Jews the hop from somewhere else to the United States would land them in college in a single generational jump and not, as with me, in two. Recently, I began to collect information about America's Jews — anecdotes, impressions, anthropological shards, what a colleague remembered about his or her family. Nothing formal, never organized, certainly not planned or systematic. Just scraps stuffed in the crannies of the mind. I wondered how I could distill the essence of all this information. I did not want to write a formal history; that had been done more than once. In its place I decided to collect bubbe mayses, grandmothers' tales. I would tape-record a wide sample of American Jews, asking each in turn to recall and to recount his or her personal and family history.

I set out to trap memory, however imperfect, in electronic amber. Over a four-year period, I carried my tape recorder across the United States, targeting some places, falling into others. I called on friends — Jews and non-Jews — asking for help, setting forth the kinds of people I was looking for who would consent to be interviewed and share their memories with me for publication. In some cases I knew what I was after — pre–Revolutionary War families, German Jews, merchants, kosher innkeepers, persons raised on the Lower East Side of New York City. In other cases, friends old and new led me to people and places that had been strange to me but turned out to be rich in Jewish heritage.

I was overwhelmed by the generosity with which people, mostly strangers, opened their doors and memories to me. Altogether, I interviewed 227 people — young and old, rich and poor, educated and uneducated — from Maine to California and Alaska to Florida. As a general rule, I interviewed only those Jews who still identify themselves as Jews. Two notable exceptions are William Cohen, Republican senator from Maine, and Barry Goldwater, former Republican senator from Arizona.

Soon after starting, I found my list of potential interviewees was considerably altered as friends and relatives would say, "You must interview my . . ." or "Did you know that . . . ?" In the end, I selected certain people from the growing list because they promised to be especially interesting about particular aspects of my search or their stories seemed compelling. In each case, I would explain to the interviewee what I was trying to do, that whatever he or she said was for publication, that I might use all of it, some of it, or none of it, and that I would edit the transcript. Very few of those I approached, perhaps a handful, turned me down. If someone balked, I immediately withdrew the request for an interview.

The burden of my quest was to re-create aspects of the Jewish experience in the United States. I wanted to tell a story, to make some narrative sense out of it all. And I wanted to use other people's words and memories and views.

From the very first, Jewish immigrants have availed themselves of every opportunity of this ample democracy. They plowed its land; fought its enemies; governed its communities; saved its monuments; made its discoveries; ministered to it when it was ill; fought prejudice; spurred its labor movement; wrote its literature and drama and comedy; ventured capital and brainpower; and, above all, spread ubiquitously, like dandelion feathers traveling on the wind of freedom, to the next community or the next opportunity to take root and dwell and become involved.

I grew up in a heavily Italian Catholic neighborhood, liberally sprinkled with Irish Catholics; indeed, it was in the shadow of the Cathedral of the Immaculate Conception in Albany, New York. Most but not all of my friends were Jewish. I was a member of a Jewish Boy Scout troop; went to Hebrew school; attended Jewish day and summer camps; belonged to a Jewish high school fraternity; and spent hours at the Jewish Community Center, the common meeting ground for the Jews who had made it, the "uptowners," and those who hadn't, the "downtowners"; and roamed the shabby South End, where were located the Jewish stores and shuls and the city's core population of poor Jews.

My father was born in Poland and came to the United States at about age ten with his father. He never went beyond high school. He lost a clothing store to bankruptcy in the Depression, was out of work for a few years, and then became a workaday agent for a large insurance company until his retirement. When the family business failed, my mother went to work as a saleslady in a children's store. Later, she worked for city, county and state governments until, unhappily, she was forced to retire at about the age of seventy-five.

It was my mother who introduced me to bubbe mayses. She was born on Henry Street on the Lower East Side, but exactly when we are uncertain; New York City never could locate her birth certificate.

She spoke ungrammatical English. Her Yiddish was benignly profane, usually directed at uncaring merchants. She was warm and gregarious and had a natural wit. One of my favorite mother stories is one that Bob Levine, family friend and one of Albany's undertakers, tells about her. When she was in her seventies and widowed, she would leave her house once or twice a week and trek downtown to tend to her affairs. She would stand on a corner of New Scotland Avenue and wait for the bus. Bob once drove by, stopped, rolled down his window, and offered my mother a ride. "I'm not ready for you," she said, and declined his offer.

Because of my mother's example, I grew up thinking all Jews were funny. Jewish humor, to me, has always been a given. Even miserable Jews could find humor in misery. Daniel Bell, the eminent Harvard scholar, longs to write a scholarly study of Jewish humor and has the skeleton of an elaborate, intellectual approach about how it has evolved and been shaped. My own view is derived from my mother's cooking, and she was not a good cook. When she made cabbage borsht, she would throw in a handful of brown sugar to sweeten the soup and then several crystals of citric acid to sour it. This act came to symbolize for me the sweet and sour of Jewish life and, derivatively, the sweet and sour that is the rich flavor of Jewish humor.

Although even their years in America were sweet and sour, for many Jewish immigrants they were anything but grim. Certainly there was discrimination, sometimes manifested as pure hate; and there were opportunities denied because of religion; and there were hardships. But on balance America has been, as advertised, a land of opportunity. Nonetheless, many have chosen to abandon their identification; have elected, instead, "to pass." And pass they have. By my crude and unscientific sampling, I calculate that the Jewish population of the United States — if measured by the original religion of the immigrant ancestor — would easily be twice, perhaps three times, the population of the roughly five million and a half who identify themselves as Jews today. Because they could not find Jews to marry, some married non-Jews and converted to the religion of the spouse. Others wanted to run from Judaism. They were tired of anti-Semitism, wary of rejection, hungering for acceptance. They changed their names; they converted; some even fooled their families.

There are other closet hints. More than once, interviewees in small communities, especially in the South and Midwest, told me that after the Six Day War, when Israel scored its most celebrated victory over the Arabs, people not hitherto identified as Jews in the community would approach Jewish leaders and offer congratulations and money for Israel. They also offered the sometimes startling information that a grandparent or great-grandparent had been Jewish.

It was not just a matter of assimilation. Rather, it seems that a goodly number of East European Jews wanted to be, in effect, German Jews — prominent, well-to-do, accepted and acceptable, and members of a Reform congregation. And many German Jews wanted to be Christians — with services on Sunday, music, choirs, flowers, reverends rather than rabbis. They wanted total acceptance in Christian society, at their schools, in their service organizations, at their balls and parties, and above all at their clubs.

While the struggle for acceptance was going on — and continues to this day — others were desperately trying to maintain their Jewishness in an alien environment. Some did it by keeping kosher, sometimes in remote regions where it might have been thought impossible. Jerry Green, a furrier in Anchorage, Alaska, whose father and aunt and uncle were pioneers in that distant land shortly after World War I, recounted:

"My father met Archie Zoper and Archie's wife, Aunt Annie, in Cordova. She was very religious, very scrupulous in her kashrut, you might say, probably to the point where it would be a little burdensome to Archie, although Archie toed the line.

"Archie and Aunt Annie," Jerry Green said, "shipped in their meat by Alaska Steamship, which was the shipping line in those days. From Seattle, I would say. Fish, of course, was in abundance. She would not eat anything except kosher meat. I know that for a fact."

This story is repeated and repeated, even today in small communities, where the kosher butcher is an extinct species of merchant; Jews wait for the delivery of kosher meats from afar.

Finally, again mostly in the small towns of America, Jews organized weekly, monthly and yearly visits or affairs, tying one family or a few Jewish families in a small town to Jewish families in other small towns in the surrounding geography.

Harry Popkin remembered: "In the South, in every little community around, there were two or three Jewish families. A Mr. Meyer Saul 'owned' a little town called Canoe, Georgia, and once a year he invited all the Jews within a radius of about fifty miles to come to his place for a barbecue. He never barbecued pig. He barbecued chicken and goats but never a pig. As a kid I remember running around — there may have been a hundred people there, because he would invite everybody that he could, to come for this annual barbecue at Canoe, Georgia.

"Not only would you get to know other Jewish kids," Popkin said, "but the Jewish families made their own Jewish life, because there wasn't enough in any one town — one or two families. They would gather at somebody's home on a Sunday. The men would play poker. They would play pinochle. The women would do other things. But they would always meet at somebody else's house on a regular sort of schedule, maybe once a month or once every two or three weeks, to keep the social contact among all the Jewish families in south Georgia. They were very close. They all had dry goods stores. They all had businesses. They all did things similar, but they were not in competition, because they were maybe fifteen, twenty, thirty, fifty miles apart, but they made sure that they kept that contact."

In the larger cities of the Northeast and Midwest, there was less need to etch an identity. Jews knew they were Jewish. They were surrounded by other Jews and shuls and culture and Yiddish. There was critical Jewish mass.

Anti-Semitism had a lot to do with people's running away from Judaism or with their clinging to it. Not everyone says he or she experienced anti-Semitism. Indeed, it seems that there was far more of it in the northern and midwestern cities than in southern and western communities. Of those interviewed, almost all the former ghetto youngsters from the North talked about fighting their way to and from school or playground as they traveled through predominantly Catholic neighborhoods. Not so in the South.

"First of all," said Jack Bass, who grew up in a tiny South Carolina town with the unlikely name of North, "it's important to understand the South was always very, very open to the Jews for several reasons, and a large part of that was because in the South Jews were white. The blacks became the scapegoats for everything, and the outcasts. Jews weren't cast into that role, so they weren't viewed so much as outsiders, but as someone who was different. Because of the Old Testament religious orientation of many of the Protestant evangelicals in the South, the concept of the Chosen People was still very much alive."

If some Jews escaped anti-Semitism, others felt its lash and were forever scarred by it. I was startled to discover that people in their seventies and eighties could recall the day, time, place, and most often the full name of the anti-Semite who first assaulted them. More often than not, it was another child. When I asked Jack Cohen of New Haven, Connecticut, "Any anti-Semitism?" he replied, "I never came across it. As a matter of fact, I think it was reversed. The Jews didn't think that the Italians came up to snuff and certainly not the blacks." His wife, Mildred, had a different story to tell:

"We lived in a three-family house at one time, and there was a family that lived over us. We were on the middle floor. It was a lovely Gentile family that lived on the first floor. And a couple and a small boy that lived on the third floor. They would mutter under their breath, as they went by, 'Jew.' I never had that kind of confrontation before. Our method of dealing with it was to ignore it and pretend it wasn't there. But I remember being scared all the time and feeling insignificant because people could do that to me and make me feel small. And it never happened otherwise. I went to school with Gentiles, almost entirely. Never ran into that. Had good friends. Played with kids all in the neighborhood. My brothers did, too. But that was just a sick family. So that was pretty direct, and I still feel the squirm."

Many Jewish immigrants and ghetto dwellers, victimized by non-Jews in Europe and in the urban slums of the New World, were as bitterly anti-Christian as some Christians were bitterly anti-Semitic. Ironically, often the Jew, who showed his contempt for the Christian with a derisive phrase like "goyisha kop" — literally "Christian head" and loosely "empty head" — was oblivious of his own intolerance.

I think today anti-Semitism is far less virulent than it was before World War II; nonetheless, anti-Semitism in the United States remains a latent virus ready to be activated if the right stimuli are introduced.

Diminishing, too, is the feeling of being "different," expressed by many of the people I interviewed. No matter how comfortable Jews were, how accepted and secure, how much "at home" in America, most still felt different. It gnawed at them not necessarily in a grating, negative sense, but rather like a sporadic itch or annoying tic that is neither life-threatening nor serious, yet is an irritant, a reminder. Lorine Friedman Hertz, eighty-nine, grew up in Point Pleasant, West Virginia, on the Ohio River, a member of what was then the only Jewish family in town. She recalls that on Yom Kippur she and her siblings were embarrassed to stay out of school, thereby signifying that they were different. "We never wanted to be different. We wanted to be great Americans from the beginning. Now I remember, in fact, when my brother was born, the people poured in to see him because they had never seen a Jewish baby. Fortunately, he was a very handsome baby."

Whether this feeling of "differentness" results from Jews in the United States living in a predominantly Christian world and being made to feel different, whether their feeling different is imagined, whether they are different, or whether all of the above are true, I do not know. But I do know from my interviews that the one distinguishing aspect of being Jewish is this sense, this feeling, this notion, of being different.

This book is not meant to be scholarly. It is not meant to be comprehensive. It is not meant even to be representative. It is about one person's fascination with one person's experience in one extraordinary country.

The interviews that follow, with my comments, have been culled from all the interviews I conducted, sometimes because they make a particular point, sometimes because they are inherently interesting, sometimes because they express a series of folkloric memories a tad better than interviews with others. The richness of the Jewish experience is so deep, I easily could have interviewed 227 different people and achieved a similar end.

What follows are not verbatim texts. The words are the words of the people interviewed. Verbatim texts are, for the most part, incomprehensible and therefore unreadable. Few among us are such natural storytellers that we speak in fluid narrative. More among us speak in stick shift, going from first to second to neutral, back to first, and then to third. People, most especially those unused to public speaking, often begin a sentence and then do not finish, or begin a thought and interrupt themselves with an unrelated thought, or change thought direction altogether and go off on another rich reminiscence, leaving the previous memory dangling, half told. Often, I saved until the end questions about something said early in an interview so as not to break in on the speaker's memory track. Finally, I learned that many people have verbal signatures, words and phrases that repeat and repeat and repeat during a long narrative, such as "well . . ." "of course . . ." and "you know." Accordingly, I have transposed sentences and paragraphs and edited for continuity, comprehensibility, and readability. Nor does the length of each text reflect the length of the interview; instead, it represents my sense of the need to illustrate or to complement a point, to show more than one view, to make an episodic experience whole. Finally, the age given for each person was his or her age at the time of the interview.

I came away from this experiential journey more, not less, convinced that the Jewish experience in the United States is indeed unique. Unique in the sense that, more than any other immigrant group, Jews have found their way into almost every interstice of American life, have taken just about every opportunity this nation has to offer, and have given back to America in enriching ways that are wondrous. I think the Jewish immigrants, from the very beginning of their time and America's time, have come closer to realizing the American Dream than have any other group. The Jewish premium on family and religion, hard work and education, charity and public service, *is* the American Dream.

How Jews did it and why they did it is their story.

Women and Children First

THE JEWISH MOTHER is a universal symbol — a metaphor for how Jewishness is perceived. She is the mistress of the put-down, extraordinarily deft at ego deflation and just as deft at ego inflation, and often she, not the father, is the aggressive parent. Many times during my interviews, men and women would say, "My mother ran the family." Often, too, the Jewish mother is very funny, very giving, possessive, protective, smothering, and loving. In America, the Jewish woman found liberation, sometimes for herself, but mostly for her children. She worked extremely hard and made inordinate sacrifices for her sons and daughters. The newspaper publisher David Kraslow said about his immigrant mother, who lived in poverty all during her years in America, "Her only desire in life was that her children be educated and have religious freedom, because religious freedom is what she cherished above everything else."

"Jewish women in the United States have always worked outside the home," as wage earners, volunteers in service organizations, or both, said Gladys Rosen, a wife and mother who earned her Ph.D. at Columbia University in 1948. "Jewish women were also in the forefront of the feminist movement, because Jewish women were the most highly educated," she noted. "One of my young colleagues said to me, 'Wasn't it unusual in your time for women to go to college?' I told her I didn't know anyone who didn't go to college. College was taken for granted."

Lawrence Spivak, eighty-five, journalist, Washington, D.C.

My mother, who was very sensitive about her age, kept dropping three or four years with each census, so in the end she was almost my age.

I have to tell you an amusing story about it. She was at a winter resort, and on Sunday, of course, nothing could take her away from "Meet the Press." She was with some woman she had picked up there; my mother was a widow. They're watching "Meet the Press," and when I come on, the woman says, "Didn't you tell me your son was a grandfather and he had four grandchildren? He looks so young on the air, or is it makeup?" My mother says, "No, it isn't makeup. He is young." She asks, "How old is he?" My mother says, "I really don't know." So the woman says, "Aren't you his real mother?" My mother says, "Of course I'm his real mother, but that's one question I never asked him and he never told me."

Fred Schwartz, fifty-five, furrier, New York, New York

My mother is quintessentially a Jewish mother. I was honored last year to be given the Anatoly Scharansky Award by the Long Island Committee for Soviet Jews; there was a big dinner — about a thousand people. I knew I had to tell my mother about this, because she had to get a dress. But I didn't know quite how to tell her, because I didn't know what her response was going to be. I said to her, "We have to go to a dinner, and you'll have to get a dress." She said, "What's the dinner about?" I said, "I'm going to be an honoree, with Senator D'Amato," and she listened to me and listened to me and then she said, "Why you?"

I'll tell you another story about my mother. I was wearing contact lenses. She said to me, "You look very different." So I said, "I'm not wearing my glasses; I'm wearing lenses." She looked at me and she said, "You know, not every feature has to be seen."

Shirley Povich, seventy-eight, sportswriter, Washington, D.C.

My mother told how she was welcomed in Bar Harbor, Maine, by one of the patriarchs of the town who came to call on them early. His name was Mr. Stafford, a typical Yankee English name. He introduced himself to her and said, "Well, Mrs. Povich, we have customs in Bar Harbor . . . and that sort of thing. Here is what we expect from all of our people." And she said in her broken English, "Have a chair, Mr. Stafford." And he began to say what an important man he was in town, and she said, "Well, Mr. Stafford, have two chairs."

Sarah Fox, eighty-two, great-grandmother, Charleston, South Carolina

In 1916, Germany sent out messages that the mothers and young children who had tickets were permitted to leave. We went by way of Berlin by train to Rotterdam, where the boats were ready to pack the human beings like cattle. We had passage on first class, but we were down in the bottom of the boat near the kitchen, where the rats were bigger than we were. There was plenty to eat there, but we couldn't eat, we were so sick from going from one country's waters to another. They had thousands of people shoved in like animals, and the whole time we were there we did not eat.

The trip took us thirty days to New York, to Ellis Island. We sent a telegram to my dad and two sisters at the old address in America and we waited and waited and no one showed that evening. That was May 8, 1916. Ellis Island was frightening. They took us to an area where the beds were made of chains. We didn't have any blankets or anything. And we had to spend the night there. We said to one another, "This is the end. If our father and sisters don't come to claim us, we will just jump into the ocean. We'll never go back to Poland or anywheres." But the HIAS [Hebrew Immigrant Aid Society] came along with blankets and everything we needed to make us as comfortable as possible. They brought — I'll never forget — they brought sardines and rye bread. I don't remember what we drank, but we devoured it. We were famished.

We had a doctor take us apart from head to toe. Unfortunately, I got a sty on my eye after we left the ship and we thought that would cause us to be returned back home, because none of us had ever had a sty. They were very careful examining eyes, more so than any other part of your body. We were shaking like I don't know what, so afraid that this would cause it. The doctor looked at my eyes and ignored the sty and that's when we realized that it wasn't anything to be concerned about. They checked you from head to toe. And we were deloused. They completely disrobed us and put us into a room with some kind of a formula they used and sprayed us from head to toe. That was the way they deloused us, and that was another torture chamber.

We didn't have time enough to really get acquainted with anybody much for the simple reason they were all in a room and everybody wanted a bed to sit on or lie in, whatever we did at the time. We were exhausted from the trip.

Five o'clock in the morning, the next morning, we hear our name called. I don't know what language they used. I can only hear the name, the sound of the name in my ears. We should come to the auditorium, there is someone there to see us. We had no idea who. We went over to the auditorium, which was nothing but glass. We looked out and there stood our dad and my sisters. They were looking for my mother. The children, in spite of not having to eat, we still grew. Mama shrank. She was behind us, like a mother hen watching over her chickies. I saw my sister's mouth form "Mama." I moved away to show her that Mama was there. Well, they had gotten our telegram that night, but could not come for us. When we got out of Ellis Island, all of us got down on the ground and kissed it, thanking God that we made it. They took us to an apartment that was already furnished and that was home. The address is 540 Fox Street in the Bronx and that was on my birthday, May 9, 1916.

Julius Lucius Echeles, seventy-one, lawyer, Chicago, Illinois

I practice exclusively in the criminal law, appeals and postconviction matters, such as habeas corpus, et cetera.

Both my parents were born in a small shtetl in Russia somewhere near the Polish border, because they spoke Russian and Polish in the house, and Yiddish, of course. When they didn't want me to understand what they were saying, they went into Russian or Polish. Foolishly I grew up in this wonderful household but didn't learn Russian or Polish. I was teaching them to speak English and I was Americanizing them, and they should have Russianized and Polishized me. When they came, there were ten or eleven children. I was the only one born in the United States. I was born in Chicago, the last born to my mother and father. I think seventeen or eighteen children were born, all told. My birth certificate indicated that there were six who died and twelve alive at the time of my birth. Mother was about thirty-eight years old when she gave birth to me, and my father was in his forties.

My father came first, in about 1913, with my oldest brother, Louie. My father was a blacksmith, as was his father before him and his grandfather before him. So I come from a long line of itinerant blacksmiths. As he explained to me, he could take his trade all over the world and always make a living, because a horse is a horse and a shoe is a shoe. He was lucky in that respect. He can't remember when he was not in a blacksmith shop. He was an apprentice to his father, who was an apprentice to his father. He started in a blacksmith shop at age four or five or six.

My mother was a dinst, a housemaid in the town or in the shtetl. She was an orphan. Her mother and father were killed by Cossacks, I was told, as a result of some raid or burning of an inn which her father operated.

My mother was very bright and a thrillingly intellectual woman, although unschooled. She could not read and could not write, although much later in life I taught her to read a little, write a little. She always had philosophical tales and little stories that she must have remembered either from rabbinical tales or from an itinerant storyteller who I remember she said made the rounds of little villages. There was an active group of individuals who traveled from state to state just telling stories, not troubadours entertaining with violins. These storytellers were put up by various members of the little shtetl, given food and board, and then went on to another place. Maybe they collected a few rubles; I don't recall that. She remembered an awful lot of stories, one of which I use fairly successfully in trials.

It is the most appropriate exhibition of the concept of justice that I have ever read about or heard about. I remember being told it in Yiddish when I was going to be punished for some minor peccadillo. After the punishment — I was fifteen at the time — she told me the story of the rich man in the shtetl going to the rabbi to complain about a theft by the poor man. The richest man in town had three children who were thin and scrawny, even though they ate the food prepared by the rich man's cook. The poor man's three children, who were robust and husky and healthy, were standing outside the rich man's kitchen and absorbing the aroma that was flowing from the kitchen. As a consequence, the rich man concluded that they were really stealing the vital part of the food. So he went to the rabbi to complain that the poor man should be arrested and punished.

The rabbi brought in the poor man — the rabbi in a shtetl, of course, was not only the rabbi and teacher but the arbiter of disputes between members of the Jewish community. The rabbi asked the poor man, "Your children stand outside the window and smell, taka?"

"We are poor and we have no money. That's all we do. We don't touch the food. We don't steal the food. But they do smell under the window. It's the only pleasure they have."

"But your children," the rabbi said, "look at them. They are healthy; they are full-bodied. Look at the children of the rich man. I think the rich man is right, so we're going to have a trial."

The townsfolk gathered, and the rich man made the complaint that I've described: the poor man's children were outside the window stealing the aromas, breathing the flavors, stealing whatever came out of the window, the smells, and therefore they were really stealing the essence of the food. The best example was the three fat children of the poor man and the three scrawny children of the rich man.

"What do you have to say to the rabbi?"

"They go there, but they don't steal, taka."

"Mr. Rich Man, you are right," said the rabbi. "He has stolen the essence of the food. What punishment do you suggest I give them?" So the rich man, whose only concept of value in life was money, said, "Well, I don't want you to whip them or beat them or hit them, but the only way I can be satisfied is with money. They should pay me a hundred rubles." The poor man said, "I haven't got two rubles to rub together. How can I give him what he wants?" "Never mind," said the rabbi. The rabbi pulled out of his pocket some coins, put them in a bag, and made a collection amongst the community of Jews who were watching the trial. Soon he had the hundred rubles that the rich man wanted. So the rabbi said to the rich man, "Come closer." He held the bag of coins to the rich man's ear, shook the bag, shook the rubles, shook the coins in his ear, and said, "Did you hear the coins? Yes? So now you've been paid. You heard the money, and they smelled the food. That's justice."

She told it much better than I. It is a lovely story, and I frequently have had occasion to use it to show that the punishment should fit the crime. She told me many, many other stories and they always had a philosophical punchline.

My father was taciturn, quiet. He was short, pudgy around the middle, wore a huge belt, and was a blacksmith until the late 1930s, beginning 1940s. His blacksmith shop was on the West Side of Chicago. My father brought home quarters and half dollars; rarely did I see a dollar bill. Quarters and half dollars were what the peddlers paid him. Peddlers were also from the area where he came from. They peddled old rags, newspapers; some were produce peddlers; but they all had their horses shod at my father's shop.

I remember him shoeing horses. In his last years, he moved to a truck-body-building shop.

My remembrance was that seven or eight of the children lived together. Not only that, but when my oldest brother married and when my older sisters married, they didn't move out. Their spouses moved in. I never had a bed or a bedroom until shortly before my Bar Mitzvah, in 1928. I slept on an army cot. I call myself an itinerant sleeper. I was first put on a couch in the living room, but as people came in to socialize — because the house was not only a house where people were fed, but where there was a ferment of socialist talk, because my brother-in-law and older sister, who worked in the garment factories, became early organizers in the labor movement. They were all active, and socialists all. It was a hotbed of socialist discussion, especially in the 1920s and the 1930s, because all my brothers and sisters, except my older brother Louie the bootlegger, worked in the sweatshops on Van Buren Street, making dresses and clothes. Going back to itinerant sleeping: my final place of sleep was the kitchen, so I had to wait until everybody was out of it. As I explained, our house was the social center of the community. The kitchen was the social center of the house. So I'd start to sleep in one bedroom at maybe nine or ten P.M., move to the living room or somebody else's bedroom, and frequently I never got to my cot until the kitchen was empty, sometimes eleven or twelve or sometimes beyond.

My mother kept as best she could a kosher house. Of course, at Pesach there were separate sets of dishes. There was always the separation of meat dishes from dairy dishes. Always on Friday, she would bench licht, bless the candles; the lace tablecloth was spread; chicken. My mother started preparing for the Shabbes on Thursday. On her knees she'd scrub the floor. Couldn't come in Friday from school; I had to stay out of the house because the stairs going up to the second floor were kept clean.

Few brothers or sisters moved out, wives and husbands moved in, sisters-in-law and brothers-in-law moved in. Brothers-in-law who would visit before they were married and partake of my mother's cooking, they wouldn't leave. No daughter could cook like my mother.

My first remembrances of my mother are of her as a cook, and she would just cook, cook, cook, all day long. Everybody around came to eat. I don't know what the financial arrangements were, if any, but I also remember my mother selling half pints of whiskey. Where she got them from I don't know, but she would sell them to the janitors in the neighborhood, during Prohibition, of course. My brother Louie was a bootlegger, and he had his equipment not far from my father's blacksmith shop, about half a block away. One experience I had in a place called Davey Barry's in Chicago on Roosevelt near Kedzie. Davey Barry was the referee in the famous Tunney-Dempsey long count. He was Jewish, and he was the referee. He owned a restaurant. It was sort of a gathering center for sports people. Damon Runyon characters amongst the Jews would go there. It was in the center of Jewish territory. In back of the restaurant — the restaurant was legitimate — there were poker games going on, some dice. As I recall, they didn't have a bookie as such, but there were dice games and poker games. I was a kid then. This is 1929, 1930. I came from school, visited my father's blacksmith shop, visited my brother's little bootlegging enterprise, watching the liquids flow from one coil into another coil, watched how the browning took place, how the sugar was put in, and how it was all bottled. There were two or three people working, and off went my brother, distributing little bottles of liquor.

I was accepted at Barry's. I was Louie's brother and the son of the blacksmith. My father was a figure. There were quite a number of Jewish blacksmiths in the 1920s, but not in that immediate area. I sometimes went in the back part of the restaurant. "Hey, kid, get me a bottle of Coke," or "Hey, kid, bring me a sandwich." They had waiters to do that, but I was a kid, so I would deliver a soft drink. Chocolate phosphate was the big thing then, two cents or three cents. I think it gave all the Jews dyspepsia and other gastronomical difficulties.

One day in the spring of 1930 it was just like the scene in one of Ernest Hemingway's short stories that I later read, called "The Killers." Three men came in, unmasked, quiet. There was a card game going on, poker. As soon as they came in — it was early evening about four-thirty — everybody in the poker game stood up, and one man remained at the table petrified, absolutely petrified, as though he were glued. One man went up to him and shot him twice in the head; the others stood guard. All three walked out the back way, quietly, and the others, seven or eight in the room, some playing, some standing, were immobilized, absolutely immobilized. I was in terror. I was in fear. And somebody finally said, "Kid, get the hell out of here the back way." I ran to my father and told him what had happened. He said, "Schvayg!" meaning you didn't see and you didn't hear and go home. And home the hell I went.

Cecil A. Alexander, sixty-eight, architect, Atlanta, Georgia

I was about fifteen before I discovered everybody had ancestors. I was brought up thinking only the Alexanders had ancestors.

If "distinguished" means coming over early, I guess my family's distinguished. The first man that I know about, at least on the Alexander side, was Abraham Alexander, Sr. He came to Charleston, I believe, in the 1750s. I don't know a great deal about him. I know he was a reader in the Sephardic congregation there, and I have his handwritten prayer book. I'm debating about putting it where it can be better protected. My son has said, "Okay, but I want it when I get married." He wants it for the ceremony, and it was just used when my second daughter got married a couple of weeks ago.

Abraham Alexander, Sr., came over without his wife, and there's no record of his first wife. He married a woman here who was not Jewish, but she converted and became very much of a Jew. As far as I know they had no children, so the family line would come down through his son Abraham Alexander, Jr., who followed him to this country. I have a copy of his naturalization papers, and I believe they were about 1796.

Abraham Alexander's war record intrigues me, because he started out fighting with the Revolutionary forces, and then when the British took Charleston he apparently made his peace with them and then later went back and fought them again with Francis Marion, the Swamp Fox. In the synagogue in Charleston is a mural done by Halsey, who's a native artist there related to Admiral Halsey, and it shows Abraham on horseback — a very stylized and glorified image of the man.

Did anybody fight in 1812? A midshipman named Phillips who was on the *Constellation*. He was drowned. I think the launch he was in was sunk and he couldn't swim. But that's the only record I know of anybody in my ancestry who was in the navy around that time.

Aaron, who was Abraham Jr.'s son, I believe came from Athens, Georgia, to Atlanta in 1848. He bought a piece of property which is now right in the heart of Atlanta. It was a hundred feet on Peachtree Street and went back four hundred feet to the street behind it, and he paid $150 for it. His son or grandson sold it in 1913 or 1914 for $75,000, which to me is more amazing than the original price, because at the time that Aaron bought it, Atlanta was maybe twelve or fifteen thousand people, if that. Atlanta even during the Civil War was only twenty-five thousand people.

My grandfather, Julius M. Alexander, was seventeen or eighteen years old when he was a top sergeant in the Confederate Army. He was fighting around Savannah, and one of the stories, which I don't think is apocryphal, was that the trenches were very close together and that on a dare, or whatever, this kid jumps up on the Confederate trenches and waves a Confederate flag. The Federals just held fire and let him do it, and he got back down. If they had been a little more aggressive, I wouldn't be here. He died just before I was born.

Let me talk about my uncle for a few minutes, because he's a very interesting man. My uncle was a lawyer and he went to the University of Georgia and then got his law degree at the University of Virginia. He came back to Atlanta. He was, I think, at the time probably the first and only Jewish member of the Georgia legislature. He only lasted one term, because he was a man who said what he thought and acted on it. If it was politically good, fine; if it wasn't, the hell with it. In the early days in Atlanta, apparently the Jewish and the Christian communities commingled socially and so on. He went out with "society women." But he got mixed up in the Leo Frank case, and he was one of Leo Frank's lawyers and appealed the case to the Supreme Court.

He was convinced that Frank was innocent and based a lot on the note that was left. The handwriting experts said that it was not Frank's handwriting. Of course, Frank's being lynched was a bitter experience. It had a real effect on all the Jews of Atlanta, and on my family very much so. A lynch mob headed out to the Governor's Mansion. Governor Slaton had commuted Frank's sentence just before he went out of office. My uncle went out there to be with the governor. This was before I was born. I heard it so often as I grew up, I feel as if I remember it. This mob started in downtown Atlanta, and the Governor's Mansion was out in Buckhead, which is now very much in Atlanta but was then a little sort of isolated town. We lived on Forrest Avenue, which was named for Nathan Bedford Forrest, who was prominent in the founding of the Klan. My mother heard this mob a block away, yelling for Slaton and Alexander. She liked my uncle, but my uncle and my father looked something alike, and she was really worried they were going to get my father accidentally.

Well, the mob got there and the governor called out the guards and had them surround the house. This real tough Scotsman was the commander, and he said to the mob, "I know you guys," and he called the leaders by name. I'm sure he used some pretty rough language, and his men had rifles and were ready to fire. He said, "If you take one more step forward, these men are ordered to fire and I don't care who the hell you are." They dispersed. My uncle was there with the governor during this business, and it really had a profound effect, or something did, because he became very absorbed and interested in Jewish matters at that point.

You know, with the name Alexander and this pug nose, which was attributed in part to boxing, I used to get exposed to what I've always called "locker room anti-Semitism." I really had a chip on my shoulder about it. I never let it pass. The only real anti-Semitism that I recall was when I was in high school. I was asked to join fraternities until they found out I was Jewish, and then I was dropped. I remember one case in particular, where the son of a friend of my father's was in a fraternity and this man went with us to a meeting. I got blackballed because I was Jewish. I was conscious of it. I was conscious of being different, but I was raised at a time when our rabbi in Atlanta was number one, an American, and number two, Jewish. The religion was a religion, and he didn't believe we were an ethnic group or people. We just were Americans who practiced the Jewish religion, and he was very, very much into the community and very highly regarded and respected. So I sort of grew up in the Reform temple with that attitude. But to say that I wasn't conscious of it, that I wasn't brought up on the Frank case, would be wrong. I knew I was different from my Christian friends.

More Than Frank

LEO FRANK was lynched in Georgia in 1915, a victim of the anti-Semitism that has dogged and stalked and murdered Jews throughout the world for thousands of years. His brutal death spooked the Jews of Georgia and far beyond. Many families fled Atlanta, some never to return. Others sent their children away. All were afraid that they, too, would be felled by the same recurring hate virus. Southern cossacks had chopped down a man most Jews knew to be innocent. Ironically, the Frank case gave rise at the same time to the Anti-Defamation League of B'nai B'rith, the Jewish fraternal organization, and to a resurgence of the moribund Ku Klux Klan. It took decades to exonerate Frank; clearing his name became the pursuit of young Jews who continued to trip over Frank's shadow. Meanwhile, the Klan, albeit much diminished in numbers and power, continues to taunt and threaten Jews and other minorities, and the ADL, for its part, continues to monitor the activities of the Klan and other hate groups.

Dale Marvin Schwartz, forty-two, lawyer, Atlanta, Georgia

I was born during World War II in Columbus, Georgia. Both my parents were from New York and they were just temporarily in Columbus. When I was less than a year old they moved back to the Bronx.

The earliest memories that I have are from New York and living two blocks from Yankee Stadium, in fact. We lived in New York until I was about seven years old. My father worked for Klein's, the clothing chain from New York — Klein's on the Square — and he got transferred around the country. I was almost like an army brat. We lived for a couple years each in places such as Huntington, West Virginia, Chattanooga, Tennessee, Macon, Georgia. Finally, my father was offered an opportunity to buy into his uncle's business in a small town called Winder, Georgia. It was the home of Senator Richard Russell among other things.

My uncle really wanted to retire and brought my father in to run a small department store, a clothing store.

I guess I had just turned twelve when we moved to Winder, and I left at sixteen to go off to college. So I lived in Winder maybe four years. There were four of us — my mother, father, younger brother, and myself.

Winder was a little town with a population of five thousand. The county, Barrow County, had about thirteen thousand people. It was a garment-manufacturing area; it was the work clothes center of the United States. There were a number of plants there that manufactured men's dungarees and work clothing. At the time, we were the only Jewish family living in Winder. My uncle had been there a number of years and had occupied different political positions, and I think was very well liked in Winder. When my mom and dad came in, they didn't know that we weren't supposed to hire black sales help in our store, and they proceeded to do so. Our moving to Winder was greeted by a revival of activity of the Ku Klux Klan in the countryside. Crosses were burned, our house was shot at, windows were broken, the back of my father's car was blown away with a shotgun blast or something one time. It was a harrowing experience when we first moved there. This was about 1953 or 1954, in the earliest days of the civil rights movement.

I got in a few fights in school when somebody would call me a "dirty Jew" or "kike" or something like that. Not that often, though; I was fairly popular in school. The people who did that were what I labeled the "redneck" ilk from out in the country.

My parents were fairly liberal people. But my parents weren't really picked on that much. In later years, my mother and father both served as the president of the local county Chamber of Commerce. My mother was the first woman in Georgia, we think, to have been elected president of a Chamber. Among the business and professional people in the community, my parents were very well accepted. There's always some underlying anti-Semitism, I guess, and we would sometimes feel that. There were certain people in the city who would never shop in our store. We used to think it was ironic that whenever we sold a lot of white sheets we knew there was going to be a Klan meeting.

That's not apocryphal. That's true. In fact, there was a time that the Klan used to meet in a Masonic Lodge which was on the fourth floor of my father's store building. When my father made it known to the Masons that he didn't want the Klan meeting there, they had to stop letting them use their facilities. My uncle owned the building. Sometimes friends of mine who were not Jewish and I would hear about a Klan meeting or a cross-burning out in the country. In those days, we would sneak within a half mile of the place and park the car, turn the lights out, and walk across some field to let the air out of the tires of some of the yahoos' cars there. Now that I'm a member of the national board of directors of the Anti-Defamation League, I think back to how dangerous that must have been, though at the time we didn't think of it as being particularly dangerous. If we'd been caught, I imagine bad things could have happened to us.

Winder is almost fifty miles northeast of Atlanta, and it's about fourteen miles southwest of Athens, Georgia, so we belonged to a temple in Athens. That's where my brother and I were both Bar Mitzvahed. We used to travel a couple times a week on a Greyhound bus, after school, for Hebrew lessons with the then resident rabbi in Athens. But I also had a grandmother who was active in business in the Catskill Mountains in New York. She would lease out coffee shops and night club bar-and-grill concessions in different Catskill Mountain hotels over the summers, and my brother and I spent a lot of summers with her in the Catskills. She lived in Miami Beach in the wintertime, so around December vacation we would go down to Florida and spend some time with her. It was like we had a foot in both worlds. That was a fascinating experience, as a kid, getting the chance to work as a camp counselor and waiter and bus boy and that sort of thing up in the Catskills. It was, I guess, our biggest involvement with lots of other Jewish people, because in Winder that just didn't exist.

Interestingly enough, going back to the small town for a minute, right through the 1950s they had something like family circles. There would be, in every small town like Winder, one or two Jewish families. And once or twice a month, usually on a Sunday, they would all get together for a luncheon or a barbecue or just kind of a general socializing at one of the other families' houses in towns like Winder, Athens, Madison, Monroe, and Gainesville.

It was a way for the Jewish people in these small towns to keep their identity as being Jewish. Out of those meetings grew, I think, several marriages.

Does the shadow of Leo Frank still hang over the Jewish community here in Atlanta? I think it does to some extent. The scars are certainly still there. You have to put it in context. Leo Frank came to Atlanta about 1910, and at that time the Jewish community he found here was a very interesting community. It was a well-to-do community by and large. It was what I call a Deutsche Jewish community. Elements of Russian and Polish Jews were just beginning to arrive in Atlanta. They were ostracized, by and large, by the older line people, who had done a very good job of assimilating into the Gentile community here in Atlanta. Back then, as is still the case today, Jews did not belong to the exclusive country clubs. They formed their own country clubs, in effect, which became to some extent even more exclusive than their Gentile counterparts. But Jews were accepted in society in Atlanta in most ways. They were prominent doctors, lawyers, dentists, bankers, store owners — that sort of thing. There was a very thriving Jewish community in the Atlanta that Leo Frank found when he arrived back in 1910, 1911.

He was from Brooklyn, New York. His family was prominent. He was related to the Montagus here in Atlanta, I believe. The company that Leo Frank managed was the National Pencil Company. It manufactured lead pencils, not the mechanical kind, but the old-fashioned regular pencils. That company through a series of acquisitions later became the Scripto Corporation.

Leo Frank came to Atlanta; he got elected president of the oldest B'nai B'rith lodge in Atlanta. It's now called the Gate City Lodge of B'nai B'rith. He married a Selig girl, whose family were very prominent in Atlanta, and seemed to be doing well here until the incident occurred where this little girl was found murdered in his factory basement one weekend. It's a fascinating story, because nobody believed that Leo Frank would be convicted of this crime. Nobody but Leo Frank.

He had a foreboding sense about it all. There was a phenomenon going on in Atlanta, and I guess throughout the South, although I'm not that much of an historian, but I've done a lot of reading on the Leo Frank era. Atlanta up until that time was primarily a transportation center. It was one of the last stops on the northern railroad, where southern farmers would bring their cotton into Atlanta. In fact, at one time the town had been called Terminus. It was the terminal point on the railroad. I'm sure that by 1910 the railroad went on to Birmingham and New Orleans and places like that, but Atlanta was then, as it is today, primarily a transportation center. That really hasn't changed. But you have to think about what was going on back around 1910 to 1915 in the South, and in Atlanta in particular.

The industrial revolution had come upon the United States, and mills were growing up everywhere, particularly in Atlanta. Atlanta had become a mill town. There were a lot of factories here. There were a lot of sweatshops that employed young teenagers at ten-cents-an-hour wages, and a lot of them were owned by Jewish people, particularly Jews from up north — Boston, New York, Philadelphia, places like that. So there was a growing resentment against the owners of these factories, particularly the northern Yankee Jewish owners. That was going on. At the same time there had been a disaster out in the rural areas with regard to agriculture in the South. I think there was a real depression going on in the farmlands. The cotton crops, which had been prosperous for so many years, were petering out. The boll weevil had taken its toll; the land was worked out; and thousands and thousands of people were moving off these farms in Georgia and moving

into the big cities like Atlanta. As I put it, they brought with them the bag
and baggage of whatever prejudices they had out in the rural area. Prejudices
against Negroes and Jews and Catholics, in particular. So there was this
underlying, seething current going on that nobody really had identified at
that point in time.

Another interesting phenomenon was that as a result of the Frank trial
and the subsequent lynching of Leo Frank, the Ku Klux Klan was revitalized.
In fact, the same twenty-five men or so who found Leo Frank in a rural
Milledgeville, Georgia, prison farm jail and brought him back to Atlanta
in the middle of the night and then lynched him — that same group of
people met several weeks later on top of Stone Mountain and burned a
cross. They had called themselves the Knights of Mary Phagan; that was
the name of the little girl who had been murdered. They burned a cross on
top of Stone Mountain after the Frank lynching and they renamed themselves something like the Reconstituted Knights of the Ku Klux Klan of
Georgia.

These were not necessarily yahoos or rednecks. These were some prominent business people from the Marietta, Georgia, area, which is a separate
town but sort of a suburb of Atlanta. It's ironic that the Anti-Defamation
League was formed and the Ku Klux Klan reborn in the same year, primarily
as result of the same incident. That's the Leo Frank trial.

What happened was this. Mary Phagan was found in the basement of
the National Pencil Company factory on the day after Confederate Memorial Day. There had been a big parade downtown and she came down
to collect her $1.10 pay envelope. She had not worked full time the previous
week because they had run out of copper. Her job was to put the little
copper things that hold the erasers on the top of the pencils. She came up
to collect her paycheck. She announced to Mr. Frank what her payroll
number was — she was number fifty-one or something like that. He pulled
her paycheck out. She asked him if the copper had arrived. He said no, it
hadn't come in yet, but he expected it next week. Check back with him.
And she left. She was never seen alive again.

Late that night, I think very late that night, a night watchman making
rounds in the building came across her body in the basement, down in the
coal bin, and called the police in. It's a very complicated factual story, you
know, as to what happened. But after a series of people, including the night
watchman, were arrested for suspicion of the murder, they finally arrested
a fellow named Jim Conley, who was a black porter — a sweeper, as he
was called — in the factory. At first he denied any knowledge of the crime,
and then he gave a series of four affidavits, all contradictory, but further
and further implicating Leo Frank. He finally said that Mr. Frank had put
him on watch to make sure that nobody came in the building, and that Mr.

Frank was planning on raping this little girl when she came to collect her paycheck. And that after he raped her, he strangled her to death, murdered her, and paid Conley the then enormous sum of $200 to dispose of the body down in the basement or the incinerator or something.

Conley said that he helped Leo Frank carry the body across the floor of the third story of the factory, where the crime was supposed to have been committed, onto this new elevator and down into the basement of the building. That became very significant in the trial, because it was an old-fashioned elevator. I think it used to work with a rope pull. It had recently been converted to electricity, and Frank had one of the few keys for the little box that would unlock the switch to turn the elevator on and off. The testimony was that the elevator wasn't turned on that weekend, and that nobody had used it, although Conley said that Frank unlocked the box and they took the body down to the basement.

The body was found in the basement in a large pool of blood and soot. In fact, the little girl's body was so covered with soot and blood that when they found her with the lanterns, they couldn't tell if she was a white girl or a black girl. They had literally to pull her clothes off to see what color her skin was. There never was any blood found up on the top floor of the factory, where the murder was supposed to have taken place, which is rather significant if she'd been bludgeoned up there as Conley said. Also, it's almost embarrassing to talk about this, but when the police found the body, it was near the bottom of the elevator shaft. It wasn't in the elevator shaft. But inside the elevator shaft, in the bottom of the shaft, they found a pile of what the police report described as human feces, in its undisturbed state. Somebody had obviously gone to the bathroom at the bottom of that elevator.

When Conley was questioned the next day, he told the police he often went down to the basement to take a snooze and have a pull at his bottle. There wasn't any bathroom down there; there wasn't any colored bathroom, I think, anywhere in the building. And that he would often go to the bathroom in the bottom of this elevator shaft. He said he had, in fact, gone to the bathroom early on Saturday morning after he first came to work. Conley was a notorious drunk and a bully and an abuser of people. He borrowed nickels and dimes from people to buy corn whiskey and never paid them back. He had, in fact, tried to borrow a lot of money from people there that day and nobody wanted to lend him money because he would never pay them back. In any event, he'd said he'd gone to the bathroom that morning in the bottom of the elevator shaft.

Now, the following morning, when they brought Leo Frank down to the factory, the police wanted to get down into the basement. There were no steps down from the main part of the building into the basement. There was a package chute, like a coal chute, that went down, and there was a trap door with a ladder you could climb down. But the best way to get there was on the elevator. So the police officers asked Frank to come down in the elevator. It was an old-fashioned elevator and it didn't have springs in the bottom of it, and when the elevator landed on the bottom, it squashed the feces that were there, which somebody should have figured out would have proved that Conley was lying about using the elevator to take the body down.

There was a trial. The newspapers made Frank out to be a philanderer, you know. Frank had been married for about a year or two by the time this incident happened. They tried to tarnish his reputation in the newspapers. Rumors just were running rampant throughout the city. Ironically, there had been a whole wave of murders of young children in Atlanta back in those days, which repeated itself more recently. And the newspapers had been openly calling for the district attorney's resignation. His name was Hugh Dorsey and he wanted to run for governor, and this wasn't doing him any good. So he was hell-bent to solve this crime. Initially, they arrested Conley and then Conley implicated Frank and they arrested Leo Frank as well.

Frank had very fine lawyers representing him. The trial lasted twenty-nine days, and each day during the trial, as they would bring the jury from the hotel down the street to the courthouse, the crowd outside the courthouse was ever increasing. It was the number one show in Atlanta. For example, as the jury came in every day, the crowd outside was reported by the press to chant "Hang the Jew or we'll hang you." There were lots of windows being broken. Somebody told me, and I don't know if this is accurate or not, Rich's Department Store had a standing order to replace their plate glass windows every morning during this period. There was a lot of anti-Semitism floating around. They called Frank "the rich Jew from Brooklyn," you know; "the Yankee sweatshop owner" — all sorts of rumors about his sex life. They had him everything from philandering young boys to raping young girls who worked in his factory. None of that was true. It all came out at the trial that none of that was true, but the jury just didn't seem to care. They were determined, I think, to convict Leo Frank.

In fact, the judge had no idea that Frank would be convicted, because there just was no evidence implicating him in the crime at all, other than Jim Conley's testimony. Interestingly enough, if you read the judge's charge to the jury — in those days this was a legal charge in southern states, I later learned — he said, "Ladies and gentlemen of the jury, you have heard the testimony of Jim Conley, a nigger in this case." And he said, "We all know that niggers don't tell the truth unless they're forced to. And you don't have to believe the testimony of this nigger if you don't want to, against the testimony of white witnesses." That was a legal charge in the courtrooms in the South. No white man had been convicted of a capital offense in the South, up to that time, based solely on the testimony of a black witness — anywhere in the South, we're told.

Historians have told that when the Frank case came to trial in 1913, it occupied tremendous amounts of column inches of newspaper space. It was one of the lead stories throughout the United States that year. It was covered extensively by newspapers such as the *New York Times* and others around the country.

Frank was convicted by the jury and sentenced to hang. At that point, Jewish organizations and Jewish people throughout the country got involved in raising money for an appeal. Newspaper articles were being written demanding his pardon and his release, and it became a real cause for lots of different groups.

Finally, the lawyer who represented Jim Conley, the black sweeper, went first to the trial judge and then to the then governor of Georgia, John Slaton. There was an episode in the television version of John Kennedy's *Profiles in Courage,* about what Governor Slaton did in this case, because it truly was a courageous act. Slaton was a very popular governor, and in Georgia in those days governors served two-year terms. He was planning on running for the United States Senate, and everybody pretty well conceded that he would be a shoo-in for that position. The lawyer for Jim Conley went to the governor after having gone to the trial judge, who agreed to do something about it but then died before he had an opportunity to do so. Conley's lawyer, whose name was William Smith, a young criminal trial lawyer in Atlanta, went to Governor Slaton and told the governor that he knew that his client Conley was guilty and that Leo Frank was innocent and they couldn't let an innocent man hang. Smith called a press conference and told that to the press, and pretty much got run out of town for having said that.

Now, the governor of Georgia was considering commuting Leo Frank's sentence. The game plan, so to speak, was to commute Frank's sentence to life imprisonment, and when the heat was off and people cooled down in a few months, they were probably going to pardon him and let him out of jail altogether. Governor Slaton, while he was considering the commutation, had to call out the National Guard and lots of friends to guard the Governor's Mansion, because the Klan-type people were out there every night, burning crosses and raising hell and hanging him in effigy and things like that. Actually the effigy hanging came after he granted the commutation.

He stayed up all night one night just a few weeks before his term as governor was about to end, and around dawn he woke up his wife and he said, "Look, this is the right thing to do, but it's going to mean my political death if I do it here in Georgia." But he said, "I can't let this man go to the gallows. I believe in my heart he's innocent, and can't do that." And she made what has now become a famous saying. She told her husband that "I would rather be the widow of a brave and honorable man than the wife of a coward." He granted the commutation order and then took an around-the-world extended vacation. He wound up settling in Kansas someplace, and didn't come back to Atlanta for many, many years. He never got elected to anything again, I think, other than the bar association presidency in Atlanta. But it really was a profiles-in-courage story.

After he commuted Frank's sentence, they took Frank seventy-five miles from Atlanta to Milledgeville to hide him out at a state prison farm, because they knew that the angry mobs would try to lynch him. In fact, the judge insisted, when they brought the jury verdict in, that Leo Frank not be present when they announced the verdict, because the judge presumed that the verdict would be innocent and that the mobs outside might just come in and do their own form of justice. So Frank stayed in jail while they announced the verdict, which was the basis of an appeal. The famous Louis Marshall handled Frank's appeal to the United States Supreme Court, and argued that in a mob-type atmosphere one could not get a fair trial in a state. The U.S. Supreme Court — I think it was a seven-to-two decision — said that the Supreme Court had no business telling a state how to run a criminal trial.

Eight years later, the Supreme Court reversed itself in that case, and ruled that it was a violation of federal constitutional due process to try somebody in a mob-rule atmosphere — in a case with some young blacks from Alabama who had been tried and railroaded, so to speak. But it was too late to do Leo Frank any good. After his sentence was commuted by the governor, this mob finally found him in Milledgeville. They cut the telephone lines and met with no resistance — his throat had been cut by another inmate in a fight in that institution just weeks earlier. In fact, I have a picture in my office of Leo Frank hanging from a tree, and you can see the scar of the knife wound on his neck. Some white inmate had accused him of being a raper of young white Christian girls or something. Anyway, they got Frank out of this jail and brought him back to an oak tree that was within sight of the place where Mary Phagan had been born outside of Atlanta, and they lynched him from this tree.

Lynchings were not unusual in Georgia. Lynchings of white people were. Something like an average of four blacks a month got lynched in Georgia during that era. But it was always customary to cut the body down from the tree immediately after the lynching and then everybody disappeared and went fishing. You know, had alibis. They let Frank hang from the tree for a number of hours. Thousands of people came to see it when they heard about the lynching. Finally, some prominent citizen came and got up on his car and urged everybody to stop doing this, that it wasn't a very nice thing to do, and they cut him down. His body got trampled by the crowd. People tore pieces of his clothing; he had prison garb on — pieces of the lynch rope. To this day there are some families that have preserved little pieces of this rope that they used to lynch Leo Frank. They've used them as Bible markers over the years. That was the common thing to do.

Photographs were taken, and postcards were being sold. It was a regular carnival atmosphere. Finally, Frank's body was sent back to Brooklyn. Rabbi Marks at the temple here in Atlanta and a friend of Leo Frank's accompanied the body on the train for burial in Brooklyn. He's buried in Mount Carmel Cemetery — I think it's Queens, not Brooklyn.

Frank left no children. A distant cousin called me a few months ago and told me they'd been out to visit the cemetery plot that Leo Frank is buried in — nobody had been out there in years, apparently. There is a Latin inscription, they told us, on his tombstone. I haven't been there to verify this myself, but they thought it was unusual to have a Latin inscription on a Jewish tombstone, not Yiddish, not Hebrew, not English. It said *Semper idem*. They came back and asked somebody in the family to tell them what that meant, and it means "Always the same" or "Nothing really changes." Somebody was pretty prophetic seventy years ago to put that on Frank's tombstone.

In the aftermath of the trial, the most vehement anti-Semitism came out. Not to say that there wasn't a lot during the trial. At that point, several rabble-rousing newspapers, including one owned by Tom Watson, who later became a U.S. senator as a result of this matter, were really doing diatribes against the Jewish community. They did Shylock caricatures and caricatures of the Pope and just lots of slurs about how Jews control the newspapers and the railroads. You know, everything bad in life was blamed on the Jews. It was a scapegoat kind of a thing. The public really got riled up a lot. A lot of Jewish husbands sent their wives and kids out of the state. Lots of people were sent to Birmingham and Montgomery and New York and other places until things cooled off.

There are very few of these people left now. They would be in their late eighties and nineties. I think there are a few people at the Jewish Home who were around here as youngsters during that era who remember some of this.

It truly was a panic, because the Jewish community was in a state of shock. You have to remember it was a very assimilated community, and yet this blew them wide open. They were really afraid. The attitude was: If they could do this to Leo Frank, what about the rest of us? For years after the lynching the community kept the lid on this story. Rabbi Marks refused to discuss it with anybody. Leo Frank's papers were locked up at the temple here in Atlanta and nobody could have access to them. In later years, when Harry Golden was writing his book *A Little Girl Is Dead,* which is an interesting account of the Frank case, his researchers were not granted access by the temple to these materials. Everybody just wanted to forget it and put it behind them.

Then in 1983, an eyewitness to the case came forward. His name was Alonzo Mann, and he had been a fourteen-year-old boy working for Leo Frank at this factory. Lonnie Mann testified that he came to work that day. It was a Saturday and he was working some extra hours to make a few extra dimes. He said that Mr. Frank had always been nice to him and gave him pennies to go out and buy candies and sodas and things like that. He had left because it was Confederate Memorial Day and his mother said she would meet him downtown to watch the parade with him. His mother had also told him she was going to buy a hat, and if she was late, he could either stay and watch the parade or just go on home on the trolley. He said that folks were kind of rowdy and drunk. He was a frail little boy, and he was rather intimidated by these crowds, and when he couldn't find his mother he decided to go back to the pencil factory. This was during the lunch hour.

He says he opened the front door of the pencil factory — by now everybody had collected his or her pay and was supposed to have been gone. He was startled because he saw Jim Conley carrying the limp body of this little blond girl, Mary Phagan, down the steps and into the main part of the factory, walking toward the chute to the basement. When Conley saw him, he yelled at him and he told him to halt or stop or something and he lunged out to grab him. Now Lonnie Mann didn't think that the little girl was dead. He didn't envision that she was dead. It just looked like she had fainted or something, he said. He turned around and ran through the door and jumped on a trolley car and went home.

As he ran out the door, he said, Conley hollered after him, "If you say anything about this, I'll kill you." He went home and told his mother and stepfather what happened. At that point the little girl wasn't missing, so nobody was really too concerned. His mother did what a lot of mothers would do. His mother and stepfather told him, "Don't get involved." Later, when they arrested Leo Frank, he told his mother again that he wanted to go tell the police what he saw. And they said, "Naw, it will work itself out. Don't get involved."

Lonnie Mann got subpoenaed to come to the trial as one of 139 character witnesses for Leo Frank. Nobody had any idea he knew anything about the case other than as a character witness for Frank. He says that he made up his mind that morning on the trolley that he was going to blurt out in court and tell what he had seen that day. He says that when he got into the courthouse, there were thousands of people — the local newspapers estimated crowds of more than five thousand outside the courthouse. This was pre–air conditioning days, and the courthouse was on the second floor. People were climbing up in trees and sitting in the windows. Each time a question was asked a witness, somebody in the window would repeat it to the crowd down below. If it was something favorable to the prosecutor, everybody would cheer; if it was favorable to Leo Frank, people would boo.

Lonnie Mann said he was scared to death; people had guns in their back pockets. He said they were just a bunch of rednecks in and out of the courthouse and he had to make his way through them. And when he got in there, Jim Conley was sitting at a table or something and gave him, as he put it, the evil eye and stared him down.

He got so frightened that when they asked him his name he started stuttering. He'd never stuttered before, but he stuttered very, very badly and whispered. They could barely hear his answers because there was so much noise and confusion there in the courthouse. The judge could not control the audience or the crowd or anything. Finally, after two or three questions, the judge excused Lonnie Mann as a witness because nobody could hear him and he was too young. He ran out of the courthouse crying, never having had a chance to tell his story. Well, he says that over the years he has tried to tell this story a number of times to reporters — he wound up owning a restaurant in downtown Atlanta down the street from the *Journal-Constitution* newspaper building. Everybody just said, "Lonnie, let sleeping dogs lie; let's not bring up this story again." He finally moved away to Bristol, Virginia, and had a heart problem and a pacemaker installed. At age eighty-two, I believe it was, or eighty-four, he decided that before he died he wanted to set the record straight and clear his conscience.

We brought him to Georgia. We did a two-hour videotape of him under oath telling the pardon and parole board the story. Then a group of Jewish organizations got together and applied for a posthumous pardon for Leo Frank. That case sat at the pardon and parole board for over a year, and a day or two before Christmas, in 1983, the board decided they had not been convinced beyond any doubt whatsoever of Leo Frank's innocence, and therefore they refused to grant the pardon — a very unusual legal standard, "beyond any doubt whatsoever."

I was asked to be the attorney for the group of organizations and I doubt whether I would have spent literally thousands of hours of my life working on that case if I had known that they were going to use that kind of impossible legal standard.

We have some hope to go back to the board and try to get them to reconsider the matter and we are working on that.

How has our attempt to get a pardon been greeted by the Jewish com-

munity and the non-Jewish community? It's been very interesting. We had
a meeting at the Jewish Community Center when this first came to light.
We brought Lonnie Mann to Atlanta. He got up and told his story and
there were some elderly people there who had been around during those
days who got up and thought this was just terrible — that we were resur-
recting these old ghosts. They used phrases like "dragging skeletons out of
closets." For years they had suppressed this story. I think of it on a smaller
scale; it's like Holocaust survivors who refuse to talk about their experiences
at Auschwitz. They just suppressed it. It was such a horrible era in Jewish
history in the South and in America. I think Leo Frank is probably the only
Jewish man who ever got lynched in this country. It set off a wave of anti-
Semitism in the South, revitalization of the Ku Klux Klan, and all these
horrible experiences flowed out of this case.

For years the Jewish community suppressed the story, and I think there
were some people, particularly the older ones, who were horrified that we
were bringing it up again. But after a while, it was almost like a catharsis,
and once we let it out of the closet, so to speak, then people were interested
in seeing that justice finally was done in the Frank case, which, of course,
today has not yet been done. Hundreds of newspaper editorials all over the
country supported the pardon application.

I think we had a whole lot more support from the non-Jewish community
than we expected we would have. Church groups rallied to our support,
particularly after the pardon was denied. The press were horrified; the
Jewish community was shocked. I think even the Christian community,
which fully well expected the pardon would and should be issued, were
mad about it. The Metropolitan Council of Churches issued statements,
and organizations like that came to our rally. So, to some extent, there was
some good that came out of the pardon application; not a whole lot, but
some anyway.

Today anti-Semitism takes a whole lot more subtle form than it did back
in those days. It's pretty gauche nowadays in a Christian community to go
around calling people Jews or kikes or Christ-killers or anything like that.
But one senses that underneath there are much more subtle forms of anti-
Semitism and discrimination. Jews are still not allowed in those country
clubs. But by and large, the Jewish community in Atlanta is a very thriving
community. I think it's one of the best Jewish communities in the United
States. We have some sixty thousand Jewish people in the metropolitan
area. A lot of professionals. Jews are involved in every walk of life in this
city, in its politics — just highly accepted. But still one senses down deep
inside that there's still some anti-Semitism around. It's just much subtler
than it used to be. You can live in Atlanta, Georgia, and be Jewish and be

very comfortable being Jewish in this city. I think that's a credit to the Jewish community and also to the Gentile community here.

Postscript: On Wednesday, March 12, 1986, the *Atlantic Constitution* carried a banner headline on its front page: 70 YEARS LATER, LEO FRANK PARDONED.

The story began: "Seventy years after he was lynched by an angry mob, Leo M. Frank was pardoned Tuesday for the murder of a teenage girl.

"The State Board of Pardons and Paroles pardoned Frank 'without attempting to address the question of guilt or innocence' according to a statement issued by the board."

The pardon was granted, said the board, because the state had failed to protect Leo Frank or to bring the lynchers to justice.

Wayne Snow, chairman of the five-member Georgia Board of Pardons and Paroles, commenting on the pardon, said, "Hopefully, this will put the Leo Frank case behind us and redress what was a very poor episode in the state's history."

4

Steerage and Peerage

BETWEEN 1881 AND 1914, roughly two million Jews immigrated to the United States, my father and all four grandparents among them. Most came from Eastern Europe. Most were labeled Russian Jews, whether they came from Poland or Rumania or Hungary. When they got here, many of them were welcomed by members of the Hebrew Immigrant Aid Society, or HIAS. But they were not welcomed by their immigrant predecessors, the German Jews. "Oh, yes," recalled Leo Despres, a Chicago lawyer and descendant of French Jews, "Russian immigrants would be referred to as kikes." Moreover, he said, there "were certainly great social distinctions, until I was eighteen or nineteen or twenty years old, for sure. When I attended the university, I think my feelings about Russian Jews broke down; not entirely though, because I really felt that German Jews were superior. But I began to deal with Russian Jews on the basis of equality, and of course it didn't take very long for the distinction to disappear, but it was there, all right."

And the "Russian Jews" remained unwelcomed by their richer, snootier, and more assimilated German Jewish coreligionists until World War II, when Hitler unwittingly forced the two strands together.

*Edward M. Benton, seventy-seven, lawyer, New York,
New York*

My father arrived at eighteen, alone, the only one in his family. He had an uncle in Hoboken, I believe, who had a factory, and his first job was in the factory. He went to school as quickly as he could at night and became a stenographer. I don't know at what stage, but in the meantime he brought over his mother and his brother and his stepsister. I guess he just lived modestly and accumulated enough money. He got a job with a non-Jewish law firm, strangely enough, in New York City. He worked there for a number of years and went to law school at night.

HIAS is some 103 or 104 years old. Its beginnings were peculiar. The Jewish community on the Lower East Side discovered that there was a Jewish person who had died on a ship coming into the harbor, and they were very exercised about giving him a Jewish burial. So they sent somebody over to the ship for that purpose, and that led to the idea that some way ought to be found to meet people who came in as immigrants who were Jewish. My father, John L. Bernstein, who was a lawyer most of his life, was one of the founders. So a little group was formed that established what was called a "sheltering house," which was really a way station where they served food and had sleeping accommodations for immigrants.

Then they decided that they needed immigration help as well as shelter, and established a Hebrew Immigrant Aid Society. I don't know whether I made clear that the first group was the Hebrew Sheltering House and the second group was the Hebrew Immigrant Aid Society. Within ten or fifteen years, they had merged into the Hebrew Sheltering and Immigrant Aid Society. By that time, they had developed a system of sending somebody to meet every immigrant who came in — at that time at Castle Garden, which is now part of the Battery. Immigrants didn't go to Ellis Island. They came directly to shore at Castle Garden. There was an immigration station there.

The HIAS offices were on the Lower East Side, on East Broadway. They became well known among the Jewish immigrant group because they were doing a good piece of work, and the community supported them with very small contributions — two or three dollars a year, or something like that. Shortly after World War I, an enormous number of people began to come in. I think immigration reached a million in one year. Not all Jews, but a large number. Very serious concerns were the situations in Europe of refugees who were on their way across the ocean, got stuck in Europe, were taken care of to some extent by local populations in way camps and such. One of the biggest, and I know a little more about it than other places because my father and mother went there, was in Gdynia, which is near Gdansk, the port for Poland, then known as Danzig. They had a big immigration station and it was too much for the local population to take care of. There was insufficient organization and all of that. Well, HIAS by that time got a crew of people over there and organized it so that the food got distributed in a reasonable way.

At that time relatives here could send money for their relatives abroad, but no bank in this country would send dollars. They would accept dollars and pay out in local currencies, which were inflating by the minute. Also, it wasn't always easy to find the recipient. So the bank would receive the money here, send it abroad, then the local bank abroad wouldn't find the immigrant, and if they did find him, two, three, four, ten weeks later, the money was worth one-tenth what it was before. So we established a bank, a New York bank. It was called the HIAS Immigrant Bank, chartered by New York for the purpose only of transmitting funds. We didn't take deposits as such. We took only transmittals, and we paid out in dollars. And we used our facilities to locate people who weren't otherwise easily located.

I'm talking about the 1920s. I was still either abroad or in school. I'm repeating what I knew from my folks. The organization grew and it bought the old Astor Library on Lafayette Street in the twenties, which is a huge building, and established dormitories and two kitchens — one fleyshik and one milchik — and served enormous numbers of people. Also, during the Depression they fed breadlines, whether they were immigrants or not. I remember lines outside.

We operated all through World War II and the refugee situation. By that time we had offices in half the countries in the world. But going back to the outcome of World War I, there were a substantial number of refugees who came from Eastern Europe through China into Japan and got stuck in Japan trying to come here. Conditions were, as everywhere where the local population was unprepared, awful. We sent people to Japan to alleviate that situation and eventually got most of the refugees out. They weren't persecuted there; they simply didn't have the facilities to take care of them. This is after World War I.

I joined HIAS probably around 1934, 1935. I can't remember the date exactly, but I had already finished law school and come back to New York. My father had been president of HIAS for seven or eight years. When he left the presidency he remained as chairman of the executive committee and very active, and he interested me in it and I became a director at that time and have continued as director since. I think I'm senior in service on the board.

HIAS was very active during and after World War II and still is. We did a huge job on the Russians when they came in in numbers, and we're still operating, though not in that level of numbers, with Iranians and a few from the Iron Curtain countries, like Rumanians, a few Polish girls.

How does it work? Let's say for someone coming from Iran? We can't do anything until you get out. When you're out, you learn through the grapevine that if you go to HIAS, you'll get some help. You'll start in Turkey. That's the most likely. There you'll be directed to the Catholic organization in Turkey, which, finding you're a Jew, will direct you to HIAS in Vienna, and will give you the fare and all that. In Vienna, our people start moving them out of Vienna to Italy, because Vienna discourages long stays, and besides it's a hotbed of espionage and we don't want to be there. We send them to Italy, where we have a staff. In Italy, they're prepared to take care of these people for as long as necessary to get the documentation and the examinations and all that to come to the United States. Then they come to the United States.

We know all about them by the time they arrive from the reports we get, and it depends upon where they're going. If a community — and we have contact with all of the communities — in Cleveland says it can take two Iranian boys, for example, we'll meet them at the plane here in New York and put them right on a plane to Cleveland. The Cleveland local organization is ready to pick them up and take care of them. If they're to remain in New York, the similar organization in New York is called New York Association for New Americans, popularly known as NYANA. They are the resettlement arm of the machinery for settlement in the United States. And this is true of all of them.

Occasionally, we get something special. Syria will not allow anybody out of the country. Certainly no Jews, but for some strange reason they are convinced that it would be all right to send unmarried Jewish girls out because they can't find men in Syria to marry. So we get a handful of Jewish girls every year who go immediately to the Brooklyn community of Syrian Jews. There's a large and quite prosperous community there with a synagogue and all that. They take charge of these girls, and they've arranged a number of marriages.

HIAS is *the* major Jewish immigrant group and pretty nearly the only one. Whatever else there is is very minor and doesn't have the facilities and the machinery and so forth. HIAS is a professional organization. We have very few volunteers. For long periods we never had volunteers. Most of our support up to fairly recently has been the support of people who were helped or their children. It still occurs. Esther and I, as the firm of Benton and Benton, are in charge of the legacies to HIAS, and we have 150 to 200 a year. Many of them are from people who remember HIAS as having helped them or their parents and their grandparents. Some of them are substantial sums, because some of the people did well.

Esther Benton, seventy-six, lawyer, New York, New York

When the immigration station moved from Castle Garden to Ellis Island, HIAS was given permission to have a kosher kitchen there. Then when seder came around, they had big seders there. One of our men was always at Ellis Island to take care of people generally, to try to get them through the rather stringent immigration requirements — the physicals and all that sort of thing. If there was a danger of deportation, and there often was, he would promptly get to the courts with it. My father did some of that work there on a *pro bono* basis.

I'll tell you something about my own mother in HIAS in the early days. She came, as nearly as I can make out, in 1891. She was nineteen years old, the first member of her family. She came all alone as a nineteen-year-old adventurer. Her mother scraped together the money to send her. The reason she left was that her older sister had been married off to a young man from another community whom she'd never seen before, and my mother was a great reader of romance novels; she was not about to let herself be married off that way. She was always very independent, way ahead of her time. She came by herself after thirty days in steerage, seasick every minute of the time. In fact, many years later when I took my first sea voyage with her, I was nineteen, and before we passed the Statue of Liberty she was flat on her back and seasick — just being on the water was enough. She was met at the boat by the predecessor of HIAS.

There was this young girl who arrived at Castle Garden. All she had was the address of a landsman, and they would not send her there. First of all, they took her to this shelter, gave her a bath, and cleaned her up. In the meantime, they investigated to see if the landsman was a respectable man. The landsman was a man with a wife and five kids, so they said all right, she could go and stay with the landsman. For the rest of her life, there was a little pushka on the kitchen cabinet for HIAS, and we were taught as kids when we got our allowance we put pennies in the HIAS pushka. There were other pushkas, but the one that I remember was the HIAS pushka from my earliest childhood. I never forgot it, and that's where most of our support came from in the early days.

Evelyn Squire, seventy-three, retired teacher, Lake Lucerne, New York

My mom was one of two children living in a very, very small village in Lithuania. Her father was murdered by Cossacks. He was a seller of wood, and as he was going with his wagon from one spot to another, he was ambushed, his money stolen, his horses stolen, and he was murdered. So my grandmother had a very, very hard life. Now, she knew that there was no future for her children. She was able to save money and send her firstborn to America. He came here at age seventeen, saved money, and when he was eighteen he got enough money to send for my mother, who was then twelve, in 1905. I am not going to go into detail how my grandmother prepared my mother not to get involved with strange men. She told her about prostitutes. She hid her money under her petticoats and told her, "If anybody asks you if you have money, you say no."

My mother comes to Castle Garden and there was nobody there to meet her. She was petrified. She was kept overnight and the next day no one came. People from the HIAS came to help her. She thought that they would send her back, that maybe she had a sickness. It was a very, very traumatic type of thing. She was told that her brother had died two days before at Mount Sinai Hospital from a burst appendix. You can imagine, a twelve-year-old coming in. This gives me a background to understand my mother through the years. I only knew this much later. In a few days she was taken to a factory and taught to become an operator, and she worked on overalls for a company called Orr.

Ida Stack, sixty-three, retired Yiddish teacher, St. Louis, Missouri

What I shall never forget is when we were all on the ship; we came over not on a tugboat or anything. We came over on the *Mauritania,* which was a big ship. But at dawn, we entered the New York Harbor and there was the Statue of Liberty and everybody just fell on their knees, thanking God that they were seeing this Lady with the Lamp. Then all I remember of Ellis Island was a very, very sad place. People were deathly afraid that they might be diseased or hard of hearing or something, because right away, oh, before we even got on to Ellis, we were deloused. I can even smell it. Like kerosene in the hair. It was a very unattractive place. People just huddled together; families huddled together and they were all afraid lest they be sent back or not allowed. We were there for just a very short time, because Father's brother and my father's uncle came and they met us and took us to their home.

Martin Bucksbaum, sixty-four, shopping center developer, Des Moines, Iowa

My father told me hundreds of times that they weren't faring too well in what was Austria-Hungary at the time, and all the senior members decided to go to the rabbi in the area and ask his advice as to what they should do. He suggested that they should go to the United States. So the father, the oldest son, and our father, the next oldest son of a large family of seven children, left in approximately 1912 and headed for the United States. En route they were asked if they would have any objection to going to some place other than New York City. Not knowing the difference, they said, "Fine." So the boat docked at Baltimore briefly and then went to Galveston,

Texas. They got to Galveston and, he says, they divided them up into different groups. They were sending them to Iowa at that particular time. Some of the people ended up in Davenport, Iowa. Our father and his brother and father ended up in Cedar Rapids, Iowa. Some were sent to Marshalltown, Iowa. Some came to Des Moines, Iowa. And I remember, growing up, that whenever we traveled to those cities, he would look up his friends or he would hear about his friends in those different localities.

To go back to their arrival in Galveston: HIAS was the agency that directed them and put them on a train and sent them, in his case to Cedar Rapids. In Cedar Rapids there was a fellow named Goldberg who met them at the train. Every time we saw Goldberg he used to jokingly complain. He said he had had one shipment come in that day and it was late in the evening and he had just gotten home and then he got called that there was another group that had come in on a later train. So he went back, and our father and his father and brother were included in that group.

Our dad used to tell us that HIAS gave them either five or ten dollars. It was a pretty meaningless amount of money, but that was what they had when they landed in Cedar Rapids.

Henry Morgenthau III, sixty-nine, writer and former television producer, Cambridge, Massachusetts

I am at present writing a Morgenthau family social history.

The first Morgenthaus that I know anything about were my great-grandfather Lazarus Morgenthau's family. Lazarus was born in 1815 in Bavaria. He was a very interesting character and like some of his descendants had a powerful ego. He was very optimistic about getting ahead in the world at a time when it was not at all easy. At twenty-seven, just before he married, he wrote a short memoir in which he tells us a good deal about himself and his parents. His father, Moses Morgenthau, was a shochet — a ritual butcher — a cantor, and a Hebrew teacher. He was married to a rabbi's daughter and he had a lot of children. He expected his sons to become cantors and started them in that direction.

It got to the point where being a cantor was no longer a very lucrative profession for a nice Jewish boy. So Lazarus went into tailoring, which we now think of as a stereotypical Jewish occupation. But in those days Jews were peddlers or they were in strictly Jewish trades, like butchers, cantors, et cetera. But they weren't very much in the crafts, including tailoring. Lazarus was apprenticed at times to Christian master tailors.

The Morgenthaus lived a very traditional, what we would think of as an Orthodox, Jewish life. Moses had trouble keeping his family together, and it soon disintegrated. The sons went into various crafts: tailoring, shoe-making, carpentry.

When Lazarus was very much a struggling young tailor, working very hard just to make ends meet, he wrote in his memoir that should his family ever prosper, he wanted them to know how it was to live poor. What made him think he was going to prosper then, I don't know, but he did. First of all, he married up a bit socially. The men in our family tended to advance their lot through marriage. That meant marrying into a family that had residence rights in some particular town. Lazarus married a woman by the name of Babette Guggenheim. It would seem very likely that this was the same Guggenheim family that immigrated to the United States and became copper magnates — although I haven't really tracked that down — because they all came from a town in Switzerland a generation earlier, some time in the eighteenth century. They were well established in the southern Bavarian town of Hürben. That was where Lazarus settled and became a tailor. He had a total of only about two years of schooling, according to his memoir, so he hired both a secular and a religious tutor, because he didn't know anything about his religion and he was concerned about that. He also didn't have any general learning. So he would be tutored at night. But his education always remained limited.

Then as a tailor he started making neckties or, as they were called, cravats. He began peddling them first door to door and then at fairs. He recalled a situation in a town where they had different booths for Jews and Christians. This time they didn't have any of the Jewish booths left and so they put him in a booth for Christians and business was better there. He added dressing gowns to his line. At some point he added what one would call men's notions. He also added cigars. In those days in the Rhine Valley, the Palatinate, they grew tobacco — something like the Connecticut Valley tobacco. Soon Lazarus was buying and selling tobacco. Then the family moved up the river or up the river to Ludwigshafen, which was just being established by King Ludwig of Bavaria. It was across the Rhine from Mannheim, which was in the independent archduchy of Baden. He could see that all the action was over there in Mannheim. Lazarus had a younger brother who, in 1850, went to San Francisco. The brother arrived as a peddler and wrote back and said there was a very good market for expensive cigars, and he sent some money to get a business started. In no time at all, Lazarus had become a tremendously successful cigar manufacturer in Mannheim with branch factories in other towns.

At the time my grandfather was born in Mannheim in 1856, the family was very well off. Then the American Civil War came along, and there were high tariffs put on all kinds of things, including cigars. Since the business was primarily export to the United States, it was clobbered. Lazarus decided to move his big family to America. In 1865 or 1866, he sent three of his older children to establish a beachhead, to prepare things for the rest of the family. They went to Brooklyn. The next year the whole family came over. There were about thirteen children. A couple had died, but at least one was born in New York. My grandfather was in the middle, perhaps the ninth child.

There is evidence that the Morgenthaus sailed from Bremen to New York first class. It wasn't steerage anyway. My grandfather was a great pack rat, a keeper of all papers, which he gave to the Library of Congress. Among other things, there was a newspaper clipping listing Lazarus among the heads of families who were passengers arriving on the S.S. *Hermann* from Bremen. Lazarus brought $30,000 with him, which was a lot of money. I figure it might be close to a million dollars now. But things did not go well for him when he arrived here. I don't know why, because there were quite a few Jews in the cigar business doing well, but he never went back into the cigar or the tobacco business, or into the clothing business.

He tried various things. I think he never was at all comfortable with the English language. That wasn't as much of a handicap then as it would have been later, because the German Jews identified very strongly with the Germans and they had their newspapers and their clubs. They had a community. There were a lot of people in this country who used English as a second language.

Lazarus went into the wine business, and he bought a restaurant. It burned down, and things did not go at all well. The money that he had brought began to go. At the same time, he was very interested in keeping up appearances. He moved quickly from Brooklyn to Manhattan, although there were certainly sections of Brooklyn, particularly in the German community there, which were considered fashionable and respectable. He moved over to the East Side of Manhattan. The family was big and his wife put all the kids right into school. But they didn't really have enough money to live on; they always had at least one boarder. The father was yanking his children out of school and making them go to work.

Lazarus could not really support this big family, but he wanted to make a very good impression. Part of it was practical, in terms of just getting the best possible marriages for his children. He joined a Reform temple whose rabbi was David Einhorn, an extreme Reform rabbi who had been kicked out of a congregation in Budapest, where he was considered too radical. He had been in Baltimore before coming to New York. Temple Emanu-El was already established. His was Temple Beth El. It was not quite socially on the level with Temple Emanu-El. Jacob Schiff belonged to both; sort of noblesse oblige.

In those days City College, and perhaps college generally, was really more like high school. You could go to City College right out of the eighth grade. My grandfather began to do very well. He would rank one, two, or three in his class, although he was still having trouble with his English. He was extremely good in math and worked very hard. They had a kind of transitional year in which if one hadn't gone to high school one could go to City College and take really the whole of high school in one year, and then go on. But his father yanked Henry out after he had been there only a short time and made him go to work. Later he decided he wanted to become a lawyer. He started working in a law office, doing what was called reading the law — which was an acceptable way of becoming a lawyer. But he decided that was really not a very good way of learning the law, so he got into Columbia Law School. He taught night school to support himself. His students were working-class immigrants who needed to learn basic English. Meanwhile, he started to have trouble with his eyes. He thought it came from eyestrain, working in bad light. His eyes were always sensitive. He didn't like tobacco smoke. He offered all of his grandchildren a thousand dollars if we didn't smoke until we were twenty-one. It was partly because he didn't approve of it and partly he didn't like it around him.

Grandpa took a trip back to Germany in 1873. A lot of German Jewish families did keep contact with their old country relatives up until World War I. I think the anti-German feeling then was more intense than in World War II, and German Jews particularly were concerned about their allegiance being questioned. At that point they severed relationships permanently. But before that, most of these families had relatives whom they went back to visit. The Morgenthaus never did. There must have been some relatives who remained in Germany, but they weren't in touch with them, and I don't know who any of them are. When my grandfather returned, he didn't go back to where his family came from. He went to Kiel in the north, which was considered a healthy place on the sea. This was a Prussian seaport where they were building up their navy. It was right after the Franco-Prussian War. General von Moltke, the great war hero, came and spoke. My grandfather went and heard him. After that, he started writing about the military threat of the Germans in his diary. It wasn't like things had been in Bavaria, when he remembered the Gemütlichkeit of his childhood. But in Prussia he had sensed the harsher mood of the people. From then on, for the rest of his life, he remained wary of the recurring threat of German militarism to world peace.

Grandpa came back and he formed a law partnership and began to get into business as well. His first business venture was through one of his clients, who manufactured celluloid piano keys. At the time there was an ivory shortage. The business prospered. Then he got into the real estate business in Manhattan, and then he got married. His wife was named Josephine Sykes. Her father was born in Manchester, England, but he had married a German Jewish woman, and they had settled in Detroit. He was in the clothing business. At the beginning of the Civil War, he got a contract — I'm not sure whether it was for uniforms or just clothing — for the Michigan state militia. He made a lot of money and then, only in his thirties, he sold his business to his brother-in-law and retired. He may have been in bad health. He and his wife went abroad and traveled in Germany and other European countries.

My grandmother was born in Stuttgart, but actually the family had already settled here in this country. Her father died when he was quite young, but he left his wife in very good financial condition. This family was socially above the Morgenthaus. The Morgenthau family, by that time, was under a cloud because Lazarus really went nuts. In fact, they had him in an asylum for a while. I think it was a combination of this kind of big ego and losing control of the family; they weren't listening to him, particularly on matters like marriages. But to keep up his ego, he tried various businesses, including insurance. The insurance business was not a thing that many Jews went into, but he was apparently a good salesman. Then Lazarus started raising money for charity in New York. He invented and patented a system for selling pages in books for various benefits. He had something called the *Golden Books of Life* and the less expensive *Silver Books*. He raised money for Mount Sinai Hospital in New York and things like that. He raised quite a lot of money and he got quite a lot of publicity out of it. I think occasionally he took something out for his own expenses and maybe there were some questions about just how he was handling these funds.

Lazarus became quite disturbed, and he and his wife were either divorced or separated, which was quite unusual in those days. This was at the time when my grandfather was engaged to get married. Josephine's mother really did not approve of the marriage. But they did get married, and he did very well in the real estate business in New York. He had four children. My father, who was the third, had two older sisters and a younger sister.

Although my grandfather was very interested in probing various religions, I think, he never thought of converting. He would go around town and listen to spellbinding preachers. There was a Quaker doctor who was a boarder in his parents' house and my grandfather became interested in the Friends' religion for a time. Then he became associated with the Ethical Culture movement. Late in life he was attracted to Christian Science. There were some of the family who became Christian Scientists; some of them are right up here in Boston. My grandmother's family, quite a few of them came to Boston. I think there was one sister who became a Mrs. Weil, and one of her daughters married whichever Filene brother it was that got married.

But my grandfather never converted. In fact, he was very active in Jewish affairs. He became an intimate friend of Rabbi Stephen Wise and was the founding president of his Free Synagogue. He was never a tremendously wealthy man in terms of the great Jewish fortunes like the Strauses, the Schiffs, and the Lehmans. He was never in that league at all, but he liked to make an impression and give liberally. He gave $5000 a year to the Free Synagogue, which was a lot of money. In fact, $5000 seems to be what he gave to a number of charitable and political activities. It was, I guess, enough to make an impression. He was generous, too. I shouldn't put him down. He was very interested in the social-action side of Stephen Wise's work. Stephen Wise had two things that he was very active in: one was social reform, and the other, of course, was Zionism. My grandfather was never a Zionist, and eventually became militantly anti-Zionist.

The Free Synagogue had their services in Carnegie Hall, and Stephen Wise himself was a great spellbinder, but he would also invite people like William Jennings Bryan and Jane Addams. When the Free Synagogue had its fifth anniversary they invited Woodrow Wilson, governor of New Jersey, and Senator Borah to speak after dinner. My grandfather, as president of the synagogue, sat next to Wilson, and according to what he wrote, he was immediately taken with Mr. Wilson and decided on the spot that he would go out of business and devote himself completely to Wilson's political future. He gave Wilson $5000 at a time when Wilson was very much of a presidential dark horse. Grandpa was made chairman of the Finance Committee and chief fund raiser. He also put the campaign on a business basis so that they actually ended up with a small surplus, which was unheard of.

After the election my grandfather was ambivalent. On the one hand he wanted to be treated just as an American, not as a hyphenated Jewish-American; and on the other hand he felt that politically something was owed to the Jews. He saw himself, I guess, as a Democratic equivalent of Oscar Straus, who had been the first Jew in a Cabinet in the Teddy Roosevelt administration. He wanted some kind of Cabinet or policymaking job. Wilson offered him the ambassadorship to Turkey. He was very insulted because this was a Jewish slot. In fact, Oscar Straus himself was three times our diplomatic representative in Turkey, minister and later ambassador, before and after he'd been in the Cabinet. Jews, ironically, were accepted in Turkey, which was a Muslim country — socially acceptable in a way that they would not have been in a European Christian capital. Wilson argued that he could do so much for his people — because Palestine was part of the Ottoman Empire, and there were also a lot of Jews in Syria and in Turkey itself. When Wilson said, "You can do so much for your people," that really did it. My grandfather said his people were the American people, not the Jewish people. So he turned the offer down and went off to Europe on a vacation. Stephen Wise went after him and told him he had to take the assignment for the same reasons Wilson had advanced. My grandfather said, "Okay, you can talk to Wilson, and if he wants to do it, let me know. I'll think about it." Wilson offered it again, and Grandpa took it.

He went off to Turkey and he had a great time. He was very much impressed with what the Zionists were doing in Palestine. At this point, he came as close to being a Zionist as at any time in his life. But, for reasons which unfortunately still have some validity today, he thought that this was not something that could be successful: couldn't support that many people; there would be trouble with the Arabs; and so forth. He thought that these Jewish settlements were good. He was interested because the main idea was to help the Jews in Russia and Poland and get them out. He was very sympathetic, but not converted to Zionism. But then World War I came along. He was afraid that the Turks would turn on the Jews the way they were already turning on the Armenians and the way they were persecuting all non-Muslims. And certainly if the Zionists started pushing the idea of an independent state, that would be the thing that would turn the Turks against them.

The war came, and the Jewish community in Palestine — Jerusalem particularly — was cut off. My grandfather wired back to the States, and through Jacob Schiff and the American Jewish Committee raised initially $50,000. He had it delivered in gold coins on an American gunboat by his son-in-law, Maurice Wertheim, who was Barbara Tuchman's father. This was very key to the survival of the community. There is now a street named after my grandfather in Jerusalem.

Then he became very much interested in the Armenians. In 1915 the Turks began massacring the entire Armenian nation, something which they still, to this day, deny. They just say it didn't happen, that the Armenians were war casualties. My grandfather, as a result of what he did, is a saint in the Armenian community. When they have the anniversary of the massacre, particularly when they have something special every five years, I get invited to go around and speak and read from his book, *Ambassador Morgenthau's Story*. Somebody said, "Well, every Armenian child has memorized that book." Although he was not successful in helping in a big way, he did help some, and he also publicized their plight when he came back to this country. These efforts led to the development of the Near East relief, a great outpouring of American generosity. Remember, "the starving Armenians" became an American outcry. He also became very much aware of the German military presence in Turkey and what the Germans were doing. They were the only people then who really could have done anything to stem the atrocities. He believed that they were actually encouraging the Turks. They certainly did nothing to stop them, and they certainly could have, because they were running Turkey at that time.

My father was born in 1891. He visited my grandfather frequently in Turkey. As the only son, he was the apple of my grandfather's eye. They were very close. Unlike my grandfather, my father was not a good student at all. He had a lot of trouble in school. Undoubtedly, he had what we would now recognize as a learning disability. I've seen it in other members of the family, including myself. I was a slow reader and that sort of thing. It was very difficult for him. My grandfather decided, and I guess my father agreed, too, that a conventional career pattern was not for him. For German Jews, business was the thing. If you look at the American pattern, the German Jews — there were certainly some exceptions — on the whole were in business. And the ones who succeeded, succeeded in business. Success was measured in money, on the whole. Later, then maybe they began to get into public life. My grandfather was something of an exception, but not unique; the Straus family did that too, and some others. With the exception of law, which is very close to business anyway, always was and still is, and a little bit into medicine, there were not many intellectuals. They didn't even have rabbis. They imported their rabbis.

My father went to Exeter, and he hated it. I don't think there were many Jews there. I think that was not so much the problem. It was the matter of not doing well in schoolwork. My grandfather had the feeling that there must be something wrong with the school — there could be nothing wrong with his son — so he yanked him out. Then he had the idea they would go into business together, into real estate. My father would be an architect, and he would design the buildings, and my grandfather would finance and build them. So he went to Cornell in the department of architecture, and he didn't like that. He got typhoid then, and he left and went to recuperate on a ranch in Texas. When he was there, he suddenly decided he wanted to become a farmer. I suspect maybe my grandfather pushed him in this direction as well. Grandpa believed that if you couldn't do well in business, farming was a good substitute. He suggested, for example, that his younger brother, whom he was very fond of and who had problems, go into farming. Jews seemed to have the idea, at that time, that some of them should become farmers. The idea of owning land was sort of romantic and appealing. It seemed like a good thing to do.

When my father decided he wanted to go into farming, he went back to Cornell for one year more and took a year in agriculture. He never graduated. That was the end of his formal education. Then he decided he would really go into farming. My grandfather had this grand manner about things — if you want to go into farming, you should go and talk to the Secretary of Agriculture. So he sent my father down to Washington — this was about 1913, right after Wilson was elected. The secretary released an expert to accompany my father at his expense. He took a long trip around the United States to look at farms, and he ended up buying a farm in Dutchess County, New York. Although my father, I know, thinks that he discovered that location himself as the ideal place to go, it is interesting that as a young man my grandfather had gone to a boarding house in the village of Hopewell Junction for his vacations, almost on the borders of these farmlands.

My father was very much under my grandfather's guidance, and Grandpa liked to have my father with him in Constantinople. He liked to have all of his family around him, partly to admire him and partly — this was something my father did himself later on — to see that what he was doing was really for the family, to elevate the family. So Grandpa was constantly yanking my father over to Constantinople. But my father was interested in the farm, and he was beginning to do well with it. There were letters he wrote to my mother at the time — they were not married — which talk about all of this.

My mother was a good student. She went to Vassar. In those days, women didn't go to college very much unless they had some special reason, and Jewish women went even less. If you really felt you had to go to college, you could go to Barnard and live at home. My mother was from New York City. Her father was Morris Fatman, a woolens manufacturer, Raritan Mills. He was born in Cincinnati, as far as I know. His wife was Lisette ("Settie") Lehman, who was the sister of Herbert and Irving Lehman. Settie was also the sister of the Aunt Hattie to whom Stephen Birmingham attributes the term *our crowd*. She was Hattie Lehman Goodhart. She and her sister, my grandmother, had adjoining houses their father had built for them on West Eighty-first Street.

Going to Vassar was considered a very adventurous thing to do. There certainly were not very many Jews there. In fact, they were such a rarity that I don't think it was a problem. There's one woman I've interviewed at great length who was a year ahead of my mother at Vassar, class of 1912. They became lifelong friends, and she just says, "Absolutely not." Many of the women who went there came from genteel families, but if they didn't get married, they'd have to have jobs as teachers or missionaries. Many of them were daughters of missionaries and preachers.

My mother and father were not at all religious when they got married. That was the height of the era of assimilation. They were married by Rabbi Stephen Wise. They had no doubt they were Jewish, but at this point they had screened out just about everything that was Jewish. This was where I came into the world. To the extent you thought about being Jewish at all, it was negative. It was a problem. It was never something to be proud of or happy about. To compliment somebody, you would say, "So-and-so doesn't look very Jewish."

Part of spending time on the farm was that it gave us an escape route from the very tight German Jewish circle in New York and Westchester County. On the other hand, in my parents' generation there seemed to be little doubt that you would marry a Jew — a German Jew. You could marry into one of the old Sephardic Jewish families, but there weren't many of them left. There were some, like the Sulzbergers — the mother of Arthur Sulzberger, publisher of the *New York Times,* was a Hays, and she looked down on the German Jews. But those Sephardic Jews had either long since become converted to Christianity or they had more or less been absorbed into the German Jewish community. There are a few of those families that continued — the Cardozos, the Benjamins, the Nathans.

On one hand, we never talked about being Jewish. There was nothing Jewish going on at home, in terms of rituals, symbols, and artifacts. And because we had this farm and went away for weekends, we never went to temple, even on the High Holidays in those days, though we did later on. On the other hand, all of the kids I played with were Jewish and came from the same group. When we got to be teenagers there were dances; there were organized parties. It was just expected that we would attend. In those days it seemed as though things would just continue as they had been forever — to marry a German Jew. Then there were law firms and Mount Sinai was a Jewish hospital, so you had Jewish doctors and Jewish lawyers and Jewish friends. It was a completely Jewish life without anyone's ever mentioning it. It was considered bad form to mention it. So you used all kinds of dodges; like Aunt Hattie, you'd talk about "our crowd" and "people of our persuasion" and all these euphemisms. It was all very constipated ambivalence. You didn't say "Jewish"; you never used the word.

When I got a little older we did go to funerals at Temple Emanu-El. Nathan Straus, Sr., was a Zionist, which was very unusual in "our crowd," and the Strauses continued their interest in Judaism. The Nathan Straus, Jr., family, who had four sons in my generation, had what they called Bible class in their house. This was conducted by Rabbi Wise's son, who was a great renegade actually. He became wealthy as a friend of Picasso, who allowed him to be the dealer for many of his paintings. We had the Bible classes, and I remember enjoying them quite a lot, but not the other kids, who were a very unruly group. We were there under duress. Wise would tell stories from the Bible, in English, as though it were kind of history or literature.

My grandfather had an idea that right after the United States went into the war, in 1917, they could get Turkey out of the war. This was just before the Russians got out. It was also just before the Balfour Declaration. So he went and talked to Secretary of State Robert Lansing about his plan, and Lansing talked to President Wilson about it. They thought it was a real long shot. My grandfather said it was a real long shot, but why not give it a try; they had nothing to lose. As he set out on his mission, my grandfather took along with him a young man by the name of Felix Frankfurter, who was a Zionist closely associated with Justice Brandeis, who was on the Supreme Court and was a leading American Zionist.

My grandfather thought he could make a deal with the Turkish leaders. Turkey was really falling apart and the Turks were not happy with their German relationship, where they could see they were being had. So it was a real possibility. The cover for this mission was that they were going to see what could be done to help the Jews in Palestine. Frankfurter did a whole chapter in his oral history in which he rips into my grandfather. He thought he was a pompous fool and so forth. At this point, the British decided that they really didn't want Turkey out of the war, because they were about to launch the Allenby campaign. That was after Gallipoli. My grandfather had been there during Gallipoli, and my father was there during the storming of the Dardanelles, and visited the front lines.

The British then decided that they didn't really want this mission to proceed. But they thought the Americans wanted it. So they sent Chaim Weizmann as their representative. Weizmann was opposed to the plan because the Balfour Declaration was in the offing — it came out a few months later. He also saw it as locking in the *status quo* — that part of the deal with the Turks would probably be, if they got out of the war, to let them keep most of the Ottoman Empire, which would have included Syria. And Palestine was part of Syria. There was no Palestine as such. It didn't have any geographical boundary. Actually, as things turned out, they probably would have been better off with the Turks than they were with the British. But at that time, they didn't think so. Weizmann representing the British and somebody representing the French met with my grandfather at Gibraltar, and they talked him out of this mission. He sent Frankfurter back to Washington to report, and he stayed on in Europe. What Frankfurter had to say when he came back, God only knows. I haven't really gotten to the bottom of all this. But partly because of what had occurred, my grandfather began to feel really betrayed by the Zionists.

Shortly after that, he felt that Stephen Wise went behind his back to Wilson and got him to endorse the Balfour Declaration. Wilson became quite pro-Zionist. It fitted in with his self-determination policy. My grandfather eventually had a very bitter falling-out with Stephen Wise. They began to say terrible things about each other. From then on Grandpa was just bitterly opposed to Zionist aspirations. He also, I think, saw Zionism as some of that immigrant generation did, the business of dual allegiance.

My dad, by the way, was very pro-Zionist. When he got out of the Treasury, he devoted the latter part of his life, until he got ill, to Jewish affairs. He became national chairman of the United Jewish Appeal and then the first American chairman of the Israel Bond drive. Grandpa died in 1946 at the age of a little over ninety. I was living with him at the time. I was out of the army after the war, and he was very much opposed to my father getting involved in Jewish affairs. It was a very bitter thing for him. At the end of my father's career in the Treasury, he became very emotionally committed to the plight of European Jewry. After all, he was really responsible for getting the War Refugee Board organized, late as it was. Stephen Wise and various people began coming to see him because of his position in the Treasury and his closeness to President Roosevelt.

How did he hook up with Roosevelt? Again, I think my grandfather had great talent for spotting political comers. He began seeing Roosevelt as a promising political figure when Roosevelt was Assistant Secretary of the Navy in the Wilson administration. But you see, in Dutchess County my father and Roosevelt, though they weren't actually neighbors, shared local interests. Just how they met, I don't know. There weren't very many Democrats in Dutchess County for one thing. The first official thing my father did for FDR was to organize a welcome-home celebration in Hyde Park when he was nominated as Vice-President in 1920. At the same time, my mother became a very good friend of Eleanor Roosevelt and got active working in the women's division of the Democratic Party. I think the two Eleanors were persistently sort of pushing my father's career behind the scenes. When Roosevelt ran for governor, my father was an advance man for him on the campaign trail. Then his first job as a state officeholder was as chairman of an agricultural advisory committee for Roosevelt. Later he made him Conservation Commissioner. Meanwhile, he was publishing an agricultural newspaper called the *American Agriculturist*. So his interests were all very definitely in agriculture and his real ambition was to be Secretary of Agriculture.

New York is a major agricultural state, but the rest of the country doesn't think of it that way, and the idea of having a Secretary of Agriculture from New York State who was a Jew, I'm sure didn't seem like a very good idea. Roosevelt, by that time, was taking care of some "Republicans for Roosevelt," and he put Henry Wallace in his original Cabinet — Wallace's father had been Secretary of Agriculture under Harding.

He told my father he had something much better for him. That was when they were creating all these alphabet agencies. My father was appointed governor of the old Farm Board along with heading a new agency called the Farm Credit Administration. That was the first financial operation that he was fully responsible for. William Woodin, who was Secretary of Treasury, was ailing. Dean Acheson was the Under Secretary of the Treasury, and he was opposed to going off the gold standard. Roosevelt decided that was what he wanted to do, so he removed Acheson and put my father in as Under and Acting Secretary. When Woodin died, my father became Secretary.

There were quite a few Jews who were close to Roosevelt. None of them, including Frankfurter, really did anything to push Roosevelt in the direction of assisting the Jewish victims of Hitler. My father was a very emotional kind of person. When he began to hear about the troubles in Europe, which was late, probably around 1943, he was very shocked. At the end of his career in Washington this became completely obsessive with him. First of all, he discovered that the State Department — particularly Assistant Secretary Breckenridge Long — was not only anti-Semitic but actually covering up and suppressing information. At the urging of three men in the Treasury, all of whom were Christians, he came up with a plan for the War Refugee Board. Had people like them in the State Department made a similar effort, they wouldn't have survived. My father presented his proposal to the President, and at a very late date the President did appoint a War Refugee Board, consisting of Cordell Hull, Henry Stimson, and my father. Hull wasn't interested at all, and Stimson, I think, was concerned that it might hamper the winning of the war. Although the two other Cabinet officers didn't actually oppose the board, they certainly did nothing to advance its work. It was run out of the Treasury by a brilliant young lawyer named John Pehle. To the extent that they were able to do anything, as it was very late, it was Pehle with my father's backing that did it.

My father also had the idea for the so-called Morgenthau Plan. The Morgenthau Plan, particularly the idea of demilitarizing Germany, was an obsession with him. Harry Dexter White was involved in this. White remains an enigmatic figure. In view of the things that White was in favor of, there doesn't seem to be much indication that he was a communist; particularly the Bretton Woods, of which he was the principal architect, was certainly not any kind of a communist plot. White had a lot to do with preparing the memorandum, which Roosevelt — and my father, who accompanied him — took to the Quebec conference with Churchill. The idea was not simply to demilitarize and dismember Germany, but to deindustrialize the entire country, making it dependent on its agriculture and light industry. My father was talking to Roosevelt about the Morgenthau Plan up to the time that Roosevelt died. He had dinner with Roosevelt at Warm Springs, Georgia, the night before Roosevelt died. The only other guests at the table were three women — Mrs. Lucy Mercer Rutherfurd, Roosevelt's cousin Laura Delano, and a woman painter Mrs. Rutherfurd had brought down there to do a portrait of FDR for herself.

The Morgenthau Plan, as I said, became an obsession, to the point that when Truman became President, my father wanted to go over to Europe to see that it would be implemented under the American military government. Partly because each President wants his own people, but also with my father's obsession with the Morgenthau Plan, which was not rightfully Treasury business, Truman asked for his resignation. My father would have liked to have become President of the World Bank, because he had given birth to it at Bretton Woods. It was through American leadership, with the architecting primarily of Keynes and White, that the Bretton Woods agreement was hatched. So Dad would have liked to have gone from the Treasury to the Bank. But it didn't happen. The last part of his life, he found himself immersed in Jewish affairs until his health really got very bad, and he was out of things completely.

I was brought up insulated from being Jewish, and at the same time, just without ever discussing it, knowing that all these people, the families and friends that I associated with, came out of the same mold. I went to a day school, Lincoln School. There were Christian families there that we associated with. But when it came to social life, we separated. The school actually was financed by the Rockefellers, and the Rockefellers went there, and maybe a few upper-class families of that kind, but not many. We would just be locked out of that sort of social life, anyway. There was no thought of really invading it, I don't think. For instance, although we would see the Roosevelt family as families, the Roosevelt boys went to Saint Bernard's School in New York and then on to Groton and Harvard. They had their own parties and there was no thought of even wanting to be involved in those things at that point.

My mother was quite adventurous about getting out of this gilded ghetto. First of all, living on the farm, we had a life of our own there. This German Jewish life was very carefully orchestrated. It was primarily on the West Side of New York, and then it began moving over to the East Side. It was mostly in that Central Park West area. There was the Harmonie Club and the Century Country Club in Westchester. I think the Century gave my father a life membership when he went into the Treasury, but we never went there. I don't ever remember going to the Harmonie Club. I don't ever remember going to Temple Emanu-El except for funerals. My mother did something that was quite radical, in that we had non-Jewish doctors, although my father had a Jewish doctor, Dr. Kessel. In those days, even if you weren't terribly well-off, you had probably five servants in the house. The employer had a kind of tacit responsibility to take care of everything, including their health. I remember my mother saying, and she was shocked to learn of it, that Dr. Kessel would not take care of the servants. He had his assistant, Dr. Harold Heyman, take care of the servants. Later, Dr. Heyman became our family doctor. I remember our pediatrician was not Dr. Schloss, whom everybody else had, but Dr. Curly. We had all these Christian doctors, which was quite unusual. Most people used the Mount Sinai circuit.

My father's lawyer was his old friend Eddie Greenbaum. Then we began experimenting. Summer resorts were all segregated, too. Most of the families we knew had first gone down to the Jersey shore, to Elberon and Deal. Then they went to the Adirondacks, where they had what they called camps, which were clubs of perhaps a half dozen families. My grandfather had started one of those, which I've gone back to visit. It was called Eagle Nest. But after his experience in diplomacy, Grandpa experimented with summering at Bar Harbor, Maine, which was more or less on the level with Newport. He became a member of the Bar Harbor Club, and must have been the only Jew in it. We began going to places where my mother had access through some of her Vassar College friends. They weren't places where very wealthy Christians went. We started going to a Quaker resort in Rhode Island, the Weekapaug Inn. Of course, Quakers had associated a good deal with Jews and sometimes married them. Then when my father was Conservation Commissioner, because a lot of wealthy Christians were interested in the preservation of the Adirondacks, we went to a place where I guess there were no Jews at all. Even then, I didn't think about it very much. It was called the Ausable Club in Keene Valley.

In my experience in living at home, I can never remember a rabbi being a guest in the house for any purpose, but I remember the Reverend Henry Sloane Coffin being invited. It was something special, and I think my mother was a bit nervous about this. I seemed to be protected from anti-Semitism when I went to day school and to boarding school at Deerfield Academy in Massachusetts. There was a whole group of Lincoln School boys who went *en bloc*. We didn't keep to ourselves. As a matter of fact, there was a tendency to do just the opposite, to keep away from each other. Anti-

Semitism really hit me for the first time when I went to Princeton. Then I really got it, full in the face. I was in the class of 1939. I went there in the fall of 1935. You joined one of the eating clubs in the middle of sophomore year. I was not invited to join any of the good clubs.

In 1936 my father was Secretary of the Treasury. The social life in Washington had suddenly opened up to us. You were treated as kind of honorary Aryans if your father was in that kind of high government position. I must say, I was very intrigued with all this. I loved it. It didn't bother me at all that other Jews wouldn't be accepted, that I was an exception and I wasn't taking anybody with me — that I was entering not only a Christian but an anti-Semitic world. This went on simultaneously with my Princeton experience.

At Princeton I began to learn in a negative way about Jewishness and anti-Semitism, experiencing it in a very painful way because, at the same time, I was willing to do most anything to be accepted in the social mainstream. I didn't really resolve this gross ambivalence until much later.

I went into the army and I was in the Third Army in Europe in the mechanized cavalry for four years. Then when I came back I got involved in Jewish affairs. I became chairman of the junior division of the New York City United Jewish Appeal, and began to get interested in Jewish things. But I guess I didn't get fully involved until I got married, which was rather late in my life. My wife, Ruth Schachter, came out of an Orthodox family that had been through the Hitler experience, although she hasn't led the life of an Orthodox woman. She has found her own way. She teaches political science at Brandeis University. Judaism was really more a part of her than she knew, and part of something that I never had known. I found it very interesting and very appealing. Then when we had children she felt very strongly, well, that one doesn't give mixed signals. In my family we'd always celebrated Christmas. We'd had Christmas trees, Santa Claus, and stockings, and all the rest of it. We had Easter egg hunts. The whole bit.

Ruth thought that things were bad enough when one lives in a secular world here in Cambridge. It was just going to be confusing for the children. Certainly no Christmas celebration at all, and the children would have to have a Jewish education. Then I got interested. Our wedding, of course, was Orthodox, because Ruth's father particularly felt very strongly about this. Then I began to learn Hebrew and I got involved in Harvard-Radcliffe Hillel through the children's Sunday school classes.

Despite all of this, the children are not very Jewish. Mainstream life, and particularly here, is so open, one gets sucked into it painlessly. All three of our children have had a Jewish education. Our daughter was Bat Mitzvahed and our two boys were Bar Mitzvahed and went to Camp Ramah. They can spout off the blessings and we try to keep Friday night, and we do have Chanukah, when we give presents. We try to have them home for the High Holidays and Pesach. They go along with that, but I don't know who they're going to marry. We'll have to see what happens.

5

World of Their Fathers

I AM STILL ASTOUNDED by how many Jews, as very young boys or as fathers, left their homelands in the late nineteenth and early twentieth centuries to travel alone to the United States. Often the reason was to escape military service, which in Russia could be for as long as twenty-five years; or there was the deep urge to find the proverbial better life, which meant religious freedom, freedom from persecution, and a better education. One, two, five, ten years later they sent for their families, usually siblings and wives, but not always in that order, and then mothers and fathers. Most, if not all, were illiterate in English. And they were impoverished. Some brought a radical ferment with them from Germany, especially after the disorders of 1848 and later; others brought a new radicalism from pre-Revolutionary Russia. Some established secular schools to teach not the Jewish religion, but Yiddish and socialism. They argued, debated, created tumult, went to plays, listened to lectures, and argued some more.

As the Washington lawyer Leonard Garment put it: "Generally, almost all the places where I lived, and worked occasionally as a kid, were densely packed with immigrants and children of immigrants. They were places of mixed language — English, Jewish, German, Russian; yelling, incomprehensible language, muttering, screaming — very lively."

Zita Cogan, who was raised in Chicago and is a university concert manager there, remembered how, late in her life, she learned a startling fact about her parents:

"My mother and father were never married. They were part of a group who came from Europe, in probably 1908 or 1909, who defied convention. They were part of a group of these freethinkers; let's call them that, because I don't think they considered themselves intellectuals. They were interested in politics; they were interested in changing the world maybe, but there wasn't that much to change at that time. They did a lot of reading and they would discuss. I don't know what they discussed, but I remember they used to discuss. Then, of course, when Bolshevism came on the scene, that's when you began to have splits in these freethinking ways. Some became socialists; some became communists."

Daniel Bell, sixty-eight, professor, Cambridge, Massachusetts

I am a professor at Harvard University. My mother and father both came from the area between Poland and Russia, about thirty miles northeast of Bialystok, the area which shifted back and forth constantly. But they didn't know each other in the old country.

My mother came as one of five sisters; she was the middle one of the five. A brother was left behind and died in Poland. My mother's father was a melamed, a teacher, and he stayed, and I was named after him. My father came with his father. My grandfather was the eldest of about eight or nine boys, most of whom, as far as I recall, came over, and there was one sister. His family name was Bolotsky, but as I found out later that was not actually the original name. His father or grandfather, probably his father, had been named Karlinsky. There was this edict in Russia that if you were a younger son you were eligible for service in the army, so younger sons were often placed in other families or moved away and took different names in order to seem to be only children. He took the name Bolotsky.

He came over here and for most of his life he worked, having a small business which was coal in the wintertime and seltzer and ice in the summertime. He had a horse and wagon, and one of my earliest memories was working with him, riding on a horse and wagon through the Lower East Side, saying, "Giddyup." That's the closest I've ever come to nature. It reminds me of Bernard Malamud's marvelous story where he goes out to Eugene, Oregon, and the character in the story is called Levin. Levin goes into the fields and looks with amazement and he says, "It's the first time a Levin has ever seen a cow, and the first time a cow has ever seen a Levin."

I grew up on the Lower East Side. I had an older brother. My mother was a dressmaker and my father worked as a pattern maker, cutting dress patterns in shops. My father died in January 1920, when I was about eight months old. So when I grew up, we lived for about the first six or seven years with different relatives, usually with one of my mother's sisters. But my grandfather also lived nearby on the Lower East Side, so I would go over there in the afternoons. My grandparents moved up to the Bronx when I was about five years old, but we remained on the Lower East Side because my mother worked in a garment factory. I was put in what was called then a "day orphanage." It was a peculiar institution. It was partly a day care center, partly an orphanage, because there were many children like myself who came from families where one or the other parent had died.

It was called a Hebrew day orphanage, actually. It was supported by the community; it didn't have any city or state money. There was no such thing. It was supported by the local businessmen. It was a peculiar arrangement in that about three or four months a year, sometimes five months a year, I would stay there for weeks at a time. The other times of the year, I would only be there for the day, the reason being, of course, that particular situation known as "slack." In other words, in the garment industry, because of the seasons, there are long periods when you work ten or more hours a day. So I'd be there in the morning and I never knew in the evening whether my mother would come to pick me up. If she was working late, I'd sleep over. If there was slack and there was no work, she would come and pick me up. So I used to joke, when the revolution comes I have the perfect proletariat background — both parents were workers, deprived, broken home, every situation of that kind. There was another orphanage that I recall where the real orphans would stay, but these sorts of day orphanages were quite common on the Lower East Side. And again, it was one of these interesting illustrations of the way you had a self-help pattern, which was very important: providing a sense of support. Today, it would be called "network support."

I had about seven or eight uncles and aunts from my father's side. When I was about ten or eleven years old, my legal guardian was my father's younger brother. He was a dentist. His name was Samuel Bolotsky, and he used to have an office on the Lower East Side. He was moving up to Second Avenue and then to the Bronx. They thought Bolotsky didn't fit well. Actually, a group of the cousins came together to change their names and they took three different names. Some took the name Bell, which is what my uncle Sam took. Some took the name Ballin. And some cousins took the name Ballot. He changed our names legally; that's when I became Bell.

I remember the Lower East Side very, very vividly, because when I was about eight or nine years old I refused to go into the day orphanage. I didn't like it there and I was the vilda in the family, so my grandfather and my aunts and uncles would not want to have me around. I was always running around, breaking in. My brother was the quiet one, so he would be taken in. First, you went to cheder. For two hours after school, you went to cheder. I went to cheder five days a week. It was one of these typical East Side Jewish cheders in which you translated not from Hebrew into English;

you translated from Hebrew into Yiddish, because everyone spoke Yiddish. Just to backtrack for a moment, I didn't learn English until I went to school. I learned a little bit of English, knew bits of words, but I spoke to my mother and spoke to my relatives in Yiddish.

So to that extent, Yiddish was my first language, and English was always a second language and it gave one a sense later of the nature and vicissitudes of language. Yiddish is a very fruity language; it's more like Elizabethan English, and you can express yourself in Yiddish in ways which are genteelly wrong in English. Emotionally I would speak in Yiddish. Many years later I was in psychoanalysis. Fortunately, I had an analyst who knew Yiddish, because quite often when I would revert to certain emotional strains I would begin thinking and speaking in Yiddish. It was natural. Yiddish is a language in which one can express oneself very readily.

It goes back to what I was saying earlier, which is this interest I have always had in Jewish humor. My retirement project is a theme called "Some Serious Thoughts about Jewish Humor." I have tried to understand what it is that makes Jewish humor so readily available as a medium of aggression and discourse. And yet, in its own way, it is radically different from almost all humor to some extent, except black humor, in its willingness to even talk back to God, so to speak. I think the answer, at least one of the answers, is that Jewish humor has a certain tension. Yiddish humor, that is, has a certain tension because Hebrew theology is deeply conservative. It has a view of human nature which is radically pessimistic. The world is full of chayas. There's Sodom, there's Gomorrah, there's Babylon, and therefore the world is a place of terror. The Orthodox are always very conservative, even politically so, because of this radically pessimistic view of human nature. But Jewish experience is radicalizing because it's the experience of humiliation. You are forced to kowtow, as in Poland, where you couldn't sit down at school; you had to stand in the ghetto benches. You were smarter than these people and yet you were humiliated.

Humiliation, I've always felt, has been one of the strongest mainsprings to Jewish radicalism, so when you have the experience being radicalized but the theology being conservative, you get a peculiar tension. And the humor begins to express that kind of tension, which is the sense that the world is one which is basically hostile. You cope with it by being aggressive in your humor and showing you are smarter. I mean, if you look at Freud's *Jokes and the Unconscious*, there's a whole series of stories that Freud tells which involve ratiocination, complicated reasoning, pilpul, the very thing you learn in Talmud. Pilpul simply means pepper, so when you learn pilpul, which is "why here and not there," it goes on this way.

Let me just take a minute, because I think it is crucial to understanding certain notions of education and why to some extent Jewish education predisposes certain kinds of Jewish children to a way of thinking which is radically different instinctively than most of the formal education. Because when you go to cheder, as I did, you start in with the chumish, the five books of Moses, and you start reading — to show the rabbi how smart you are — "Bereshith barah." The rabbi says, "Wait a minute, wait a minute. What's the first word in the Bible? The chumish?"

"Bereshith. In the beginning." "But what's the first letter?" "*Beth*." "God is beginning the world. God is not a capricious God; there has to be a reason for what He does. Why does God begin the world with the letter *b*?" You say, "I don't know. Why does God begin the world with the letter *b*?" He says, "Well, look, yold" — you were always being told you were a yold in school; you were always being sort of put back on your heels so you'd have to either crumple or you'd answer back, "Why didn't God begin the world with the letter *shin*, which is the sign you put on the tfillin on your hand; which is one of the ineffable names of God; which the Kohens hold their hands up this way on Yom Kippur; which you will find on certain Jewish gravestones?" *Shin* stands for Shaddai, one of the ineffable names of God. Why not begin the world with the letter *shin*? Well, if God began the world with the letter *shin*, the world would be too compromised, because *shin* also stands for sheker, which is a lie.

"Why not begin the world with the letter *tav*, for Torah?" Well, *tav* is also the sign of death, which God will place on the front heads of men. "Why not begin the world with the letter *daled*, which stands for the Hebrew word din, which is justice?" So you go through every letter of the alphabet until the only one that's left is *beth*, which stands for baruch, which is blessed, and blessed are those who accept the word of God.

There's a lovely little book by Ben Shahn I think called *The Alphabet of Creation*, in which he illustrates this process, and when I once wrote an essay on Hannah Arendt's *Eichmann in Jerusalem* I ended with this story. And I used it in the essay that is in my book *The Winding Passage*, which I call "The Alphabet of Justice," the way in which you have to weigh each letter to understand it. But also it leads to the kind of pilpul: "Why here, not there? Why this and not that?" When we'd go to school later, we'd drive our teachers crazy. The teacher would start a poem: "Into the valley of death rode the six hundred." "Say, teacher, why six hundred? Why not five hundred? Why not seven hundred?" She didn't know. So you would say, "If into the valley of death rode seven hundred, it would be a hundred too many. If into the valley of death rode five hundred, it would be a hundred too few. So into the valley of death rode the six hundred." And I thought of this the other day, because there was a marvelous story in the *Times* that they had found some papers of Tennyson, who'd written the poem, in which it was pointed out to him that actually into the valley of death had ridden seven hundred. But he didn't like seven hundred because metrically it didn't fit in, so he made it six hundred. So actually the logic was absolutely right. But you see, you learn this way of thinking, and instinctively it's always . . . You turn things around; you turn them upside down — why this way, why not another way? — and therefore it shows you the different, multifaceted nature of all thought. It leaves you with a certain kind of questioning, a certain degree of distance, and therefore certain ways and modes of evaluation.

Now this form of thinking, as I say, becomes instinctive. That's why many Jews go into law, where you eventually have to sort of tease the ultimate principle out of the whole muck of cases; in physics, where you are trying to find the underlying structural principle for the different combination of things. So there're some interesting reasons why certain occupations — theoretical physics as opposed to experimental physics, elements of the law — are themselves modes of intellectual work where certain kinds of Jewish modes of thinking fit so readily and predispose people to be more successful.

That's cheder. What about the street gangs? They were made up of kids like myself and we would run around the streets. We were involved in the typical things called turf wars. People think of turf wars as things which are going on now, but we had them on the Lower East Side. The Jewish turf, so to speak, was roughly from about Second Street to Twelfth Street and from Avenue D to Avenue B. Above Twelfth Street was the Italian section. Above Avenue B was the Ukrainian and Polish section. So when you were passing through, there was always the matter of getting beaten up by kids. The big arena of conflict was Tompkins Square Park, which is now the place where the new art scene has developed in the last couple of years. That's the place where I used to play as a boy. And we'd go skating and you always risked being attacked by a gang and your skates' being taken away. So obviously everyone traveled in gangs. And there were wars. Sometimes it got very rancid. I never engaged in a war, but we knew of situations where guys would take potatoes and put razors inside the potatoes and throw them. You can get awfully hurt with something like that. But you also had shields; the tops of the garbage cans would be the shields.

I remember the pushcarts. You bought from the pushcarts on Avenue C, on First Avenue. In fact, as a boy I used to be embarrassed. One remembers odd little things. My mother would bargain. There were tomatoes. The tomatoes would be, I don't know, five cents apiece, and she said, "I will give you four cents apiece." And I would say, "Mama, it's not nice. Don't do it." And she'd say, "Don't be silly. It's a penny from him; it's better a penny for you." That was her attitude, you see. The pushcarts were the daily life of the time. Besides which when we were in these street gangs the pushcart people would go over to get the crates of tomatoes and radishes and other things and that's when we would go over with them and sort of take things off the crates for ourselves.

Pushcarts were always parked in the same place. They were licensed. You had to have a license from the city. You had the same place. Then, of course, the city thought it was unsanitary and didn't like it. And towards the end of the 1930s they tried to build these large, inside markets to get the pushcarts off the streets. And when my stepfather had a store — he had a store on Eleventh Street between First and Second avenues, which was an Italian section — there were pushcarts along the street there and along First Avenue.

But the other thing which was most important, actually, is that this was the Depression. And the garbage scows used to tie up on the docks, on the Lower East Side, and next to them would be these little cubicles, these little tin shacks where people lived. You'd see people scrambling all over the garbage scows for food, and this is an indelible impression. At the same time you also saw a lot of screwing. The dock was the place, there was an open area, particularly around stanchions and what they call the edge of the scow, and you'd see a hell of a lot of screwing. So there was a lot of peeping. So it was an initiation into life, so to speak, in a double sense; namely, that you saw what the Depression really meant and you saw open sex in a way which I suppose any protected middle-class kid in an American town would never see, at least in this way. So those, in a sense, were the indelible impressions from growing up on the Lower East Side, and they clearly predisposed me to become a socialist.

When I was thirteen years old I joined the YPSL, the Young People's Socialist League, and immediately you get into the whole question of tactics of the revolution. One of the problems that came up was the fact that a revolution would be more difficult in America than in France. Why? In France they have cobblestones. They can dig up the cobblestones and throw the cobblestones, which is the revolutionary tactic from the French Revolution to the Commune. But where were the cobblestones in New York? And obviously one revolutionary faction being very into it would say, "Fool. What you do is, the revolutionary women go upstairs; you barricade the streets. When the police come in you throw down hot water on them." [Laughs.] Well, you adapt the tactics of the gang wars for revolutionary tactics.

Curiously enough, if you look at immigrant experience in America, there has always been the myth, largely put forth, some suggest, by the dominant press, if you want to call it that, that immigrants tend to be radicals or "foreigners"; "un-American." If you look at the works of various historians of immigrant groups, it turns out to be quite true the other way around, rather: the majority of the immigrants were conservative. They were eager to make their way; they worked hard; they didn't want to have much do with these elements; so that particularly the German groups and others were much more conservative. But there is always a minority that is much more vocal, radical, angry. And in any situation of this kind, the minority gets the attention. They are more visible. It's always the problem, the problem of selective attention. That those who are the more aggressively radical are visible, and therefore you generalize and say, "Look at all the radicals," and they never learned their old mode of reasoning from the Talmud, which says, "An example is not proof." The trouble is that newspapers, you see, always go by example.

But it wasn't just New York. You found this radicalization wherever you found these kinds of globules in these sorts of concentrations. You could find this in Montreal; read some of Mordecai Richler's stories of Montreal. You can find this in Winnipeg, where there's a Jewish community out in Canada. You find this, of course, in Chicago, because later on you always seek each other out. There was a whole Chicago contingent — Saul Bellow, Isaac Rosenfeld, Oscar Tarcov, and various others — who had gone through the same experiences we had. Not necessarily as orphans and such, but essentially the experience of radicalization and the Jewish life. There has to be a concentration, and those who grew up in the South, who were in small towns, probably were totally outside of these things.

There were certain occupational concentrations. Mostly, proletarian Jews in New York worked in dress factories or in men's clothing factories. Therefore, the unions were Jewish unions. So there were three major Jewish unions in New York: the ILGWU, which David Dubinsky headed; the Amalgamated Clothing Workers of Sidney Hillman; and the Hat, Cap, and Millinery Workers of Max Zoritsky. Alex Rose came out of that. He was never the head of the union, but he came out of the Hat, Cap, and Millinery. My mother was a union member. Naturally she was a union member. This was something you simply accepted as part of the ordinary radical activities of the lot. When I worked in the summertime, I worked as a pusher. When I tell people I worked as a pusher, they think, "My God, what the hell is going on? A drug pusher?" When I worked as a pusher, I mean I used to push these racks of dresses through the streets on Seventh Avenue. So I was a pusher. I worked for an uncle of mine. Naturally; how else do you get a job? And I remember very vividly in 1932 I worked in the summertime from about eight-thirty in the morning to about five-thirty or six at night and a half day on Saturday until about three o'clock. I was getting, I think, originally eight dollars a week and then nine dollars a week. Then the National Recovery Administration came in. My uncle had to pay me twelve dollars a week. Naturally I was for Roosevelt. Who says government can't help people? Here I was, getting a fifty percent increase in salary because the government said so. My uncle was furious — it was going to drive him out of business. He made more money, all right. But still, this was the situation. I got fired, interestingly enough, the next year. His partner insisted I be fired. Why? Because I was trying to organize a union among the pushers. We were not included in the union contract. Later they tried to organize; they are called shipping clerks.

I also learned, and someday if I ever write my memoirs, I am going to do it in peculiar form, not to write straight history; that makes no sense to me. But to take experiences that are focal experiences, which last one's lifetime and pose issues of an extraordinary kind. Let me tell you a major one of this sort. In 1933, 1934, we were helping the ILG organize. This was during the NRA days and such and the big push of organizing. We had heard some disturbing rumors that the ILGWU was hiring gangsters to beat up scabs. So we sent a delegation to a man named Julius Hochman, who was the manager of the joint dress board of the union. I was in the delegation. We said, "Comrade Hochman, we understand" — in righteous indignation — "that the ILG is hiring gangsters to beat up scabs." This was the time of Lepke and Gurrah and the whole era of gangster racketeering. And to our surprise, Hochman, instead of denying it, said, "Look, my young comrades, I'll tell you the truth. Yes, we hire gangsters to beat up scabs. You have to understand something. A strike is an important thing in a worker's life. If a scab takes his job, there's no milk for the children, there's no bread on the table. Then tell me, my young comrades, can you imagine a little Jewish cloakmaker beating up a scab?" Well, at that point, we were taken aback and one of our characters, a shtarker, you know, a man named Jerry Coleman, who later, oddly enough, became the head of the millinery union and a member of the New York City Planning Commission, said suddenly, "All right. We'll do it." And this time, Hochman was the one who was really taken aback. He hadn't expected this. His bluff was being called.

The next day we come about nine-thirty in the morning, and the assistant manager is with us. A guy comes downstairs clutching a package and the assistant manager says, "There's the scab; go give him a k'nach." So we all push each other forward and Jerry's up front and Jerry gets ahold of the guy. Unfortunately, he doesn't understand professional. He's a YPSL. He gets the guy by the lapel. He starts making a speech: "You're a scab. You take away the milk from the worker's children! You take away bread from the worker's table! You're a scab! You're a scab!" The guy yells out, "Help! Police!" Jerry gets rattled, grabs the guy's package for some inexplicable reason, starts running down the street, the cops come, grab Jerry, and arrest him for petty larceny. And the next day the ILG went back to using gangsters to beat up scabs.

But it raised a question, though in a crazy way: this is means and ends. Is it legitimate to use violence? To use gangsters to beat up scabs? And in its own crazy way, odd as it may sound, one can look at a whole array of problems about means and ends, the justification of actions, in these terms. And here I was, fourteen years old, you know, facing that immediately and having to think about it, and it stayed with me my whole life.

Was there any crime in the Lower East Side? Of course there was Jewish crime. There was a lot of Jewish crime. In fact, there are some great novels about it. There is a novel by Sam Ornitz called *Haunch, paunch and jowl*, which is about the Jewish lawyers and the Jewish gangsters. First of all, there was prostitution. Jewish prostitution. In fact, there is a great play by Sholem Asch called *Gott fun Nekomeh — The God of Vengeance —* about a Jewish brothelkeeper whose daughter ends up in a brothel, to his great dismay. He wanted her to become respectable. Allen Street, which was the continuation of what then later became First Avenue, was where you used to have the whole row of Jewish prostitutes. They were called "nafkas" in Yiddish, or sometimes "kurvas," and there was the old Jewish joke, of course, where the mother would say to a son, "I don't want you to go driving in this country. It's crazy. It's meshuga. There are signs that say CURVES AHEAD." You know, crazy little jokes. So there was a lot of Jewish prostitution. So there were pimps.

And then, of course, there was the industrial racketeering. The biggest gang was Lepke and Gurrah. He was a man who had difficulty speaking and he would always say, "Gurroutahere" — "Get out of here." Oddly enough, he got the name of Gurrah. Lepke is the diminutive for Louis. Lepke was executed when Thomas E. Dewey was the prosecutor. The reason was very simple. The garment industry was a great mess. And there's always been a movement — this is something again a lot of people don't want to think of in American economic history — there has been monopoly and stabilization to eliminate competition. Industry after industry always moved towards this. Now in the major monopolistic industries — steel, automobile, et cetera — the big firms became oligopolistic. In the other industries, the unions tended to do this, the reason being to eliminate wages as a competitive factor between the firms, because if you've got cutthroat competition, you do it by squeezing wages. In the garment industry the union began to enforce the so-called price lines, $3.95, $5.95, $7.95, depending upon the kind of work and style. But the gangsters were the ones who did the job of enforcement.

Now, for example, Lepke and Gurrah had a monopoly. This wasn't done simply by beating people over the head. This was a very sophisticated mode of racketeering. Lepke and Gurrah had a monopoly on what's called cloth finishing, meaning that all cloth normally was finished so that you could make it shrink-resistant. When the manufacturers bought cloth from the mills down south, it would all be sent to this single firm in New York which did the cloth shrinking. That was the payoff to Lepke and Gurrah. At the same time, they enforced price regulation among the contractors and the manufacturers. What happened was that when the NRA came in, what before had been done illegally, but understood, now became a legal situation, and you no longer needed these people. What before had been a quasi-economic function now becomes extortion and the administration can move in as Dewey did to prosecute these people.

You had bootlegging. You had gambling, numbers, industrial racketeering. I wrote about this in, I suppose, one of my most famous essays, "Crime Is an American Way of Life," which is in *The End of Ideology*, in which I tried to point out that there was a succession of ethnic groups. This story is really one of the most crucial ones for understanding ethnic life in America and the succession of ethnic life. In this essay I tried to show there was a kind of Irish gangster, then Jewish gangster, and then Italian gangster, taking over different functions. But it wasn't just gangsters and crime. There was an interplay between racketeering, wealth, and politics.

If you generated wealth in these ways, you were able to support a group of bright lawyers and to give money to political machines. The early political machines before patronage, and before the great degree of federal monies, came essentially from monies raised in this way. People forget Lincoln got money from the gamblers in New York when he ran for President of the United States. In the same way, a large part of the local political machines were financed by this kind of wealth. Now a lot of it was reinforced by political contract. For example, in New York City there were three people, when I was growing up, who were crucial. There was a man named Sam Rosoff, who was a building contractor, who did most of the subways; Generoso Pope, who later owned *Il Progresso*, who had a monopoly on the concrete mix thing for building construction; and a man named Bill McCormack, who controlled the trucking, the teamsters. Now these three men, essentially, were political contractors: McCormack in trucking, Generoso Pope in construction and the concrete mix, and Sam Rosoff in the digging. McCormack, for example, would haul away the ashes and cinders from the schools and give them to Sam Rosoff, who used them to pave the street. You never miss a trick this way. This novel by Sam Ornitz called *Hauch, paunch and jowl* is very revealing about this. This interplay of racketeering, wealth, politics, law, was essentially the way this worked.

There always were Jewish political machines. The boss on the Lower East Side was a Republican. Many Jews were Republicans the way the Italians were Republicans. People forget in the 1920s, 1930s, the Republicans were liberals. You had George Norris, for example. The Midwest progressives were Republicans against the southern Democrats, who were reactionaries. Sam Koenig was the Republican boss on the Lower East Side, and his protégé was a man named Louis Lefkowitz, who later became the attorney general of the State of New York. There were always political machines, and almost all the judges came out of these political machines. But these political machines were fueled by the wealth, this interplay of wealth. I'm not saying all of it. The German Jewish wealth came, of course, from the banking families. But a large part of the Russian Jewish wealth, the next generation — a lot of it — came out of this interplay.

Were all the young socialists Jewish? Yes. So much so that you never even thought about it. The story of my joining the YPSL, curious story. One never joins something purely — you don't go up and say, "I apply," you know. Someone always recruits you. You are always part of your own milieu. When I was in junior high school, a group of us began reading — and I found this true of a lot of people — there are certain books that suddenly hit you for a peculiar psychological reason, and this book was Upton Sinclair's *The Jungle*. Here was a story of the immigrant family in Chicago being exploited. At the end, this man who's broken and such goes into a hall and he hears a speech, and actually it's a speech of Gene Debs — his great vision of socialism and such. There's a young boy by the name of Leonard Weidman, I remember, who's the younger brother of the novelist Jerome Weidman, né Julius Weidman. He was named Julius but he never liked it so he called himself Jerome and he gave himself yichus. But through him, I joined the YPSL circle. I went to the melamed who was teaching me my Haftarah for the Bar Mitzvah. And I said to him, "Look, I found the truth. I don't believe in God. I'm joining the Young People's Socialist League. I'll put on tfillin once, in memory of my dead father, but that's all." He looked at me and he said: "Yingel, you found the truth? You don't believe in God?" He says, "Tell me, do you think God cares?" I was absolutely furious, absolutely furious.

In later years, I realized this was the actual, traditional answer. Many,

many years later there was a study circle — I've always worked in study circles. This was with Irving Kristol and Nathan Glazer and Milton Himmelfarb, and a strange man named Jacob Taubes, about whom one can spin endless stories. A European. And we met every Sunday evening and read Maimonides' *Mishneh Torah*, a line-by-line analysis, real pilpul. In Maimonides there is a fascinating discussion in which he says, in effect, to a skeptic, to a disbeliever, he says, "Look, who are you to say 'I believe or don't believe'? Who are you to say 'I believe in God'? Believe or don't believe; that's your business. Just obey the law." And that again, you see, is real Yiddish chachma. It's arrogance for you to say "I believe or don't believe." I thought of this later on, in a peculiar way. It must have been about twenty years or so later that Elliot Cohen, the founding editor of *Commentary*, ohav shalom, had in his house Martin Buber, the Jewish philosopher. Elliot had gathered a large number of the young Jewish intellectuals, contributors to *Commentary*, to meet Buber. There was Kristol and Bob Warshaw, Clement Greenberg and myself. And I've never forgotten. Buber was sitting in the corner of the room. Small man. Trimmed beard. Very elegantly attired. White hair coming down over his forehead. And he was saying, in this kind of grandiloquent way, with his hands weaving arabesques, "We must reach out. We must speak to God. If God won't listen we must clutch Him even by the lapels. There must be an I-Thou relationship; otherwise the world becomes smothered in I-It. We must make a dialogue, I and Thou. And we must speak out to God." And suddenly, that old story of my Bar Mitzvah came back. "What do you mean, 'Speak out to God'? Do you think God cares?"

And I thought, you see, this is curious, because what Buber was teaching was a form of existential Judaism. I said, "You know I can't be an existentialist Jew." Actually, I wrote about this subsequently without mentioning Buber in an essay of mine called "Reflections on Jewish Identity," in which I say that one is a Jew by fate. You are there. Everyone is identified by the way you live in the tension of the parochial and the universal. We all want to be cosmopolitan. But if you are totally cosmopolitan, you become deracinated. If you are totally parochial, you become crabbed and orthodox. Yet you can't deny who you are, because in a modern sense you say to someone, "Who are you?" You say, "I am me; I come out of myself." It makes no sense. And the traditionalists say, "You say I am Yitzhak ben Avram; I'm Ali ben Ahmed; I am Ivan Petrovitch. I am the son of my father." There is a sense of continuity. You cannot deny the parochial element, but, as I say, if you are entirely parochial, you are purely narrow; if you are entirely cosmopolitan, you are deracinated.

So one lives in this tension. But the notion somehow that you can become an existential Jew and sort of reach out and speak to God goes against all the grain of historic Jewish thought. So I could never become an existential Jew in Buber's sense, and since I am Jewish, I am not a Jew by faith in the fundamentalist sense; I'm not a believer in the narrow sense. I am a Jew by fate, in terms of who we are. And that, it seems to me, has always been true, that Judaism has never been a religion. Judaism is defined as being a people. And you are defined by history, defined by history as the shaping experience of history and culture. I did an essay about a year or so ago which has now caused a big furor in France; it was published in *Commentaire*. It was published here with less attention in *Moment*. It's called "New York or Jerusalem?" in which I was trying to say the experience of the galut is just as relevant as the experience of Israel, because you cannot deny several thousand years of history and say, "We will leap over it," and simply return. Yet the history of the Jewish people is a history where you identify from history and culture; the experience of the galut and living in the galut is as relevant.

In fact, what I've said is the curious thing about the idea of going back to Israel, and only in Israel could you live a normal life and outside you couldn't because it was always the historic extension of being Jewish. I said the odd part is that today in America, more than any other time in human history, Jews live what could be most practically a normal life, and in Israel they live an abnormal life in terms of all the pressure cookers. So you find this odd paradox. I never was a Zionist; I mean, I always identified obviously with Israel but never with the Zionist cause. And the notion that somehow everything is illegitimate always struck me as wrong. But it goes back, you see, like all these things, this early experience here. I had this Bar Mitzvah. Suddenly, there's rebuff. It comes back in this extraordinary way many years later in listening to Buber at that conversation and then reflecting upon it and saying, "But I can't be that kind of Jew." But in what sense am I a Jew? I'm a Jew by fate, by the continuity of my people.

And what I've also tried to argue is that the most important element in Jewish life is memory; what keeps the continuity is memory. Most people live by memory, but curiously enough, this is in an essay I did on Jewish identity. Jewish memory is reinforced four times a year when you say Yizkor: "May God remember the name of . . ." Since I was a boy one thing I never did was to miss Yizkor or miss Kaddish for my father.

The trouble is, as you see, one thing leads to another in any free association; I can't give you an orderly disquisition.

There are two things which were important about the YPSL. One was there was this intensive pressure to learn and study. So that you went to school, to a Sunday school, but actually it was a Sunday school for a Marxian text. There is also the Rand School of Social Science in New York City, which is the old socialist school. I've never forgotten when I was fifteen years old I took courses in dialectical materialism. Like all these things, there are little funny threads that come up later. A few years ago I met a man named Francis Low. Francis Low is a very great theoretical physicist and had been provost at MIT, a man who was one of the major figures in theoretical physics. When I met him I said, "You know, it will amuse you to learn that your father taught me dialectical materialism at the Rand School." His father was Béla Low, an engineer and a socialist, but he taught dialectical materialism.

Also, curiously enough, Béla Low's wife, Francis's mother, was a woman named Eugenia Ingerman, a physician, a very well-known physician. She lived on Washington Square, and her father, Sergei Ingerman, was one of the Menshevik delegation who left Russia in 1922, 1923. I met him at the Rand School through his son-in-law and he was saying to me, "All you young people joined the radical movement. You don't know any history. You don't know what the Bolsheviks did. You don't know what they did at Kronstadt and what they did at other places, because during the Depression you didn't care; you became radical." At that time I was moving towards the communists; a lot of people were because of the Great Depression. It goes back to a famous remark of John Dos Passos in which he said joining the Socialist Party was like drinking near beer, which you remember was that thin, pre-Prohibition beer. But through people like Sergei Ingerman and through some anarchist cousins, who I used to see in the summertime when I'd go up for a week or so to the Mohegan Colony outside of Peekskill, I read anarchist pamphlets. Particularly, I still have some of them called "The Truth about Bolysheviki," sort of an odd spelling. So we'd get into debates with the members of the Young Communist League, because we were constantly having ferocious debates, and they'd talk about the need for revolution and I'd say, "What happened at Kronstadt?" They'd say, "Where's Kronstadt?" So you learn, you see, the advantages of esoteric knowledge.

The Mohegan Colony still exists — it's right near Peekskill, New York. In the 1920s, a number of anarchists and then later some socialists and communists bought land to set up summer homes, but some people live there all year round. They had Attica School, the Ferrer School. Later there was one called Three Arrows, which the socialists built farther up in New York. They had cultural programs. They had speakers every week at the schoolhouse. It was a very active, live thing. There also were factions among the anarchists and socialists and communists. All Jewish, a few maybe not, but again it never came up. It never came up as a question. It was simply part of a normal life, so to speak. It was a shtetl.

Surrounded by Jews? Not surrounded. You were in. What do you mean

surrounded? You are Jewish. It's a shtetl except that you don't have the
pressures immediately of the outside goyisha world on you. It's a world.
It's a real shtetl just as later on, among the New York intellectuals, we had
the Upper West Side kibbutz. You know, we had these parties back and
forth in each other's houses. It's part of a milieu that you took for granted.

When we were in study groups we'd read *Kapital* line by line, and I was
the chachem, because I could tell you on which page any footnote appeared,
the left-hand side of the page, the right-hand side of the page, how many
lines there were. We were like little puppies or little goats butting each other.
This was the coin of the realm: learning a text, being more adroit and
quicker to use a text and know the relevant quotation than anybody else.
So, in a crazy way, the kind of turf wars of the Lower East Side carried
over into the intellectual turf wars so that at City College all this came to
a head. Irving Kristol has written about this in a very famous essay called
"Memoirs of a Trotskyist," which is in his book *Reflections of a Neoconservative*. And there was Irving Kristol, and Melvin Lasky, who became the
editor of *Encounter*, and Irving Howe, and myself. And these little wars in
the alcoves of City College move out later on to the wider culture.

But there we were, battling away with each other. Lasky was a Trotskyist.
Kristol was a Trotskyist. Howe was a Trotskyist. I was a social democrat.
At least we could talk to one another. Why? Because we all hated the
communists. They were in another alcove. Then there was the Lovestonite
alcove; Jay Lovestone, who later became the adviser to the AFL-CIO. Irving
Brown is a Lovestonite; "that paskudnyak"; that's what we'd say. But things
came to a head in these alcove battles. We very rarely went to school, I
mean to classes. We organized our own classes: we had Footnote Writing
100, Barricades 202. This was 1935 to 1939 at City College.

None stayed radical in the old sense. Many stayed liberal. In his memoirs,
Irving Kristol said Dan was the rarity among us, a social democrat who
believed in a mixed economy and such. In those days we used to attack him
from the left, now we attack him from all sides of the ideological canvas.
No. Irving Howe was a Trotskyist later than anybody else; now he thinks
of himself as a social democrat. Mel Lasky, who's been editing *Encounter*
for about twenty-five years, I suppose moved over to the right. Kristol, of
course, has become a strong neoconservative. Nat Glazer, well, Nat succeeded me as co-editor of *The Public Interest* when I decided to leave because
I didn't want to get into the constant fights with Irving, and I said to Irving,
"Look, friendship is more important than ideology. There's no point in
hassling with you. I want to get out and remain friends. Otherwise, it will
just break up." And Nat presumably was supposed to be the balance wheel;
he moved more over to the right. Marty Lipset, who's a sociologist at

Stanford, stayed sort of center, left of center. And there are many others, less well known.

All Jewish? Entirely, and again, without any self-consciousness. One didn't think who was Jewish and who was non-Jewish. City College, at that time, these circles at least, was entirely Jewish. We had classmates we never knew about. Julius Rosenberg was a classmate. But he was in science, oddly enough, and so we never met — we met a few of the scientists, but he was also a communist. So again we were walled off by the double fact that he was in science and he was a communist. But those who were in science — Bill Gomberg, who later went to Pennsylvania, an engineer who started most of the time-motion studies for the unions, was at City College with us at the time; various others. But mostly it was people in history and in economics and sociology and literature; these were the alcoves.

Were the professors Jewish? The younger ones. The older ones often not, so there was a split in that respect. And the young ones were often radicals, so there was a large collection in the Communist Party and there were battles between them and us. This came to a head during the Rapp-Coudert Committee, which was one of the very first of the investigation committees. In 1940, the New York legislature, after the Nazi-Soviet Pact, set up an investigating committee and they bounced quite a few radical teachers.

I'll give you a little footnote which winds its way out into the world at large. Curiously enough my main work at City College was in ancient history. And you say why ancient history? Well, it's logical. I had a teacher named Moses Finkelstein, very brilliant young man, only a few years older than I. And he said, "Look, you want to know about the world? You want to become a sociologist? Learn ancient history." I said, "Why?" He said, "Look, you can either study anthropology or you can study ancient history, which is the antecedent to what comes up here. You can also see them as relatively homogeneous cultures, the Egyptian culture, ancient Greek, Roman culture, and therefore you will get a sense both of different social structures as well as Western history." He says, "If you read anthropology, what will you read?" For example, I read a book by John Whiting, who later was a colleague here, called *Becoming a Kwoma*, which was a small tribal study. And I said, "What else would he bekwoma?" So through the influence of Moses Finkelstein I studied ancient history.

Now Moe Finkelstein also had been the secretary, in 1939, of a committee called the American Committee for Democracy and Intellectual Freedom, or some such title, which was a communist front, headed by Franz Boas. Against him Sidney Hook had organized the American Committee for Cultural Freedom with John Dewey, and there was this big fight among the intellectuals. There was a famous denouement: in August of 1939 the com-

mittee which Finkelstein headed gathered four hundred signatures to de-
nounce the rumors which were going around that there might be a
rapprochement between the Soviet Union and Nazi Germany. They said
this is ignominious, this is a slander, et cetera, et cetera. And they got four
hundred signatures. They published the list in the issue of *The New Republic*
that was dated September 3 and came out that way and that was it.

Anyway, Finkelstein had been my teacher and I liked him enormously,
even though, as I say, he was a communist. We had great fights. He dropped
out of sight for many years — I don't know where he was working — and
surfaced in the late forties and early fifties at Rutgers. He was called up
before one of the investigating committees and he told them he wouldn't
name any names and he refused to talk. At first, he was protected, but then,
under pressure, Rutgers decided to fire him. So he was fired from Rutgers
University, and a man named Arnoldo Momigliano, a great figure in history — an Italian Jew who taught in England — got Finkelstein a fellowship
at Jesus College in Cambridge. And Moe Finkelstein went to Jesus College
in Cambridge. When he went there he changed his name to Finley — Moses
I. Finley. He became the reader in ancient history in Cambridge; became
professor of ancient history in Cambridge; became master of Darwin College
in Cambridge; was knighted as Sir Moses Finley. Unfortunately he died last
year. Here's a Moses Finkelstein from City College and he got to be Sir
Moses Finley, one of the leading luminaries of modern scholarship, by the
crazy accident of being bounced out of Rutgers. Who knows what would
have happened if he stayed in Rutgers? But there it is: a peek at how the Jews
go anywhere.

Before the war and even in the early years of the war there was never
any expectation that you'd get an academic job. If I think of my friends,
people I knew, Irving Kristol's first job was as a mechanic in the Brooklyn
Navy Yard; Melvin Lasky, who had finished an M.A. at Michigan, his first
job he became what's called a junior historical archivist, which meant he
was put in the Statue of Liberty as a guide to tell people what was going
on up there; Clem Greenberg was a customs agent, even though he's *the*
foremost art critic; Harold Rosenberg worked on the WPA. So again there
was never any sense that you were going to have an academic career. This
was true of almost everybody I knew at the time. There was never any
expectation that you would be able to be placed anywhere. It simply wasn't
there.

There's an old remark of George Orwell that said in the old proletarian
feelings one should never rise out of one's class but should rise *with* one's
class. With us, the whole class rose, the whole Jewish lower class rose, and
we all became intellectuals or whatever.

Arthur J. Goldberg, seventy-seven, Marshall, Virginia

I am former counselor for the labor movement, former Secretary of Labor, former Justice of the Supreme Court, former ambassador to the United Nations, and a former ambassador-at-large.

My father came over in 1894. He came over as a deserter from conscription in the Czar's army. He came from a town called Zinkov, which I later visited by courtesy of the Soviet government, which was in the pale of settlement about two hundred miles from Kiev. Nothing was there. All the Jews were gone. My mother lived in an adjoining town. It was an agricultural town, much like Tevye's in *Fiddler on the Roof*. My father had somewhat of an education, apparently, because he was the town clerk, the Jewish town clerk. He was not a rabbi. My grandfather was, but my father was not. He was, in other words, the Jewish registrar of births, deaths, et cetera.

The townspeople raised enough money for him to go because they were against impression, which might have lasted twelve years at the time. The Czar's army used to go around impressing Jews. And one of the conditions was — he was very young and married — that if you were a young person, you served twelve years and then you could have a permit to live anywhere you wanted to, which was not accorded to most Jews. That was the *quid pro quo*. But he was not ready to accept that, so he went over the border and took a ship. He came over the Manchurian border, interestingly enough.

He could not bring my mother and my oldest sister. We started as a family of nine, but twins died in the old country, so we emerged as a family of seven. My oldest sister was born there, and the rest of us were born here.

He peddled for two years in Texas. There's an anecdote that you'll be interested in about this. When I was appointed Secretary of Labor, I was having a drink with Sam Rayburn. He asked me the question you asked. And I told him. And he said, "So you are a Texan." Texan? My father was there two years, peddling. There were rich ranchers. My father died when I was eight, but I remember as a child his telling me that. There were rich Jewish ranchers in Texas and they gave him the back of their hand, this poor illiterate — by their token, although he spoke Russian and Yiddish. He didn't speak English. He resented the treatment he got very much. Rayburn called the leadership of the House in and to my amusement and astonishment, he told the House leadership, "I want to say something. The Secretary of Labor is a Texan, and I want him to get everything he wants." And while the conventional wisdom is that the Kennedy administration got no legislation, it got more legislation in the almost two years I served than under any Labor Secretary in history. I don't give myself credit for it. Sam Rayburn.

In any event, my father sent my mother some money and she went to England with my oldest sister and she was a housemaid until they jointly got enough money to come. Then she came through Ellis Island. Well, they finally got together and moved to Chicago. Why Chicago? Because in those days, 1896 to early 1900, you went where there were people from your locality. Indeed, as a boy, before my father died, I slept in the kitchen. Why? Because he located the house — had a little apartment, a cold flat, one toilet for everybody — near the old B and O railroad. Why? Because he and my older brothers could take the cart and every new immigrant from Zinkov was received and brought into our house and remained there until they found a job and an apartment. So I slept in the kitchen and I didn't resent it.

My family was apolitical, unlike Dave Dubinsky, a Bundist and so on. I never heard the word *socialism* until I went to law school and I was the editor-in-chief of what was then called *The Yellow Lion Roars* and is now *The Northwestern* and I got interested in Sacco and Vanzetti. That's the first time. I had to find the way myself to the liberal movement.

The immigrants who came, poor, impoverished, could only live in the poorer section, and so you naturally lived there, and you lived there also to receive the new people. You regarded it as your obligation. My father was illiterate in English, so he could not get any job in this country. And he was not, by nature, an entrepreneur, like so many who surmounted the language. So he drove a blind horse — that's all he could afford — and hauled potatoes from what was called a commission house — wholesale vendor — from Old Water Street. Four o'clock in the morning he would go — he was a sort of independent contractor — and load up with potatoes and deliver them to hotels. That was his business.

He died of cancer when I was eight. I still have the candelabra at my farm, presented to my father for being president of a Jewish fraternal organization — I've forgotten the name; it's on the menorah. That's the only inheritance I have. My oldest sister, before she died, gave it to me. He was president. And it was a verein, of which there were many. It was really a burial society, which, as we know, was very important to Jews. The poor were buried, and those who could afford it paid fees. They arranged Jewish burials and basically, I think, the fraternal society was that. I could not find any evidence that they did anything else.

Then we had to struggle, all the kids, to support my mother, who was illiterate. She did not possess my father's education. Typical of the immigrant families. The other brothers and sisters helped until they got married. Then it was my job. And I never resented it. It's a very interesting thing. We had a discussion in the family. One of my grandchildren said, "Do you feel badly that as a kid twelve and a half years old" — I got through with grammar school at twelve and a half and went to high school — "that you had to work after school?" I said, "No. I accepted it. Everybody was poor. We had no concept that the world around us wasn't everybody's. We didn't like it. I am just like you. I would have loved to go to the prom and so on. But I recognized the realities of what occurred."

Irving Howe's book, and the other books, I don't think catch the flavor of the Jewish experience. I shall say why. They have concentrated on the small stratum of Jews who were well educated and politically minded. The great bulk were not. They were not. Politics did not enter into our life at all. You know what the most popular newspaper in our house was? It was the Hearst paper. Why the Hearst paper? Because it was for free immigration. And therefore it was the Hearst papers, with all of their jingoism — and you know what the Hearst papers were like: yellow journalism . . . But that was our paper. I vaguely recall we did not subscribe to the *Forward*. That was a socialist paper. My father would read the *Tag*. That was middle of the road. But it's a very interesting thing that the books that have been written, which I have read — Howe's *Maxwell Street*, others — I think miss the essence. Most of the Jewish immigrants were apolitical. They didn't know anything about the Bund. That was for educated people. They were not educated. They lived in these little shtetls, and they had no time for that. They had to make a living and scratch it out under great restraint — the Czar's regime. So they had no time for politics. Politics didn't enter. I never heard it mentioned.

The neighborhood was called the Old West Side and it centered around Maxwell Street, where the bazaars were. It was very much like if you go to Borough Park. When I was United Nations ambassador, my law clerk at the time was Alan Dershowitz, this little boy who has become nationally known, which gives me great pleasure. He came from Borough Park, which is the very religious section of New York. And I liked Alan. He was, at that time, a little, modest fellow and Orthodox. He's not any longer. Anyhow, when it came to worshiping on the High Holidays, he and his family invited us — I was ambassador — to come to them and worship in their Orthodox synagogue, and we did. And I saw in Borough Park a repetition of my childhood. Shops all closed. People walked to the synagogue. That's the atmosphere I recall in Chicago.

You see, you must remember Jews came from all over, and *bazaar* is a term used in the Middle East. It was a bunch of secondhand stores which were open on Sunday because Orthodox Jews could not open on Saturday, for which I have been duly critical of the Supreme Court in articles I have written — my former court — for holding that they were not entitled to an exemption from the law about Sunday closing. I think that's a dreadful decision. It required that Orthodox Jews then had to choose economic necessity or their religion.

There were stalls, secondhand shops, hookers who tried to pull you in, all kinds of merchandise, from suits to vegetables and so on. And Jews who felt very inferior. They were afraid to go to the big stores, but they spoke Yiddish here; they could go here. And they felt more comfortable. And also it was very social. You argued with the proprietor. He knew a great many of the people and you haggled, but in a department store you had to pay one price. This was a familiar atmosphere. I never had a suit until I became Bar Mitzvah, and to get a Bar Mitzvah suit of course you went to Maxwell Street.

There was an Orthodox Jewish environment. My father was the president of a little Jewish synagogue. My grandfather was a kind of itinerant rabbi, and when my father died, he was the one who trained me for my Bar Mitzvah.

My Bar Mitzvah was in the little synagogue that my father had been president of. I remember very distinctly and it taught me a great lesson. They think the British are understated. When we got finished I thought I'd done remarkably well. You know how a kid of thirteen . . . So I said, "Well, Grandpa?" I spoke some Yiddish. He spoke only Yiddish. So I said, "How did I do?" He says, "Nisht kashruth," not kosher. People get confused; translation — not so bad. But he was a wise old man. Not terribly well educated. He was a rabbi from a little shtetl. Not all rabbis were well educated. He wasn't. But he was a wise old man and he made a statement which when translated into English is understated praise, which is better than saying, "You're terrific. We're terrific." I always remembered that.

After, downstairs, we had to serve shmaltz herring and booze, but I learned that Jews had a hierarchy. It's funny how things stick in your mind. I wanted to give the shamus an aleeyah. The rabbi said no. Hierarchy. We don't call the janitor, the shamus, to the Torah. It was a very snobbish thing, wasn't it? That really existed.

By present standards my wife's family, they weren't rich, but were ten stages above us. My father-in-law was a salesman for a garment firm. His own garment firm had gone bankrupt. And they lived on a standard far higher than we did. We were a damn poor family and yet without resentment. I emphasize that. It's very interesting we never conceived that something was wrong.

We lived in this enclave because we were so poor — the first railroad train I ever took was to the Bar in Springfield. But we moved at various points. The Jewish emigration shifted. First it shifted to the neighborhood of the old Cubs' park on Polk Street and we lived there for a while. That's where my father died. Then we moved to Ashland Boulevard. We had a little house. How we ever got the money to pay for the little house amazes me. We rented it. And that was the next stage. Finally we moved to the Lawndale district, which was the up-and-coming Jewish district. We lived there for many years while I went to grammar school and high school. I'm the only member of my family who ever went to high school.

I was admitted to Harvard. I just applied. I heard of Harvard. I didn't know much about it. I applied and because I was the first person in my class in high school I was admitted. But I had no money. So I went to the community college, the first one in America. It was called then Crane Junior College, in an old dilapidated high school. My wife later went; although her family was better off, her father would spend it on outfitting Ann or other things, not on providing a college education. But afterward, she was horrified to find all of her classmates — see, they lived in a better area, Humboldt Park — all went to college but she didn't. There was no money. She went to the same one, two years after I did. When I became a lawyer and could scrape up a few dollars, I sent her back to school. She is a graduate of the University of Chicago. But I went to the community college and then I realized I'd never get into law school if I didn't hurry. So I also, at the same time, went to De Paul, a Catholic school, and got thirty semester credits the same year. I had to prove to the registrar at Northwestern Law School I was the same guy. They didn't believe you could get thirty credits. But I always had to work, and I worked at the post office, the library, construction work, always without a sense of grievance. I emphasize that because today kids don't learn that. I can't persuade my grandchildren. I'm not telling you a sob story or Horatio Alger. I would like to discuss with you why I didn't feel grieved. I didn't. Because everybody was more or less in the same state.

Nobody can explain to me how I suddenly had liberal points of view. I cannot explain that. Why the hell did I march around as a law student when Sacco and Vanzetti were executed? I did. How did I write the company communication for my own law adviser taking issue with the dean? How did I do it? I can't tell you. It is an astonishing thing. How did I get that attitude? I cannot explain it except reading. I was an omnivorous reader, so I must have picked up journals of opinion and so on. There was no interplay among the people in my neighborhood. And certainly the law school . . . Northwestern, for example, was a very conservative law school at that time.

Then I got a job with the law firm of Pritzker and Pritzker, but I left there after two years because I did not conceive that my life should be devoted at that time to foreclosing gold bond issues. I opened my own law firm.

Anti-Semitism? That we knew. Crawford Avenue, when we lived on Lawndale, was the demarcation point between us and the Poles. And as a kid, all the anti-Semitism of the old country carried over. I remember as a kid there were fights and I was an ammunition bearer — that's a fact. I passed bricks to my brothers. If the Poles invaded our area, it was defended by throwing bricks, and as a kid six or seven years old, my job was to pass out bricks, and my brothers stood on the roofs and threw them at the Polish kids. I don't know what the hell got into me — all the Jewish kids went to a mostly Jewish high school. I didn't. I went to a high school where the Jews were in a minority and Polish and Czechoslovene kids were a majority. Had to fight my way home every day. Yes. Every day. It sounds like an exaggeration, but the Polish kids would lie around and when Jewish kids would want to walk home — there were some — we had to fight our way home.

The interesting thing is that I owe a great debt to the labor movement. When I got involved representing labor, a whole new world opened to me. Phil Murray was Scotch Irish. Jimmy Carey was Irish. At the beginning I represented no Jewish unions. I came here to Washington and became general counsel to the CIO, among people I had to deal with who were largely non-Jewish. Later I represented the Amalgamated and the textile workers and met the Jewish unions. Until then, no. So all of a sudden I recognized a new world where the nexus was their common interest in improving wages and working conditions. Van Bittner of the coal miners, John Daugherty, Joe Germano, an Italian, who was director of the Gary works and became a friend. All of a sudden I had a different perspective.

Ultimately, I represented all three Jewish unions — Dubinsky of the ILGWU, Hillman and later Jacob Potofsky of the Amalgamated, and Alex Rose of the Hat Workers. I learned something. They were the morality of the labor movement. See, they were Bundists mostly. And Bundists are socialists and they pinched a penny more than you can imagine. It was other people's money, to use Brandeis's phrase. I was a director of the Amalgamated bank in Chicago. Even when I was general counsel of the CIO, I'd go to at least one meeting of directors a year. There was an Italian vice-president. He would save a fee. He'd carry it around in his pocket, I think, for a whole year until I came. The enormous compensation of one hundred dollars. It cost me a fortune to get there. The Chicago bank has since been sold. The union still owns the New York bank. Do you know why it was formed? I inquired then. The union population — all Jewish; there may have been a few Italians — would want to send packages and some money to their relatives in Russia and Poland. There were unscrupulous travel agents who skimmed, gave them bad rates of exchange, and so on. So the Amalgamated banks were formed primarily for the purpose of providing a banking way to send money. And peculiarly enough, worked out arrangements with the Bolshevik regime and the Polish regime to be recognized as authorized agencies to get a fair rate of exchange.

The morality was very interesting. It was a socialist morality. You know — that they owed to the workers. The obligation to conserve their resources, to live frugally; they had modest salaries. None of the stuff that you see with Jackie Presser and the teamsters and so on.

Jews, who place a great premium on justice, found their horizons were very limited. How many Jews were in the newspaper industry? Not many. Jews didn't know investment banking; couldn't get a job in a bank. Executive suites were closed to them. The garment industry was open to you if you had some money. We had none. Where the hell could Jews go? Somehow you could get a job in a law office or hang out your shingle.

How about the Jewish seat on the Court? People have misunderstood me. I have spoken against *a* Jewish seat. They always forget the second sentence. I point out that Hoover had two Jews — Cardozo and Brandeis — sitting at the same time. And I've said many times I'm against the tokenism. I don't see why there can't be two or three. Same with women, you see. The Court is still basically a Protestant institution. Nobody talks about it up at the Court. One Catholic. They have one woman. The rest are all Protestants. Now I thought, and still think, that is not healthy. They have one black, Marshall. I think that's very unhealthy. We're a pluralistic country and it is not an appropriate composition of our highest court.

I think the one thing I want to emphasize to you is what I emphasized in the beginning. The big defect I found in the Jewish stories is they concentrated on intellectuals, and most Jews were not. They came over to this country. They were illiterate. They lived in the pale of settlement. They were nonpolitical, like my family. What the other books have described are the worthy, socialist elite who went to the Café Royale. We never heard of the Café Royale. And it's a distorted view. And they read the *Forvarts*. Most Jews did not. They read the *Tag* and the other papers, and I find it very distorted. I do not recognize the description, and that isn't the Jewish community that I knew. The Jewish community that I knew revolved around the synagogue and these little vereins. Nonpolitical. We were never told who Theodor Herzl was, and I went to the Theodor Herzl Grammar School. That's a fact.

Arthur Weinberg, seventy, writer, Chicago, Illinois

I was a reporter for thirty-three years for Fairchild Publications. In later years I did book reviews for *Women's Wear Daily*; my specialty was writing for *Home Furnishings Daily* on electronics, television, and home appliances. My wife and I have written seven books.

My experience as a Jewish boy in Chicago might be a little bit different from most. I was brought up in a nonreligious home, but a very ethical and moral home. I was not Bar Mitzvahed. I went for many, many years — in fact, was graduated from — the Arbeiter Ring, the Workmen's Circle, and went to their high school for a while. The center of my Jewish activity was around the Arbeiter Ring, which was organized as a fraternal organization. It offered insurance and various medical care for the immigrant Jew who came into the United States. It also was founded as the "Red Cross" to the labor movement. In those days, the labor movement was poor and needed financial help, and the Arbeiter Ring was there always to help them. That was the adult organization.

My father wanted to belong to the Workmen's Circle. They had forums. He participated in that. I used to go with him as a kid. Most of them were on the West Side in what was, at that time, called the Douglas Park Auditorium. It was really a continuing-education program. This was in Yiddish. The way it was operated — and I've always wanted to see forums like that operated again and I've never been able to see them — they'd have the speaker, and after the speaker finished they'd have a question period. But it was only questions, no speeches. After the questions were asked, either the speaker would answer them one by one or he'd wait until all the questions were asked. After that they'd have a discussion period, where the audience would be able to take issue with the speaker. This would go on and then the speaker would have the final word. I think there may have been some refreshments sold between the speaker and the question period. Those were fascinating programs.

There was a little forum in Humboldt Park — it was the anarchist forum called the Free Society Forum. I think the audience was predominantly Jewish. They would discuss subjects such as "Is capitalism at its end?" "Zionism versus socialism, where are we going?" or something like that. It was always exciting. The forums in Douglas Park Auditorium were in Yiddish. The anarchists were in English. In fact, it was at the anarchist place that I saw the operation for the first time of the lie detector test — the guy who created it demonstrated it there. They'd have some authors come in and speak.

Then they had the Yiddish schools. In the Yiddish schools we learned how to read, write, talk Yiddish. We learned Jewish history. We met Yiddish poets. While they didn't call it Bible studies, we really learned the history of the Jews through the stories of the Bible. We learned about the Jews who were active in the revolutionary movement here in the United States and also in Europe.

The school was three times a week: twice during the week and once on the weekend, either a Saturday or Sunday. During the week, our class was reading and writing Yiddish, speaking Yiddish in class. We put out a little Yiddish magazine every so often. We put on plays. Saturday or Sunday was history day. It was then the teacher would give us the history of the Jews. We learned about the Maccabees, Haman — the whole history of the Jews. Socialism would be taught on Sundays. It would become part of the whole social philosophy of the school. There was a freedom there; there was a questioning that we always were permitted. We had some wonderful teachers. As I look back, much of the stuff I learned there helped me in history and in the social sciences once I got into high school and college. We put on some plays that were adapted from Sholem Aleichem — a beautiful little story about the knife. We put on a translation of the *Happy Prince*. It was all in Yiddish. We were both boys and girls. The whole atmosphere was a very strong relationship between the people.

The schools began disappearing in the 1940s and 1950s. The Depression had nothing to do with them. During the Depression in the 1930s there was pretty strong organization. I think it began disappearing with World War II.

My family came from Poland. My father had to flee Poland on the day his father was on his deathbed because the police were looking for him. My father apparently was a lookout for something, and they were after him. He came here when he was about sixteen. My mother soon followed. They knew each other in the old country. My parents both became active in radical movements here, particularly the anarchist movement. My father was a 1910 striker at Hart, Schaffner and Marx. He was a cutter in the garment business and worked for Hart, Schaffner and Marx for over sixty years. My father was active in the Amalgamated Clothing Workers. My mother was a housewife who raised two children.

Being active in the anarchist movement in those days — in the 1920s and 1930s — meant selling raffle tickets for helping the Spanish Civil War. It meant collecting money for the Kentucky miners on strike. I never heard either one of my parents or any of their friends who were anarchists ever speak in terms of violence. It was always a dream of how they could attain a society in which people lived together without the need of a state which told them "You've got to do this."

We spoke Yiddish at home. We were very identified as Jews. I don't remember it, but they tell me that when I was five or six my father told me the story of the imprisonment of Eugene Victor Debs, and I decided I had to do something about it. So I collected as many friends as I had in the neighborhood on the back porch and began speaking to them in Yiddish on the injustice of the imprisonment of Debs. The home was a Jewish home. In fact, I have part of my father's library in Yiddish still. I've been very sorry that I gave up the other half.

We celebrated the culture. On Pesach, we'd have a dinner. We never went through the ceremony. If we did do any of the ceremony, it was the four questions. It was a joyous thing, nothing serious. We celebrated Chanukah. We always took off from work on Rosh Hashonah and Yom Kippur because my father wanted people to know that he was Jewish. It really meant nothing to him — my father, incidentally, was a yeshiva bocher in the old country. While crossing the ocean, he threw his tfillin into the ocean. I would say he was not a shul-going person, but as an individual he was very, very religious. I didn't go to shul; I didn't go to cheder. My folks never went to shul.

We lived most of the time around Humboldt Park. One of the exciting things about Humboldt Park, and it was in other areas, too, they had soapbox speakers on the corners. At least two or three nights a week you'd have soapboxers there. Some of them were in Yiddish. You had hecklers, but there was a certain orderliness to it. The biggest problem, if I remember it correctly, were the commies, who tried to break up meetings of anybody. I remember — this was on Fairfield and North, which is also Humboldt Park — the International Workers of the World were having a meeting and the Young Communist League decided that they wanted to have a meeting across the street. This was in the early thirties. The speaker for the IWW was Ralph Chapman, who was author of the song "Solidarity Forever." The way they tried to break up the IWW meeting was by singing "Solidarity Forever," apparently not knowing that he was the guy who wrote it. At soapbox meetings you'd get instant analysis of the news, like you get on television now. Immediately, somebody would be on a soapbox, and you had some good speakers there. Then you had the famous Bughouse Square, which was right across the street from Newberry Library, where there's a park. They had speakers all along the street, though that wasn't Jewish. You also had soapbox speakers on the West Side, and there would be a lot of Jewish speakers in Douglas Park.

We discussed Palestine. You see, among socialists in those days prior to Israel there was always this argument of is the answer to the Jewish question a homeland for the Jews? There was a lot of antagonism among socialists toward Zionism. The socialists felt the Jewish question was not a question unto itself. In other words, in order for the Jewish question to be solved, you've got to solve the working-class question, et cetera. With Hitler, a complete change came over the Jewish socialist movement. Many of them took on a Zionist tinge.

I think Jews primarily have this sort of radicalism. For our last book on Darrow — that my wife and I wrote — we found a statement by him to the effect that he would not want to live in a world where there weren't Jews, because the Jews are always there to protest. They're always there to arouse, to make you think. That's the kind of world he wanted to live in. I think Jews are more on the liberal side, at least until recently. What's going to happen now, I don't know.

I think I still consider myself a philosophical anarchist. I have dreams that if we're ever going to attain a better society, it's got to be based on a society where there is mutual aid and cooperation, rather than competition. I believe that basically democracy, in its truest form, is anarchism.

I've got to emphasize that while I may not have been identified, except at the Arbeiter Ring, as a Jew, I was always conscious and always aware that I was Jewish. And I never denied it.

6

Names

WHEN I QUESTIONED people about the derivation of their names, at least a half dozen asked me whether I knew about the Jewish man named Shane Ferguson. Well, they would say, the Jewish immigrant would arrive at Ellis Island, and when the immigration officers there asked him his name, he would shrug his shoulders and say, "Shoyn fargesn," which in Yiddish means "Already I've forgotten."

Alan Finberg, fifty-six, lawyer, New York, New York

There is a wonderful old story in our family. It goes back to when my father's father, as a boy, came to this country from Poland with his father and three brothers, all of about the same age. They were perhaps in their very early or middle teens. They all came, obviously, from the same shtetl in Poland. All came in the same boat, steerage, probably holding hands. They came to Boston because some of the family had come to Boston earlier, so you always go where there is already family. This would have been in about 1880-something.

The four boys got off the boat. There was this great crowd at the immigration station, and somehow they got separated. Each of the four went through a different immigration gate. I should tell you now that when they left Poland their name was Mikiloshansky with variations as to its transliteration.

When they came through these four separate immigration gates, having been interviewed by four separate immigration inspectors, my grandfather's name was Finberg, which was the name of the mayor of the shtetl. One of his brothers was Friedman. One of his brothers was Reddinov. And one was Rubinstein.

That's the story of the four branches of the family in Boston. None of them went back to Mikiloshansky.

Abraham Lincoln Marovitz, eighty, U.S. District Court judge, Chicago, Illinois

My father and mother come from Kovno, part of Lithuania at the time. Dad must have come here as a comparatively young man, because he got his citizenship papers in 1894, and he had to be a resident for five years, so he must have been here at least in 1889. Mother was one of five or six children, and her brothers preceded her. One brother left Kovno and went to Dublin, Ireland, before the turn of the century; one went to Johannesburg, South Africa; one went to Melbourne, Australia; and one came to the United States — her oldest brother.

My mother was fifteen; she was brought here by her older brother, along with her younger sister Lena, who was thirteen. He got Mother a job in the sweatshops in New York. She didn't have any education in the old country and she wanted to learn and she went to the settlement houses to hear some lectures. Of the many lectures that Mother heard, two were most impressive. One was on Samuel Gompers, who was a Jew and founded the American Federation of Labor. The other was on Abraham Lincoln.

First, she saw pictures of Abraham Lincoln — he had a beard, his name was Abraham, father of our people. And one of the speakers said, "He was shot in the temple." She thought that was the synagogue and she really thought he was Jewish.

To her dying day, no one could convince her he wasn't.

She made up her mind that one of her boys had to be named Abraham Lincoln — kindly man, tolerant. So when my brother Harold was born two years before I was born, my mother wanted to name the boy Abraham Lincoln. But my father wanted him named after *his* father. Shortly before I was born, my father's mother said to my mother, "I have no right to ask you, Ruchel, but there is no one named after my father. And I wondered, if it's a boy, will you do me the honor — my own four daughters haven't done it — to name him after my father?" My mother said, "What was your father's name?" She said, "Avram." My mother said, "No problem."

So when I was born she named me Abraham Lincoln; that's what my birth certificate shows. Matter of fact, she died right in this room and we were all around her bedside and she thought she'd suffered a stroke. And I pinched her thigh; she had hardening of the arteries. I said, "Can't you feel that, Mother?" She said, "Sure. Who is that?" I said, "Abe." She said, "Ah, my Abraham Lincoln," and she expired; the last words she said.

Shirley Povich, seventy-eight, sportswriter, Washington, D.C.

I am aware of the family of Goldie Ahearn, the prizefighter, a former champion of the American Expeditionary Forces in France in World War I, who
came back to Washington, D.C., to be a professional fighter as well. Goldie
Ahearn, the fighter, Johnny Goldstein, the restaurateur in Washington, and
Sammy Lewis, the actor, were brothers. This is partially explained by the
fact that it was thought to be useful in those days for all fighters to have
an Irish name, typifying violent pugilism, or whatever you want to call it.
So Isadore Goldstein became Goldie Ahearn, Johnny Goldstein retained the
family name, and Sammy Lewis thought it would be more appropriate to
be known as Sammy Lewis rather than Sammy Goldstein.

*Edward M. Benton, seventy-seven, lawyer, New York,
New York*

I was born Bernstein. My father didn't change his name, ever. My father
was a lawyer and had been a lawyer for many years by the time I became
a lawyer. I came into his office when I first got out of school in 1931, and
I was with him for two or three years, during which he said, "You should
change your name. The atmosphere is hostile. There is no reason why you
should bear the burden. It's going to interfere with your practice, and why
don't you change your name?" After a good deal of resistance, I did. I just
didn't feel right about it. But I did change my name. He was absolutely
right, because of that atmosphere in certain areas.

I remember particularly dealing with the trust departments in banks. You
dealt with an officer of the trust department who, of course, was never
Jewish. If you wanted something and introduced yourself as Bernstein, you
got a very cold shoulder. If you introduced yourself as Benton, it was entirely
different, much more cooperative. So in that sense he was right.

I was embarrassed for a time, but after a while it didn't matter.

The reason I chose the name Benton was because a cousin of mine had
changed his name to Benton from Bernstein. He was my father's brother's
son. He went to Oberlin and concentrated in psychology. When he was
ready with his doctorate, there was a question of getting a job. This was
again in the thirties, later than my years and really depressing years. His
mentors at Oberlin said, "We won't be able to place you at all with the
name Bernstein, but if you change your name, we think we can place you."
They said, "The problem isn't really anti-Semitism; it's the way it looks in
the catalogue." So that whether you are Jewish or not is not the problem.

It is how it will look. That's what he was told. So he changed his name to Benton. And he didn't get a job.

He came back to New York. He looked for possibilities, and one of the favorable interviews he got was with a Talmud Torah in Brooklyn, and they asked him whom he knew in New York. He told them who his father was and his uncle was. They said, "You changed your name? We can't hire you."

And he wasn't hired.

David Goldring, seventy, physician and professor of pediatrics,
St. Louis, Missouri

It has to do with one of my uncles who came over to this country long before my family did, and his name in Russia was Mack. When he came over to this country — and I can't, for the life of me, understand the rationale behind it — believe it or not, he changed his name to Weinberger.

7

The American Shtetl

THE UNITED STATES always has provided a rich broth for experimenters in communal or community living. Many such communities had a strong religious content; others, none at all: the Amana villages and Oneida Community, the Shaker colonies, the Greenbelt communities of the Great Depression, and more recently the various attempts at communal living that grew out of the tempestuous 1960s. Jewish immigrants were no exception. They had their communal experiences, too.

Groups of East European Jews were extricated from their impoverishment in the small Jewish shtetls of Eastern Europe that were made universally known and glamorized by *Fiddler on the Roof*. Many immigrants were taken out by European and American Jewish philanthropists and settled in various areas of the United States, where they were expected to establish farming communities, regardless of whether or not they had been farmers in the old country.

Other groups banded together in the small towns and cities of America, where they retained their shtetl mentality. Often they dubbed their urban shtetl Little Jerusalem; the sobriquet was adopted by many such communities of Jews who immigrated to the eastern United States between 1880 and 1910. The American shtetl, essentially, was a clone of the Eastern European one, heavily dependent on religion for its character, its social life, and, above all, its cohesiveness. While they lasted, they were as vibrant and colorful as Tevye's shtetl.

Molly Kravitz Greenblatt, who was born in one of the New Jersey farming communities in 1893, remembered that it was a "very, very tight unit. Everyone knew everyone else. It was like a big family. When there was trouble, they all tried to console if there was one person troubled. When there was happiness or happy occasions, everyone was happy. The synagogue was the focal point."

There was no mayor in her small community. "It was just the synagogue people decided what was to be done," she recalled. "Each one was a free person to do what he pleased as long as he didn't hurt anybody else. If there was someone who needed to be reminded that he should do the right thing, they told him."

Only remnants and memories of these once thriving communities exist today, but for those who have tasted of my mother's borsht of the bitter and the sweet, somehow the American shtetl memories are invariably sweet.

Leo Libove, retired farmer, Roosevelt, New Jersey

I used to be a farmer here in this community. I was born in the U.S. My parents came from Russia, and they always had a dream of having an independent life on a farm.

I always wanted to be my own boss, not responsible to anybody and not have anybody tell me what to do. I went to an agricultural school in Doylestown, Pennsylvania, after I graduated from high school. I couldn't afford to go to college and this was a chance to get some kind of a college education free. It was called the National Farm School at the time. Today, it's an accredited college called the Delaware Valley College of Science and Agriculture. At the time, I was living in Brooklyn, New York. They were advertising for eligible students. You had to be in the top five percent of your class in order to qualify.

Almost all were Jewish students at the time. Today, of course, I don't believe there's ten percent Jewish students. The school was established by a Dr. Krauskopf, and he was a rabbi. He felt that the Jews should be on the land to avoid all kinds of persecution. He felt that if they were part of the landed community, they would be accepted by the rest of the population. But in order to be a farmer, you had to know how to farm. So he established this school. I think the first year was 1909. They only had about a dozen graduates altogether that first year, but later on when I went, in 1929, there were about three hundred students. I graduated in 1932 in the midst of the Depression. I was the valedictorian of my class. I was a good farmer. They gave me good training there. It was very good.

I took up farm machinery. At that time we farmed with horses, but I knew that in the future it would be mechanized. I wanted to learn the mechanical part of farming, which I did. It's almost the same kind of a course as an auto mechanic, but here you deal with farm machinery of various sorts. We learned everything from poultry and dairy and beef cattle to raising corn and wheat and soybeans, and floriculture and horticulture. I was in the orchards for a while. I sprayed trees and picked apples and things like that, and I found it very interesting. It reinforced my desire to be a farmer. But nowadays farming is such a poor occupation, I don't believe there's ten farmers in the whole school. They may study in related fields, like food.

Dr. Krauskopf was gone when I got there. There was a board of trustees that took care of the school. His widow and his horse were still alive when I went there.

I got a job on a dairy farm in Pittstown, New Jersey. I worked there for a while. Then I got another job on a poultry farm. None of these paid enough to make it worthwhile. So I went back to Brooklyn, and when we got to Brooklyn shortly afterwards my mother-in-law noted an item in the Jewish press that there was a community going to be built by the government to establish a project for the needle-trade workers of New York. Because their season was so short, they couldn't make a living. At that time, Rexford Tugwell was, I think, in the Department of Interior, and the government was inclined to establish Greenbelt communities for some of the low-income trades. This one was for the needle-trade workers. They established a community for the miners in Kentucky. I believe there were over a hundred different communities established at the time. I don't believe any of them succeeded. Perhaps the one in Maryland succeeded as a housing community. If they were going to be producing communities, they didn't work out. We couldn't compete with the open market. It's that plain and simple.

The people in this area didn't like the idea of a Jewish community here at all. They called us Bolsheviks and reds and pinkos and whatnot. Hightstown was noted in the early days for its conservatism and its Ku Klux Klan. Here's a Jewish community being set up under their noses, and they certainly didn't like it. But after a while, when we became a little wealthier, we began to do business in Hightstown. We shopped there and we used the bank there. So they accepted us, grudgingly perhaps, but they accepted us. After a while, we established pretty good relationships. Also, our children went to the high school in Hightstown, and our children were bright children and went to some of the best colleges in the country. It didn't make friends for us, but we survived all this and we finally made a place for ourselves here.

We had twelve hundred acres to farm. It was called an agro-industrial community. They had a factory to make ladies' garments. We had a fifty-cow dairy and we had a large poultry plant. But I can't say that we were successful, because the prices were so low and we had more labor than was necessary in many cases. We had to do something with the people here. We couldn't let them just hang around. The needle-trade workers had a place in the factory. The poultry farmers had a place on the poultry farm. I think there were seven farmers altogether. The rest of the community, about a hundred, were needle-trade workers. So we were really a minority. The board of directors that controlled the farm, I think, consisted of seven needle-trade workers and two or three farmers; something like that. We had one farmer on the board of the garment producers. We didn't understand their problems, and I don't think they understood ours at all. They were supposed to help us in the busy season, picking potatoes and things like that. But it couldn't work out. They were people who'd been sitting at a machine. They were middle-aged, most of them. You'd come out to a potato field and tell them to pick potatoes. Their backs began to hurt, and they'd decide it's easier to go swimming, to hell with this. They were making, I think, $1.25 an hour at the time, and the farmers were making twenty-five cents an hour, the lowest paid industry there is. I think I made sixteen or eighteen dollars a week. I had to put in a lot of hours.

It wasn't easy, and the thing folded up. Actually, what happened was the government got tired of subsidizing it. They decided they were going to sell the houses to the people living in them; sell the land to the farmers, which is what they did. They divided the land into a house and so many acres, and we picked straws to see who would get what. It so happened, I got 130 acres and a house. Most of the people got between 130 and 160 acres; something like that. We paid for it. The Jewish Agricultural Society was a society in New York, originally established for the purpose of helping Jews get on the farm. They would give you a loan. They would lend you money at six percent at the time, I think, which was a pretty high rate then. But they did help. They gave me a loan. I got a second mortgage from them to buy the farm that I had. Happily, I paid everything off after twenty years.

The others, all Jewish farmers, dropped by the wayside rather quickly once they bought the property. They found other means of employment, because farming didn't pay at that time. I was getting sixty cents a hundred for potatoes, and twenty-eight cents a dozen for eggs. I had five thousand laying chickens at the time. I built the barn there myself, most of it. It was very hard to make a living. So I decided either you have to get bigger or get out. I couldn't get bigger, because I didn't have the means. So I began to work outside. Every winter I worked on different kinds of jobs. One winter I was a carpenter, another winter I was a hat blocker; anything I could get. I had to feed the chickens and feed the cows. So I worked for them. They didn't work for me; I worked for them.

I rented out the land because I couldn't make a go of it. I made out pretty well for about ten years, made a nice profit. The last ten years, I just barely made it. And the last year that I farmed, I think I made $500 for my whole year's work. I grew corn, wheat, soybeans, vegetables, tomatoes. I raised thirty cows a year, dairy head. I never milked them, but I sold them as soon as they became springers, as soon as they dropped a calf.

After twenty years, I got a different kind of job. I learned how to do other work. I worked in a high-vacuum metalizing factory, where they metalize plastics, made them look very pretty. Then I got a job with Continental Can Company in Ohio. When I came back from Ohio after two and a half years, I got a job at the James Forrestal Research Laboratory in Princeton.

Helen Barth, fifty-five, school secretary, Roosevelt, New Jersey

I came to Roosevelt in 1936.

My father, Abe Topal, responded to an ad in the *Jewish Daily Forward* with regard to interest in the community. He was a garment worker. In about 1936, they decided to make the move to Roosevelt. They were not socialists nor were they communists, but my father was a very liberal Democrat. I think the idea of finding work in the garment industry, living in the country, and raising children in the country had tremendous appeal, more than the ideology of a socialistic kind of life style. That was their reason for coming. He was a member, as were many others, of the ILGWU, which is seasonal work. But my father did have a job in a sweatshop; my mother did work in the needle trade, also. We lived in the Mosholu Parkway section of the Bronx, which was not the Lower East Side. So I think, in my particular circumstance, my parents just wanted to provide fresh air and sunshine.

In 1936 we moved to Roosevelt, then called Jersey Homesteads. My parents were required to make a $500 cash deposit as a share in the community. In return, they got a share in the cooperative — a share in the factory, a share in the retail store, a share in the grocery store, a share in whatever this community was supposed to have been. The town was basically set up to provide industry. There was to have been a garment factory with a retail outlet. The factory was to make ladies' coats and suits. My father's specialty was pockets.

Benjamin Brown conceived the idea of the community. He owned property nearby, and he was a money man. He was an entrepreneur and he had a vision and he convinced the government they should subsidize it. I understand that Eleanor Roosevelt, for whatever reason, was very supportive of the project. I believe Brown was a socialist and wanted something like a moshav in Israel today, not like the kibbutz, but more like the moshav, because you own your home or you live in your home and you farm, yet you work in the cooperative factory. That's what Jersey Homesteads was to have been, but it never happened. The government financed it. It was financed under the National Recovery Act, built by WPA labor. They built the homes, the factory, the school, everything that you would see here.

Every little house like ours had a half acre, and my father, who lived in the Bronx and in a shtetl as a boy in Poland, had a garden every year until two years before he died. He gardened every year, and they canned tomatoes in the heat of the summer, and made tomato juice, and did these wonderful things that I recollect.

I remember the community as family. There were as many meetings and as many organizations as there were people, and everyone was involved and yet everybody was family. Times were hard, but we never felt that we were poor. Our family never had a car. There may have been a half-dozen cars in town, and we would hitchhike into Hightstown, where all the services were — the kosher butcher, the food store, the movie theater Saturday afternoons.

I remember the limitations as well as all these wonderful things. There were ten children that graduated with me in my class. So I had ten friends, five boys and five girls. If I was in fifth grade, one of the sixth-grade girls might allow me to play with her. Again, that's really like family. It's like sibling rivalry: "You can't cross my line today." Our parents weren't able to provide what we, as parents, were able to provide for our children when we moved back. We were limited in our relationships here. Our parents went to work, came home from work, and life revolved around the community. The children were always included in meetings. We weren't excluded. There was no such thing as a baby sitter. Everybody turned out. We would have New Year's Eve celebrations at the school, and the children came as well as the parents. The children went home early and fell asleep, of course, and the parents probably continued partying and maybe the older brother stayed and watched. I really don't know, but when we came back we realized the limitations of the community and we made a very active effort to involve our children in organizations and car pools, to get the boys involved in Little League. My daughter wanted Little League, so she did Little League, and then she wanted gymnastics, so I shlepped her to Princeton to gymnastics.

There was a synagogue. Originally I'm not sure where the synagogue met, but I know that prior to World War II there was something like a construction shack. It may have been the construction shack that was left, and there was a synagogue and that's where people congregated. It looked like an army barracks. Ultimately, about 1955 or so, they built another, very fancy synagogue on another street. So this community, which is now a mixed community, has a synagogue. We don't have a church, but we do have a synagogue.

Mostly Jews? I would say ninety-nine percent, if not a hundred percent.

I think maybe the manager was not Jewish, and he happened to live in town. Most everyone went to shul on the High Holidays. My parents didn't impose that on me personally. I have my grandmother's Shabbes candlesticks, but I don't bench licht Friday night. I hope maybe my daughter will someday. Christmas didn't exist. It just didn't exist. As far as I'm concerned, it still doesn't exist.

My brother went to Hebrew school. Although there was an Orthodox synagogue in town, my parents did not conduct themselves in an Orthodox manner and felt that I would benefit more from a Yiddish culture experience than the Hebrew school. So I went to a Yiddish volkshul, and I learned to read and write and speak Yiddish. I'm not as fluent as I used to be, because I don't hear it anymore, but I can still carry on a conversation and certainly I understand it. The *Forward* was delivered here and the *Tag,* but my father's preference was the *Forward.* Some people were very frugal. After one person read the *Forward* they would trade with somebody who got the *Tag.*

I remember May Day and our mother's making costumes, ornate costumes. We were flowers, bunny rabbits, butterflies. There would be bonfires and singing and everybody would provide coffee and cake, because that's the Jewish experience.

Lots of organizations, yes. My father belonged to Workmen's Circle, for example, and his ultimate goal was that when he became old he would not become dependent upon his children and he could go to the old-age home in Elizabeth. We wouldn't allow that. He moved in with us. He lived around the corner when we moved back to Roosevelt, after we married.

I hate to use the term *unique,* because it's overused in our community, but a unique feature of our community is that we have free burial. Anyone who is a resident of our community can be buried in the community. If one has lived here for twenty-five years, they have a right to free burial in the community. Unmarried children of residents can be buried here free. It's a municipal cemetery, with a very large Jewish section. There is also a section that the synagogue owns so that those people who want to be buried in Roosevelt who don't qualify, as long as they maintain their membership in the synagogue, will have the right to be buried in Roosevelt.

People who were born in the thirties who lived in Roosevelt and grew up in the forties had a reunion. All of our elementary teachers, my nursery school teacher, came to this reunion, and the electricity, the excitement! Here we were, a group of people that shared a common experience that nobody else in the world did. Our parents were all founders of a community; all came from the same socioeconomic circumstance, worked in the same industry, had the same goals for their children. See the sewing machine that is now a planter? I wanted to learn how to sew. My parents found every excuse in the world for me not to ever use that sewing machine, because that's how I would end up. I didn't learn how to sew until after I was married and out of the house. They wanted to educate their children, the things that they could not have. These were intellectuals, like the custodian in the school. They all worked with their hands, and I can't describe the intellectual climate that was here, and this is how we all grew up.

When we all got together — I don't know how many people we were — the realization came to us then that what we share is so special. There was a table full of liquor, and those bottles were just as full at the end of the day as they were at the beginning, because everybody was just so charged by seeing one another and sharing experiences. We got together and somebody said, "Okay, do you remember the old Roosevelt school song?" Here we are, a bunch of fifty-year-olds singing the eighth-grade song. That feeling still exists today.

How did the name Roosevelt come about? It was Jersey Homesteads, this pioneering spirit. But because the community was funded under the programs of FDR, and there was this very strong Democratic community in this surrounding of Ku Klux Klan in Allentown and Republicans in Hightstown, and the tremendous anti-Semitism that we experienced in Allentown High School — when FDR died, it was just natural, some two days later, the emotions were so overwhelming, that we should change the name of the town to Roosevelt. As far as I know, the monument that we have here is the only monument that exists to FDR. That was done by Ben Shahn's son.

Ben Shahn came here in 1936 under the WPA. They sponsored artists. He painted a mural in our school and became enamored with the community, with the intellectual climate. I think he had another commission and moved elsewhere for several years, but then because his recollections and his memories of Roosevelt were so wonderful, he came back here and lived here until he died. His widow is here today, and his son has moved here since.

What about the charge of communism, that the surrounding people thought this was a communistic society? It was very strange. Here was this group of people who came and spoke with accents, who voted straight Democrat. As I said, the Ku Klux Klan was in Allentown. Hightstown had always been a Republican community. What else would they think?

The factory failed after two or three years. My father went to work in Philadelphia. He commuted two hours every day, back and forth to Philadelphia. He was able to find employment there. Some people went back to New York. Other people moved. The majority of the people remained. They worked in the garment industry, commuted to Philadelphia, commuted back to New York, and then factories opened in Freehold and in Jamesburg, in the surrounding communities. So for many, many years my father worked in Freehold, and we were able to remain in Roosevelt.

What does one do now in Roosevelt? What one does in any other suburban community. We're still a very active, vital, interested community. Town meetings, school board meetings. They're alive. There are opinions, and they are expressed. People become overinvolved. We're a community of volunteers. And a lot of that sense of family, even though the community is really a microcosm of the United States, a lot of that sense of family still exists. The community still draws together in time of great joy and in time of tragedy. We're really still family. Was I aware when I was growing up that I lived in a totally Jewish environment in the middle of New Jersey? No, it wasn't until I left Roosevelt. It wasn't until I went to Allentown High School that I realized everybody here was the same. I realized that Hightstown was different, yes. We knew that one of the storekeepers was anti-Semitic, and we didn't go in there and buy clothing from him. We just knew these things. What our parents did was, without ever really defining or spelling out or being specific, they set a standard for us, a moral code, a code of ethics, goals, achievements, without ever really being specific. It was the atmosphere in the community. I think we all became overachievers.

The government could not sell all of the homes to the pioneers, because I think they had commissioned two hundred homes and they had only sold about half. I don't know how many commitments there were, but by that time the cooperative failed. So what the government did was rent the homes. Initially they were all rented, but then the government divested itself of the community and sold them off. But the people who came into the community were still mostly Jewish. A handful, maybe a dozen, non-Jews.

After World War II, much later, children returned. I returned.

The community has been a tremendous success. Did my father feel it was a success? Yes, he stayed, absolutely. He could work. He could live in the country. He could plant his garden. He could maintain his intellectual stimulation, and live not in an apartment, but in his own home that he paid for. He paid $4200 for that home, and that was hard-earned money, but it was his own home and he had tremendous pride in that, definitely.

This was one of ninety-nine communities planned by the New Deal, and the only one left.

Augusta Chasan, eighty-four, housewife, Roosevelt, New Jersey

I was born in Russia. I came here when I was three years old. My father had lived here three years before he sent for us. We were four children at the time.

My husband lived in the next building to where we lived. His two sisters were in my grade in school. We'd play around together and then we'd talk about boys, you know. I would say the kind of boy I would like to meet, like kids do, and my girl friend would say, "How about my brother?" I said, "He doesn't like me," because when I'd come in he was studying. When I'd come in, he'd say, "Get that noisy kid out of this house." Then he joined the navy. He was seventeen and it was World War I. When he was in the navy, he began to write letters to me. When I was sixteen, he sent me a telegram and a gift, and he signed it *Love*. Well, was I excited! Then, two years later he got out of the navy, and we were married. We started life together on a shoestring.

He was an electrician. He had gone to the Hebrew Technical University at the time. He graduated when he was fifteen years old. The Hebrew Technical University in New York City was for teaching trades to young Jewish boys. He was taking an electrical engineering trade. He was very brilliant.

In 1932, I think, or 1934, they advertised in the Jewish papers for people who would like to move, especially needle-trade workers, who weren't having much work at the time, to a country place and start a cooperative colony. So my father-in-law was very, very interested. He came to my husband and said, "How about you going out there?" He said, "I would go, but I'm too old." So my husband said, "I'll look into it. It sounds interesting." And he did, and we decided we'll go to a meeting. We used to meet in New York at that Jewish building somewhere on Ninety-second Street. We liked the people that came there. We liked the whole idea. We were going to get a house, and we'd have a factory here and have a little co-op store. It all sounded so good. I always dreamed that someday I would like to have a little country house. So this was great to me. By 1936 they were ready for us, and we came out here.

My husband came here as an electrician. They didn't have electrical work yet, because the laborers were the people who were working here. So they said, "Look, we need a truck driver to bring in the material from New York to the factory here, and then to bring it out, take it to different co-ops on the East Coast." They asked him if he'd like to be the truck driver. So my husband said, "Sure, I'll do anything." While we were at the meeting place, they said the people that they selected had to be under fifty. They were all in their forties. We were in our thirties. I looked around and I found a young couple sitting there. I said, "How would you like to be friends with me?" And she said, "I'd love it." We became friends. As the houses were being settled, as they needed the workers, whoever they needed more than the houses had to board with the people who already had houses. This couple that I was with were farmers. He was one of the farmers that was chosen, a very brilliant man who lives across the street now. So we decided whoever gets here first, the second one will live with them. Well, we were both called at the same time, and they gave us the house because I had an eleven-year-old boy, and they were just married. They were younger, in their twenties. We became friends and we're still friends, fifty-one years. We're still in the same houses.

The community was a hundred percent Jewish. They had people from different Jewish organizations. They had a small group of religious ones, and one from the IWW and then from the Workmen's Circle. We all came with no money really, and we came for the same purpose. We really enjoyed ourselves. We had so much fun together. We used to tell everybody, "Come in here, come in here," and we'd serve bread and jelly. See, we had an apple orchard here, and we could pick the apples. We'd make apple jelly. We had bread and apple jelly and tea, because you didn't need milk for it. People could come here and just have the most wonderful time, and that's what we did. We just lived with each other. It was just beautiful.

We decided, after we were here almost a year, we were going to have our own government, because the people in Hightstown didn't like us because we were Jewish. Yet we had to shop there and we had to buy our shoes and clothing there, and the bank was there. Yet somehow they didn't like us. So we decided we were going to have our own government. We elected a mayor, a police chief, and a fire department.

When they decided on the fire department, they called for volunteers. Most of the people that sit at the machine and sew, what do they know about fighting fires? So they said, "Come on, volunteers." Very few of them had sons old enough to take. So we had just a few. They said, "Come on, somebody." I said, "I'll be a fireman." So they said, "Okay." They took me up. At that time we had a newsman who worked for the government. He was here to report everything that was going on. He got it across the country about the first "fire lady" in the United States. I had reporters from everywhere come here to photograph me, to ask me questions. Before I knew it, I was getting letters from all over the country, saying, "Please send me a button off your uniform." They were very excited. Fred Allen — remember him? — invited me to come on his program.

Did I ever fight fires? Oh, yes, I really was a fire lady.

Aaron Goldberg, twenty-nine, lawyer, Burlington, Vermont

I am a sixth-generation member of the Jewish community of Burlington, Vermont. My daughter is a seventh-generation member.

My family is a very large family that consisted of a couple named Jacob and Toby Fine Rosenberg, who had seven sons, who each had a very long life and had many, many children. In fact, one of their seven sons married three times and had eighteen children. The family, all of the sons except two, came to Burlington. One went to Chicago and one went to New Jersey. When I was in college, I did some extensive histories about Burlington, including the residential patterns of the communities, which showed a tremendous desire to adapt to American styles but still attempt to transplant an Eastern European culture into the Burlington environment.

Most of the children spoke Yiddish through the third generation of the community, and, at least until World War II, most of the people would live very close to the synagogues and moved continuously closer as they prospered. Then after World War II, people of course moved as the next generation was a little more secularized and moved away from the synagogues of the old North End community and up the hill towards the university.

It's my belief and opinion that one of the reasons that Burlington was able to perpetuate this Eastern European tradition was its geographic isolation. In fact, I would venture to say that's true not only of the Burlington Jewish community but true of the other ethnic communities. We have very large and thriving French Canadian communities here, and there are smaller groups of Lebanese and Syrians. It's a very mixed community.

One of the other papers that I did at college was an extensive family history. I came up with a five-page questionnaire and sent that to all family members I had access to, and in addition to that, I did oral interviews with as many people as I could find of the family who were nearby.

When I got done I was able to do statistical analyses based on occupation, average income, number of children per generation, longevity. All the generations have had large families. Many have had more than four children. Even to this day, the family continues to have four or five children in some cases. In terms of longevity, the family is close to eighty-five or eighty-six — men and women.

But what fascinated me was the actual immigration patterns. I was able to determine that the original couple did not come over first, as thought. Two or three of the sons came over first and then sent for their wives. In fact, in one instance, one of the sons had his brother bring his wife and children over; he didn't want them to come over alone. Then they sent for the remaining brothers and the parents. All five of the Rosenberg sons were founders of the community.

The family came from Kovno, Lithuania. Apparently they crossed the German border by wagon and went to Hamburg and then got a boat in Hamburg to New York. They did not stay in New York any length of time, since many other family friends and other kin were already in Burlington.

As I see it, there was a virtual transplantation of a part of this town of Kovno to Burlington. Many of these other families also came from Kovno — the Samuelsons, the Lamports, and other families. They, in turn, would write back to the town — to friends and relatives — and ask them to come over, too. That also may have been a factor in the perpetuation of the shtetl mentality, because there were so many of these families that were all from the same town.

I don't know if there was a shortage of women or not. But in many instances in my family there are both first cousins' and second cousins' marriages. In addition, two brothers or three brothers of one family would marry two or three sisters of another family. That happened on more than one occasion, and that's in our family tree. Beyond that, though, what was also interesting, the family members cooperated extensively in business enterprises, where one brother would have his brother working for him in his grocery, and then when he wanted to expand, he would go to another store and then the second brother would take over his store, and there was all kinds of renting of rooms to family members and other relatives or other families that were distantly related. There was also an extensive network of care of the elderly. Over and over, I found that parents lived until they died with their children, and in some cases they required critical care. Some of these people were blind and deaf.

I must have hundreds of cousins, but not in Vermont now. What's interesting, of course, now there really are only three families that are descendants of the Rosenbergs in Burlington. There's my roots, the Goldberg root. There are the Pauls; Allen Paul is a very successful attorney also in Burlington. His wife, Elsie, is a first cousin of my mother. Then there are the Londons — and I am married to a London. My wife and I are third cousins and third cousins once removed, because I am in two generations, since my grandparents were first cousins and first cousins once removed.

Barney Cohen, seventy-seven, retired wholesale distributor,
Burlington, Vermont

When we were growing up it was Little Jerusalem, East European. They all had cows, a lot of cows in the back yards. They used to go right through the streets on their way to pasture, just outside of town. They were all quite a religious community, as I said. They had three shuls. Had a minyan every morning in three different shuls. They lived according to the way they lived in Russia. Their manners were the same: very little respect one for another. Couldn't keep a rabbi because every man in the community felt as though he knew more than the rabbi. Yiddish was a common language. As kids, I think most of us couldn't speak English before we went to public school.

And as kids, we had quite a Hebrew education, very, very extensive. We were taught to do everything.

Jack H. Press, seventy, retired wholesale distributor, Burlington, Vermont

My mother's father and mother came from that old Vilna area, where most of the Jews of Burlington came from, because Burlington, originally, was a hotbed of Litvaks. Galitzianers weren't too readily accepted in this town, you know. They were always called ferd ganovim, et cetera. But after the war, of course, they filtered in here. Now the derivations are forgotten. But it was a strong Litvak community. Very strong. Everybody had the same accent in Yiddish, naturally.

What made it a shtetl? Well, because we were basically in a little Jewish village. Everybody lived together. Everybody was fairly poor. Basically, there were very few professionals; they all were working people. Some were cattle dealers, a few storekeepers, and butchers, and so forth. Living so close together, everybody knew each other. Because the tradition of Orthodoxy came with them from Russia, they more or less extended it here. And God help you if you weren't really Orthodox; you were an oysvorf, you were a goy, you were no good. If you didn't go to shul, they called you a goy. Of course, we all went to the same Hebrew school; we all played together. There were a few little cliques among us. But we weren't divided in the day school by money. We were divided by likes and dislikes. We all did the same things.

We all went to Hebrew school six days a week basically, and even on Saturdays we had to go to shul. We all more or less were tough kids, because as you might have heard, we all had to fight our way home from school. We were "Christ killers," "Jew bagels," and whatever they wanted to call us; "sheenies" and other names they derived from where I don't know.

Most of the kids in my group spoke Yiddish. When we got into the kindergarten and then first grade, we couldn't speak much English. Burlington was known for various names either by trade styles or by derogatory names. You had Cohen the baker, Cohen from Vergennes; you had Kershner the short, Kershner the tall. You had derogatory names. You had one who was called the fartzer; he was known for that.

Arthur Bloomberg, seventy-two, retired state tax auditor and legislator, Burlington, Vermont

When I grew up in Burlington — I was born there — we were a real Jewish community. We had three synagogues at the time. I went to Hebrew school about seven days a week, including the Saturday services. We had teachers who could not talk English, so we were a Yiddish community.

Everybody was kosher then. If you were found not to be kosher, you were on the s list. You didn't count. You almost got thrown out of the synagogue. We were limited with the amount of kosher foods we had. A couple of Jewish butchers and then we had Colodny's market, where we used to get the processed meats and stuff from New York, Hebrew National. We had a Jewish bakery, so we got our bread there. We didn't buy anything in the so-called goyisha stores, nothing except maybe sugar and coffee and stuff like that. But we did grow up in a very tight Jewish community. Like going to the movies on Saturday; we used to have to buy our tickets ahead of time so we could go to the movie. I remember wearing tsitsis to school.

I don't think the kids any longer wear tsitsis like we used to in school. I remember going to high school and undressing in the gym. The goyim would ask us what that was and we'd say chest protectors. One guy gave me a zetz and knocked me flat on my ass. He said, "It didn't protect your chest." Younger kids don't do that.

We used to have a lot of anti-Semitism. In the wintertime, we had to walk to the high school in groups to protect ourselves, to work together in a snowball fight. This is no longer true. We have now been accepted. We are no longer a minority people. I have a friend of mine who said once, "If you scratch a goy, you find an anti-Semite." And sometimes that happens. It's different than people who grew up in New York City, where you grew up as a Jewish person and no one had the guts to call you a "goddamn Jew," because he would get his head bashed in. Here it was different. I grew up next to a Catholic school, and the first paragraph in the catechism at that time was that the Jews killed Christ. And when they used to walk in front of my father's shoe store and we would be out there, they used to call us Christ killers, the kids. That no longer exists. It's not in the catechism anymore, but this is the sort of community we grew up in.

We had a lot of fun. We stuck together. We celebrated all the holidays. I remember on yontif going to tashlich down at the river. We don't do that anymore. There were things that were going on; we had a tight Jewish community.

There wasn't much difference between here and a ghetto in Europe really, or a shtetl. We grew up that way. Yiddish was our language. In fact, we used to have a football team, the Jewish boys did, and they had one black on the team, and they taught him Yiddish. So the signals were all in Yiddish. Finally the goyim learned the yiddish codes and we couldn't use them after a while.

Marshall G. London, fifty-six, doctor, Burlington, Vermont

It was a fairly sizable Jewish community for the size of the town itself, which was reasonably cohesive as far as the outside world was concerned, even though it was not cohesive from the inside. And I think it left a significant influence on the community around it. Little things, like the way the Jews would take care of their own people. There was never a pauper that died who couldn't have a proper burial. How successful they were economically! How hard they worked! Even though they themselves were poor, along with the rest, they rose up higher. And then the Jewish community itself stuck together so well. It really was a ghetto. From all I can read, it was a ghetto without the external forces; forces to hold the people together were all transmitted from Europe to here with a little influence of America. In such a small community there was a lot of social pressure not to break through the lines and the rules of the ghetto. So for a boy to date a non-Jewish girl, which would be a little ahead of my time, was — my God, the talk of the community. For someone to move to the Wasp area of town — my God, that was forbidden. Or to try and join the country club or swim in a certain area that was restricted. This news got around pretty fast.

So it became a fairly cohesive group, and some very influential, bright people were in this community, intellectual in their dealings with the non-Jewish community, but primarily at that time with their knowledge of the Talmud, their study of the Talmud. They set up this little community. And everybody was Orthodox. You had to be Orthodox. It was a shame if you didn't keep kosher. You didn't do things you weren't supposed to do on the Shabbes. They stretched it a little bit so that when I was a child after shul they would give us a few coins to go to the movies on Saturday afternoon. We are talking about the late 1930s.

It had a great deal of influence on me, going to the Talmud Torah and studying at the Talmud Torah and the Sabbath and then the flavor of home-style Judaism, both custom and ritual, primarily in my Grandfather Gladstone's home. We spent a lot of time there because it was my mother's home. The seder, the traditional seder, the traditional foods, going with my grandmother to the shochet to see a chicken slaughtered ritually, influenced me a great deal as a young boy, and I'm talking about when I was seven, eight years old. The warmth around the table and the guests that would come, the university students they would bring down for meals and holidays, the warmth that exuded from the family, left a great impression upon me.

There are advantages and disadvantages to that ghetto atmosphere. Not only just the ghetto atmosphere but the more concentrated Hebrew education that I had, even though I learned a great deal of what I did by rote. It left me with an emotional feeling towards Judaism and towards the Hebrew language that in subsequent years I have filled in by study of the significance of many of those things and have read a great deal about Judaism. But in years that I went to Talmud Torah, everything was by rote. It was how fast you could read the Shemona Esray. You raced through it. It made no difference what it meant. It was the speed of the thing and the sound of the words, but the sounds of the words left a great impression on me, and those melodies still linger; I love to hear them again, nostalgically, the melodies that I grew up with. But I am sure that the children today don't have that same sort of feeling. They know a lot more about Judaism and its significance as young people than I did at that particular age, but I don't think they have the sense of attachment to it that I did, which is, I think, unfortunate.

They are also more worldly than I was. I have, all through my life, been much more comfortable in the presence of Jews than in the presence of non-Jews. My children, I find, are equally comfortable in both groups. It was a difficult thing for me in adult life to mix socially and to feel comfortable in the presence of non-Jews.

Max B. Wall, seventy-eight, rabbi, Burlington, Vermont

When I came here, most of the Jewish people were still living in the North End. They were slowly moving, the younger people. The war broke everything open, you understand. But most of them were still living around there. The Talmud Torah was there. The shuls were all there. Remember, this was an Orthodox community for years. That didn't mean they lived it Orthodox. That's like Mark Twain, who said if I don't go to church, the church I never go to is the Methodist church. Most of the Jews were not very observant, even when I came here in 1946. Yet some people were slightly observant. They would go to shul on Shabbes, yes. But people came in to pay them rent and they'd say, "Put the rent under the tablecloth." They were not observant Orthodox.

It was a Yiddish-speaking community, Yiddish-understanding community. Even the young people understood Yiddish. They all came from Lithuania. The synagogue ritual was strictly Litvish. I would call it dry as compared to a spirited, romantic, Chasidic-type community. More rational than emotional; intellectual. So even the people who are apikorsim at least knew something, because otherwise you are not an apikoros, you're not. You are just simply an ignoramus. There was a tendency on the part of the Litvisher community always to pay a lot of attention to reason. And their study of Talmud was in terms of reason; those who observed, observed very meticulously.

When I came on the first Friday nights and started to sing "Adon Olam" at the end of the service, they looked at me as if I was crazy. "Who's singing in shul?" It was that kind of a service. Now we do a great deal of singing.

Today, you've got three congregations. The synagogue is no longer the center of focus of all activities. Jews have proliferated in every aspect of private enterprise, of public service, from governor to judges to lawyers to doctors to engineers. Burlington is a modern American community. Has there been a return, as there has in some communities, to being more Jewish, both religiously and in practice? There is on the part of a good many young people. We have a sizable group. They are the ones who are the core of our active Conservative congregation as such. There's an Orthodox synagogue. I don't know how many are Orthodox in their observance. It's not viable. Reform is very viable. It's growing. It's young. I think they are just building their own building. For the last ten years they rented space in a church. And they have a wonderful rabbi now and I think he's the difference between existing in the doldrums and really taking off. Young people, I think, are going to contribute to the total Jewish community because the American Jewish community is not singular any longer. It may not be recognized by a person who was accustomed to Jewish life fifty years ago, but *c'est la vie.*

Lena Rosenzweig, eighty, housewife, Savannah, Georgia

I was Lena Feinberg and I married my husband in 1926. My father had a sister who was married to someone who was related to someone who lived in Savannah. The someone who lived here was connected with the police department and he brought my uncle over and gave him a job on the police force.

The cousin that brought him over was Charlie Garfunkel and he was chief of the police department. I think that was the title he had, chief of police. He gave my uncle a job on what they call the Black Maria. In those days there was a little box on each corner. If a policeman caught someone stealing, he'd take them to this little box and call in the police force. They sent the Black Maria out. It was a black horse and a black wagon. They would put the prisoner in and take him to jail. So they gave my uncle this job. Then, after my aunt was settled here a short period of time, she brought over three brothers. One of those brothers was my father. That was about 1894, 1895.

When the Jews came over at the turn of the century they were all very, very poor. All they brought was a tallit and their tfillin. The women brought their candlesticks, a copper fish pot, and a perenah. Other than that, they had very little. They were all under twenty — the men — because they came over to escape the military training. They were really poor and they weren't too educated, because everybody couldn't become a melamed and everybody couldn't become a rabbi, so they had to go out and make a living. They all became like laborers. One a tailor, one a shoemaker.

There was a Garfunkel family, who were Orthodox, and one of them particularly, Mr. Abe Garfunkel, was quite an intelligent man and he took an unusual interest in the new immigrants. He took them in immediately and prepared them for citizenship. In fact, I remember as a child they told the story that one of the Jewish men was so flustered when the judge asked him who was President of the United States, he said, "Mr. Abe Garfunkel." But Mr. Garfunkel, being Orthodox himself, took a very great interest, because the German Jews who came over before sort of looked down on the Eastern Jews a little bit. I do not know what it was; either they thought they were richer or what have you. But gosh, I don't know what we thought they were. We thought they were God's pets because they had everything in the world — cars and homes, and they spoke English so beautifully. I remember when the first Reform boy married the first Orthodox girl, why it was like marrying a non-Jew.

My mother opened up a shop in 1898 on the main street. It was a little shop of pots and pans in a Jewish neighborhood. She did it because Pesach was an important holiday, and we made a nice little living. Anyhow, the pots got holes in them and my father found out that he could fix these holes. He went out and started buying a piece of lead and he learned that he could melt the lead and solder the pots. The only medium of heat at that time was a little stove that was called a hot stub and you put it into the chimney, but you had to have pipes to go up into the elbow and pipes to go into the fireplace. So my father took into my mother's shop these little hot stubs. First thing, you know, they asked my father would he come and put them up. Well, you have to have pipes to put them up. My father learned how to make the pipes and gradually opened up a little workshop in the back. He fixed pots and pans and made pipes and elbows, and I think that I personally could make a pipe in two minutes. He had the machinery to make it and I could make it right now. He spread it out, and that's how we made a living.

They were very observant. At that time, the Jews who came here were religious. But very few kept their little shops closed on Rosh Hashonah and Shabbat, because they just couldn't. But they were religious. All mothers kept kosher. All mothers went to mikvah. The men worked during the day but at night they davened mincha and mayrev. They kept up the religion from the little shtetl that they came from.

Unfortunately, as the years went by, that chain became less, and unfortunately today it's not too much around, is it? There's not too much of an Orthodox community, you know. But my mother was determined that we were going to be shomer Shabbes. She had four children. She had had seven; three died. And all four of us still remain shomer Shabbes. We are Sabbath observers.

I can remember the Jews that came over. I can remember from five years old. Those Jews that came over at the turn of the century all seemed to have gathered in the west part of Savannah. It was a village called Yamacraw village. The village was named after an Indian tribe, the Yamacraw. There were a few Jews here already who had been here maybe five years earlier or ten years earlier and they were what we would call "shoyn aus gegrint," but the green ones that came over all gathered in this little section. They all lived in little wooden houses; two-story wooden houses with little porches. They had a yard full of chickens; everybody had a yard full of chickens, and everybody had a cow. The scene that is indelible in my mind is going down to that neighborhood where I had cousins. It was a familiar sight, in the afternoon, to see the mothers sitting on the porch with the goose on their laps, stuffing the goose as they did in Europe. There would be a familiar sight to see them taking the dead goose and picking the underfeathers, what they call the puch, to make a perenah for their daughter who would soon be getting married.

Late in the evening the oldest daughter would go to the pasture and get the cows. And I can see these beautiful fifteen-, sixteen-, seventeen-year-old girls with long hair, bare feet. They'd be driving the cows up to their homes and then each one would milk their own little cows, watching the milk come out of it. It was quite a memory to me. They're beautiful memories. The life might have been rough, but we didn't know any better. Like they say, ignorance is bliss, and we were happy.

We didn't go to the undertakers in those days. The body was washed in the home and all the funerals were from the house, most of them. The women that were having babies — and they were having them because there was no such thing as birth control in those days — never went to a doctor. They were too modest, unless, God forbid, there was an operation or something. But they had the babies and the midwife would come. I remember a lot of superstition. I remember when a little baby was born they stuck a red bow on the cradle so that the evil eye wouldn't get there. If my mother was hungry at the time, I know that the midwife would wait until after in case she gave her the evil eye. They wouldn't feed Mom. And I thought that was kind of cruel. I knew it was time for her to eat; I thought there was a lot of superstition at the time.

Unfortunately, they had cows but they did not pasteurize the milk, and there was a lot of diphtheria. There was always a sign on somebody's house, a yellow sign with red letters: DIPHTHERIA — SCARLET FEVER, because the milk wasn't really pasteurized.

I still remember a wedding that took place in Yamacraw. People at that time thought it was a mitzvah, a good deed, to help a bride get married. Not too many came over that were unmarried, but there were a few. They would get together and make the wedding. I remember one of the back yards in Yamacraw — the shochet was there killing those chickens and flinging them over into a barrel, and there were a bunch of Jewish women right there picking them, and one would give them to the other woman, she'd singe them, then the other woman would open them up. They had a group that would kashrut them; you know — make them kosher. The wedding really was made by the whole little group of neighbors that came in. They even baked their own challah.

In those days when you went to a wedding, as poor as people were, they would send a horse and buggy for you. I don't know why they did it, but I remember they sent it for my mother and daddy and the kids. I remember the sensation of going over the cobblestones in Yamacraw. And when we got there, there was a big room and on the table there were long thin vases and they would have celery stuck in them with the leaves up for flowers. There was a man by the name of Mr. Lippman who played the violin. He had four sons and they were all musicians. He was there in the corner playing the violin with his sons. We ate — we had a wonderful meal. In order to dance, they stood against the wall, the women against the wall in one room and the men against the wall. I don't know what you'd call it. They just would move around to the tune of the Jewish music. It was just great. They were happy. We just thought it was great. We didn't need any hotels or anything at that time. We didn't know any better, I guess.

We had one baker. He would come at eight o'clock with the horse and buggy and stop on the main street, where the Jews would surround him. He'd ring a big bell. Well, nobody had a telephone, so everybody ran out to get the bread to find out from Mr. Gottlieb, whose grandchildren still operate the bakery, to find out who died during the night, who had a baby during the night. We'd all wait in the house eagerly. The daddies always went to buy the rolls. It was ten cents a dozen, I remember. They'd come in and everybody would eagerly wait to say well, Mr. So-and-so died or Mrs. Kaminsky had a yingel, a baby, during the night. That's how we got the news from Mr. Gottlieb. That's how we really got the news of what was going on. It was a warm community.

We had the city market where we had four Jewish butchers at the time. The women that went to the market, that would be the gathering place, around the butcher. What would take them fifteen minutes, they stayed two hours. That's where they got the gossip and the news; everything centered around the butcher's little stall. It was a lovely little community.

The old city market was where everybody practically bought everything they needed. It was about a ten-minute walk from Yamacraw, which was the Jewish village. You bought a live chicken and we had Mr. Kaplan, the shochet, kill the chicken down in the basement for a nickel. There was a little lady next to him, Miss Shapiro, and she would pick it for a nickel. But in those days you thought twice before you had your chicken picked, because that nickel would buy a pound of ground meat for the family.

I could pick one with my eyes shut right now. I knew exactly — flock one leg, then the other leg, then the breast, then turn it over, and go through the back part of it, then lift the neck. I could do it right now if I had a chicken.

Friday evening dinner in my house was exactly like it was in Kovno and what it is today. You know, you either got heartburn right then or you had to wait an hour. It was the same thing — gefilte fish and you had your chicken soup and your chicken. That was the meal. In the winter, Friday night and Saturday you got your cholent; that was a Shabbes dinner. Then, everybody had the same meal. We ate meat during the week and we had chicken for Shabbes. Meat was very cheap at that time. My mother made her own gefilte fish. She made it a little different than the modern gefilte fish. She would cut the fish into slices, take it out of the skin, and fill it back into the skin, so when she cooked it, it looked like a fish that was sliced. The natural skin was around it, which I guess gave it the name of gefilte fish — you filled the fish, whereas today we don't use the skin anymore. We make fish balls. It's all made in a different shape. But everybody had cholent and everybody had gribiness, I guess that's why they didn't live too long.

During the week, we bought bread from the bakery, but everybody made challah on Friday and you'd get home from school you ate gribiness on a fresh tsibila kuchen, on an onion bun. It was a must. We were young. God was good to us. People did not live too long when I was a child. I don't know, they seemed to live between fifty and fifty-five, maybe sixty. The man who worked and struggled and when he was able to enjoy life a little bit, he'd have a coronary thrombosis. I guess from the gribiness.

This little village — Yamacraw village that I'm telling you about — where they stuffed the geese, the more shmaltz, the more chicken grease you had in gallon jars, the better housekeeper you were. They thrived on the cholesterol. Strokes were very common. Coronary thrombosis — they would all drop dead from hardening of the arteries or what have you. Of course, I have a son now that says, "Mother, I'd give five years of my life to eat a gribiness sandwich." But since we've become aware of cholesterol . . .

We made petcha. That gives you a heartburn two hours before cholent, I think. That's what you get it first from — the petcha. It's the feet of the calves and it's like Jell-O. You boil it down and you season it with a little garlic and take it up, put hard-boiled eggs in it, put it in a Pyrex. I make it. Of course it's heavy. The older we get, the more modern food we eat.

Everybody had pushkas. That was part of tsedaka, part of your religion. Everybody knew that you had to have pushkas on the wall and the misholoch would come, and how much did he get? If he got five dollars, that was a lot of money in those days, because before you would bench licht — light your candles — you'd put in a nickel. Today, I think we put in eighteen cents. But, we don't have pushkas today; we have JNF [Jewish National Fund] boxes, Mizrachi boxes, the blue box for Hadassah. We still have pushkas, but it is a more modern way. Instead of five dollars, you might have fifty dollars in them.

I remember there were no intermarriages when I was a child. The first intermarriage I remember, the family sat shiva for the girl. She had run off and married a goy. She turned Catholic and she raised her children Catholic. Nice family and raised very fine children, but we lost her as a Jew. Fortunately, we didn't have many intermarriages. We didn't.

It's something beautiful about this community that the Jews and Christians get along just beautifully. We never had any problems. The Jews have always sort of mingled with the goyim to the extent there was no anti-Semitism; really wasn't. I must say. We've never had any trouble with the blacks. Help was cheap and every Jewish woman had a black or two blacks and I think the Jewish mother and housekeeper had a lot more compassion for them than the goyim did, much more. We accepted them and took them in our homes. I know I personally had one for fifty-three years. I helped my husband in the business and she really took over. My son was going to Hebrew school and he just hated to have to study. I came home one day, and in order that he shouldn't get a whipping, Bernice had written all the *alephs* and the *beths* out for him on the paper with the lines. I said, "Marvin, did you get it done?" And he said, "Yes." Sure enough, Bernice knew that Daddy would probably reprimand him and she did it for him. She was with me all those years. She knew everything about us. I always used to say

"Gee, if you could just marry a nice Jewish boy." She knew everything about kashrut, and if you'd sit down sometime without a yarmulka, she'd grab that yarmulka and stick it on your head.

Jay Greenblatt, forty-seven, lawyer, Vineland, New Jersey

What we're dealing with in this story is the forty-three families which banded together and came here from Russia in 1882, funded by a back-to-the-land movement out of Paris. When they arrived in the United States at Ellis Island in May 1882 from Odessa, Kiev, and what later became Stalingrad, their funding was taken up by various other organizations, among which were the Hebrew Immigrant Aid Society. I believe at that time it was known as the Hebrew Emigrant Aid Society; HIAS now, HEAS then. Also the Baron de Hirsch Fund, the London Mansion House, and the Jewish Agricultural and Industrial Aid Society. This group of forty-three families from Ellis Island sent out what they like to dramatize as "scouts." I get a picture of these men riding out from Ellis Island into the boondock area of south Jersey looking for appropriate land. They came down and found an area which is a hundred miles from New York, fifty miles from Philadelphia. It was located on the Central Railroad, in the southeast corner of Salem County, about five miles outside of Vineland, New Jersey. They brought their group down in the summer, I believe, of 1882. They got down here to this railroad terminal and they had absolutely no place to live. So very quickly the local politicians in Vineland somehow got through to the Secretary of War, and a resolution was passed in Congress — it's Resolution 230 — providing twelve hundred army tents for a group of Hebrews stranded outside of Vineland. By wintertime, the forty-three families built barracks and they called that Castle Garden.

These barracks had cubicles eight foot by fourteen foot in which each family was lodged. They ate in a communal manner in a dining hall and lived in a communal manner, as I understand it, the children being cared for communally while the parents went out and did the next step of their work. And as waves came in, in the years thereafter, that's what would happen. They would first go into the Castle Garden and then build and move out into their homes. In the spring of 1883, with the help of the Baron de Hirsch Fund, each of these forty-three families got a home. What they did was this.

The fund purchased large tracts of land. The land was then divided up into fifteen-acre parcels, and for $350 you got fifteen acres of farmland, as it were. They had to then remove the stumps that were left and that took them more than a year or two to do. They got a house, which was one room downstairs with a loft room above it; a twenty-five-foot well. Although it's not anywhere in the literature, I assume an outhouse, and a mortgage, because they put no money down whatsoever, but bought it with the $350. The records that I've been able to find show that in most cases no principal was paid for many years, and only interest was paid to carry these mortgages. The bank in Salem held them and cooperated beautifully in carrying them for many years thereafter. Three of those original houses still remain. Two of them are houses of the original families.

They are all in Alliance. Alliance grew up with the help of the Christians of the area. There were Quakers who lived in the area. Salem was a Quaker settlement, and the Quakers farmed the area up over to Cumberland County. There are many old Christian families whose names still exist in the area. The land that they went in to farm was not the best farmland in the world, very sandy. You could only use it for limited types of crops, but you have to get a picture here of forty-three families in unusual garb, speaking a foreign tongue, not even knowing what a plow looked like. It is consistent with the picture of sending a man to the moon and not knowing what he's going to find when he gets there, with the exception that there's no one to communicate with, and here they couldn't communicate. When you think of an experiment that's doomed to failure, you would think that that's got to be it.

With the help of their neighbors and with the help of the politicians and without any federal funds at the time, really, except for what the Secretary of War gave them, but with a tremendous amount of hard work, they took the land and they did learn how to farm. Contrary to what their grandchildren and great-grandchildren would have you believe, they were not the best farmers in the world. They were not the best farmers, but they survived and they got A and A-plus grades as U.S. citizens. It took five years to qualify for citizenship, and most of the immigrants applied for citizenship right at the anniversary date on the fifth year. They were very proud of their American citizenship.

They voted, and within a very short period of time there was a change in the area. They called it the Alliance Colony. Within the first year, one of the first things they did was to form a chevra kedisha, a holy brotherhood for the burial of the dead, and they formed an array of organizations, such as a library, a school, a very large, beautiful synagogue. They had a board of trade; they had a men's club and a women's club. They had a benevolent association. They didn't have a government as such. This was Pittsgrove Township, Salem County, as far as government was concerned. But it was their shtetl out in the woods on the Morris River. They picked it because it had a river running right alongside it, which served as the mikvah of the area. It had a railroad siding or a railhead right at the end of the colony.

When the post office came in, they had to have a name for it. The station-master's daughter was named Norma, so they named it Norma, New Jersey. That's how it got its name, and that is at the southern end of the colony.

At the northern end of the colony, which is about two and a half miles away, a man named Brotman came in close to the turn of the century and built a factory there where piece goods were brought in from the Philadelphia area and worked on. He also laid out a plat plan for the streets. You'll find that almost all of the streets of the colony are named after benefactors — Lewisohn, Schiff, Isaacs. These are all names of Jews who were well-known philanthropists of the time. Mr. Brotman's area he called Brotmanville. My dad was born in Brotmanville in 1896. His father came there in the 1880s. He wasn't one of the first forty-three families, but we refer to the first forty-three families as "the forty-three settlers." A pioneer of the area is anybody that came within about ten years thereafter.

Now these two suburbs, one at the northern end and one at the southern end, had people who were extremely chauvinistic. I have interviewed people who came from Brotmanville who simply didn't know people of the same age living in Norma, and vice versa. By 1902, let's say, with the exception of the synagogue in Norma, which was built around 1905, you had three separate sets of organizations. There was a men's club of Norma, a men's club of Brotmanville. There was a women's club and a benevolent association; there was a synagogue in Alliance; there was a synagogue in Brotmanville; and then, as I say, there was a synagogue in Norma; and there was another synagogue in Alliance. The second synagogue was built in Alliance within a couple of years of the first synagogue. So you had four synagogues by around 1905 or 1908 within this tiny little area.

How important was Judaism to the colony? Judaism as a philosophy, I don't know, but the maintenance of the religion was mandatory. My father says that if somebody wasn't in synagogue when he was supposed to be, they'd find out where he was. I mean, you just were there. Everyone was there. My father tells the story how in order to make additional money, because he wanted to go to college — and even throughout college — he picked blackberries in the summertime and had a blackberry route in order to make his tuition at the University of Pennsylvania Law School. Before that he contacted the Gentile farmers of the area for their blackberry crops so that he could pick them up and take them to market in Salem. Now Salem is twenty-some miles away, and it was an overnight trip. He had to go all night long, get there in the morning, sell, and then turn the horse and wagon around, sleep over at some farmhouse, and get back, or sleep while the horse moved. He snuck out on a Saturday while his family went to synagogue. His father caught him when he came back and took a whip to him. It just simply wasn't done. Everything centered around the synagogue, everything social, everything educational, everything cultural. It was totally the synagogue, with the exception, of course, within the family itself.

As I'm told, they didn't have any locks on the doors. They had no crime in the area. They had large families. They had athletic clubs. Each one had its own softball team or baseball team. In those days, all the towns around here had semi-pro, if not social, baseball teams and clubs. The Norma baseball team was fairly well known and did fairly well, and was a source of intercourse, I think, with the non-Jews of the area. A man by the name of Maurice Fels, of Fels Naphtha soap, took an interest in the area. He opened up an experimental farm called the Allvine or Allivine Farm, which was very famous. It was a contraction of Alliance and Vineland. There was a canning factory there and an experimental farm. Leonard Lewisohn of New York, a philanthropist at the time, sent down a sewing machine for every household so that they would be able to sew their own clothes as well as take piece goods home from the factory, work on them at home, and bring them back to make extra money.

By 1897, there were 512 inhabitants, 96 families. By 1905, there were 891 residents, 165 families. The Jewish Agricultural Society decided before the turn of the century that they needed to help bring culture to the area, so they hired a man named Professor Louis Mounier. He was a Unitarian minister. Professor Mounier was hired not just for this colony, but for other colonies which followed. There was a colony in Carmel; there was a colony in Rosenhayn, smaller; and there was Woodbine. Professor Mounier was to bring culture, and the Jewish Agricultural Society built halls. Mounier brought in, for instance, the old lantern slides and showed pictures of what was going on outside this colony in the rest of the world. He would tell them something of geography. I guess it might be much like reading *National Geographic* magazine. They spoke and wrote Yiddish, so they didn't have anything else. He would talk to them about current events, tell them what was going on in the world. This is what I am told by my father and others who listened to him. Also, Mr. Fels did another thing. He built a workshop in Alliance, where the boys of the community could learn manual arts — woodworking and metalworking. He built a cottage where the girls were taught domestic sciences — sewing and cooking.

The kids grew up. Most of them got good schooling. They first went to school right there locally in Alliance. My father tells me that there was a school for the first through the fifth grades, with the sixth through the eighth grades on the second floor. One teacher taught first through fifth; another teacher taught sixth through eighth. Brotmanville eventually had its own grade school, but then for high school they went first to Vineland and then to Bridgeton. To get there, they had to go by horse and wagon and then take a train to get to Bridgeton, but they went on and got good education, and then went on to higher education. Joseph Perskie, who was the first Justice of the Supreme Court of New Jersey, came from that area. The Bayuk sons went on to Philadelphia and formed Philly Cigars. Gilbert Seldes was dean of the Annenberg School of Communications. George Seldes, who published *In Fact,* was a journalist and a publisher and a liberal patriot. Herbert Kraft built the Roxy Theater. Gershon Agronsky was the editor and owner of the *Jerusalem Post.* Benjamin Golder was the youngest congressman from Pennsylvania, at the age of thirty-three. Frank Golder was on Wilson's panel at Versailles and was on a board for Hoover.

The parents of those, as they got older, got out, most of them. A few remained and died on the land there; only a handful. The others moved to the city, the city being Vineland mainly. Or they might have gone to Philadelphia if their children were there or something like that. By the time you got into the 1930s, it was starting to disappear. You had the old buildings.

When you talk to people who grew up in the area, they at first remember all the goodness and the sweetness, but then as they talk more and more, they start talking about some of the more bitter things of the times. How really hard it was. Children died young. You go out there to the cemetery and you see the children's graves, and you can tell with the early settlers there were a lot of infant deaths. The whole family would work, large families. My father's family was eleven. I believe there were twelve; one died as an infant in Russia. The whole family would work in the summer months, and they'd even pull the kids out of school when the picking would begin in the fields, especially berries, because it was extra money. It was a small amount, maybe ten cents for whatever had to be filled for the day.

My grandfather was a carpenter. He came here without the family at first and walked around looking for work. Then he brought the rest of the family over a couple of years later. He helped build the synagogues and he helped build all the homes of the area, and then when everything was built and there was no more carpentry work to do, he just switched his job and became the butcher. So he was the butcher of the Brotmanville area. My father tells a story how they would get up on a winter morning when it was just pitch black outside. My grandmother would have wrapped the meat for the two different wagons and my aunt Molly would take a wagon one way and my father would take a wagon the other way and they would go and make all their deliveries in the bitter winter with a horse and wagon, and then come back and have hot sweet potatoes for breakfast and then go to school. That was a daily thing. The sacrifices that they would make for each other were just amazing. They would do all of their schooling, and yet do all of this work. I'm talking about children of ten and eleven years old. It might be unheard of in our society or thought of as even being cruel now, but it didn't do them any harm. I think it's just interesting, for an outsider looking in, that those are not the things that are remembered first. Those are the afterthoughts. The things that are remembered first are the sweeter things. Maybe that's what the mind does to people. I don't know.

In the thirties, a new wave of immigrants came in; again persecution. They found an area here that was readymade for them. There were some old synagogues; not so old at that time. There were people in the area who spoke Yiddish, and there was the poultry industry that was growing, and they were funded, again, by the Jewish Agricultural and Industrial Aid Society. In they came, and took up where the others were leaving off. They were mainly German at that time, I think.

After the war, another wave, and again as a result of persecution. Again, filling up this void. You know how wind doesn't really blow; it sucks into a low-pressure zone. So here is a void, and it's readymade and it's a point of least resistance, where they don't have to tolerate the fact that they can't speak the language, and you have a readymade situation. And they became the members of the congregation and so forth. The third wave was mostly Holocaust survivors.

So now you're into the fifties, and the poultry industry then starts dying, and they're moving out and you have only a handful, two or three, of the representatives of the original families remaining in the area. Just about everybody else is gone. By the time you get to the seventies for sure, because the children of even the survivors' families are now growing and leaving and the parents are beginning to think of leaving. So you get into the late seventies and for some unknown reason I decide to go back to Pittsgrove Township and I find that there's a piece of land there that I want to build a house on, and I wind up buying it and starting to build a home. I've always heard the stories of the area. Nearby is a town called Gouldtown, which is the oldest black community in the United States. It was founded in the 1700s. Right within striking distance of each other, you have the oldest black community in the U.S. and one of the first Jewish farming communities in the U.S. As you may know, there were Jewish farming communities in the Dakotas and in Colorado and they spread in several other different areas. They may have only lasted a year or two. This one lasted.

For the hundredth anniversary, I put together three ladies and had them go out to prepare a map of the area where all the original homes were. I'm talking about at the turn of the century. I went out with them and by the first hour they were fighting with each other so much that I just left them. They came back with a beautiful map, which we then had printed up to hand out to people, thinking that maybe somebody would be a grandchild of somebody and they would want to know where Grandma's house used to be. We sent out about two hundred invitations to descendants, and the only way we made up a mailing list was just to have these people sit down and try and remember who was where. We had over seven hundred descendants show up.

8

Growing Up Jewish

WE HAD so-called Jewish neighborhoods in Albany, New York, when I grew up there. Dr. Stanley Talpers, a practicing internist in Washington, D.C., is my contemporary. Whereas I grew up surrounded by other Jews and was grafted to them psychologically, sociologically, and religiously, his experience in Casper, Wyoming, was vastly different. "When I was growing up, there were maybe forty Jewish people altogether in that town and some from just out of town," he told me. "Some of them were spinsters, some bachelors, and some were families, but there weren't many kids. In my high school of eleven hundred, which was four grades, when I was a senior there was a freshman girl who was Jewish. The rest of the time I was in high school there were no other Jewish kids." Growing up Jewish in the United States meant similar experiences and disparate experiences. And where and when one grew up seems to have influenced significantly one's attitude toward non-Jews.

In St. Louis, Missouri, I interviewed at the same time eighty-year-old Al Fleishman, an advertising executive, and forty-seven-year-old Michael Newmark, a lawyer. Fleishman grew up in a traditional Jewish American urban ghetto, and Newmark in what might be characterized as a golden suburban ghetto. This is some of what they had to say.

NEWMARK: I grew up in Saint Louis, lived here most of my life. I grew up Jewish. It was very easy to do. I don't think I ever thought very much about it. I lived in Clayton, Missouri. I'd say about one quarter of the community was Jewish; certainly one quarter or more of my classmates in public schools were Jewish. I'd say through most of high school I never thought very much about it. I went one summer to Jewish camp; a couple of times to Boy Scout camp. I was not Bar Mitzvahed; I was confirmed from United Hebrew Temple. Both parents were Reform, although their parents on one side had been Orthodox, and on the other, I guess, Reform. My parents were both born in this country. I feel an entirely different person than the [much older Jewish] people [you've just interviewed]. No attachment to that history you've just heard [about ghettoes and anti-Semitism]. I mean I'm attached to it, but no part of it.

FLEISHMAN: I found anti-Semitism when I went to high school. I was chased down the street; rocks were thrown at me. My grandfather, when he went to shul, wore a silk hat and they threw snowballs. Newmark didn't have any of that. I still see it in the ghetto. I remember when we played non-Jews at Yateman Park, and God help us if we won. We had to run all the way home because we were Jews. Yet none of that was present in his life at all.

I happened to grow up in an atmosphere in which they say on Sunday, "Only through my blood shall ye be saved, saith the Lord Jesus Christ." That meant I'm out. I grew up in an atmosphere where they sang Christmas carols, and I was out. We didn't know any different. So I have this innate suspicion of the Falwells and all the rest of them that Newmark may or may not have. He talked about bridge building. I'm willing to build bridges, but I know that back here I'm different. I've heard it all. I lived through the Hitler period. He didn't. I was secretary of the Jewish Community Relations Council. I met with the chief of the FBI on December 7, 1941, to give him the list of the members of the German American Bund. We had it in our Jewish Community Council, you see, because it wasn't illegal, as you know, to be a Nazi prior to December 7. We lived through that. We had spies in the German American Bund and they almost got killed, and the whole business, you see. He didn't live through that. He only knows it from my retelling it. So I have this feeling that someplace down the line, comes the revolution, we're out again.

This low-grade but constant fear of anti-Semitism, of being "dealt out," as Al Fleishman put it, is a recurring nightmare of most older Jews and, surprisingly, of even some younger Jews. Fleishman's is an acquired apprehension, rarely expressed openly.

Nicholas Lemann, thirty-two, journalist, Pelham, New York

It would seem to me odd if they operated a plantation before the Civil War and didn't have slaves. Maybe they didn't. One would certainly want to think that one's ancestors were that noble, and I hope they were, but I'd always assumed that they did hold slaves. There's a little black town near Donaldsonville called Lemannville. It's unincorporated and it's just a little cluster of houses, all black. I don't know what that means.

The New Orleans I grew up in was the uptown part of New Orleans and I was completely unaware of life in the suburbs. It would be like growing up in New York on the East Side. You just wouldn't have any sense of life in New Jersey. There were people in other parts of New Orleans who would have been closer than I was to what is considered a typical Jewish experience in America. In my world, New Orleans had a small Jewish community. I always heard five thousand people in the city, which is less than one percent, I think. It might be more than that, but anyway very small. Everybody very German; again, not totally, but on the whole German. Everybody knew everybody else. Everybody married everybody else. Everybody was related to everybody else, it seemed like, and by northern lights, very assimilated. Nobody ate lox and bagels.

So you had this sort of assimilationist, prosperous, conservative German Jewish community; small-rooted. The people were in business; like a small version of New York. The big businesses that people were in were retailing, finance, merchants, shippers. United Fruit Company, the old Kohlmeyer stock brokerage firm, Godchaux's department store, Gus Meyer; there's another Godchaux who had a sugar company. These were the big Jewish businesses in New Orleans; a lot of doctors and lawyers as you got into my father's generation. Basically, I think that one of the differences between German Jews and East European Jews is German Jews are not interested in politics. They're very interested in culture. You had absolutely none of the socialist tradition that existed in New York. That was just completely foreign to people in New Orleans. To the extent there was liberal politics in New Orleans, it was Jewish. But it wasn't liberal by New York standards. The neoconservative reaction never happened in New Orleans either. The typical German Jews in New Orleans were just much more interested in art and culture, opera, museums, than in changing the world.

The most dominant Jewish family in New Orleans was the Sterns. Mr. Stern came from just a typical, big New Orleans German Jewish family. Mrs. Stern was the daughter of Julius Rosenwald. They were the richest family in New Orleans, and lived in a huge estate. She was more liberal than the typical New Orleans Jew. Although also very interested in culture, she was really the dominant figure in the city. My grandfather was Monty Lemann. His full name was Montefiore Mordecai Lemann, named after Sir Moses Montefiore. He was Mrs. Stern's husband's lawyer and best friend. My father grew up with their son Phil Stern and was his best friend. The typical family history of Jews in New Orleans was — came there from

Germany, everybody started as a peddler according to legend, walking around the plantations peddling off their back, and went on from there.

That's how people naturally got into retailing and also into finance, because it all flowed from being a peddler. Often the peddlers would lend money to plantation owners. Some, like my great-great-grandfather, would then repossess the plantation. My cousins in Donaldsonville, the male head of the family, is a Lemann, and his wife is from the Ayraud family, who were foreclosed on by my great-great-grandfather. It was considered very ironic for them to marry and be reunited, both branches, in the old family home. It's not like Tara. It's not huge. It's a two-story house with about twelve rooms. It's not this grand mansion, but it's a beautiful old house. They're farmers, basically. They grow sugar cane. In the Jewish community there was assimilation, and my family was especially assimilationist and is known for that in the Jewish community in New Orleans. Not without some resentment, I think, even within the family.

The reason is, I think, my grandfather was a very, very respected lawyer with a national reputation. He was so respected, he was courted by all elements of New Orleans. His law partner, Mr. Monroe, was in society and was not Jewish. By the way, it's quite common, and is an oddity of New Orleans, that the Jews and non-Jews are often in business together but don't socialize together. So for the Monroe and Lemann law firm to be half Jewish and half high society is not considered something about which to raise eyebrows. My grandfather had that tie to the non-Jewish world. And also, Mrs. Stern founded a school called Country Day in New Orleans that was part of the national Country Day School movement. Most of the Jews in New Orleans send their kids to Newman, which is uptown. Country Day is out in Metairie. But because of my grandfather's ties to the Sterns, my father was sent to Country Day, where, from boyhood, he was friends with a non-Jewish group. His circle of school friends was Jewish and non-Jewish both.

The head of United Fruit was Sam Zemurray, an immigrant from Bessarabia. My grandfather was his lawyer also. He was Jewish, of course. His general counsel was a man named Montgomery, not Jewish. Montgomery's son and my father are best friends. Montgomery was from a vaguely social family, but married a woman from an extremely social family, sort of the queen family of society in New Orleans. The Montgomerys are really the nerve center of social New Orleans. It is their Christmas party to which my family goes. My father is very, very close to George Montgomery. They have a friendship that seems unlikely to outsiders, because they have very little obvious in common. But they are devoted to each other. George Montgomery has, over the years, used my father as the James Meredith of Mardi

Gras, and invited him to be the first Jew invited to this ball or that ball. My father's never really gone whole hog about it. He is totally uninterested in actually being in these kinds of things. It's just not him at all, because it's all these guys who sit around and drink and party, and my father doesn't drink or party at all. He's touched by his friend's desire to do this for him, and he knows that he's sticking his neck out and he thinks it will be good for the Jews. I know it seems like an odd goal for the Jews to have, to get into New Orleans society, but my father's contention is it would be better for them to be in than not to be in. He believes that slowly, over the years, the barriers will fall, and this is all a part of that.

Jews are excluded from the most socially prestigious of the Mardi Gras organizations. There are many, many Mardi Gras organizations. Some of them all black, et cetera. The really high society, prestigious ones, Jews are excluded from. Comos has no Jewish members; Rex, which is another Mardi Gras krewe, does have Jewish members. Jews are in Rex, because that's considered more Chamber of Commerce-ish and public. The really social ones have no Jewish members. They just let the first Jews into the Junior League in New Orleans, I think, last year. I believe no Jew has ever been inside the Boston Club, where Mr. Monroe until his retirement ate lunch every day. Certainly it doesn't have any Jewish members, and I don't think you're allowed to take a Jew in as a guest. The change has been very minimal, and New Orleans society still excludes Jews.

I don't think there's any law firm in New Orleans that doesn't have a Jew. For some reason, that happened. I guess there's no law firm in New York that doesn't have a Jew. But very recently you were hearing things about that. Looking for housing around New York, I constantly heard rumors about co-ops that don't let Jews in; there are suburbs that don't let Jews in. You never hear that in New Orleans. You never hear that a Jew can't buy a house in this neighborhood; a Jew can't get a job at this company. But on the other hand, it is true that a Jew can't join various clubs or Mardi Gras krewes. There still have not been any Jewish debutantes in New Orleans. One is tempted to say about this, "Who cares?" which is my attitude, although I guess if you live there, you care. Most of the Jews in New Orleans, I don't think really care that much. They feel, We've got a nice life; we're in our own little social world. It's not something that cuts deep. Although if you really question them about it, you get anger.

It's remarkable in a way that this social anti-Semitism still exists in New Orleans. It's a real relic; it's an antique. You can't defend it. It's not Nazis. I know these people. I know what they're like. They're good ole boys; they're not haters. Some of them are haters, but they're mostly the country club set. I don't like the country club set anywhere. I don't like the Jewish country club set. That's just not me.

My parents say — my father just doesn't talk about it — my mother said when she went to these balls — it must have been a very strange scene, because there are all these people who they know but they're all masked, so you can't exactly tell who they are — she said she got a lot of cold stares from people. I remember various comments over the years when I was growing up in school. Nothing vicious or virulent or anything like that, but I remember being aware of it. Once I remember when I was in seventh or eighth grade they would roll a penny down the aisle past my desk, the joke being that I was a Jew so I would dive and grab it. The bottom line is that I found this whole situation I'm describing sort of creepy. The main reason I left New Orleans was because I just fell in love with journalism at a very early age and decided that if I was going to do this well and seriously, I had to leave. I didn't have much stomach for that whole role that I'm describing my father playing.

What has been the relationship between the New Orleans Jewish community I've described and blacks and civil rights? There hasn't been the same kind of bitterness that there's been in other cities. The Jewish community in New Orleans absolutely took the lead in civil rights, Mrs. Stern and my cousin Julian, the rabbi, in particular. It's just absolutely true that the Jews were out in front of everybody else on civil rights and integration and giving to black charities, giving to Xavier University, giving to Dillard University, giving to Flint-Goodridge Hospital, supporting black candidates for political office. They really have been ahead on that. The other side of it, I'm sure there is some black anti-Semitism.

What I see as the friction points between Jews and blacks don't exist to the same extent that they do in New York City. On the Jewish side, to my mind one big friction point is affirmative action. Affirmative action is just not an important factor in New Orleans life, because Jews work in family businesses that don't have affirmative action. They don't care that much about college admissions and such. If they want to apply to Harvard, they'll probably get in just because Harvard doesn't get that many applicants from New Orleans. So that's not a factor that causes incredible bitterness the way it does in some northern cities. This whole issue of the black leaders being anti-Israel and the Jewish community being pro-Israel, that's not a big deal in New Orleans either, partly because the Jewish community is not as pro-Israel and partly because Palestine isn't as big a deal in the black community, or isn't a big deal at all, as far as I can see.

The other friction point on the black side is the Jewish store owner–landlord phenomenon. There's a little bit of that in one neighborhood, but it's really long forgotten. Most of the Jewish community in New Orleans has not been in those businesses and didn't use those businesses as its route to success. There's this one strip in New Orleans called Dryades Street —

which is like what you see for miles in Chicago, where there're all these Jewish department stores, former synagogues turned into AME Baptist churches — but it's only about four blocks. That's the only place in New Orleans that's like that. So most of the black neighborhoods don't have this formerly Jewish feeling to them.

I had a lot of Jewish friends growing up, and a lot of non-Jewish friends. I was sent to Sunday school, but left in about seventh grade. So I wasn't confirmed. My cousin was the rabbi. My father was the president of the board of the temple. My father would take us to temple once a year on Thanksgiving. Did the High Holidays mean anything? Not really. Now my sister and I go on the High Holidays. My father, I think, goes sometimes on the High Holidays, but for some reason when we were growing up he didn't take us on the High Holidays. I never had a seder until I went away to college. We had a Christmas tree and exchanged gifts. I remember when I got married, and I said to the rabbi in Westchester County — I was describing my family — there is a concept that one should be sort of Jewish but not too Jewish. And that really is the operative feeling of Jewish New Orleans. Say that to a New Yorker, they'll just look at you with contempt. Maybe it's contemptible, but the feeling in New Orleans is that what they really scorn is a Jew who pretends not to be a Jew because he feels that it will help him or get him ahead in the world. That scene is really beneath contempt. The kind of Jews who change their names or convert to Unitarianism. This is what you are and you should be proud of it. They really don't go in for New York–style Jewish life, ethnic Jewish life. It seems too ethnic to them. My father has a long history of these United Jewish Appeal battles. It would be very easy for a New Yorker to paint him as a self-hater because he doesn't go to temple on the High Holidays, et cetera, but he's been very, very active in all Jewish civic activities in New Orleans his whole life.

The most unattractive side of the world of New Orleans is Jewish anti-Semitism. That's what you didn't ask me about. I don't know if the world you grew up in had such a thing as Jewish anti-Semitism. This is true in my mother's family, also, in New Jersey. I grew up in a world where there was some Jewish anti-Semitism. Again, to draw a black comparison, it's very much like growing up in the old, light-skinned black elite. There is an element in this world that thinks, Well, the Mardi Gras people — the reason they don't like Jews, they're not completely off-base about some Jews, not us, but other Jews. The ones in New York. That's the creepiest thing about it.

Remember Me to God by Myron Kaufmann is a wonderful book. It's very depressing, but it's about being Jewish at Harvard in the 1930s. It's

Jewish self-hatred. The days when Weinberger was there. Somebody my age just can't connect with the world of that, and *Gentleman's Agreement,* and what it was like.

I do a lot of work as a journalist in ghettoes, and you always hear about how the Jews control America. It's not the way they say it, but I've grown up with the idea that Jews really do control America in some way. I grew up with this social anti-Semitism that I'm talking about. But by the time I got to Harvard the world in which a Jew couldn't get tenure at Harvard and a Jew couldn't be a partner in a big law firm and that kind of thing — just seemed a million miles away.

When I got to Harvard I felt a real affinity for other Jews, even though I had this completely different experience. Most of my close friends at Harvard were Jewish, although not all by any means. But the "other Jews" were shocked by me. They would say to me, "You're a self-hater." And I would say, "Just because this world I came out of was so different, why am I a self-hater? What did I do?" There's an element of that, but a lot of it is just it's a totally different milieu that is nonetheless Jewish. Part of our discussion that we were just having is somehow if you are Jewish, it always comes out. One Jewish student used to call me Finzi-Contini. We didn't get along, and this was part of it. When I'd come into a room he would start to speak either Hebrew or Yiddish to his friends to make the point: "Nick won't understand this now because he's such a self-hater."

I have a theory that the German Jews have disappeared as an ethnic group, as a coherent group. Maybe not in New York; I don't know what that world of the Harmonie Club is like. There's a summer resort where my family has gone for years and years: Charlevoix, Michigan. This one street, Michigan Avenue, was the German Jewish street. It was a few blocks long, and everybody who lived there was a German Jew. At one time, and especially in the nineteenth century, since the German Jewish communities were so small, there was a lot of cross-pollination among the German Jewish communities in New Orleans, Cincinnati, Saint Louis, and Chicago, which were the big cities with German Jewish populations, partly I think with the idea of setting up marriages. My great-great-grandfather who came to America, his son, the first Bernard Lemann, married a girl from Cincinnati named Harriet Friedheim, and he met her at some social event set up explicitly to introduce young German Jews from different cities to each other. At that time the state of Donaldsonville was such that you wouldn't marry the local Catholic girl. So you had to hit the road to meet German Jews. Charlevoix had German Jews from Cincinnati, a lot from Chicago, Saint Louis, and New Orleans. There were some Charlevoix romances that led to marriage. But going there last summer, which we did, for the first time in twenty years, it seemed to have fallen apart. There were some of the old people there, but it just wasn't — the same. The street wasn't all Jewish. You had the sense that this very cohesive world no longer existed.

I'll tell you a great story. My aunt in Chicago goes on and on about things like the Lake Shore Country Club, which was the old Jewish country club, and she says today it's in tatters; you can't keep it up anymore, she said. I guess back in the 1930s or 1940s they were living in the near North Side of Chicago and they actually moved because Ann Pritzker moved to their block. You couldn't have that. Part of what happened to the German Jews is that there came a time when the Jewish community in America just became dominated by Eastern European Jews, who were much more proud of their Jewishness. And also I think the culturalism of the German Jews was part of their downfall in a way. Not downfall, but everybody in Charlevoix that you met — all the people of my generation — were museum curators, in grad school in anthropology . . . They got so refined, they couldn't dream of going into the family business, or so I felt, keeping these sort of dynastic Jewish businesses going.

Larry King, fifty, radio talk-show host, Washington, D.C.

The name was changed to King in 1959, when I started in radio. It was legally changed. But the birth name was Larry Zeiger.

I was Larry Zeiger until I was twenty-six, and then it was changed for radio purposes. Now they wouldn't change it, by the way, if you were starting today. Then it was the thing to do. You had to have a name that was immediately recognizable, easy to remember. I don't know if part of it was anti-Semitic. I think they would have changed the name if it was Gamboli. They wanted a name like King, like Smith. But any kind of ethnic name wasn't big. You had to change it. And I changed it legally. My mother used to go around in Miami — she lived the last years of her life there, where all my broadcast career was — and go to the butcher shop and she used to say, "You have good lamb chops?" And the butcher would say, "Well?" She would say, "Perhaps, perhaps you know my son. His name is Larry King. I am Mrs. Zeiger, the mother of Larry King." She sent me a birthday card once to Larry King: "Dear Larry King." She signed it "Love, your mother."

I grew up in Brownsville in Brooklyn until I was ten and then my father died and we used what little was left of the insurance to move to Bensonhurst, which was a nicer section, where Mother's sister lived. My mother came here with six sisters. Seven girls altogether. Their name was Gitlitz and they came from Minsk. My father came from Pinsk. They met here. They married. All the sisters married. I guess there were twenty or twenty-one children from the seven sisters, and I am the only one who did not go to college. Even all the girls went through college.

My father owned a bar and grill in Brooklyn, in Brownsville, and was a hard-working, tummler kind of guy, I gather. When the war broke out my father tried to enlist; he was a patriot. You know, the Jewish patriots at that time were zealots. He tried to enlist and they wouldn't take him because he was just over forty. So he sold the business to work in a defense plant. He had to help America because America was so good to him. He worked the overnight shift in a shipbuilding plant in Kearny, New Jersey. And died of a heart attack one night. I guess he was forty-four and I was ten. I had a younger brother, Marty.

We were on welfare for a year. There weren't many Jews who were on welfare. My father, as I say, was a tummler and, as best as I can gather, a kind of guy who went to ball games, bet horses. He was a good provider but not much on bank accounts. We had meager insurance and when we moved to Bensonhurst we lived on the third floor, an attic apartment in a very nice residential section, and I remember the rent was forty-three dollars per month. For the first year after we moved — my brother was six and I was ten — my mother had to take care of us. There was limited insurance funds. So we were on New York City welfare. New York City bought me my first pair of glasses. I remember that my mother couldn't work because she had to take care of the two little ones. The welfare inspector would come every two weeks. What she would do — on the side she was a seamstress — she would take in the neighborhood clothing to mend. They would never tell you when the welfare inspector was coming. You couldn't make extra money. If you made extra money on the side, you were off welfare. So we'd get the cue downstairs if one of the kids saw the welfare inspector coming, and we would have to hide dresses and stuff that she was mending. The welfare inspector would come up and, I remember, open the refrigerator, and he would say to her, "Mrs. Zeiger, why are you buying grade A meat? You know, grade C meat is just as good. You don't have to buy grade A meat." And she would always say, "I'm sorry." But she was the typical, classic Jewish mother. She would eat chicken so we could have lamb chops. She would never buy less than grade A kosher meat. We were on welfare for a year and then she went to work and she worked as a seamstress and then as a foreman in a factory.

She sent me to the Eddie Cantor Camp at Surprise Lake, New York, for two weeks. You had to be poor. No money. What always hurt me later on was when people would call the radio show and discuss "the Jews are rich" or "Jews have always had everything in this country or an edge." Everyone at that camp was Jewish, as I remember, and they were all poor. In fact, I think it was union money that buried my father. Even though he wasn't in the union, I think my mother had had a membership. I wasn't happy at camp because my father had died and I was really tied to my mother and it was the first time that I was away. My little brother was having a good time, but I was miserable. I missed the city. I was very much a city person. At the end, the last two or three days, I was getting to enjoy it. But it wasn't the warmest remembrance for me.

Bensonhurst was wonderful. I'm so glad I grew up there. Bensonhurst was a mixed community near Gravesend Bay and ten minutes from Coney Island. I would say it was sixty percent Jewish and forty percent Italian and the two groups were generally very friendly. The Italian mothers and the Jewish mothers were very similar types.

We had no idea what a Protestant was. We knew blacks much better than Protestants. There were blacks in the neighborhood. They were largely superintendents of the apartment buildings. Blacks turned on the lights on Friday nights in the synagogue. Mario Cuomo was on my show recently and told a wonderful story. When he was growing up in his neighborhood in Queens, Cuomo was the Shabbes goy and had to turn on the lights Friday night and do whatever he had to do on Saturday. Then on Sunday he was a choir boy.

There would be the occasional "you killed Christ" fights, but we were not a fighting neighborhood.

Basketball was the theme of the neighborhood. The Jewish kids then were so predominant in basketball. Sandy Koufax and I grew up about six blocks from each other. We were friendly. We had a group called the Warriors. We used to meet in the club room. We had jackets, reversible jackets, wool on one side and satin on the other. We played in the Jewish Community House on Bay Parkway. There were some twenty-one guys, and we've remained very friendly. We had a reunion just six months ago. One of the wives got in touch with all twenty-one, and nineteen of them came. It was really remarkable.

We had a club room and a guy named Bernie Horowitz had this house and we used his basement.

His father always played pinochle with us; he would come downstairs. We were then, I'm talking ages fourteen to nineteen — all the experiences centered around the club room. Bernie's mother was very much the Jewish mother. Bernie was funny. On Chanukah he would buy her a fielder's mitt. She would say, "Bernie, it's a lovely mitt. I don't have any use for it; why don't you use it?" "Thank you, Ma." He'd get her basketball tickets; tickets to a Knicks game. She was wonderful. I remember a cute story about her.

Jews didn't fight. Never fought. Never punched each other. Screamed a lot. Argued. Never punched. We are about seventeen. Herbie Cohen and I are hanging around the neighborhood — I don't know where the rest of the guys were — and we meet two girls who are known as "loose." We had never been with a woman. And these two girls say, "We heard a lot about your club room. Let's go down there." Angela and Teresa. So we go down to the club room. There's no one there. Me and Herbie. Angela and Teresa. We had couches. Herbie's sitting on one couch with Angela and I'm sitting with Teresa and we shut out the lights. We are downstairs in Bernie's basement, our club room, we're starting to neck, and one of the girls says, "I won't do anything without music," and our record player was broken. So Herbie says, "Larry, why don't you go upstairs and get Bernie's radio?" I run upstairs to get the radio and I'm about to go downstairs when Bernie's mother blocks the entrance. She's making chopped liver and she's got this big wooden bowl and she's pounding. She says, "Vhere are you going?" I say, "I've got Bernie's radio. Herbie and I are downstairs and we want to listen to the radio. Ball game." She says, "I think I heard a girl's voice." I say, "No girl." She says, "There's a girl. You ain't taking the radio." I say, "Mrs. Horowitz, I'm taking the radio." She's blocking the entrance to go downstairs.

Then I hear Herbie yell, "Larry, come on with the radio," so I ran right through her. The chopped liver went up in the air and she went down on the floor and there was chopped liver all over the ceiling and it was a mess. The girls had to leave. She was screaming, and the father came running.

Next day, we are all on the corner. Bernie comes over to me, walking down the street really angry. He says, "You beat up my mother last night. And I am going to tell you what I'm going to do." And we all wait, you know. A Jew angered. He says, "I'm going over to your house. I'm going to kick your mother in the face." I say, "You kick my mother in the face, I'll punch your mother in the stomach." He says, "You punch my mother in the stomach, and I'll drag your mother along the ground." None of us are touching each other. We are just making violent threats to the mothers.

We were a very close group. We weren't religious, but all the homes, as I remember, kept kosher. My mother always changed the plates. We went to synagogue on the holy days. I certainly didn't observe the Sabbath. I went to ball games, ate bacon outside the house. But inside the house was always very Jewish. The Jewish values were very important. Family. Loyalty. Later on, I went to Miami and got married and got divorced. Divorce would have been unheard of in the neighborhood. It was a word we never used. Also, there was a solid approach. Nobody moved. Your friends were your friends. There was no such thing as transit. You weren't "in transit." People were there. There was a lot of caring, the extended family. It wasn't just your own family, but the family of your friends. You learned a lot about giving then. Even the poorest Jews, as I remember, contributed. That essence to give. My mother, if she had ten dollars left and someone needed five, she gave it. And that wasn't unusual; that was typical of the neighborhood.

I was the only one without a father. Therefore it was a little hard on me. It was low-middle income and I was low income. The guys would have five dollars and I'd have a dollar. It was tough. I worked after school. I delivered groceries for Willie the grocer. I'd go out on a bike and deliver stuff and try to help my mother out. Also, unusual, most of the Jewish kids were fairly good students and I was a nonattentive student. I think I lived a lot off the fact that my father wasn't alive and I think, looking back, I even used that; you know, "I'm the poor kid without a father." My mother would go to school when I would have problems. I wouldn't have truancy problems. I would have problems of not paying attention in class. "Why isn't Larry doing better? Larry is bright; why is he getting bad marks?" She used to go in and always blame someone else. Had to be the school. "You don't understand Larry." It was never Larry's fault. "Come over to the house," she said to the dean of boys once. "Come over to the house, we'll have some soup, we'll talk." Herbie once said that if I blew up a bank, killed thirty people, the classic, you know, arrest him, my mother would say, "Maybe the bank made a mistake on his checking account. Maybe they misplaced five dollars, he was angry."

She was always very protective of her two boys. Love, I think, was the essence of the Jewish heritage then. Love and caring and caring about others.

Also, political involvement very early. We were all Democrats. We gave out fliers on the corner for the American Labor Party. I remember sitting in the balcony of Madison Square Garden when Adlai Stevenson ran for President, sitting way up and remembering: Vote Row B. The Democratic Party was Row B. You didn't have to know who was running; you just went in and voted Row B. First, the American Labor Party and then the Democratic Party. Very politically oriented. Activists. I remember, growing up, we didn't know why we hated Hoover, but we did. *Tooooey* with Hoover, you used to say. Roosevelt was god. Remember the day Roosevelt died? It was like your uncle died — your favorite uncle. It was just the eeriest thing in a Jewish neighborhood. Italian neighborhood, too. I would guess that that neighborhood would have voted for Roosevelt ninety-six percent. No Republicans. We didn't know any Republicans.

We were so into sports — that was another big thing in New York — Brooklyn boys, Jewish boys, and sports. It was an extension of us. I do know it was very important. If you were not a sports fan, you had trouble. You were kind of out. We did not have other things. We weren't able to ski and play tennis and do things other kids do today. But sports — Ebbets Field was a big part of our center of activity. Going to Ebbets Field. Going to Dodgers' games. Basketball. The Garden. NYU. There were a lot of Jews in basketball. Our heroes as kids were the Sid Tannenbaums and the guys who played basketball in New York City. There were a lot of great Jewish players. Sid Luckman was a hero. I remember as a kid hearing legends of Sid Luckman, the Jewish quarterback. When we were very young, we would look at the Chicago Bears. We'd read "Marshall Goldberg." We had great pride in the fact — and I think that was because they were Jewish.

But the Jewish kid knew he was going to go to college. Most of the baseball players produced in the era when we grew up got out of high school and went right to play, and the Jews had goals beyond that. Now the Jewish basketball player knew he was going to go to college, had to go to college. You didn't go from high school to the NBA. So you went to college. Hence, the Jewish basketball player. Hence, the non-Jewish baseball player.

Then we branched out and learned of the Jewish intellectuals. But sports was the neighborhood thing to do. And urban basketball was cheap. We had no tennis players. We had no golf. Who knew from golf? We played a lot of basketball. We played softball. We played baseball. The Police Athletic League used to take us to baseball games. Poor kids.

We played stickball, squareball, punchball. Stickball tournaments. Stickball for money. Punchball for money. There were punchball games on Sunday where the really good punchball players came. Punchball is like stickball, except you hit the ball yourself. Spaulding — you used the red Spaulding — rap it with your hand and then run to first base, second base, third base on the streets. Get the street cleared. Guys would move their cars, and the cops would cooperate and clear off Eighty-fourth Street and Twenty-first Avenue on Sunday morning. They would bet on the games — the men in the neighborhood; the fathers, the uncles, would bet. I would umpire third base sometimes. These guys were wonderful ball players.

There was stoopball, stickball, triangle — you'd play in a smaller area — pitching stickball, hitting-by-yourself stickball. Punchball was the famous game where "three sewers" came from. Can you punch a ball three sewers? How far can you hit a ball? And we measured it by sewers. The quality of a guy. A three-sewer man was like Dave Kingman. Sports was very much a part of it. We argued it. I saw the first game Jackie Robinson played.

Koufax joined the Dodgers and came up from spring training. They were playing the Yankees in an exhibition. Every year before the season began, the Dodgers played the Yankees. They played one game in Yankee Stadium, two in Ebbets Field, or two in Yankee Stadium and one in Ebbets Field. Koufax is now on the Dodgers, but he is still like one of us. Spring has ended. The season is about to begin. And it is Passover. We took matzo sandwiches to Ebbets Field, with chicken fat. We go to the dugout to give it to Sandy. And he's saying, "Get out. Get away. They are crazy. They are tummlers." Jackie Robinson came over and said, "What's this?" "Matzo." We had the whole Dodger bench eating matzo and chicken fat. We were handing it out. The starting pitcher was Joe Hatten, and he ate matzo and chicken fat and he got knocked out in the first inning when the Yankees belted him. The fans around us were blaming us because we gave him the matzo and chicken fat. And Sandy was burying his face in his hands. Sandy was a very heymisher Jewish boy. Would not pitch on the religious holidays.

About once a year, I talk to him. Sandy wore his Jewishness. He married Richard Widmark's daughter and she had to convert or he wouldn't marry her. I remember, I was in Miami and they were in the World Series and I did a phone interview with him, and the World Series was opening the next day, which was Rosh Hashonah. He wouldn't pitch or dress or go. So we taped the day before and he kept saying to me, "Remember, Larry, I know that you are playing this on Rosh Hashonah. Announce that it was taped yesterday." It was very, very important to him. He had a lot of those values.

We went to movies a lot. And we went to theater when we were fairly young. We would read the reviews. I'm talking about in our teens. If a play got good reviews, one of the guys would collect money. I remember *South Pacific* was a $2.40 matinee in the balcony. One guy would go and buy tickets for the other guys.

Girls were very late. First sexual experiences were late. We were into the guys and boasting about things that didn't happen. A girl was bad if she let you touch her. Jewish girls. Couldn't touch a Jewish girl. I remember when I started to smoke, I took out a Jewish girl. I think I had been smoking two days. I was eighteen, and I took out a Jewish girl. We went and had Chinese food and then to a movie. I wasn't used to smoking. I thought I was a big man. I took her home and I didn't expect her to kiss me good night, because on the first date Jewish girls never kissed you goodnight. It was cold and I had my hands in my pockets and I walked her upstairs and I had a cigarette dangling out of my lip and suddenly she puckered up. I was totally shocked. So I kissed her with the cigarette. She screamed. I guess I put a hole in her bottom lip.

We were funny kids. The candy store was the other center of our existence. You couldn't stay sequestered in the club room the whole time. So we went to the candy store and hung around. The candy store was owned by Sam Maltz. "Buy something. Don't sit around. Buy something." Sam Maltz had a very pretty daughter who was built pretty good, and we started to look at her and grabbed the *New York Daily News* and the *New York Mirror* and read everything we could and argued over baseball. One day, Sam Maltz was yelling at us that we don't spend enough. One of the guys said to him, "What do you make off the juke box?" He said, "I get half. You put in a nickel, I get two and a half cents." "So if we play the juke box, can we stay?" He says, "Of course." So we played Frankie Laine's "My Heart Knows What the Wild Goose Knows" a hundred times. Sam Maltz threw the juke box out on the street. He was singing, "Enough with the goose."

We were meddlesome kids, but no one ever got in trouble. No one ever had problems of that kind. We didn't always come home on time. We played ball late. We were good kids.

But we were very, very involved — we had a lot of not just sports discussions, but political discussions. We were very politically aware. We were very street-smart. But I discovered that all the kids in New York were street-smart — I don't think that was a Jewish thing. By the way, the Italians talk about having Mafia people as heroes. Jewish gangsters were our heroes. Louis Lepke who founded Murder, Incorporated. We were proud of that for some reason. There's a Jewish pride factor, which I understand a lot with blacks. A black may rap Jesse Jackson, but don't you rap him. I can be that way. I can go on the air and talk about Israel and disagree with what Israel did in Lebanon and make that statement; criticize Israel. If someone calls in and I can detect that it's a non-Jew, criticizing Israel, I get defensive, even though they are agreeing with my opinion. I get very defensive. Because we tended to be very much that way. Even in Miami, Meyer Lansky — and this was hard for the non-Jew to understand and the *Miami Herald* never understood it — Meyer Lansky was respected. Why?

Here's a guy who's never been in jail, forty years, Mafia. He planned all their finances. He skimmed all their money. He was the guy who taught them how to deal with money, how to deal with cash, how to launder money. Meyer invented laundering money. Well, there were very few Jewish people that wanted Meyer Lansky arrested. And when the *Miami Herald* then, which had an image of being anti-Semitic, would run Meyer Lansky stories, prominent Jews at meetings — I remember B'nai B'rith meetings — would always say, "We are not proud of things Meyer Lansky has done, but if you read that editorial, it was more than Meyer Lansky . . ."

I met Meyer a couple of times. Jewish gangsters are wonderful.

I'm at a restaurant called the Embers, and Meyer Lansky sits down at the next table. The first time I met him I was doing a radio show at the Fontainbleau Hotel and he was in the coffee shop and he called me over to the table. He's sitting. When he walked into a room everybody stopped, even though he looked like a haberdasher. He had a little Jewish accent. He called me over and he says to me, "You making a dollar?" With him is Jimmy Blue Eyes, who was famous as a Jewish killer. Meyer never killed anyone. Meyer never carried arms, even though as a kid he was part of a very tough Jewish gang in New York City. There were gangs of poor Jewish kids on the East Side of New York who were as tough as the Mafia kids or the black kids. Meyer was one of those gang guys, and Jimmy Blue Eyes, who had the most beautiful blue eyes I ever saw in my life; I mean prettier than Paul Newman — beautiful blue eyes. He was known as Meyer's killer. When Meyer got mad at a guy, Jimmy killed him. There were books that credit Jimmy with forty killings, fifty killings, in his life. He also never went to jail.

Now, they are at the next table with their wives in this restaurant. Meyer's seventy-two; Jimmy Blue Eyes is seventy-one. The waiters would come over and the plates would jangle; they were nervous. I'm sitting next to them, just with a date.

Everybody asked later, "What did they talk about?" It was very crowded. "What did they talk about?" So here you are, sitting with a famous gangster, a killer, and they are Jews. Here's the conversation:

"I can't eat Roquefort anymore. My stomach. I used to love Roquefort."

"So what do they make you take?"

"Ah. The oil. The oil and vinegar."

Meyer to Jimmy: "Jimmy, why don't you move down here? It's warm. It's twenty-eight in New York today."

"Ahh, I don't know, Meyer. I still got friends in New York. I'm comfortable there."

It could have been any two people anywhere. And it was just touching to me. Even the bad ones were heroes to us. We didn't understand Louie Lepke and Abe Reles; these were Murder, Incorporated, guys. But yet there was this Jewish camaraderie, which still exists, I think. There is a knit to the Jewish community that binds it. There might be some pompousness to it, too. But there's a knit. And the Jew is always laughing.

You know, it always intrigued me about Jewish comedians, why so many comedians are Jewish. I've learned that there were an unbelievable number of Jewish comedians in concentration camps. I interviewed a man once who spent five years at Dachau, and he was the camp comedian and he kept alive by being the camp comedian. They made jokes about dying to keep together, to laugh. The Jew has always been able to laugh at himself. There's a Jewish kind of ironic sense of humor. Now, it's not inbred as Milton Berle would tell you. Charlie Chaplin wasn't Jewish, and there were other great comedians that weren't Jewish. But there's so many that are.

I have rarely in my life met a Jewish person who did not have a sense of humor, who did not enjoy a good laugh or know timing or respond to something that was funny. I don't know any Jewish person who does not laugh a lot, and most can tell a story well. I remember my mother going to the Yiddish stage and talking about Paul Muni. You see, we were proud of a Jewish actor. When we heard that Paul Newman was Jewish, that was a big day. "Paul Newman's Jewish, ah-ha!" George Segal's Jewish; I'm proud of that. As if, wow, we can do these things, too. But I remember the

Yiddish stage, I remember Menashe Skulnik, the hero he was to the Jewish community.

Do you know what's helped the Jewish culture? Television. The gags, the Jewish gags. Johnny Carson with Mel Brooks talking about the Jewish idioms. Like we never saw a Protestant, I met people in Miami who had come to live there from Alabama who did not know what a Jew was, who didn't know what you mean by Jewish. They weren't anti-Semitic. They didn't know what a Jew was. What does a Jew do? What does he sound like? They didn't know. The media now has made the Jew part of the culture. I think it has reduced anti-Semitism. It has increased an awareness.

We had a lot of passion. We didn't have many laid-back Jewish guys. Cool. Cool was not an aspect of Judaism. There were very few cool Jewish guys. We admired cool guys. I remember, Wouldn't you like to be cool; wouldn't you like to just let things float off your back and just be cool about it? Lenny Bruce, I knew Lenny very well, and he used to talk a lot about Jewish influence in America, which was almost bizarre. What is Jewish and what is not Jewish? He used to do a wonderful routine on New York is Jewish and Montana is not Jewish. That means that if you are Jewish and you live in Montana, you are not Jewish, but if you are black and you live in New York, you are Jewish. Rye bread is Jewish; white bread is not. Lettuce is Jewish, garni is not. He'd go through this kind of thing, and what's amazing to me is the Jewish influence in America.

It's incredible to me. We are three percent of the population. The involvement in the media, the involvement in the beginning of the motion picture industry, the effect we have on the thinking in America is incredible. A guy called me up the other night. He wasn't a bigot or anything. He was a black guy. He says, "There's something I don't understand. Blacks are twelve percent of the American population, maybe fourteen percent, and Jews are three percent. The Democratic Party is worried that Jesse Jackson is going to hurt the Jewish vote. Why isn't the Democratic Party worried about the black vote?" They talk about we need the Jewish vote. He said, "I really don't understand. There are so many more blacks than Jews. Why are they so worried about the Jews? They should be worried about the blacks." It's amazing to me the kind of impact we've had in America.

Godfrey Cambridge told me once — the black; he died; he was a wonderful man — he said to me in an interview, "Do you know what blacks need? The Jewish p.r. league." And I said, "What is it?" He said, "There's a Jewish p.r. league. It's worldwide. It's strictly Jewish. It's inherently Judaism. There's no president. There's no vice-president. Every Jew is a member of the Jewish p.r. league." I said, "What do you mean?"

He said, "I didn't hear that polio was cured. I heard a Jewish doctor cured polio today." Which is really very true. We would look in box scores and root for Sid Gordon to get hits. It was very important to us that a Jewish person did well. That's why I think blacks and Jews, while there's a lot of discord, there's also a lot of empathy. In other words, while the Jews may be upset by Jesse Jackson, they all understand why the blacks are voting for him, because we voted that way. I mean, who are we kidding? Italians voted for a guy who was Italian. And we rooted for Jewish players. We looked up and Koufax did well and we wanted him to do well; apart from just being Koufax, he was Jewish. It was pride to us.

I've been married twice. Both girls I married are not Jewish. I think I would have married a Jewish girl had I stayed in New York. I went to Miami, and while there were Jews in Miami, I got into a culture larger than that. When we grew up, shiksas were bad girls. All shiksas were bad. There were certain things about Jewish girls that I did not like. I did not like the Jewish American princess. "Where are we going tonight?" and "What kind of food is this?" and that kind of thing. Good girls and "you can't touch me" and that kind of thing. Yet now that I am a father and my daughter's sixteen, I'm trying to make her a Jewish American princess.

I'm certainly not a believer and I am not a religious person; I don't go to synagogue. I go on Yom Kippur and say Yizkor. I don't know why I go and say Yizkor; I don't think there's a God listening to me. I really don't think that. But I go in the hope that maybe — I don't know what it is — maybe it's infantile to think that maybe there is and you want Him to watch or out of respect for my mother. But lately I have more and more feelings about my Judaism. For a long time I didn't. It was part of me, but I didn't think about it. Like when you called and talked about doing this, there was a pride in that. I'm glad to see this kind of work being done. And I didn't think much about that five or six years ago. Maybe it was turning fifty. Maybe being fifty years old and starting to think more and dwelling back on the Jewish star. I've never taken my chai off.

I sort of strayed. I went the Miami route and I was like the bad boy. I think I was the only one of the guys who didn't marry a Jewish girl.

I went to Miami in 1957 and broke into radio and then did radio and television all those years there. Didn't leave to come to Washington until 1978. I moved my mother down in 1968, and she lived her last eight years in Miami.

There was a Jewish Miami. Now there is no Jewish Miami, it's spread out so much. When I go down to visit, Jewish people have moved to Broward County, Fort Lauderdale, unheard of then. Fort Lauderdale to us was goys. Jewish Miami was Miami Beach and North Miami.

Miami Beach was all Jewish. All Jewish. I broadcast at Pumperniks and that was a famous restaurant. Wolfie's. There were a lot of kosher restaurants. Pumper's and Wolfie's were Jewish-style restaurants. Duke Zeibert's here in Washington, D.C., is a Jewish-style restaurant. Duke's is not a Jewish restaurant. Jewish restaurants change plates; wouldn't serve meat on a dairy dish. A real Jewish restaurant is Sammy's Hungarian in New York; no butter. They have meat dishes. They put a lot of pastrami on rye bread, they give you that Jewish kind of feeling, pickles on the table. But if you really want a Jewish item, you call them on that. Duke's Passover — I said to him, "You got matzobrei?" The chefs don't know how to make it. I grew up with matzobrei. Now, in New York, the restaurants have matzobrei. So it's Jewish style.

Wolfie's was twenty-four hours. It was show business. It was the hangout. Pickles on the table, bread. "So what do you want?" The Lindy's kind of person. The waiter. The shtick of hanging around, and Steve Lawrence comes in and Milton Berle. I did a show at Pumperniks, which was very similar to Wolfie's. And a lot of rolls, a lot of rolls on the table. Lots of Jewish people would take the rolls home. Now these were people not without money; I'm not talking about poor. But the fresh rolls, they'd bring little bags and take the rolls home.

I remember a *Time* essay once, we were in Miami and we were all upset. They did an essay on being Jewish in America. This has to be 1967. Wolfie's was one of the examples they used. The huge lemon meringue pie. The eight-layer cakes. The huge pastrami sandwiches. They explained that as Jewish feelings of inferiority. Not personally inferior; feelings that you are not going to be here tomorrow, that the Holocaust is so drummed into us and the thought that nothing is permanent that that's why we eat the overstuffed sandwiches. There were great arguments in Miami; we did radio shows on this. A guy came down from *Time* and debated people. We had psychology people come over and discuss this.

It was one of *Time*'s first essays; it was on Judaism in America. There were people writing letters that this is an anti-Semitic piece, et cetera. I bought it. I thought it made some sense. Why these overstuffed sandwiches? Why did the pastrami have to be this big? Why does the rye bread fall off? Even though you didn't order the cake, why did the cake have to be this big? Why were big portions so essential? Big portions; give them a lot. They were saying because they came from a culture in Eastern Europe that didn't know if they would have a meal the next day, so it was "Eat up! Eat up!" Boy, I had to finish; you had to finish. My mother, when I would take her to Pumperniks or Wolfie's, that was to be expected. If you only gave six slices of corned beef, something was the matter. It was very interesting. But that was one of the themes — overstuffed sandwiches. Lots of portions. You'll eat a lot. Oy vey. You'll sit a lot; you'll be hungry.

Now, Miami Beach is three-quarters Spanish, I would say three-quarters.

Then, it was New York South. It was Delancey Street with nice weather. It was Pumperniks and Wolfie's and Passover and it was a feeling of New York with good weather. I remember my mother couldn't believe she would come over to my house and see an orange tree. An orange tree? To her, oranges were at the vegetable stand. To actually see an orange tree just blew her mind. But the Jewish community in Miami was activist, very influential politically. I went to Miami and the mayor of Miami was Jewish. Now, Miami's Jewish population was minimal, but Jews had tremendous influence. There were still private clubs in Miami. See, I never saw a private club in New York.

The Jewish community in Miami was as fortified as it was in New York, as politically active as it was in New York. The Jewish community had an enormous deal to do with causing integration in Miami. The Jews and blacks worked very hard together. We were all in the Urban League. There were a lot of wonderful Jewish people around. But a lot of it also became the embarrassed Jew; the Jewish visitor with the white-on-white shirt, with the limos, with the fancy cars, the big cars, the Jewish kind of thing that would sometimes get you embarrassed. I remember I took my wife out to dinner. We'd go to a famous restaurant, let's say a Jewish restaurant. The Jew who was loud, the Jew who was boisterous. She was very kind of quiet and refined, and I was embarrassed for my own. You'll still get that way sometimes. I'll be in Duke's sometimes, and I'll see people yell, "Hey, Phil, how are you?" Even though I can do that very same thing, there's a part that cringes about it.

New York mayor Edward Koch represents a lot of what I don't like about Jews. An incredible ego. Every sentence begins with "I." That kind of "I did this" and "I know what's right" and "They don't listen to me" and "They are crazy." All those kinds of things. Also, everything that people dislike about Jewish people, about what people dislike about New Yorkers, he represents. That brashness. The first thing he said on the air when I said "Thank you for coming," he said, "Come back to New York. What are you doing here? Why are you living somewhere else? New Yorkers should be back." Yet the outpouring for him — his book is an enormous seller. Simon and Schuster — Michael Korda — said they can't believe where it's selling. Why? People call up and say, "You are my kind of guy. You are my kind of guy." Is it the fact that he says Carter is an idiot and Jody Powell's a jerk, he said "shmuck" on the air? "Jody Powell's a shmuck," he says. "Jewish people know it. He's a shmuck." Is it that? What is it?

President Carter was more interesting off the air than on. Begin drove him crazy. "God," he says, "he drove me crazy. He drove me crazy. I don't know how Sadat took him. Sadat took him better than I did." He said, "I used to have to learn tricks to handle him. One of the ways to handle him is to talk about his family. His grandchildren make him cry. And I tried to have understanding. I tried to say this man saw his parents killed and his sister killed. But it was hard: *t*'s and *i*'s. Dot the *i,* cross the *t*. Wait a minute. But wait a minute. This is to my face he told me: 'I don't trust you. Don't trust any of you.' Sadat he trusted. 'You I trust. You I don't trust.' " He said that to Carter.

Carter couldn't stand Begin. Begin drove him up the wall. He said, "I have great respect for Jewish people and I never met one like this, like him. Obstinate. Immovable. And I kept trying to say this guy went through things that I didn't go through." Begin never forgot the Holocaust.

That's something that the *Time* essay said: that we are raised to remember it. Hannah Arendt said that the Holocaust is much more part of the Jewish culture than any other culture. I mean, we talk about it, we thrive on it. She contended that we thrived on it. That's kind of a cop-out. That we've used it — you know, remember the Holocaust, remember the Holocaust, remember the Holocaust.

Judith Nelson Drucker, fifty-four, temple cultural director,
Miami Beach, Florida

I come from a wonderful Jewish background. My mother's father was a very well-known rabbi in Brownsville in Brooklyn. His name was Rabbi Solomon Levine. He was also a mohel. My mother's family was one of the best known in Brooklyn because of my papa. When I was a child, Grandpa — Papa — would come to the house, and there was always great reverence and respect. My mother's mother was the matriarch of the family. They came from Lithuania. Actually, their name was Handelman, but when they came here they took her maiden name, which was Levine. There was sort of a dynasty in Brooklyn, a huge house. Uncle Arthur, who was the real brains of the family, became the doctor, and he was the chief obstetrician and gynecologist of the Brooklyn Women's Jewish Hospital. Uncle Harry was the dentist. Uncle Dave was the lawyer. Actually, David was a grand-child and they brought him up as a child, a brother. And the ones who made all the money were Uncle Ben and Al, because they went into the hosiery business. The Benal Hosiery Company became one of the leading hosiery companies in New York and North Carolina. In fact, when Uncle Ben died at the ripe old age of forty-three years of cancer of the jaw, he had half a page in the *New York Times* because he had established the first boys' club in America, which was in Brooklyn.

Mom was the one living daughter. The family also lived next door to Murder, Incorporated. My mother knew that Lepke and that bunch lived next door to them. They were looked up to in the community. They were the ones who also gave philanthropically. Then, once, the house was bombed.

My father is a Katznelson, and they came from Russia. He has the famous cousin called Beryl Katznelson. My father was Yidel Katznelson, and when he came to this country they said, "Your name is now Nelson." So when I was singing professionally they'd say, "What's your real name?" I'd say, "Judy Nelson," and nobody believed me. My father's family were also great educators and lovers of the book, as Jewish people are. My father came to this country at the age of fourteen with three dollars. He got a job, and at night he went to high school. He learned how to read and write English. He refused to speak Russian. One dollar a week he saved, one dollar he spent for rent, and one dollar for food. He brought his whole family over here from Russia. His particular business, the Leading Lady Dress and Costume Company in New York, became one of the biggest dress manufacturers in New York City. The whole firm was occupied by relatives, from the top down to the shipping clerk. His brother Julius became famous later on. His cousin Julius Nelson had the Nelson Towers on the corner of Thirty-fourth and Broadway.

I was brought up first in Brooklyn in a big seventeen-room home that was quite Jewish. Life in Brooklyn was terrific. I was very sad when my parents told me they were leaving Brooklyn because my brother was an asthmatic. The doctor said that he would either have to go to Phoenix or to Florida to live. This was in 1936. My family moved down here to Miami and I hated it. I went into sort of a cultural shock. We lived here from 1936 to about 1938, and we really were quite unhappy at the time. We also found tremendous anti-Semitism.

We moved from Miami Beach to southwest Miami. I became friendly with a little girl who then came to my house. Her father was a policeman. She cried and said she couldn't play with me anymore, because her parents found out I was Jewish. I remember very vividly that I didn't even know what that meant, but I was very hurt. When that happened, and my father realized how bad it was down here, he made plans to move back up north. I remember at Coral Way Elementary School the teacher particularly pointing me out and saying everybody got up in the morning to say the Lord's Prayer, but that little girl over there who's Jewish doesn't have to get up. I wanted to get up and say the Lord's Prayer, because I knew it as something I was brought up with anyway.

Because of the unhappiness, my father decided to move back up north. We moved back to the Bronx, to 2720 Grand Concourse. We lived in the Bronx until I was about thirteen, and I loved it. I was admitted to the High School of Music and Art, because at that time I discovered that I had a voice. At eleven, I did the role of Buttercup in our junior high play, and I also studied the piano. I forgot to tell you that the most important part of our family life is my mother, who was a concert singer and pianist. But being the daughter of a rabbi, she was never allowed to proceed with a big career, because you were not allowed to take money for it. It was considered not Jewish to take money for entertaining. It was considered undignified. You did it for philanthropic purposes.

Then all of a sudden my father told us, when I was thirteen, that the business world was not good. It was the war years, and he couldn't stand the pressure. He was getting ulcers, and he decided to retire and move back to Miami. This to me was an absolute death blow. At the age of thirteen I felt my life was over. I had to leave my musical friends and my piano pals, everything that I had been building up to, because I knew that at that age I really wanted to have a career. I moved back to Miami and once again went into a slump. This was about 1941. We moved back to Miami Beach and built a house on Michigan Avenue.

There wasn't a great preponderance of Jewish people in those days, as much as people always say. Miami Beach was so identified with being Jewish. It was mostly very wealthy Gentiles. We sort of felt like interlopers. I remember Miami Beach High School. The most important kids there were the Gentiles who belonged to the Surf Club and the Bath Club and those kind of places. We found out before long, in those days, that you really couldn't get into the social world, because it was barred to Jewish people. Many of the hotels said NO JEWS ALLOWED or NO JEWS AND DOGS or SELECTED CLIENTELE. There were many hotels — the Deauville, which was owned then by Bernarr Macfadden, the Kenilworth, the Seaview, so many. You even were afraid to go near the Ronay Plaza, because even though it was a Schine hotel, a lot of the Jews in those days didn't profess to being Jews. We just kept our own lives.

We went to the Miami Beach Jewish Center. I belonged to the B'nai B'rith Girls; my brother became a member of AZA, Aleph Zadek Aleph. We surrounded ourselves with that, but we kept our distance from other things. In BBG, we all knew we were Jewish, so we felt comfortable. We worked for various Jewish causes. We had cake sales and the money went to the Jewish National Fund a lot. Plant a tree in Israel, because there was an Israel to work for. Money went to the B'nai B'rith. We used to have conventions, and I used to sing at them. We used to go over the State of Florida in buses and meet other Jewish kids from other places, which was so important.

My other brother, who is only fourteen months younger than I, wasn't that secure in his Judaism. I guess it's the middle-child syndrome, and he went over to the other side. We had a name like Nelson, so he never told anybody he was Jewish. He became a member of the Macfadden Health Club at the Deauville Hotel and at the age of fourteen he became a lifeguard, and he went out with all the Gentiles — to their parties and their balls. Of course, my mother and father couldn't believe this, but they went along with it. The interesting thing is my parents always went along with things, feeling that the kids would grow out of it, and they did. You go through these periods where you don't like it. I never did. I always liked it. In fact, when I finally got to college, they called me the all-American Jewish girl.

I went to the University of Miami here, and every Friday night I had to sing in shul. Every Sunday morning I sang in church. I found tremendous anti-Semitism. When I was in high school, I recall going to meet my older brother, who was already at the University of Florida — the one who turned down Harvard. I went up on the bus, and I recall the bus driver — I was fourteen — saying, "Where do you come from, little girl?" I told him Miami Beach, and he said, "How could you live down there with all those dirty Jews?" It was very hard for me to handle, but it was good for me. It set me back, as if someone had just punched me in the jaw. I was more aware of it. The problem we had in Miami Beach through those years was that we tended to put ourselves in little cliques and little circles, and pretend that other things didn't exist. If you belonged to your AZA group or your BBG group and you went to school, your whole life was in this little enclave. A lot of kids never were touched with anti-Semitism before. They didn't even know it existed. If you asked them if it exists even now, they don't know it exists. But it exists.

Miami Beach opened up to the Jews only in the 1940s. I would say more after the war. They would start coming down and spending winters in hotels, because we didn't have condominiums in those days. You never went to Fort Lauderdale, because you just knew Jews weren't welcome, and perish forbid, you never went to Palm Beach. If Saturday night you went out on a date, the big thrill was you got in the car and drove all the way to Fort Lauderdale and back. It was like "I'll show them."

We found a lot of anti-Semitism after we looked around, and Jews not being able to go into places. I even recall, when I was married, trying to check into the Pan American Motel about 1950, and they looked at my name, Drucker, and told me there were no rooms available. There is still a hotel, believe it or not, right now on Key Biscayne and there's a huge sign outside on the lawn — I don't know if it's still there; it was last year — and it says SELECTED CLIENTELE ONLY. We still have it now. There are clubs that do not allow Jews. Whenever an organization or a friend of mine invites me for dinner and for lunch or something, I say I can't go. They wonder why, and I say, "Because no Jews are allowed." They say, "Oh, well, it's okay; I'll put in a good word for you because you're my friend." You know, "You're special." "You're different." So it still exists.

My mother and father, I think, felt secure that even if we dated a Gentile, nothing much would come of it. They would sort of watch it from the side. I dated a lot of Gentile soldiers during the war. I was interested in speaking to them. In fact, I went out with one wonderful guy whose last name happened to be Albee, and I didn't know he was the great playwright Edward Albee. I met, also, a George Albee, who was related to him. It was on the highest level. They were very bright guys, and I would always bring them home. I dated Gentile men, but I knew I'd never marry one. My older brother, Teddy, is the most Jewish of heart in the family. He met a girl in the Masada group and they married. My brother Don, being sort of the lost one all those years, ended up marrying a Jewish girl first and then a Gentile girl second. Even though he loves being Jewish, I don't think he ever was really comfortable with it.

Jewish foods, I think, are the most important part of growing up. I think even if you don't identify with anything else, you become a gastronomic Jew. My father would always go down to the delicatessens or to the Jewish butchers and bring home all the stuff. The house was always filled with salamis. In those days, you couldn't get delicatessen in Miami. There were no delicatessens. You couldn't get corned beef or a good salami. My uncle Izzie Isaacson ran the counter at Rappaport's. So whenever my father would go up to New York, he'd come back with a big box of salamis. That was a big thing. So we identified with the salami. Then when the Jewish places started opening up, of course we would frequent them the most. There was one place I remember in the city of Miami, in southwest Miami, called the Rosedale. It was a delicatessen, and my father would always go out of his way to take us there for stuffed kishka and everything like that so we'd keep remembering.

I think if my father and my mother hadn't continued with these things in the house, we very easily could have become assimilated, because there was no reason to have to be Jewish. It was a tradition that every Sunday the whole family came to our house, because we had the big house. So the whole family came and there was huge whitefish and noodle puddings and lox and bagels. So as far as my father could in those days, he'd always go out and get the bagels and lox. We were three boys and a girl, and the boys always ate so much that the house was always filled with food. Food became a big issue in our home. I still feel today that you keep the family together Jewishly, if no other way, by everybody getting together and sitting around the table. I think that's very important. I've continued that way.

Starting about three or four years ago, or whenever it was that Carter allowed the Marielitos to come in here, we had the influx of the Cuban community. There was no place to house them and feed them, so they put them down in the small hotels in South Beach and all over, and crime came to this community, where we never had it before. A lot of the elderly Jewish people didn't want to come back to those areas, and by their not coming back, more of the underprivileged Cubans moved in. What happened was we started getting a bad reputation and we were not chic anymore, so the wealthier, more affluent Jews decided they had to go to Palm Beach and Delray and Boca. Boca is like the new Castle Garden of the South. They moved away from their apartments here on Collins Avenue and moved up there.

So many apartments that used to be occupied by our "winter snowbirds," as we call them, are not occupied now, and rents went down. Miami Beach went through a terrible slump. Things are picking up now, because everybody's fighting so hard to change our image. It's much less Jewish than it used to be. I don't know the exact percentage. Miami Beach is no more the place where people send down their elderly mothers and fathers to spend the winter. They're either staying home now or going to Palm Beach and other places, which has affected me and our cultural program greatly. I was here starting this cultural program at the temple at a very propitious time, because these snowbirds first started coming here about ten years ago. People would walk into my office and just say, "How much should I make out the check for for the tickets?" because, of course, they knew it was tax deductible anyway. So they'd throw an extra hundred dollars in.

The New York–Boston–Philadelphia crowd that had apartments here were delighted to go to the finest concerts in the world. So we never even had to advertise or print a brochure. We were sold out immediately. For fifteen years, our series was on top of the crest, and in the past three or four years we have found that ten to fifteen percent of our audience has disappeared and moved northward. It's affected the temples and affected the Jewish way of life here drastically.

When my folks first came to Miami, I recall in 1936, we stayed in a hotel — I think it was the Evans Hotel or something like that — where they also had meals. There were a couple of kosher restaurants, mostly like little houses down the street, but there were no kosher hotels. Oddly enough, they've sprung up in the past five, six years here. They're the ones doing the best, especially during the holidays. You can't get into them, the Saxony and those hotels.

We have now an interesting influx of a different type of Jew in Miami Beach. On Forty-first Street, right around here, we've got a whole bunch of Lubavitchers and Chasidim. On a Saturday here, you think you're in Meah Shearim in Jerusalem. They're all walking around with the shtraymels. The whole configuration of this town is changing. It came up from the days when the Jews weren't important here, because Flagler and those guys were the ones that made this place, and the old Coral Gables crowd were very

Gentile. When people say to me today, "Oh, it's only loaded with Jews," I say, "I wish it were." The days of the 1940s to 1965 or 1970, I think, were the best days, because the Jewish community flourished here. It's changing and going back a lot to the 1940s. I feel anti-Semitism creeping up again. I feel it in the structure. The leaders of our community are not the leaders on the beach anymore. They're the leaders in the city of Miami.

9

Jewish Growing Up

WHEN I WAS in junior high school I wore tsitsis until the first day I had to undress for swimming class. I was so embarrassed that I never wore them again. Nor would I have thought of wearing a yarmulka outside the synagogue. (I'm on the yarmulka side of the line dividing generations between the Yiddish for skullcap and its Hebrew equivalent, kipah.) Today, youngsters all over the United States wear both, unabashedly. It is a testament to their own comfort with their religion and to the tolerance of contemporary America. For many American Jews, religion was and is paramount, and there has been a resurgence of Orthodoxy. For others, more secular-minded, paramount was and is the importance of knowing and feeling comfortable with their Jewishness.

Part of this Jewishness is the emphasis on family, especially on keeping it intact. When my mother's mother died after giving birth to her fifth child, her unmarried sister was forced to marry my mother's father and look after the children. She produced four more children. They all felt part of one family.

By one of those happy flukes, while I was finishing this book I happened on a 1907 edition of *The Americana,* described as a "Universal Reference Library," which had this to say:

> Combined with the absence of this vice [drunkenness], there are other virtues engrafted on the Jew for centuries, all of which tend to the preservation of his self-respect and his self-esteem. Among them are the love of home, the inherent desire to preserve the purity of the family, and the remarkable eagerness which he shows for education and self-improvement.

With this emphasis on the value of family and education, it is fashionable to suggest that the Asian American represents the "new Jew." A *Time* magazine cover story in late summer 1987 said that many Asian-American students are making the U.S. education system work better for them than it has for any other immigrant group since the arrival of East European Jews began in the 1880s. Like the Asians, the Jews viewed education as the ticket to success. Both groups "feel an obligation to excel intellectually," says New York University mathematician Sylvain Cappell, who as a Jewish immigrant feels a kinship with his Asian-American students. The two groups share a powerful belief in the value of hard work and a zealous regard for the role of the family.

Hasse Halley, forty-four, English teacher and principal of a Hebrew school, Burlington, Vermont

I grew up in Rochester, New York. My zeyde lived with us. My father came from Vilna. My mother was born in Pittsburgh. We were really first-generation Americans. My father belonged to the Orthodox shul, and I was just telling my kids the other day that when the High Holidays came, my father didn't stay with us, because he wouldn't ride. He stayed in a rooming house [near the shul]; and we stayed home.

We came here twelve years ago. My husband was transferred with IBM. I'll never forget my first impression: I had come to Yankeeland. I mean, I knew I came to Yankeeland. And I wanted to come here. We were part of a back-to-basics movement. We had four kids — little kids. We wanted to have our own farm and grow vegetables and fruit and make our own bread and all that stuff. I mean, I was really into it. But, of course, there is a part of me — the Jewish part of me — that knew I had to be in a Jewish community. I knew there was a synagogue, so I wasn't at all concerned. I knew that it was Conservative, so I wasn't concerned; I knew that there would be a kosher butcher here. Of course. Right? I looked in the Yellow Pages. I looked under "Meat." There wasn't anything. I looked under "Kosher." There wasn't anything. I tried every possible cross-reference that I could think of, and there wasn't anything. For a moment, a part of me died. I couldn't believe that we had accepted a transfer to come to the north country and there wasn't even a place where I could buy kosher meat.

So today we get our meat imported from Albany; it comes on the bus, frozen, in three hours and we pay postage. Like you pay for a passenger, we pay for meat. Or, along with a lot of other people here, we go to Boston or we go to Montreal to get meat.

We lasted in the country for about six years, and then we moved into Burlington after we had had our fifth child. I took my daughter to Israel four years ago for her Bat Mitzvah. When I came back I wanted to uproot the entire Halley family, seven of us, and move immediately to Israel. I didn't care if we lived in the desert. I wanted to move to Israel. At that point, maybe we were looking for something; maybe I was returning to the traditional Jew that I always was as I was growing up. My husband was Reform. He grew up in a very secular family. He didn't know about anything.

We were obviously looking for something. I think that's what sort of drove me to go to Israel the first year with my twelve-year-old daughter and my six-year-old son. The second year we all went together, the seven of us. My oldest son stayed and went on a kibbutz ulpan. My other children came back reluctantly. As a matter of fact, Adam, who was then a senior in high school, wore his Israeli army uniform to school every single day at Burlington High School until the kids were going to pool their funds together to send him back to Israel. We tried to create an environment in our own lives that would be like Israel. It's hard for me to explain.

We all became shomer Shabbat by choice, not by shoving it down anyone's throat. We began by opening our doors to anybody who wants to come to our house on Shabbes. So we have a lot of university students. We have a lot of young professionals. We sometimes invite people from the congregation. We always invite someone who is new to Burlington, who's just moved here. We look for them. We go to kavalat Shabbat services. Then we bring home whoever doesn't have a place to go to eat. On the average Shabbes we have approximately twenty-two people. We set the table for sixteen or eighteen and then we put the overflow in the kitchen. In the winter, when the University of Vermont is in session, we can have as many as thirty-five or forty people.

My daughter and I cook the meal on Thursday night. I'm a vegetarian and a lot of people who come are vegetarians, so everything is vegetarian except for the chicken and chicken soup. But it's a fairly traditional meal, starting with chicken soup.

We have actually had people come in off the street. We were singing z'mirot one night and this young couple was walking down the street. They had been visiting two doors up. They were from the middle of Manhattan. They said they heard us singing z'mirot, so I figured they were Jewish when they said, "Z'mirot! Can we come in and join you?" It was ten-thirty at night, on a summer night. He was old and she was young, and they had a brand-new baby. So we invited them in and I held the baby, who was crying and cold and needed to be cuddled and who peed all over me, and I'll never forget it.

So we really do bring in strays. Sometimes I don't even know the names of the people. But it is very traditional. We start with Kiddush and we wash hands and we cut bread and we have chicken soup. We have chicken and then I make about eight side dishes and they are all vegetarian. I try to make six salads of some sort or another — beans with rice, pasta salad; I make a sweet kugel, because the kids love sweet kugel; and I make home fries or a potato kugel or roasted potatoes and eggplant salad. I'm a good cook. Whatever the ingredients are in the refrigerator, we make. Something with tofu, so the vegetarians have a protein. Then for dessert, my daughter makes brownies.

There are some regulars. Like I said, there are always at least sixteen — between sixteen and twenty-two. Those are my regulars. After that, there are people that come and go. We have had some kooks come and go in my house. Guys with hair down to where they sit or with no hair at all. And earrings and no earrings. I mean, it's really wild. They are almost all Jewish. But we do have non-Jewish people, especially for Pesach. We also have the same thing for Pesach. One seder we had forty-five people. One seder we had forty-eight people. We emptied the dining room and got our chairs and tables from the synagogue and set up. It was really nice. My parents come and Steve's parents come. We try to invite people who say, you know, "We've never been to a seder and we would like to come." Then, after the meal is over with we sing z'mirot like in a yeshiva, banging on the table. My table sags in the middle, and I hope one day everyone's going to pitch in and buy me a new table. They stay until ten-thirty or eleven. Sometimes I go to bed; they are still downstairs. And we bench, and the kids love it. I have a girl who has come every year for three years. She's just graduated from UVM. Her grandfather lived in Boston. He just passed away. He was so grateful that he would send us gifts for having his granddaughter participate in something like this.

The other interesting thing is now we have a lot of young professionals — a lot of young Jewish professionals here. There is a young chiropractor. There's about a half-dozen engineers at IBM, male and female. There was a female lawyer here for a short time. There's a female engineer who eats with us. There's a young woman who just moved from Dayton, who works for a packing company. She eats with us.

It's all year long and it's free. My husband Steve and I do it because we think there's a need to do it. I don't believe that a kid would choose to come to UVM if they really wanted to be Jewish, because there isn't a Jewish connection here in Burlington. I mean, you can't go downtown and feel Jewish, ethnically Jewish. There's not a kosher delicatessen. We've only had a bagel bakery for six years, seven years. You can't buy a challah in Burlington. So in order to feel Jewish here, in order to be Jewish here — you don't feel it at the university — you have to feel it in the community. And yet, in spite of the fact that I say a kid who was really steeped in Judaism wouldn't come here, even if you are not steeped in Judaism I still think that there's that connection that Jewish kids want. So they get it at our house.

For Steve and me, this is our contribution. This is our way of doing something for the Jewish community in Burlington. We give our share of donations. We give a lot of money to Israel. We give a lot of money to the synagogue. But it's not enough. That's the intangible. The tangible is seeing the kids' faces, getting cards from them, having them hug and kiss us, having them come over on a Wednesday and take our kids to the movies. Just the gratitude they show for being able to connect with the Jewish community. Just the looks on their faces. I mean, the singing on Friday night just is enough to bring anyone gratitude. There's nothing in it for us. I mean, it costs us a fortune. But it's worth it. It's really and truly worth it.

Also, of my own five kids, two are living in Israel and they are going to make aliyah; a third son is going to Yeshiva University; my daughter is planning on a program in Israel for a year and then wants to go to Stern College; and my youngest son, Ben-Israel, who is nine, just came home from an Orthodox camp. This is their social life. This is their Jewish social life in Burlington. They've made lots of friends. Friday night they wouldn't *dream* of being anywhere else but in our house. When they are away, no matter where they are — in Israel or at camp or wherever — they really wish they were at home. And that is important to me.

When I was about thirteen years old, a small group of people got together and decided to start a Conservative synagogue in my suburb of Irondequoit. So they started Temple Beth David, and my parents were founding father and mother of the synagogue. That's when we made the big switch. For me, that was the time when I made my own religious conversion because of a young rabbi who came to Rochester to be our rabbi, and I adored him and I wanted to be a rabbi or anything that I could be and I was very involved with Judaism. I kept kosher.

I grew up in a completely non-Jewish environment. We were the first Jewish people to live in Irondequoit. My brother, sister, and myself were the only Jewish children in the school. I remember when I was in first grade that the principal's son called me a kike. I marched right up to his father's office and told his father that he should put soap in the young man's mouth. I was only six. Dicky was five. Most of my friends were Catholic. As a matter of fact, none of my school friends were Jewish and none of my college friends were Jewish. Even though there were a lot of Jewish kids at Albany State, where I went to school, I was not involved at all with the Jewish life there because I was involved in theater, and there were no Jewish kids in that. The one thing I did do was teach kindergarten at Temple Israel. Just before my senior year in college, I went to encampment as a counselor through Temple Beth El in Rochester. I had decided that I wanted to go on for another degree in Jewish education, and I met this young man at encampment, who turned out to be my husband's brother. He later introduced us.

Steve, as I said earlier, was a totally secular Jew. His parents were very, very mortified that he would dream of marrying a girl who kept kosher. They thought I was way too Jewish. Now my husband has converted to being a very traditional Jew. He wears a kipah; we are shomer Shabbat. He davens three times a day. I mean, we are very traditional Jews. I'm sure that they are now even more mortified because we sort of left them out completely. We don't eat out unless we eat just vegetables or something. My children don't eat out at all. This is really unique — my kids all went to Catholic schools in Burlington, because I thought the schools were better.

Burlington is sort of a strange community, because it's hard to feel like you belong in terms of the Jewish community. You know, there is an old story that Vermonters tell that just because a cat has her kittens in an oven, you don't call them biscuits. So even though you are born here and you are first generation, like Ben-Israel, it doesn't make him a "woodchuck" in some people's eyes. Although the community is complete, in terms of its Jewishness, and we can perform every Jewish act and we have our own chevra kedisha, and I am the head of the women's chevra kedisha, my perception of this synagogue is that this is a group of nonpracticing Conservative Jews. There's a handful of us, a handful. I can probably count the number of people who are shomer Shabbat. There's a little bigger circle of people who are traditional but are not shomer Shabbat who keep kosher, who celebrate all the holidays, who come to shul, but then who wouldn't think twice about leaving shul and going downtown to go shopping. So that is sort of incongruous.

To me, Conservative Judaism is very pareve: it's not here and it's not there. I think that here in this community, when a person becomes a practicing Jew, a traditional Jew as we have, you've got to hold tight to the reins, because there is no place for a practicing Jew in a Conservative synagogue of this sort. Because the rest of the people see us as zealots, even though we have never proselytized in any way, shape, or form. What we do makes people feel guilty.

Rabbi Wall has said that Burlington was a community of nonpracticing Orthodox Jews. Now, it is a community of nonpracticing Conservative Jews. And I agree with what he said. My sons right now are downtown having their hair cut because it is after Tisha b'Ab. They are walking freely in Burlington wearing tsitsit, and no one is going to hurt them for it, but they know why they are wearing them. So while they are safe, there are a lot of Jewish people walking around here who don't even know the meaning of Shabbat. It's a bittersweet kind of a thing. Years ago you walked in bands and they didn't walk with a kipah and tsitsit, because they would have been beaten up. They disguised that. Now, while you are free to wear that because we have become such an open society, not just in Burlington, but everywhere, and so much more accepting, it's sort of watered down. What are we accepting of? What are we no longer afraid to do?

For me, the decision to become traditional was always there. The seeds were always there. It wasn't really a hard decision. It was a choice, for me, that I would have made twenty-two years ago when I got married if I could have seen ahead or been more secure or whatever. Steve, to me, was the epitome of everything that a Jewish girl could want. He was professional. He was tall and thin and handsome. My father was this short little man and he had a gas station and his hands were perpetually greasy. I didn't think of it as assimilation, but of course it was assimilation. But it wasn't assimilation into the Christian world; it was assimilation into a Jewish world that I was never a part of. So the seeds were always there for me. For the rest of my family? I think that everything else we did — moving to the country, having ponies, raising chickens — didn't have any meaning. This has so much meaning. I think that everybody looks for something to give meaning to their lives, and for us it is being Jewish and being practicing Jews and knowing that on Shabbat we always reconnect, although we may not see each other during the week. We can pray together and sing together. It just has brought such wonderful meaning to our lives.

I'll tell you a funny story. Ben-Israel, who's nine, is very, very, very religious. Very religious. He's had a unique upbringing. As you know, the Conservative movement did not call women to the Torah when I was growing up. I had my first aleeyah on my birthday when I was pregnant with Ben-Israel, so he has been coming to synagogue every Shabbes since he was conceived. He was named for my grandfather, who was a wonderful, wonderful man, who I wanted to stay alive forever and he couldn't. His name was Israel Isaac. We named our son Ben-Israel Isaac because my grandfather had a son who didn't have any sons, so this was a way of carrying on his name. My grandfather was very religious. Ben-Israel is a very religious Jew. He's nine. He wears tsitsit. He can daven like an adult. He's gone to an Orthodox camp in Pennsylvania for two years. He's the only kid in the camp who wears a Lacoste shirt and cut-off jeans. He's the only kid in the camp who doesn't go to yeshiva or day school, and there are 260 boys who go there. He won best in learning two years in a row and outstanding camper last year. This year he won a sports award. I told the rabbi who owns the camp that it's because those kids are burned out and when he gets there he's all fired up.

Ben-Israel goes to a Catholic school. At the camp, you can get up and make all these announcements on the loudspeaker during meals, and everyone sort of vies to make an announcement. When the little kids couldn't think of anything to say, they'd say their name and they'd say the school they went to. Ben-Israel decided that he would go up, but then he realized, en route to the microphone, that there was no way he could say the name of the Catholic school because they would know. He didn't want to embarrass them, he said. So he got up there and said, "BenIsraelHalley-PublicSchool," and walked away. He's very comfortable with his religion and, as a result, he's had no problem with religion taught in the Catholic schools. He's this real special character.

It seems strange that I'm not worried about the Catholic school at all. I am worried about putting him in an Orthodox environment when he goes to Hebrew school in a Conservative environment. I sent him to this Orthodox camp, and on visitors' day I'm the only woman who doesn't have a sheytel on or some other kind of head covering. What am I going to do if my ten- or eleven- or twelve-year-old son says to me, "Hey, Mom, you know you got to cover your head or I can't live here anymore." My older son's already told me I'm going to Hell. But I understand that. I've committed so many sins and broken so many Halachot that I'm doomed. But anyway, how do I reconcile with that?

I talked to the rabbi about this at great length. He said something really beautiful: "Ben-Israel knows, right into the marrow of his bones, that not only are there all kinds of people, but there are all kinds of Jews. Even at nine, he knows that there are some Jews that have peyot and there are some Jews that are hippies and there are some Jews who don't practice anything but they are accepted here in this synagogue though they have just swallowed a ham sandwich on the way in. Ben-Israel knows that." He's so well rounded; he's so accepting. He doesn't turn his back on his friends who ate the ham sandwich — and they're Jewish — and he doesn't say to them, "You shouldn't be doing that." He understands that there are Jews who do that, and that they're different. And I think that when he grows up he's going to be able to make an educated decision on what road he wants to take, and I don't think he'll ever turn his back on his parents. He's growing up in an environment where we are flexible, where we are willing to change.

My kids wouldn't eat from my dishes, so when I moved into this house a year ago, I made two sinks — a meat sink and a dairy sink. I got all new dishes. I want them to eat here; they are my children. Ben-Israel is growing up in a flexible environment, and while I have no intention of covering my head or wearing long sleeves or whatever, he knows that if that's his choice for the way he wants to live his life, he can do that.

I hope he won't reject us. I don't know. Who knows? You never know what kids will do.

But it seems so strange, you know, to worry about that now in Burlington, Vermont. I expected to come here and live on a farm and raise ponies. I didn't expect to come here and have my whole life revolve around Jewishness. Have these kids running around — I mean, I got yelled at this morning because I washed the tsitsit. They got all tangled up. I was supposed to put them in a bag. You are not supposed to put them in a dryer. They've got to be buried. None of them are any good now, I mean. We are going to Montreal tomorrow to buy more tsitsit. Can you believe it? *Can you believe that?* I mean, it's incredible.

Ari L. Goldman, thirty-six, journalist, New York, New York

I normally live in Manhattan but I'm spending the year in Cambridge, Massachusetts, at the Harvard Divinity School. I make my living as a religion writer for *The New York Times*.

What's unusual and sort of was drummed into us when we were growing up is that we are a long-time Orthodox Jewish family, not just a Jewish family, and that carried certain responsibilities. Generally, the American story is that the first generation is Orthodox, the second is Conservative, and the third is Reform, and maybe the fourth is totally assimilated, inter-married.

The only thing I know about my great-grandfather, except for his name, is that he built a mikvah in Hartford, Connecticut, and that was like the only important thing that I had to know. There's an old injunction, said to be Talmudic but probably apocryphal, that before you build a synagogue, you have to build a mikvah. That's kind of amazing to think about, but the notion of this family purity, as they call it, was so ingrained in me that this was the number one thing. So I imagined my great-grandfather getting off the boat and building a mikvah, as if he had nothing else to do.

The idea that not only we were Jewish, but that we were Orthodox was really impressed on us. It wasn't just enough to go to shul on Rosh Ha-shonah; you had to go to shul every Shabbes. Some of my worst childhood memories are of my father yanking me out of bed Saturday morning to go to shul, which I hated because he had to be there at nine o'clock. He couldn't be there five minutes late.

I went to yeshivas all the way from kindergarten through college. My yeshiva experience is interesting, because I can tell you about two kinds of yeshivas. There's the American yeshiva and there's the European yeshiva, and I really had both experiences, all in New York.

My father was a rabbi, although not a practicing rabbi. He's in real estate. My father happens to be a very religious man. He takes his Orthodoxy extremely seriously. I suspect he didn't get it from a yeshiva. There are two ways you can become a rabbi — by going to a school or you can go to one scholar and sit and study with him. My father told me that he studied with one scholar in Brooklyn.

The idea of Yeshiva University is to bring together Torah and mada.

Torah is the religious side, and mada literally means science, but it means to blend the secular and the religious. The European yeshiva, put simply, would be just Torah. But the main reason for going to school, or for being, is to study Torah. Torah means everything; it means all of Judaism. Literally, Torah means the five books of Moses, but since Judaism has this idea of an oral law that interprets the written law, the oral law is given the same weight. That was really done so that the rabbis had their hold on the religion. The Torah isn't really for everyone to open up and interpret. It's for the rabbis to interpret, and you follow what they wrote in the Talmud. So suddenly the Talmud becomes the Torah and everything is Torah.

When I went to these European yeshivas we did very little of so-called secular studies. That was sort of pushed aside. It wasn't important to know math or science or English. What was important was to know Torah. It was perfectly acceptable if you wanted just to spend your life studying Torah and never go to college. In fact, some of the schools discouraged you from getting too much secular education, because that exposed you to the real world and there were all sorts of dangers there. There's actually this institution called the koloel, where adults, you know, people in their twenties and thirties, sit and study all day. And they get paid for it. They get $100, $150 a week. They are probably supporting six kids and their wives are working. But it is the idea that being a koloel bocher is much better than being a yeshiva bocher. A bocher just means a "boy."

So the idea of a koloel was the highest good; that you should just sit and study. It was like being a graduate fellow. I run into them at Harvard all the time. They may be studying European history and they are thirty-five and they are up to their noses in debt and tuition and they are still working on their dissertation; that kind of thing. This is what koloel boys do. They know the Talmud by heart. That's the European model. Torah's what's important.

The more modern view — and it's really called modern Orthodox — is the view of places like Yeshiva University. The idea is to blend together secular knowledge and Torah. That's why the medical school is named after Albert Einstein, who probably didn't know very much Torah. But he was a Jew who represented science. It's a great ideal, but there remains a great deal of tension between the two.

In my life, I can talk to you for hours about the tension between the two and how they really don't fit, and how maybe the European model is the best way to preserve Judaism. Not to deal with the secular. To sort of hide in the koloel. Because Judaism is a very difficult system to work with in the real world.

My father was at Yeshiva University studying science and Torah. He met my mother. They had three children. The first sort of crack in that Orthodox

ideal was my parents' divorce. They were divorced when I was six years
old. That's extremely un-Orthodox, and in the 1950s it was especially taboo
in the Orthodox world. They were just unfortunately a mismatched couple,
although they shared this religious history. It's somewhat hard for me to
separate out that influence on my yeshiva-going, because there was no one
person making decisions about my life. When my father had the upper hand,
I would go to one kind of school, and when my mother had the upper hand,
I would go to another kind of school.

I began by going to a yeshiva called Dov Revel. Dov Revel was a Hebrew-
speaking school. I spoke English at home, but I had gone to synagogue and
knew the prayers and before I went to sleep I said the Shema. But again,
you're taught Hebrew, you're taught the *aleph beth* in the morning, and in
the afternoon you're taught your *abc*'s at Dov Revel, which for simplicity
I'd say was a modern Orthodox yeshiva. So it was the idea that the two
were equal, pretty much. The day was divided; say, from nine to eleven
you'd have Hebrew studies and you'd have an hour lunch, and then from
one to three you'd have English studies. They were given equal weight: you
had a Hebrew teacher; you had an English teacher. The only tough thing
for me was that in Hebrew you had to write from right to left and in the
afternoon you were writing from left to right. But it's a facility you pick
up quickly.

I went to Dov Revel for about five years. This was a coed school, boys
and girls. That's the American yeshiva model.

Did I feel uncomfortable in any way? No. It was like home. Until I was
six, I grew up in Hartford, and then I moved to Queens. Again, it wasn't
Williamsburg, but it was a Jewish neighborhood. From the time I was a
little boy I wore a yarmulka on my head on the street always. I wouldn't
go out of the house, I wouldn't walk around the house, without a yarmulka.
I'd wake up in the morning and put it on. Actually, I'd go to sleep with it
on and wake up and find it under the bed or something. Putting on a
yarmulka was like putting on my shoes. It was second nature. When I first
went to *The New York Times*, I was at Yeshiva University, and at Yeshiva
you wore a yarmulka all day. Then I was stringing for the *Times*, and I
would go down to Forty-third Street and I would take off my yarmulka
before going into the building. To this day, and I've been at the *Times* for
fifteen years, I still sort of run my hand through my head before going in.
I wouldn't say every time, but there are times when I wonder, "Am I wearing
a yarmulka?"

A yarmulka becomes part of you, so in my neighborhood, I wore a
yarmulka. It wasn't a totally Jewish neighborhood, but there were enough
Orthodox people there so you didn't feel like you were strange.

The yeshiva was liberal, modern Orthodox. I really see these as the basics to define this modern Orthodoxy: you keep kosher and you keep Shabbes. Shabbes in my house meant you didn't answer the telephone; you didn't turn on and off electric lights. You could have them set up before. There's this institution called the Shabbes clock, which probably came after the Shabbes goy; it's the automated Shabbes goy. The Shabbes goy would come in and turn off lights. No radio, no writing, no public transportation, no car. You could read. It was really a day to be at home with your family. This was the kind of thing that worked very well if you had a real family. But if you were from a broken home, it was more difficult.

We lived with my mother. My father stayed in Hartford in his home town, and we moved to New York — the three boys and my mother. My mother worked while we were growing up, so she would cook Thursday night. There was always the smell of chicken soup and kugel, and we'd go out and buy the challahs. We would check the calendar and we saw what time Shabbes started — and then nothing. No more work; no more television. I remember that very fondly and very wonderfully, and Shira, my wife, and I still have a Friday night meal and when Shabbes comes we put aside everything else and it's the night to be together and be at home. I don't keep it as I did when I was growing up, but that day is very important to me.

Dov Revel Yeshiva that I was going to was consistent. We learned about the holidays at every level, whether you did paper cutouts for the succah or you baked hamantashen, everything from arts and crafts to learning the laws of the holiday, how old you have to be to fast on Yom Kipper — all the details. It was integrated and it was very pleasant. You learned that just like you learned mathematics or history. You learned about our forefather Abraham, and in the afternoon you learned about George Washington. It all worked somehow.

We didn't speak much Hebrew, but we did learn the Torah — the five books of Moses. You start with Creation, then move on. So if it said, "Vayomer Adonoi le Moshe," we would read that in Hebrew and then we'd say, "God said to Moses." You almost didn't have to translate it after a while, because you knew it. Especially an easy sentence, you just understood. When you got to a hard word, you'd have to articulate it in English. What happened, though — and this propelled me into the European model — was that we ran out of money. We were always struggling. My mother was a school librarian. Somehow there was never any money. My father didn't help that much, and then yeshiva tuition for three boys must have been astronomical. Somehow I remember the figure $600 a year, but I don't know if that's possible. I know now we're looking at yeshiva for our son, Adam, and it's $4000 or $5000 a year.

Around fifth grade, at the end of my fourth grade, we ran out of money and we couldn't afford to go to the yeshiva. Now the modern Orthodox yeshivas have more professional staff and they charge more tuition. You don't need any money to go to the European yeshivas. They take everybody. There was one such European yeshiva called Torah V'dass, which actually means Torah and knowledge, but that's not what you learned there. This was one of my most searing childhood memories. I was probably about ten then. I went in and sat down in class. At the modern Orthodox yeshiva there was a woman who taught us Hebrew. There were men and women; it really didn't make a difference.

I walk into this class — God is sitting at the desk in front, a man with a long white beard and peyes and a black hat, holding a ruler in his hand. Everybody is set up in rows and they open their books and the class starts chanting as one, as they must have done in Vilna. They were translating from Hebrew into Yiddish. Suddenly, I was in total shock, because I didn't know anything. I had learned Hebrew all these years, and here Hebrew was a language to get away from. Hebrew was the holy language, but for some reason you had to talk in Yiddish. It was translated essentially from one foreign language to another, although I had some familiarity with the first foreign language. It was in this kind of environment that I spent the years through most of high school — very repressive, stern; in some ways some of the rebbes were downright mean-spirited. You would get whacked on the knuckles if you didn't know, and it was right out of Europe. There was such a degradation of American and secular values that it was really amazing.

I went to various yeshivas. I started at Torah V'dass, then I went to Jacob Joseph, then I went to Crown Heights Mesifta — a real European yeshiva. You'd get there at nine in the morning, and from nine to twelve there would be what was called beys midrash. That means a house of study. Here I was, thirteen years old. Everybody had a study partner and you would sit in the beys midrash and shake over your book and call out the words and try to figure it out, and then there would be a rebbe walking around making sure you weren't talking about anything else and who would answer questions if you had a rough word. You were studying Talmud on your own with another thirteen- or fourteen-year-old, shaking. It wasn't until noon that you got out of this three-hour ordeal. It was inevitably hot and uncomfortable in this room. It was packed, noisy, like a newsroom. It was bedlam; everyone was screaming; whoever could, would make the most noise, because it isn't just study, it's devotion. It's a form of worship to study the Torah.

At twelve we'd get an hour recess and lunch. There was a kosher cafeteria. All the schools had kosher lunch facilities. At one o'clock we had shiur, which means class. This meant that for two hours, until three, you would sit and the rebbe would teach the Talmud, and the next day he would test you on what you had learned in the morning. I remember in one class, Rabbi Siegel made me sit right up next to him, because my mind would wander or I wouldn't pay attention. So I was right under his thumb. At three o'clock we would start our English studies — this is in high school. You'd have your literature class or your math class. This was taught by public school teachers who were trying to make an extra buck. That was another thing: we would go to school Sunday through Thursday and we would be off Friday. That's how it was mostly. Sometimes we would have morning classes on Friday. The public school teachers were also available on Sundays. After all, what is Sunday? It is a goyisha holiday, right? We would finish at seven or eight o'clock. I would do my homework on the subway, but I did very little homework. It wasn't important. Nobody cared if you did homework. Those subjects — in New York we studied for the Regents — we studied so we could get our high school diploma. It was just going through the requirements. You talk about enrichment. I mean, there was no theater group, there was no orchestra, no baseball. Baseball may have been done on the sandlots. You know, Friday afternoon between school and Shabbes while your mother was cooking and she wanted you out of the house. There was nothing ever organized. *The Chosen* does show also the idea of the modern yeshiva and the European.

What's curious about my experience, though, is that it wasn't Chasidic. This is misnagdish. In Europe, there were the Chasidim, who followed the rebbes, and then there were the Jews who were against them. They were called misnagdim. The kinds of schools that I went to, although there was an affinity for the Chasidim, they didn't have the central figure of a rebbe. You might wonder how did I land up in this place, coming from more of a modern Orthodox family. Part of it was financial; the other part was that my family . . . I was given the analogy that we're not as extreme as they are.

Once, Rabbi Siegel saw me come into school with the *Herald Tribune* under my arm. I've said this a hundred times, but my education was reading newspapers, and that's why I became a journalist. I didn't learn anything in school, but I had a long subway trip — it was an hour on the subway from Queens to Crown Heights; everybody on the subway was reading newspapers — and I began to read newspapers zealously. I learned about sex; I learned about space; I learned about politics. That's really how I was educated. But my rebbe knew I was learning about sex and politics, and when I would walk in to class or to the beys midrash, where I was supposed to study, with a newspaper and he'd be at the door, he would take it away from me. He said, "When you wake up in the morning, you don't read that." It was considered dirty in a sexual way, pornographic, downright pornographic. So he gave me a book, a little commentary on the Talmud in Hebrew, to read on the subway. I made sure every day when I came to class I was carrying that. I threw the newspaper away on my way to school, and I walked in as if I had read the commentary on the subway.

My experience after that shifted back to the American model. I went to Yeshiva University, and there, again, college was given equal weight with the Jewish studies. So a lot of people I meet, if I describe the general yeshiva model, the modern yeshiva model to them, they think that's repressive. You couldn't go out and have a hamburger. You couldn't play ball Saturday morning. That was liberal to me, because when I was at yeshiva they said you weren't allowed to read an English book on Shabbes. On Shabbes, you'd come home — it was a holy day and you don't read a novel. One summer while I was going to these European schools I went to a Yiddish-speaking camp. It was called Camp Torah V'dass in the Catskills. There, we had very little sports. We studied Talmud under a tree, and the rebbe would teach in Yiddish. I think it was actually something I wanted to go to, because I got sort of caught up in this.

I can look back at it and say there was the mean rebbe with the ruler. But also what did I like about it? A lot of people went through this very same experience; a lot of my friends married out and didn't want to have anything to do with Judaism, rejected it all. I'm very close to Judaism and I have a real emotional feeling for it. There was something about this company of men — European yeshivas were all boys ... Here I was, an adolescent without sports, with no father around, without sex, without girls to flirt with, without anything except this fervent religious tie. It was expressed in music. At the drop of a hat we would form a circle and sing. There was a wonderful warmth to it, and even the fellow you sat across the table from every morning for three hours, he was your best friend. You knew everything about him because inevitably you would bullshit. You couldn't sit and really study. When you bullshitted you felt bad because really you should be studying, and you sort of kept each other honest. There was something very warm and very beautiful about it, and when I hear songs on records of these little boys singing, I get very emotional about it and I love that stuff. My wife is always saying that I'm a yeshiva boy at heart.

Yeshiva University is all men. There's a girls' school, Stern College, that's associated with it. There's a dating ethic. There's a basketball team, a wrestling team. I fenced for a while. It's a liberal arts college. You'd take Yiddish like you'd take French or German. The study was Hebrew to English. There was a great college newspaper, the *Commentator*. I wrote for that from my sophomore year on. I entered college in 'sixty-seven, and even at Yeshiva there was a good deal of student activism. After all, we weren't far from

City College and Columbia. We couldn't escape it. We got out of finals when Nixon bombed Cambodia. Meanwhile, in Brooklyn I'm sure those people didn't know what Vietnam was, because secular knowledge — you weren't supposed to read the newspaper. You certainly weren't supposed to watch television. I remember in 1964 when the Beatles were on, my study partner and I decided to watch them, but we were afraid to talk about them because the rebbe couldn't know that we went home and watched Ed Sullivan; you weren't allowed to watch television. But at Yeshiva, there was a television in school, at Yeshiva University, the American model of the yeshivas.

In the American yeshivas, the modern Orthodox, Israel was part of your education. We were very Zionistic. In the European yeshivas, you got a lot of negative feeling about Israel. The idea was that you can't settle the land until the Messiah comes. The whole idea of this revolutionary messianism wasn't for them. You don't go out and settle the land; you wait for God to intervene.

I thought of an anecdote that illustrates the tension that I was expressing earlier. I was thirteen years old, living in Queens, and I was already in this European yeshiva and I was walking to shul on Friday night. My mother lit the candles and then I'd go out the door and go to Friday night service. There was an old woman who walked by carrying two bags from the grocery store. She was sweating; she was uncomfortable. She was just standing at the corner trying to catch her breath, and she stopped me. She said, "I'm having a lot of trouble," and she asked me if I could help her carry this down the block. She said, "I'll give you a dime." I was so torn, because on Shabbes you're not allowed to carry, and you're certainly not allowed to handle money. But I was also taught that you're supposed to help old people. I stood there and I was in such a dilemma. My mouth was open and I didn't know what to do. I walked away from her and said, "No, I'm sorry I can't help you." I've thought of that incident a great deal when two things that I love come into conflict. I was so torn by it, it still haunts me. I wrote a story about it, because I'm still a Sabbath observer and I try to go home in time for Shabbes. I don't always make it, given the kind of job I have.

I remember once sitting in the state legislature in Albany and I'm very aware of the clock. Being a Sabbath observer, you're very in tune with the seasons: Shabbes is early now; Shabbes is late. I didn't want to violate the Sabbath, but the legislature was going on into debate, and I was sitting there in the press box and I was watching the clock and taking notes on the debate. I'd learned when I was in yeshiva on Shabbes that what you're not allowed to do is write with a pen, because that can't be erased. But if you write with a pencil, that's not as bad a sin because it can be erased. I watched the clock — here I'm a *New York Times* reporter in Albany and

I'm worrying about Shabbes — and put away my pen and took out my pencil and I covered the legislature.

I was doing the same thing, but again it's another illustration of that tension, of what's right. Do I walk out? Do I go home? Do I call up the desk and say I'm not working anymore? Some of my rabbis told me that I shouldn't be a journalist, because I was an Orthodox person first and it was going to create too many conflicts. I'd be traveling; I'd be eating treyf. I'd stray too far, even from the modern Orthodox ideal. But, again, as much as I love the Judaism, I loved the journalism. It's a tension.

I stopped wearing a yarmulka when I graduated from Yeshiva, feeling that it was too confining. I became self-conscious about it mostly. In more recent years, given the political situation in Israel, where the knitted yarmulka has taken on a whole meaning in itself, it's become more of a political statement. And I don't lay tfillin on a regular basis. But I do occasionally.

But growing up, I felt comfortable. I felt special. It's an awful word, but I felt *chosen*. As I got older, I went through my own rebellion. I described this scene in Albany. It made it sound like it was the first time I'd had to violate the Sabbath, but it wasn't. I went to Columbia Journalism School and then I went to the *Times* as a copy boy. I had to fight with the supervisors so that I wouldn't work on Friday nights or Saturday. But I'd come in after sundown on Saturday and work the night shift, and I'd trade with people. Holidays I would work something out. But again, that was the tension that I was describing. I became a reporter when I was twenty-five, and I got married when I was thirty-three. So I had many years; I sort of became a public person. When your name's in the newspaper, people get to know you, and also I was someone who dated quite a bit. I mostly went out with Jewish girls, but occasionally, yes, the shiksa had her lure. That created a tension, but not such a great one, because of my personal tradition. It would be very difficult to go out with somebody and then explain why you don't go out Friday nights, or why you can't go to McDonald's. So in a sense it kept me honest.

The things that stayed with me, though — I think they've served me well as a person, or I like to think they have . . . In a lot of these laws, you would learn the law of not carrying on Shabbes or how to wave the lulav on Succoth; that's the palm you take out and you have to wave it to the four corners of the earth. We would practice this in school, right? Otherwise the rains wouldn't come. We would learn that and maybe in the same hour we would learn the laws of honoring your father and mother. They were all on an equal level. Some of the things that stayed with me: for example, you're not allowed to sit in your father's chair or your rebbe's chair. If you left this office now, I would never sit in your chair. There are certain ideas — the idea of hakoras ha-tov, if somebody does something good for you, you're good to them in return. It means the recognition of good.

I don't want to leave with the wrong impression, but in talking about that woman with the bags — what that did was sort of tell me to redefine some of the things in Judaism, and to look at the ethics and the law. I've always wished that would happen again so that I could carry her bags and say that this is something you violate the Sabbath for. In my own life, I try to do that with the tension in Judaism and also the tension between Judaism and journalism. I guess that was the connection I missed when I jumped to the story about the pencil, because you can't always be so legalistic. There's got to be some way to bend and some way around the law or some way to be more comfortable with it or some way to do both things, both to carry her bags and to say, Well this is the more important Jewish ideal. With the idea that, yes, Sabbath is an important value and it means a great deal to me, but so does my job and covering this debate in the legislature. I can't be that legalistic, and on the other hand I can't say that journalism is my whole life. So there's got to be some way to mediate in redefining Judaism for myself, and what I want for my son. I want him to have that kind of feeling and love for it, but I also want him to be able to balance it with the real world.

Herman M. Popkin and Roger Popkin, sixty-six and thirty-five, camp owners, Hendersonville, North Carolina

HERMAN: The three of us went into service. I was in the China-Burma-India Theater, Harry was in the navy as a physical ed instructor, and my brother Ben was in the air corps. Anyway, we decided that we wanted to do something when we got out. So we wrote letters to each other trying to think what we could do with no money. I had graduated from the University of Georgia, and Harry had gone to Georgia Tech, and Ben was in college when he got drafted. We hit on this idea of a summer camp for children — for Jewish kids.

We decided we would do this. So when we got out of the service, I went to a camp up in New York, my brother Harry went to Blue Mountain Camp in Pennsylvania, and my brother Ben went to another camp down south which was run by the Jewish Community Center. We worked for one summer to see if we would like it. Then we went and talked to the non-Jewish camps. The only one that was very honest with us was a woman who ran Camp Cherokee. She said, "You ought to open a Jewish camp. None of us will accept them, and if we do, we do it on a quota system. The Jews — we don't take Jews." She said, "There's a need for it, and you boys ought to open one."

My brother Harry was on his honeymoon up in north Georgia and he called me. He says, "Come up; I've got a camp that's for rent." Dr. Jack Brooks ran a camp called Sky Lake, a big camp with a thirty-five-acre lake with two sides developed. He was using one side, and the other side was empty, so he let us rent it for the summer. We did it for two summers — 1948 and 1949. We had sixty little boys. We only took boys, from all over the South. At that time, Harry was working for B'nai B'rith Youth Organization out of New Orleans. He was their youth director. I was working for Hadassah and the Zionist Organization of America as a youth director, for the Young Judea and Junior Hadassah and the Masada programs in the South.

How I came to do that is important, because that influenced the way our camp operated. After I got out of the army, I was approached by a rabbi connected with Hebrew Union College who wanted me to be a rabbi. I told him, "Nothing doing." I wasn't qualified. I wasn't interested. He got the wrong guy. But my sisters, three of them, got married one after the other. One in October, one in November, one in December. He performed the ceremonies. I had enrolled at Northwestern in Chicago to get my master's degree. When I came home for the weddings, he got me in the corner. He says, "If you don't want to be a rabbi, I've got another job. We're looking for a director for the youth commission that we are starting to create." This was in 1946, 1947, still in Augusta, where my mother and the family were. I told him I wasn't interested. I wanted to get my degree and I wouldn't do it. After the third wedding, he twisted my arm and I consented to go to an interview with the Hadassah women in Atlanta at their regional convention, which was a mistake. Those women wouldn't let me say no. I finally said, "Let me finish this semester and then I'll take over." So I did. But I said to them, "I'm not qualified. I mean, I'm a Zionist but I don't know anything about it. My background in Judaism is nothing. You know I'm from the Deep South and I have no background." They said, "We'll train you." I said, "How?" They said, "We'll send you to Brandeis Camp." I said, "What's Brandeis Camp?"

Dr. Shlomo Bardin had started Camp Brandeis for Hadassah and for ZOA nationally in the Pocono Mountains. He got permission to name it after Justice Brandeis. I don't know if you are familiar with the series of camps he set up. They took eighteen- to twenty-five-year-old college kids, and through a combination of kibbutz, the Scandinavian adult education system, and the American camping system, in one month's time it could convert a nonbelieving Jew, really almost an anti-Semitic, assimilated Jew, into a very positive Jew. He did it beautifully.

So I went first as a student to the Poconos. This was in 1947, before the State of Israel, because he had two Israelis there, the first ones I ever met. Well, they weren't Israelis then. I met Katya Delacova and Fred Berk, too, who were doing the Israeli folk dancing and the Jewish folk dancing at that camp. Sitting out on the raft, I said then, "If I ever had my own camp, I would love to have somebody like you all teach this folk dancing." This was in 1947. He just died. She is still living. They are remarkable people. He escaped from Hitler in Germany and went from England to Cuba to here.

It was the first time I ever heard the term *modern dance* or heard of Israeli and Jewish folk dancing. I was fascinated. Bardin also had these Israelis doing the garden, and I worked with my hands, which Bardin thought was important — that you learn the dignity of self-labor. All this I acquired, and the next month I became a member of the faculty. The things I learned at Brandeis were the things which made me a better youth director.

Then my wife and I went to this Brandeis Camp in Hendersonville, North Carolina, to chaperone an intercollegiate Zionist Federation group of college kids before they went back to school. I said, "You know, we can't get a camp in Georgia" — which we wanted to do because we were Georgians. "We'll find one maybe here." We ended up buying two hundred acres and these ten little cottages, which we immediately ripped out and made into cabins. I think we charged $350 the first year. It was a short-term camp. We didn't do it full time. Five weeks the first year, six weeks the next. When we moved to North Carolina, we made it coed.

At one time we had almost nine hundred children when my brother and I were working it. About twelve years ago, maybe thirteen, Harry had a heart attack and the doctors advised him for his own health not to continue to do that. My son Roger came in with me. That's why we decided to keep it. We now have limited it to about seven hundred children at one time. Over the years we estimate about thirty thousand to forty thousand children have come to Blue Star Camp. When I retire I'm going to count, but until then I don't know the exact number.

And by the way, we take children of all races and religions. Because we can't get the Jewish staff that we want, we now take staff of all races and religions. We take about eighty foreign counselors from all over the world. In the beginning all the counselors were Jewish. They came from all over the South and all over the country. I mean, we have always attracted staff from everywhere. The children come from thirty states, predominantly southern kids, although we get kids out of New York City and seven foreign countries. Promotion is done by word of mouth, primarily. We don't do too much else. We get a lot of second-generation children now.

ROGER: What you are not focusing on really strongly is what made the camp that I went to as a camper different than other camps. Movement camps that are run by synagogue groups or agencies are supposed to be Jewish. Private camps that are owned by individuals that are supposed to have a prestige quotient involved usually jump that end of it, because being Jewish was really not that culturally significant. People wanted to assimilate, especially in the fifties and sixties. So to a certain extent that destigmatized being Jewish. Most of the children that I went to camp with that I bump into now, as adults, tell me all the time that the only place they felt comfortable understanding their heritage or their American Jewish heritage, that sort of twin background, was at Blue Star, because somehow or other it made it acceptable to be both Jewish and American, and most private camps don't do anything with that, at all.

HERMAN: We have a very unique programming. Without quite realizing it, what we decided — my brother and I — was that whatever we did that was Jewish was going to be just as much fun and just as meaningful as whatever we did on a ballfield or on the waterfront or wherever else. So that first year in north Georgia in 1950, I told my brother that I wanted to do Israeli folk dancing. My brother said, "You'd be out of your cotton-picking mind. Nobody does Israeli folk dancing and nobody does Jewish folk dancing down here." Well, I have never talked so hard in my life. Not only that, but Katya and Fred wanted a big salary. We had to get them a trailer to live in because they weren't going to live like everybody else. They were the tops in their field.

My brother said, "You can't pay them. And besides, nobody wants to do it." I won. They came to Blue Star in 1950 and I want you to know they helped us to build the camp. They had our boys and girls doing Israeli folk dancing and Jewish folk dancing without them quite realizing they were getting into it. For they knew, too, there was a certain resistance to it. But they started with us and they stayed with us for about seven years, the first seven. This is the twenty-fifth anniversary, this summer, of the Israeli folk dance workshop that Fred started at our camp for adults from all over the country — I mean from Canada to California. In fact, we've got a Fred Berk Israeli Folk Dance Pavilion named in his memory.

Once a week we'll have some kind of program that will have some Jewish content to it that the kids have to do. We give them time during the week to do it, but it's fun.

We also have a United Jewish Appeal carnival to raise money and the kids decide where it is going to go. In fact, last year they gave it to the Statue of Liberty but normally we try to do it for Jewish things.

ROGER: We have Israeli peace conferences where some of the kids will be the Arabs; some of the kids will be the Israelis, and they try to hammer out a settlement and do it in front of the group. Basically, the services are also very significant, because the Friday nights are very different. The kids write their own services. Our kids, mostly, are secular; they come out of a nontraditional background, a lot of them, so they'll write their own prayers, they'll sing songs with guitars. Our non-Jewish staff participates, so it tends to become a significant weekend program, usually culminating with some kind of an event on Sunday, in addition to Saturday.

HERMAN: This is important, too. We voluntarily teach maybe forty children, or whoever wants to learn, for their Bar Mitzvahs. They are from small country towns where they can't get lessons. We have a Hebrew teacher, we have a Living Judaism director — no rabbi, but we do invite guests to come up for a weekend or for a week even, and we've invited rabbis, but we make certain the rabbi doesn't preach his brand of Judaism. We are not interested in Reform, Conservative, Orthodox, or Reconstructionism. We're interested in just being Jews.

We observe the dietary laws. There's a basket of yarmulkas, but if the boys don't want to wear them, they don't have to. And a lot of them don't. And we don't get up and say, "When you get home, you keep kosher." They get milk before they go to sleep at night with cookies to make up for the milk they miss at their meal, but we don't tell them that's what they're to do. Somebody said, "How can you please everybody?" We don't please the real Orthodox.

ROGER: Basically, what Blue Star has been able to do is to create and to give children and staff the opportunity to delve into their own backgrounds — their Judaic and American heritages. The ability, to a certain extent, to find out who they are, to create an identity. I think for our kids, to tell you the truth, there's just a poverty of identity.

I think the core program has changed. We are much more specialty-oriented. We have tennis pros and we own our own horses and we have equestrian people and our soccer man is a trained pro. All of those things are for the prestige side of the camp. What makes the camp meaningful, however, doesn't change. That's basically adding some kind of feature that allows the kids and the staff to jointly discover their own identities. Part of what my father is talking about is what happens to kids at camp when they find out that they can stand up and do a service and write their own prayer. A lot of them have only been in a synagogue, where they listened and they talked when somebody from up there told them to. It gives them an opportunity to understand that God talks to everybody.

My feeling is that there are a lot of kids whose parents, because of affluence, feel that they don't need to be Jewish anymore, because they see it as a kind of backward pull from the old country; I mean, a lot of them do. I think the kids seem to find it an important feature of their background: where they came from, what it meant.

Stuart E. Eizenstat, forty-two, lawyer, Washington, D.C.

Camp Blue Star had as much influence on me as any other institution with which I was associated during my youth. I heard about it because it was owned and run by two brothers, Harry and Herman Popkin, who were very active in the Jewish community of Atlanta. I have a great love affair with Blue Star that I've carried on ever since. I went to Blue Star for probably six summers, and Blue Star meant many things to me. One, anecdotally, is that it was my first political experience. I was totally apolitical and I was a part of what was called Teenage Village, and there came a time when they had to elect the so-called mayor of Teenage Village, and here I was, sitting around and waiting while other people were being nominated. And suddenly someone said, "We're nominating you." I said, "You can't do that." They nominated me, and I ended up winning the election after a one-week election campaign, much to my amazement. That was probably the apex of my political career, the first and last thing I really won.

But second, it had a real impact on my Jewish identity. It was not what one would call a religious camp per se, but it observed kashruth. I still remember to this day with the fondest memories the Friday night and Saturday morning services that we would have. How Friday evenings we would dress in either all white or blue, we would eat on paper plates because there would be no cleaning Friday night, and then after dinner and services we would go and do Israeli dancing on the basketball court. I can hear the music even as we speak. It was really something that very strongly solidified my identification with Israel and my religion.

In many ways it was very formative, very important, very enriching. And it had one other advantage, which was that I really met a broad range of people, some of whom I still come in contact with. It was a southern Jewish institution; it was a place where people from small southern towns, Bessemer, Alabama, Meridian, Mississippi, the Panhandle of Florida, small towns in Louisiana even, would send their kids, because this was the only Jewish institution oftentimes in their lives. In that respect it was even more important than it was for those of us from Atlanta, which had established Jewish institutions, like the Jewish Community Center and several large synagogues. So it established a network of relationships.

The summer I was to go back — I guess it would have been my sixth or seventh summer — and become a counselor-in-training, I had what was then for my young life one of the most difficult choices that I had yet to make, because I had become very interested in and ultimately quite good at basketball. I was an honorable mention high school all-American and all-city, and there was a Georgia Tech basketball camp, and I basically hadn't decided whether I wanted to really improve my basketball skills or go back as a CIT. I ultimately chose to go to Georgia Tech basketball camp. I'm not sure I made the right choice. But, nevertheless, that was the choice I made, and that's the only reason I stopped going. And I think until my thirtieth birthday I continued to get birthday cards from Camp Blue Star.

It was an all-Jewish camp. The activities, except for the sports, were Jewish-oriented. The counselors were all Jewish. It was run with a Jewish atmosphere. Again, the Sabbath was particularly special. There was no question that you were Jewish when you went in and you felt more Jewish when you came out, but it was done in a very natural and nondidactic way. It affected a tremendous number of people. The Popkins were hands-on owners. I mean they were not absentee owners; they lived up there, their families were there. It was "Uncle Harry" and "Uncle Herman." We still talk about them to this day in that way.

Parents sent their children to Blue Star because it was a Jewish camp, and in particular those from the smaller towns. You see, in those days in the South, unlike today, when there's been such mass migration to the South and Southwest from all over the country, the Jewish community in the South and even in the large cities like Atlanta was extremely cohesive. I belonged to a group called the Devoted Sons of Israel, DSI, which some may have said was a misnomer, but it was one of the Young Judea AZA–type groups. We did everything, our whole lives revolved around that club — our social events, our parties, our softball games, our basketball games — and you competed with the Frank Garson Chapter and this chapter and that chapter. There was a sense of generational continuity. I knew people's fathers; I knew their grandfathers. They would know me. And so when you went to a camp, it was natural you would go to camp together. That kind of cohesiveness has unfortunately broken down. People have scattered throughout metropolitan Atlanta. Then we all lived in the Morningside area. My grammar school was probably seventy-five percent Jewish, and my high school was fifty percent Jewish, Grady High School. And so, again, going to camp together was a natural extension of growing up together, of being in a Jewish club together. I think people would be surprised actually at the rather intensive Jewish identification that one would have gotten in Atlanta, Georgia, in the 1950s.

We regularly went to synagogue; we were involved in the Jewish Community Center. That was where we got our activity. All of our friends were Jewish. As one looks back on it sociologically, perhaps, we were forced to have only Jewish friends because institutions were more closed than they are today. Probably, but we didn't think about it. I can really remember only two direct anti-Semitic incidents. And yet there was obviously a broader way in which the whole environment was in a sense anti-Semitic, because we did not have that much contact with non-Jews. My father's generation had quotas in schools, et cetera. In terms of actually feeling it and knowing it, because we were in such a protected cocoon, I remember only two incidents. Once, my mother was driving us to a place called Mooney's Lake and there was a RESTRICTED sign outside, and I didn't even know what it meant. I was a young kid and I asked my mother, and she said that means no Jews are allowed. And the second time was when some kids on the block, two brothers, attacked me when I came home from Hebrew school with my Hebrew books and tried to tear the books up.

Even our Cub Scouts were totally Jewish. All the dens that belonged to the pack were Jewish; the pack was Jewish. We used to meet for our city-wide pack at Shearith Israel Congregation. So there was a Jewish Cub Scouts. Now you know that in this day and age that sounds almost anachronistic. It probably is. I had very little contact with non-Jewish kids as I was growing up.

One of the funny things is that my oldest son, who is now fourteen, went to Camp Ramah in New Hampshire, a much more intensively Jewish camp, didactically so; they pray three times a day, et cetera. I had an interest in sending him to Blue Star, but my wife, who's from Massachusetts, wanted him to go there. My youngest son went away to camp last summer for the first time. I wanted him to go to Blue Star, but he ended up going to Camp Judea, also in Hendersonville.

Nicholas Lemann, thirty-two, journalist, Pelham, New York

Q: You didn't go away to camp, did you?
A: I did. I didn't go to Blue Star. In fact, I went to a camp near Blue Star. We thought that the kids at Blue Star were the revenge of the nerds.
Q: Did you go to a Jewish camp?
A: No. I went to a camp that was somewhat like Country Day, in that Jews went there, but it was not predominantly Jewish. The kids at Blue Star had to wear these little blue shorts. You know, when you're a kid, a little boy eight or nine, the idea of having to wear sort of a slightly precious uniform is just the most embarrassing thing you can ever think of. And these Blue Star kids did have to wear this. I remember vividly that they had to wear these sort of sensible shoes and socks and blue shorts.

Judith Nelson Drucker, fifty-four, temple cultural director,
Miami Beach, Florida

My kids went to Blue Star Camp, and they loved it. In fact, my husband and I used to say "Let's send the kids home and we'll stay here." I think they did a wonderful job of making kids Jewish. My kids would come home, and I tell you, it was incredible how they were. I'll never forget, we went up and we used to stay at the Lakeside Inn and we met a young couple from a town called Greeleyville, South Carolina. They were the only Jewish family in Greeleyville, and they were very Jewish. Every Friday night it was dinner and lighting the candles, and they would travel sixty miles to Charlotte and sixty miles back. One hundred and twenty miles for their son to learn his Haftarah and to be a Bar Mitzvah. I found some of those southern Jews are more Jewish than anything.

My kids would come home knowing all the Israeli songs and be very proud and be happy. They couldn't wait to go back, because they shared a great experience in being Jewish, which is in a sense how the Israelis felt, I think, in the beginning. I don't know now so much. The camaraderie is so important. In fact, it was cute, because my kids, when they got married and had children, their desire was that they could afford to send their kids to Blue Star Camp. My daughter sent her son there.

Samuel Tenenbaum, forty-two, steel executive,
Columbia, South Carolina

I went to Blue Star one time. Supposedly the food was kosher and you had Friday night services and all that kind of stuff. It was a social experience to bring young southern Jews together. I wanted the camping experience. You see, it was interesting because I went to Teenage Village, which was the hot place to be. I mean, it was — I won't say it was like Jamaica or Club Med or something, but it was close to that. Kids would tell you about these women from Miami — when you are thirteen and fourteen years old. But I wanted the camping experience and I didn't get a camping experience. I got a social experience at Blue Star.

It was sort of scary. I mean, we had a Sadie Hawkins Day. Particularly the girls from Miami, the young girls, they were five years ahead of us. I was fourteen. They were already dating guys eighteen years old, and here you are being chased by these women. It was incredible and I really felt very uncomfortable dealing with that part of it. The camping experience that I did get — the canoeing; we went down rivers — I loved it. But the social pressures put on you, particularly for us, for some people like myself, were unbearable.

Freda Hyde Lowenthal, sixty-two, Jacksonville, Florida

My mother was English and my father was Polish. His name wasn't Hyde; his name was — Gesundheidt. When he went through immigration, they said, "You are Hyde." My mother was a Bennett from England.'

My mother was dying of cancer, and my father went off somewhere and they didn't even know where he was. Left us in a house in San Antonio, Texas. We happened to have very wealthy relatives, the Bennetts. And the Bennetts did not want to take care of seven children. So they contacted the Jewish Children's Home in New Orleans and put us into it, four of us. The other three went with my father to New York but never saw him. He left them there. One of these days I would honestly like to hear their story. I never have.

I was five years old. I remember crying for a week because we were in isolation and I was scared to death. "We" were Bea, Junior, Joe, and myself. Four children in isolation. I'm five, and I don't even know what ages they were. Then we were put in with the other children and it was wonderful.

You know, this was an orphanage for the southern region. It was Texas, Louisiana, Arkansas, Mississippi, and Alabama. It wasn't just Louisiana. The Jewish Federation ran the home, which was supported by charity. We would send out letters constantly asking for funds, constantly. Originally it was the Jewish Orphans' Home but they changed it to Jewish Children's Home. It took up one complete square block in New Orleans: 5342 Saint Charles Avenue. It was a large red brick building. Three floors. I was on the third floor. There were 150 kids. We didn't wear uniforms. We had our own rooms, private rooms. Each child had their own private room.

We didn't have private bathrooms. We had showers for everybody. We were happy children. We had wonderful counselors. We had medical students from Tulane University as study supervisors. They had room and board to help pay; in other words, they didn't have to stay at the dorm at Tulane. They would stay for four years, so we got to know them.

Uncle Harry was the superintendent. He was, what would you say, into social work, but very advanced social work, where young girls and young boys bathed together. This was, you know, a very interesting thing. This was 1925 or 1927. This Harry was very far-fetched. But he was smart, I mean far advanced in child development. We used to say the minute we got bosoms and something else, we quit bathing with the boys, see. One of the girls became his girl friend. She was probably sixteen, seventeen, eighteen. Harry was forty, forty-five at that time.

We had a tremendous dining room. We had a basketball court. We had baseball diamonds. We had everything that anybody could want.

We had to clean our own room and keep it tidy. And we had kitchen duty. We had to eye the potatoes. They had the potato machine that would do everything but eye the potatoes. We had to eye them, snap the beans, wash the dishes, make lunches for all the kids when it rained — make 150 lunches, so we didn't have to walk home when it rained.

I didn't know any other home. The same was true for my brothers and sister, too. Everybody. Did people come and adopt children? No. Once or twice some parent would take a child out, like the Pulitzer brothers. The mother remarried and came into some money and she took the sons out.

Did anybody ever talk about their parents? Very seldom. I mean, it was not . . . they were somewhere else. My mother died while I was in the Home. I was probably six. My father came to see us once when we were in the Home, and it was a very unsatisfactory thing. Then my sister Bea, who is such a good person, after she was married, my father showed up on her doorstep, and do you know she took care of him until he died? She let him live with her until he died. He was a horrible, horrible person. When I say horrible, I don't mean mean; he was a sponger. Do you know what I'm trying to say? He never worked a day in his life. I don't know how he lived.

We had big brothers and sisters. I had one, but she was sort of not good. Some of the kids had wonderful ones, like Mrs. Feibelman. She had Adele and Louise — oh, she was so good to them, she was good to them. They were lucky, you know.

We were very conscious that we were Jewish children. It was just a good feeling, a happy feeling. We were really happy Jewish children. We were going to Audubon Park to swim or we were going someplace and I would sing, "We're little Jewish children. We're marching in a row. We're happy in the sunshine, because God loves us so." We all went to three synagogues. How they divided the children, I will never know. There were three synagogues in New Orleans: Reform, Conservative, and Orthodox. Families were all placed together. We were placed in the Reform. Now, my friend Lillian was placed in the Conservative, and somebody else was placed in the Orthodox. Nobody asked. It was where you went. So you had to go every Friday night and every Saturday morning, and you walked twelve blocks. They really didn't like us too much, because we used to steal the charity. "Who wants to pick up the charity from the hall — all the classes?" You would raise your hand. "Okay." Imagine all that money, so when the kids from the Home picked up the charity, the synagogue didn't get too much. All I remember is that every once in a while you had a lot of money. Don't you think they knew we were stealing at Sunday school? I would think they knew.

It was a very interesting place. The Krauss brothers were on the board and they would let us go to town and pick out our clothes from their store. It was wonderful. We didn't have to pay for them. We'd pick them out. We went to movies and we went to concerts. Tickets were donated. We had allowances. I don't remember what it was. But I remember we also had Chanukah presents and we had a big dinner and everybody would put their wish in for Chanukah and everybody would get what they asked for. On Rosh Hashonah you would have to go into the middle of the dining room and shake hands with whoever you hated and hadn't been friends with. But we did have everything we wanted.

Schooling took place at the Isadore Newman Training School, which became "Newman." Isadore Newman in his will, I guess, made provision for the children of the Home to always attend Newman School. It was about five blocks from the Children's Home. Today, it is *the* status school in New Orleans. It was then, too, because most of the children who went to the school had homes in Atlantic City and they all had chauffeurs and they all had maids. The chauffeurs would pick them up. The school was mixed between children from the orphanage and the elite.

The people we met in school were sort of brainwashed as to what we were and who we were, and they had nothing to fear from us. I think they treated us in a different way. And it was good for those children. I think it was absolutely wonderful for the very wealthy children, because I think they saw another side. By the two mixing it was good for them and it was good for us. It was good for us because it was like we accepted the fact that we could be with other people, wealthy people, and we saw the better side of things. And I believe the children that were wealthy were nicer probably than people that were poor.

Did the people in the school socialize with the people in town? Did someone say, "Can you come over and play with me? Sleep overnight? Oh, surely you could do that." I didn't do it and I don't know anybody who did, but I think if somebody had asked you, I think they could. We didn't think about it. I may be wrong and somebody else can give you a different story. I know one thing: they invited all of us to a sorority dance — Louise and Lillian and me — and they never invited us again. The fellows only danced with us. But the Home did go out and buy us all new dresses to go to that dance.

My friend Lillian had an aunt and I did go to her house sometimes on Saturdays. I never really liked it.

We always went to camp. Bay Saint Louis, Mississippi. Every summer.

Got on the train, went to camp, and we had a wonderful summer. It was a Jewish camp but it wasn't kosher. Camp was marvelous. We had bunks and we made ice cream and we boiled crabs and we had a great time, a great time.

You had to be younger than twelve to be admitted to the Home, and when you were eighteen you were — you know — placed somewhere. The first one of us out was my brother Joe Hyde. Then Bea. Then Junior, my brother Ken. And then myself. I stayed until I was eighteen. When she got to be eighteen, Bea went to Uncle Leon and Aunt Sophie in London, England. Joe Hyde was given to Sam Kamin to travel. He traveled with him, and Sam taught him the business: mattress ticking. And I don't know where Ken went. Isn't that funny?

I was sent back to Texas, to my aunt Rose Bennett. She was my uncle Julius's wife — my mother's brother. I was sent back to her. She lived in a boarding house at the time. She had a room; she got her meals. It was a little town right outside San Antonio. She had a big department store — Bennett's Department Store. Uncle Julius was dead, you see. I cried for one week. I cried. I'd never been in a house before; I'd only been in a Home. I'd never been in a home, per se. Do you understand? And I cried for a week and she finally sent me to San Antonio to her son and his wife. I went to my cousins and they found me a place to live and I got a job.

There wasn't any encouragement at the Home to go to college. And all my family did. So there must be something within you. My brother Ken graduated from Louisiana State University. Robert graduated from LSU. Bea did not. I went a couple of years to LSU. Joe Hyde never did. No desire to. People have done fairly well. Some are very wealthy. It's amazing how well they did.

The Home was dissolved when people became too affluent, when you had good times. You don't have children that are misplaced. You know, it's only in bad times. I wasn't there when it was disbanded in 1946. It was founded in the 1800s during a yellow fever epidemic. Many parents died, and the children had no place to go.

It was a wonderful place. You knew you were Jewish, yet they didn't emphasize the fact. I really feel that we had an opportunity that you missed. When I say you missed, I mean that the children in the Home had more security, feeling of security, knowing that people were taking care of us.

Mary Anna Feibelman, seventy-three, and Bernard Lemann,
eighty-one, professor of the history of architecture,
New Orleans, Louisiana

FEIBELMAN: I went to Newman School, just ordinary growing up. Isadore
Newman Manual Training School, and all the orphans from the Jewish
Children's Home went there. They lived at the Home. They went to school.
I can't really think it was too good for those children from the Home,
because they had a lot of rich children at the Newman School. I think it
caused a schism. Of course, it wasn't too many years after that they no
longer did that, because they didn't have the orphanage. But the school was
founded for them. And the history of that would be fascinating, how it
became what it is, which is the elite school here, and not just for Jewish
people, but the *elite* elite.

LEMANN: Mary Anna, it was then. You and I were elite.

FEIBELMAN: Sure. That's what I said. It was bad for the orphan children
to be there. They couldn't have as nice clothes as we had. They didn't have
any homes.

LEMANN: Mary Anna's grandfather took a special interest in the Jewish
orphans and the Jewish orphanage. He went there every Saturday, and I
think he spent time with the children. I remember my mother saying that
she would go there to rock the babies so that they would have some human
contact. I thought that perhaps your mother also did that to some extent,
but she told me no, she had not. But my recollection of the Jewish Children's
Home and the Newman School, where I also attended high school, was not
quite the same as yours. I don't recall their being so particularly set aside
or treated differently.

FEIBELMAN: They weren't set aside, except in theirselves.

LEMANN: Some of them became prominent citizens. The fact that they
had a training, and it was optional, in crafts and in business crafts, short-
hand, typing, and so on, was Mr. Newman's idea of preparing orphans,
who were more or less abandoned, to shift for themselves, make a better
life for themselves. Many of them had the advantage of an excellent high
school training that prepared them for college, because Newman, until
Country Day School was subsequently formed, was *the* one college prep
high school in New Orleans. So I'm less aware than you were of the kind
of social restrictions and less aware of the interreligious social distinctions.
In other words, I don't know what the proportions were, but it might have
been as much as half and half Jewish and non-Jewish at Newman. I think
that my friendships at Newman were about fifty-fifty.

FEIBELMAN: Bessie Margolis, who was brought up in the Jewish Children's Home and went to the Newman School, is what you are talking about. She was a rare person there. She's been in Washington all these years — she's an attorney in Washington. There were a few very bright kids in the Jewish Children's Home, and they could really benefit from Newman. But I think the majority just would not. When I got to Newman School, they were phasing out the Jewish Home.

Harold Trobe, seventy, retired Jewish agency official, Gainesville, Florida

I grew up in Beaver Falls, Pennsylvania. I got a master's degree in social work from what was then the New York School of Social Work, now the graduate school of Columbia University. I graduated in 1937, so from 1937 to 1942 I worked in the Jewish Family Welfare Service of the city of Pittsburgh. I was dealing mainly with children who had to be placed. Not orphans. Orphans constitute a very small proportion of Jewish children, even then. Split families, where the mother died.

Every Jewish community in the United States with a Jewish population in excess of twenty-five thousand, I would say, had some program for the care of children who required care outside their home. The old method was an orphanage, which was very costly and a very bad technique for dealing with it. A foster home is not the best. There's no substitute for a child's home. We didn't have an enormous number of such Jewish children in the city of Pittsburgh. Maybe we had fifty or sixty kids.

We had a Jewish population of fifty-five thousand in Pittsburgh at that time. We didn't have many children, but we had an orphanage, which I didn't have much to do with. We finally eliminated the orphanage. We placed the children in foster homes. All of the non-Jewish children who required substitute parental care were placed by the juvenile court. It was the agency to deal with that, but we had a contract with the juvenile court. They preferred to have us, the Jewish Agency, place the children in Jewish homes. The typical case was a father who couldn't take care of the child, the mother mentally ill or passed away or had deserted the family. We were able to find Orthodox homes. At that time, there were still a large number of Jews who were observant Jews.

Alcoholism among Jews at that time was very rare. When a Jew was a shicker, he was really a disgrace to everybody. There were divorces, but nothing like today. When a divorce happened, it was a scandal. We had a number of cases involving intermarriage. We even had illegitimate children. We had the same kinds of problems that the goyim had. We didn't have them in the percentage that they did, and alcoholism was not a significant problem for us. We had a few cases where the family was dependent because of an alcoholic, but nothing significant. It was so rare.

Samuel Hyams Jacobs, eighty, insurance agency executive, Charleston, South Carolina

The Hebrew Benevolent Society of Charleston is one of the oldest in the United States still in existence. The society was founded in 1784. They started out, I imagine, as a burial society, and later on they had funds and became more of a benevolent society to help the poor and the destitute Jews of the city. Even today, although the society is comfortably endowed, we loan money to needy people without interest. The Benevolent Society also helped people in a different way from the Hebrew Orphan Society. The early families that came over needed help, you see. It was a needed organization then, not just a burial society. Their idea was to help transients that would come here. You could call them "snowbirds" later on.

Today we give help primarily to students that need money to finish their education, college education mostly. We give help to people who are stranded here, families that have financial trouble, domestic problems. Primarily you have to be Jewish. We help in that way. We meet once a year also. It's open membership. I would say there are about 250 Jewish men in the city of Charleston who are members of the Hebrew Benevolent Society. It's not quite as heavily endowed as the Orphan Society is, but we do have funds, and these funds are invested. The dues, I believe, are either fifteen or eighteen dollars a year now per member. We do not depend upon the money from dues. We have a banquet once a year, and the income from the dues probably about pays for the banquet.

The Hebrew Orphan Society — the first president was David Lopez, Sr. — was founded in 1801 and is still in existence. During the Civil War, there were 180 Jewish men from this area that were in the service of the armed forces of the Confederacy, and many of them were killed in action. The widows and orphans of these young men who lost their lives for a lost cause, if you want to call it that, needed help.

It's been heavily endowed over the years, and the membership is limited to eighteen of us now. A person to be elected into membership must have accomplished something. We only meet once a year. Its affairs are handled by the secretary and treasurer, which is a joint office. I was elected secretary-treasurer for one year, and it was nine years before I could get out of office. I'm a past president of the society. Everything is handled by the officers: the president, the vice-president, the secretary-treasurer. The rest of us, we do very little, unfortunately. We keep the organization together. It's too old an organization to let go out of existence. There are too many early Jewish societies that are no more.

We men, most of us, are up in age. We're beginning to take in a few younger people, but again, a younger person hasn't had time to try himself or find himself and do necessary work in the community. It's hard to explain what the Hebrew Orphan Society does. For instance, we voted to give the Hospice Society $1500 a year, and we give to the Charleston-area senior citizens another $1500 or $2000 a year. Not to Jews only.

When the Orphan Society began, as its name implies it was to take care of the orphans and widows. Just what the book here says, "When the Hebrew Orphan Society was founded in 1801, Charleston had the largest Jewish community in the United States, about a hundred heads of families and about five hundred Jews in all." It's still there at 86 Broad Street, but we don't own the building anymore. We made a mistake selling it.

Kalman Noel Epstein, forty-five, journalist, Silver Spring, Maryland

I was born in Brooklyn, New York, November 5, 1938, just before the war. We lived kind of between Bensonhurst and Flatbush. It's a working-class neighborhood. My father was a mailer for *The New York Times*.

My father came here when he was very young, about four years old, one of twelve children. We have a very large family on my father's side. Today, in this country, just from my father's mother's side of the family — that's one quarter of my family — there are an estimated eight hundred relatives. My great-great-grandparents' names were Mordecai and Rive Nozick. They came from Osovetz, Russia. They had nine children. Eight of their children also had children; one of them didn't. She died, as I recall, an alcoholic who froze to death in the snow before they came to America. The eight children had a total of fifty-four children, an average of seven apiece.

When various branches of the family came to this country around the turn of the century and shortly afterwards, and kept coming, they established a self-help group that was called the Loyal Family Circle, Incorporated. It was incorporated in New York State in November 1929, right after the Crash. It was unrelated to the Crash. They were just poor; they didn't need the Crash to make them poorer. They came here poor. Those were very hard times, and they did remarkable things for each other. They not only lent each other money. If somebody needed money, one of them who was active, the president or the vice-president or one of the members, got on the phone and they raised as much money as the person needed. It didn't make any difference.

They created an emergency fund right off. Up to fifty dollars per family, which in those days was a fortune. We're talking about 1929. No questions asked; no identities disclosed; no interest permitted; often no repayment made at all. They just gave away money. In the 1940s, when one of the cousins needed what was then the astounding sum of $3000 for an eye operation, two Loyal Family Circle officers in New York got on the phone and overnight they raised $3000, and she got the eye operation and her eyes were saved.

There were hundreds of members, all cousins. There are the ones who settled in New York. There was a branch that settled in Providence, Rhode Island; there were others who went to Denver, Colorado. These are still active branches. There are others elsewhere in the country, in other cities. In the Washington metropolitan area today, we have between seventy and eighty members of our branch of the Loyal Family Circle. This still exists, and actively.

In 1979, we had a fiftieth anniversary reunion of the Loyal Family Circle. We rented an entire hotel in the Catskills in New York, and people came from all around the country and the world. One of my cousins, who's almost exactly my age, came from Malaysia with her husband and her children. Others came from Canada and the South. We all got together, and it was one of the most astonishing experiences I've ever had in my life. They are all descendants of those eight children, going back to the original Nozicks.

There were four hundred people who showed up out of the estimated eight hundred in the country. They tracked down extra people. They had to find them, so they asked people if they knew of anybody. There's a president, Evelyn, who's been the president for some years now. Evelyn Epstein married Sonny Solinsky. She is my first cousin, one of the three children and two daughters of my father's older brother. I send her my twenty-five-dollar dues every year.

There is a quarterly newsletter that goes out and has everything. The standard Jewish things, like best recipes, news of who's doing what, and what's happening around the country. We all keep in touch. We can't do it actively every day or every week, but down here in Washington in our local branch once a year, on Father's Day, we usually go out to the Izaak Walton Park and have a picnic. Anywhere from thirty to seventy people show up. A lot of people show up with the next generation. They do standard games for the kids — guess the numbers in the thing — and recount old times. A lot of the people down here have lived here all their lives. They're not people who came from elsewhere, as most people in the Washington area are, as I am. They grew up together; they went to the beaches together. It's great reminiscing and it's great getting together.

At the fiftieth anniversary reunion, we paid a modest price, as it was off season in November, and we got a whole hotel. All around you, everybody in the hotel is a relative. It's the most astonishing feeling. There was nobody other than the help that was not a relative. I walked in and I saw people like my father's oldest sister Mary, who is now ninety-one. They brought her in in a wheelchair from a nursing home. She was very ill, and everybody was surrounding her in the lobby. They hadn't seen her for years. My father wasn't feeling well and he couldn't even make it. There were others who hadn't seen Mary for ages. She was the oldest Epstein. In fact, there's a photo of just my father's immediate family, his brothers, sisters, and parents, which has Mary in the back as the oldest daughter holding her baby, who was also there at the reunion. Sitting on my grandmother's knee is her youngest child, Millie. Mary's daughter was older than Millie, my father's youngest sister. So the aunt was younger than the niece.

They were all there. We spent the day talking to each other, reminiscing, hugging. You can't imagine the hugs. The greatest thing about it that I found, and it's the greatest thing with this kind of an organization, is the totally spontaneous open arms. There are no questions asked. It doesn't make a damn difference who you are, what you do. You're automatically accepted, welcome — "Anything we can do for you?" — and everything is affection. We had a wonderful time. There were meetings; there were reminiscences. Some of the older members would talk about when the organization was started. They had entertainment, wonderful meals.

In the afternoon, you'd get your room, and then you'd go out to all the courts, the tennis courts, the basketball courts, the swimming pool; everybody's a relative playing games with relatives. Some of the kids — some of the grandchildren and the great-grandchildren — brought tapes to tape the grandparents and the great-grandparents talking about how it was when they came over, so they'd have it for their own histories and their own heritage and their own sense of where they came from. There was a big chart up on the wall of each of the branches of the family. A lot of people spent time at the charts, tracing who they hadn't seen and when they saw someone last, telling old stories and passing them on to the children.

What impressed me the most was the kind of self-sacrifice, the kind of commitment to family, the kind of devotion when nothing else could get in the way. Once, when a relative got sick, they formed two rosters of women, the first to visit her every week and bring her fresh fruit, and the second to make sure that the first group could go. And they took care of the children or nursing her sick husband. When one person was taking care of her, another person took care of the family. Uncle Ben got her a job in the garment industry. A couple of other cousins helped get her an apartment. Everybody donated something to the apartment. I remember that. She told Evelyn that in the bad times she wanted to die. She lived to be eighty-one.

They were telling me about this because my mother was one of the organizers and doers. I didn't know that until they told me. I knew about none of these things. I didn't know how many people needed money. Today, they still have the group and they have, for example, a college fund. Any member of the family whose children go to college, they send them a package for college — a book, a thesaurus, something else. It's all taken from that damn twenty-five dollars that they accumulate. It's a very small pot of money. They still do that. They help finance the meetings that they have. They have regular meetings in New York — the board meets, the members meet; they have white sales and collect money. They're having another reunion of the Rhode Island branch in November — the fiftieth anniversary of the Rhode Island branch, which started five years later in Providence. It's just a wonderful thing.

It's much more family and culture than religion. There are not many very Orthodox Jews in the Loyal Family Circle. It's not in the religious sense Jewish, but everything is heymish. Sure, they still talk Yiddish, which is the language my father and his brothers and sisters came over speaking. Incidentally, there are other things in here; there are intermarriages in the family between first cousins — a number of those.

They published a book. This was the second time they did it. They did it for the twenty-fifth anniversary and now they've done it for the fiftieth. It is a book that is history. It starts off with the Nozicks and shows each one of the children and their children and as many photos as they could get. They sent around the country for photos. A year beforehand they were mailing you things: "Please send us photos." It took us ages to send them photos. So when Evelyn, the president, was down in Washington, she called and we saw her — my wife and I and the children — and she had a camera with her. Anybody's photo she didn't have, she took photos. That's the only way they got our photos into the book. I bought one of those books for my wife and me and for each of my children, who now have their own books, which they will have for their families.

A footnote: My wife, who lost almost all of her family to Hitler's hell, sat at the first dinner and looked around and because she has never had the sense of large family, she sat there with tears streaming down her face, saying, "I could have had a family like this." She was an only child then, but she has a brother who was born here. She was the favorite of all the survivors. She was the only child who survived. After they resettled them in DP camps in the hills of Germany near the Czech border, she was the apple of everybody's eye. They just spoiled her to death.

10

Go West, Young Jew, Go West

HOW MANY JEWS went west across the Mississippi River before the 1800s is anyone's guess. That some did there can be no doubt. Obvious Jewish surnames show up on Catholic church records on the western side of the Mississippi; presumably the men were lone traders and peddlers furtively defying the authorities who had forbade Jews. Until the Louisiana Purchase in 1803, when France sold the United States an 800,000-square-mile chunk of North America, stretching from the Mississippi to the Rocky Mountains and from Canada to the Gulf of Mexico, it was illegal for anyone save a Roman Catholic to live in the Purchase land. So dictated the Code Noir, a fifty-four-article edict governing the life of slaves in French Louisiana. For some odd reason Article I, which apparently had nothing to do with slavery, called for the expulsion of Jews from the French colony. After the Purchase and all during the nineteenth century, Jews moved constantly westward with the rest of restless America. By the Civil War, Jews could be found sprinkled throughout the West, albeit in small numbers relative to those on the East Coast, where they tended to congregate. The great-grandfather of the New York City developer William Zeckendorf, Jr., for example, joined the Union Army in 1862 or so, enlisting in the militia from New Mexico. He was in the quartermaster corps, and when he came back, as an officer, he was sent by his brothers down to Tucson with wagonloads of merchandise that couldn't be sold in Santa Fe. The Zeckendorf brothers figured the market was so good in Tucson that they went into the dry goods business there and "eventually had one and I think probably two stores there," said the twentieth-century Zeckendorf.

"I think my great-grandfather carried a six-gun and used it. There are accounts of his leading a lynching posse and another account of his pulling his gun. And I think he was arrested for either shooting it or carrying it in Tucson."

"Is it true that he led a posse into an Apache camp?"

"That is possible," he mused. "As I say, there are a number of stories; some I am sure are true, some are probably not true. But he did evidently join in a lynching mob. Two people had murdered a friend of his. They pulled them out of jail and they noosed them."

As I explored Jewry farther West, one of the more surprising findings was what I learned about the Sephardic community of Seattle, reputedly the third largest in the United States after New York and Los Angeles. Two aspects of the community struck me as unusual. The first was the simple fact that whereas on the East Coast the Sephardic Jews arrived early, principally from Spain and Portugal, and looked down on the German Jews, who in turn looked down on the East European Jews, the situation was different on the West Coast. There, the German Jews were the earliest arrivals and looked down on the East European Jews, who in turn looked down on the Sephardic Jews, who arrived last from Greece and its islands and Turkey. The second was the extent of superstition and magical curing among the Greek immigrants at the dawn of the twentieth century, when they arrived.

Morris J. Alhadeff is president and chief executive officer of the Long Acres Race Course, which operates a racetrack by the same name on the outskirts of Seattle. He can trace back to 1349 the Alhadeff family, which came to Seattle from the Island of Rhodes, where it had existed for three hundred years. I asked him, "Was your mother superstitious about some things?" He answered, "Probably, but I can't define it exactly, because I don't remember those kinds of things. Superstition has been a large part of the Jewish religion as far as I know. But what is superstition? The fact that if you take the Lord's name in vain, you will be stricken?"

Alhadeff told me that in 1959 a man by the name of Melvin M. Firestone wrote, for a master's degree in anthropology, a thesis entitled "Magical Curing in the Seattle Sephardic Community."

"Do you remember such curing?" I asked.

"Oh, sure I do. I remember my mother doing things to me."

"Like?"

"Like, for example, putting certain types of herbs and mints on a black piece of cloth and wrapping them around my head, and also what they called a 'cura.' They would take a bean — I know this sounds rather brutal — they would take the skin off your arm and then take a garbanzo bean and insert it there and cover it and the area would become inflamed and form a hole and pus would come out of it, and the concept was that it would bring out all the evil and illness in your body."

"Did they do that to you?"

"Yes, they did that to me."

Morris Alhadeff, who is fiercely proud of his heritage and lineage, told me two other stories of his family that etched my own memory. One was about his uncle Nessim and three others, the first people from Rhodes to arrive in Seattle in about 1902 or 1903.

"He migrated together with these Sephardim and they were going to New York and the only language they could speak with anybody else in the hold of the ship was Greek. So this man said to my uncle Nessim, 'Where are you going?' He said, 'We are going to New York.' And this guy says, 'Don't go to New York. Too many people in New York. Go to Seattle; there's gold in the streets.' "

The second story had to do with my interviewing him on July 3. "It's very unusual that you are here the day before the Fourth of July," he said. "My father used to say 'The greatest gift of God was America.' I've always said, 'I'm glad my father caught the boat.' "

Barry Morris Goldwater, seventy-seven, United States senator (Republican of Arizona), Washington, D.C.

The reason my family, my father's family, never followed the Jewish faith when they came to Arizona was that there just weren't any synagogues. There were no rabbis.

My grandfather Michael was one of twenty-two children, and he left Poland when the Russians started to give the Jews a bad time. I have been trying ever since the 1930s to trace those twenty-two people, and I haven't had much luck. But Mike's brother Joe left Poland with him, and they went to France. It was a case of fighting in the French army or leaving there, so they went to England. I think this was about 1845.

Well, anyway, my grandfather Mike married an English girl named Sarah Nathan, who lived down in Whitechapel. During the war, one or two times when I was in London, I tried to find the old synagogue there, but it had been bombed. The wedding certificate and the records were destroyed in the bombing. Well, they had two children in London, Elizabeth and my uncle Morris. In 1850, Mike and Joe left London to go to California because of the Gold Rush. My grandmother Sarah and her sister, whom I never knew much about, traveled to Panama and there they rode horses across the Isthmus. They picked up the boat on the other side and went to San Francisco. My grandfather and my great-uncle arrived in San Francisco about 1850, maybe 'fifty-one, and they went to a little town called Sonora. This is a mining town up in the hills, and there my grandfather established a liquor store. The second floor was the town whorehouse. Well, my grandmother, whom I never knew, objected to the girls' working at night and raising her two children during the day.

At the same time, the two brothers had a business in San Francisco, and that really was their home. The women stayed in San Francisco and the men went back to see them. The women never moved with them, except to Los Angeles, where they opened a store down where the old Union Station was or is now.

Then, in 1860, they heard of gold in Arizona. My grandfather was never a very successful businessman. He sold a lot but he didn't make money. As I say, he maintained his home in San Francisco. He was very, very active in Jewish affairs up there; became a member of a Masonic lodge. But in 1860, he and his brother left Los Angeles and drove two wagons to what is now Yuma, Arizona. Gold had been discovered in several places along the Colorado River. They first took their wagons up to the junction of the Gila River and the Colorado and then moved up to a little town called La Paz. He stayed there until he was convinced the river changes its course so much that he could never depend on the ferry. They had flat-bottomed boats that went up the river. He could never depend on them, so he went downstream about six miles and found a little town called Ehrenberg.

Now the strange thing is, I always thought Herman Ehrenberg was a Jew. One day about 1934, 1935, I drove my old uncle down to Ehrenberg, and all that was left of our store was an adobe wall. I can see it yet. It had a beer stein painted on it: FIVE CENTS. He took me inside and said, "Now over in the corner was where your uncle Henry ran the post office. He didn't believe in delivering the mail. If they didn't come for it, he just threw it away." Well, I dug around in there and I found a letter written in German to the sheriff of San Bernadino County. I had it translated and it was a letter from Ehrenberg's brother inquiring as to the death of Herman Ehrenberg, who my uncle and my grandfather had found murdered at a trading post on one of their trips by horse from Los Angeles to Ehrenberg.

They were very, very close friends. Ehrenberg was a fabulous man — we are working on a history of his life now. But I sent the letter — this is before the war — to the library in Berlin, asking if they could put me in touch with Emil Ehrenberg, which was his brother's name. Well, I never got an answer. I went off to war and when I got back, here was a letter addressed to me from an Ehrenberg. But it was signed "Heil Hitler." I said, Well, he couldn't have been Jewish. Turned out he was a Lutheran.

They kept their business in Ehrenberg, my uncle Morris and my uncle Henry. They had a lot of interesting stories about the family. Where there was gold, the family would go looking for it. They'd never find it, but they'd do something else. They never made money until my father took over the business. My father made money. The other brothers I never knew, except

Henry. Once in a blue moon, he would show up. There were two other brothers, Sam and Ben, both of whom died quite young. They were professional gamblers and died of tuberculosis. They were about forty-five or forty-six years old. They lived in Northern California.

The family moved the store from Ehrenberg for a short while to Wickenberg; it's a little resort town. There, my grandfather and his brother ran the Vulture mine. Henry Wickenberg had discovered this fabulous gold mine. Where my uncle learned how to run a stamp mill, God only knows, but he did. Henry sold the mine and he still owed my grandfather and his brother about $90,000. So they just went out and worked the mine; kept their rifles handy. When they got their $90,000, they turned the mine over to the new owner. Well, they took $140 million out of the mine. It's the whole story of my life.

My grandfather opened a store in Phoenix about 1870. It didn't work out. They went bankrupt, but he did establish a freighting business. He hauled freight to the different army camps around that part of the state. They moved to Prescott, Arizona, which became more or less our family home, and there they opened a store. My father, Baron, came over from Los Angeles, where he was born, and my uncle Morris, and occasionally Henry. But Henry was more interested in looking for gold. He was either down in Mexico or up in California, digging for gold, so I never knew him very well.

They bought the store from my grandfather. The three brothers — Henry, Morris, and my father — bought it from Mike in 1882. Mike went back to San Francisco and spent the rest of his life there. I think Sarah died about 1903 and Mike about 1906. I never knew him. At that time, we had stores in Prescott, one each in Wickenberg, Ehrenberg, Bisbee, where there was the famous Bisbee massacre. They held the store up, threatened to kill my grandfather. They put him under the bed and put a gun on him. They killed five people. These were some outlaws. They just came in, held them up, and robbed them. A posse was quickly formed, and they caught them and in about three weeks they hung all five of them over in Tombstone. We had a store in Tombstone; a little one in Benson.

I think we had one in a little station called Fairbanks, where my great-uncle Joe married the Mexican widow of their partner. The store was, in those days, called Castañeda and Goldwater. He died, and Joe married this girl. I think I met Joe once in my life. He was shot by the Indians. He lived. They took him down to a ranch and dug two balls out of his back. He wore those balls as a watch fob until he died. I think they buried him with them on. He was very active in Jewry in Los Angeles. I think he was a big contributor to the Cedars of Lebanon Hospital and some temple. He became a very wealthy man. You are old enough to remember Boss Overalls — you remember, the one with the mule teams pulling? Well, that was his business. He had some children, but I never knew them. As I say, there were twenty-two in that family.

My father, I call him a merchant prince. He was never home a lot. He traveled when we were young, went to New York, went abroad. He'd come back home. We'd see him. He was a very handsome man, extremely well dressed. No interest in politics. He couldn't hit a nail on the head with a hammer. Never learned to drive a car. He had a great philosophy. He said, "Never do anything yourself you can pay somebody else to do." It's all right, but it gets expensive. He was a club man. He liked to play poker; he liked to play bridge and chess, billiards. So he was never a man around whom stories would grow. But my uncle who came to Arizona, he had been born in London, so when he came to Arizona in 1863 or 'sixty-four, he was fourteen or fifteen years old. He grew up with the territory.

The store in Prescott was a very successful one. My uncle Morris was in politics, he was a Mason, he was selected "Man of the Century" by his city. He was mayor of the town for twenty-seven years. He served in the territorial legislature, in the territorial senate, and was vice-president of the state's constitutional convention. Now, here's a man who never went to school. At this point was he still Jewish, maintaining his Judaism? No. But he never renounced it. He lived with this couple and the husband died, and after twenty years public opinion got the best of him. He married the woman he had been living with. They were married in the Episcopal church, but he never called himself an Episcopalian. And in his Masonic work, he only went up to the thirty-second degree by the Scottish Rite, because going up the York Rite in Masonry, you don't disown God but you don't put the great faith in God that you do in the Scottish Rite. He became Grand Master of the Lodge of Arizona. He gave me my third degree in Masonry, but I can remember on his front door there was a little tin — I don't know [mezuzah] — and in it was a little piece of paper. When he died he had a Masonic funeral.

When my father was married, he married a Gentile and they were married by an Episcopal minister, mainly because there were no rabbis. I don't think it was a case of the men in my family *wanting* to leave the faith.

There were many Jews in the early territorial days of Arizona: Zeckendorf and Steinfeld. Oh, any number of them. The Mormons had a very wide habit of establishing a town, but they always found a Jew to run the bank. That's where Zeckendorf came from. Solomonsville, a Mormon town. His family was there to run the bank. But my grandfather was always Jewish. My aunts, there were three of them. One of them stayed in San Francisco and was never married. That was Elizabeth. The other two moved to New York, and they were always Orthodox Jews. One was Lieberman and one was Butler. They are all dead. In fact, the last child, who was my age, died about three months ago, and I remember that when she married a Gentile, her father and mother disowned her; they were that Orthodox. And they used to give me hell all the time because I was an Episcopalian. I said, "I can't help it." That's just about the whole story of the family.

Did they all come to the United States? I don't know. I've started in London and I wrote or telephoned every Goldwasser, Gildwasser, Goldwater — never found a one. I found a man in Australia who I'm pretty well convinced is one of the brothers. And then the mayor of Bulawayo, Zimbabwe. I remember one day this woman came into my office, after I was senator, and she said, "You know, I think we are related. I think my husband is related to your father." And she showed me a picture, and my God, he was a spitting image of my father. So I went to Zimbabwe — then Rhodesia — and went over to the town and looked the fellow up. The father had died. But the son was the spitting image. So we became pretty fast friends, and the last I heard of him, they were looking for him because he had absconded with about a quarter of a million dollars.

I never found any more.

I remember Dr. Monroe Goldwater in New York. We were not related and he was a very, very strong Democrat. I had several pleasant meetings with him. The fire chief of Cleveland, Ohio, was Goldwater. We could never establish a relationship. There's a Catholic priest in Saint Louis named Goldwater. I've been working on this family history now since 1939, and I finally just gave up. Every once in a while I'll get a letter from somebody saying, "My mother was Goldwater," and I'll get in touch with them, but they didn't come from that part of Poland. But I have to think that we're all related.

I never knew of any anti-Semitic feelings in Arizona. But even then, when I was a boy, we had one synagogue and one rabbi. I think there are now fifty-odd rabbis in the city and a very big Jewish population. There was never any problem with joining the country club, joining the social clubs. That just didn't exist in Arizona. And it didn't exist very much in the whole West. But it was never any handicap in Arizona. It was never even brought up. You know, the West was never liberal. We were a territory of the Confederacy before we were a territory of the Union, so politically we inherited the conservatism of the Democratic South. You know, I've never given it much thought. My best friend, Harry Rosenzweig, and I have touched occasionally on the subject of why wasn't there discrimination? It just didn't exist. I think now there probably is some. But it never has been a factor in my life or the life of Harry or any of the Jewish families, and Lord knows that most of my old friends are Jewish.

Today, once in a while, if I don't vote right on a matter affecting Israel,

I'll hear. But I vote just the way I want, and people know it, so they don't bother me much. One of my best friends out there is the top rabbi; we were in the reserve forces together and we used to serve together.

My being half Jewish led to a joke during the campaign in 1964. But it wasn't me; it was my brother. He was playing golf with Bob Hope. They went up to some course on the Hudson River and brother Bob signed his name and the pro said, "Oh, I'm sorry, Mr. Goldwater, but you can't play here. We don't allow Jews to play." Bob reportedly said, "Well, can I play nine holes? I'm only half Jewish." I knew my brother wasn't that smart. This fellow used to be on the radio — he had a show, "Can You Top This?" He knew the origin of every joke. So I met him once and we were talking and he said, "You know, there are only seven basic jokes." I said, "All right, did you ever hear this story?" And I told it to him. He said, "Yeah. That was first heard when they were building the Temple of Solomon. And the Gentiles would come over with their aprons on and say, 'Can I work? I'm half Jewish.'" I don't know where my brother heard it, because I get credit for it and he's the one who told it. I still hear it. People will kid me. Even today I'll go out to dinner with good friends of mine and they'll have ham and they'll say, "Go ahead, Goldie, you can eat it; just eat half of it." It's all kidding.

Alex Singer, sixty-five, independent oil and gas producer, Tulsa, Oklahoma

My father and uncle looked for a town that was on the railroad that didn't already have a scrap dealer there.

I can't recall who started the program, some time around 1907, of bringing Jews in through Galveston, Texas, because they were stacking up on the East Coast. It was one of the early-day philanthropists. In any event, my uncle came, and he, just like many or most immigrants, went to where they had family, or landsleit. He went to Wichita, Kansas, where he had been preceded by some people from his village area. He left a wife and a child in Russia. The history has been repeated; everybody you talk to, you hear the same story.

Then he sent for my father, who was the next older brother. And my father and my aunt and my cousin, who was a young child, came next. And they worked, I guess in a packing house first. There were some junk dealers there. They worked in the scrap business. Then they started looking. Sixty years ago, every town through this part of the country that was on the railroad had a Jewish junk dealer. My relatives happened to end up in Enid, Oklahoma. They later brought over their younger brother and then they got their father out in 1914. They didn't get their mother out until after World War I, about 1920.

There were eight or ten Jewish families in Enid when I grew up there. There were two or three, four, merchants. Some of them are still there, as a matter of fact. Enid was a small town; it's not a very big town now, maybe fifty thousand. Probably in those days it was fifteen or twenty thousand. I lived there until the sixth grade. Enid had no synagogue. It used to be standard that we would get in the car on Sunday and drive to a town seventy-five or a hundred miles away to visit with other Jewish immigrants that lived in the small towns. We used to go to Ponca City; we used to go to Blackwell. Then, later on, from Oklahoma City we used to drive down to southern Oklahoma. We had family down there in Duncan. And the people got together.

My father and mother — I have a younger sister and brother — moved to Oklahoma City in 1930. Oklahoma City had a larger Jewish community. They had an organized Jewish community with both a synagogue and a temple. When we moved to Oklahoma City there was a big oil boom on. The Oklahoma City field was being developed at that time, and that was one of the reasons. There were additional business opportunities for my father in Oklahoma City. We moved into a neighborhood and rented a house in what was, I'd say, a largely blue-collar neighborhood. The kids in the neighborhood called me "Jew." Their parents did. We lived there a year or so; something like that. I don't remember ever having been particularly offended by it. I thought about it later, but I was the only Jewish kid they knew, I guess. That was my name.

There was a progression that happened all through the Southwest, not just in Oklahoma. A lot of Jews went in the scrap business, and they went in, I suppose partly, just like Greeks going in to restaurants: because other Greeks are in restaurants. And the Chinese have done the same thing. Of course, one of the big things in the junk business was you needed very, very little capital. You could save up $200 or $300 and become a peddler and get into the business. They were buying scrap, and in these areas, they were buying oil field scrap. Oil men didn't have machine shops to join a pipe that had a thread busted on it. They just threw it in a scrap yard. Then the scrap dealers started recovering usable materials from the junk pile and then they started buying abandoned leases to salvage the materials and they went more into the pipe business. Then, when they were buying an abandoned lease, there would be a well or two maybe that would still produce small amounts. So instead of plugging that well, they would go ahead and produce it. They would do the work themselves and they would keep their costs down and it could still be done profitably.

And so there was a progression from the scrap business to the pipe business to the oil business, and it was repeated many, many, many times all over this area. That, essentially, is the story of how my family got in the business, and they have been in the oil business for over fifty years at this point. Now, the next generations are being raised as engineers and geologists, and some with Harvard law degrees.

Ralph Schoenfeld, seventy-five, retired furniture store executive, Seattle, Washington

I would say a pioneer was anybody here before the State of Washington was a state, when it was a territory. It became a state in 1889. The start of the temple here in Seattle was 1899, and my grandfather and his oldest son — I was named after his oldest son, Ralph — they were founding members.

My grandfather on my father's side landed in Baltimore in 1848. He was eight years old. He was sent over here by his parents to avoid being drafted into the German army — not at the age of eight, but later on. They wanted to get him to America, and they sent him over to Baltimore because he had an aunt and uncle living in Baltimore. He came alone on the ship, an eight-year-old boy.

Louis K. Schoenfeld went to school in Baltimore, and when the Civil War started he was twenty years old and tried to enlist in the Union Army. The Union Army would not take him because his aunt and uncle had Confederate leanings. He couldn't stay in that area, being a man of fighting age, and so he went west. Just how he got west, I really don't know. Talking it over with other family members, we presume that he came over on covered wagon. He got a job on a boat on the Sacramento River and he worked on the river for a year or so and then heard of silver mine strikes in Virginia City, Nevada. So he went to Virginia City, and in 1864 he opened a small furniture store there.

There was a Jewish settlement of some kind in Virginia City. If you ever heard of the Myron Frank Department Store in Portland, Oregon, the Franks had a store in Virginia City at that time. My grandfather was married there in 1869 to a Jewish woman. A particularly good Jewish friend of mine used to remind me, "Now, remember, your grandmother and grandfather were married in my grandmother and grandfather's house in Virginia City, Nevada."

I should go back to 1864, when my grandfather opened his store; he opened it next door to what was then the *Territorial Enterprise*. You know that Sam Clemens — Mark Twain — was a feature writer for the *Enterprise*. Sam was a bachelor and my grandfather was a bachelor and they were approximately the same age and they became very good friends. My grandfather used to tell how in the afternoon, every once in a while, Sam would come to the store. There were always a few fellows gathered around the potbelly heater, and Sam would spin yarns there. They became lifelong friends and they kept in touch. Sam evidently had no money the last fifteen years of his life and he was on lecture tours and that's how he made a living. And he came through this area — Seattle, Bellingham, and so on — and my grandfather met him at the train and took good care of him. This was just three or four years before both of them died, in the same year, 1910.

My grandmother Hannah Hyman was born in Columbus, Ohio. How she got to Columbus, Ohio, I don't know. Sorry I never asked her. Just never thought of it. I never knew my grandfather. I was born about two months before he died. I don't know how her family got to Virginia City, either. The population of Virginia City then was a strong fifteen thousand, and San Francisco had a population of about thirty-five hundred. So Virginia City was a much bigger and more important city at that time than San Francisco was. Then, of course, when the mines gave out around 1878, thereabouts, why then Virginia City emptied out. They had a great fire there in the early 1870s, and that was about the height of Virginia City. My grandfather Louis's four children were born in Virginia City, including my father, Herbert, who was born there in 1874.

The family stayed on after the fire. I think they left in 1878. The town just went downhill when the mines gave out. They went to San Francisco and my grandfather opened a furniture store there. He was there for about a year or so, down the street next to the May Company. Should have stayed there. But he didn't. He heard about the new mining strikes in Tombstone, Arizona, so he took the family and they all went to Tombstone. He opened a furniture store in Tombstone. It was the Schoenfeld-Hyman Furniture Company; he and his brother-in-law were together. After they were there for a couple of years, why they realized there was need of a furniture store in Phoenix, so they opened a furniture store in Phoenix. That was also the Schoenfeld-Hyman Furniture Company.

My father died in 1933. My mother died in 'thirty-one. Fortunately, my father for a number of years always spent the winter in California. He was staying by himself in 'thirty-two. That was the first winter that he was there that he was a widower. I went down there just to keep him company. He said, "I'll tell you what I'd like to do. I'd like to just drive down to San Diego, and if I feel like it, let's go over to Tombstone." Fortunately, he felt like it.

We got to Tombstone. My father had always kept up correspondence with two or three of his school chums. One was a lady who ran a boarding house, and we stayed in her boarding house. One of his chums was the postmaster in Tombstone. I remember going into the post office and they were so happy to see each other and so on, and my father said, "I'd just like to go into the Bird Cage Theater," and the postmaster said, "I have the key to it, and here's the key. You go and take your son into the Bird Cage." We went into that Bird Cage Theater and it's just like you see in the movies. You walk in and here was a big asbestos screen. At the bottom of it, it said the elevation of Tombstone, like they used to say on the screens. Here, from the stage, were steps going into the side boxes, because the girls would go up those steps into those side boxes; and down in the main seating area there were not chairs, there were benches. Nothing had been changed in that Bird Cage Theater since the day it was opened, evidently.

Then my father said, "We have to go out to Boot Hill Cemetery." If my father hadn't known where Boot Hill Cemetery was, we never could have found it, because it was completely grown over with brambles. He finally found a tombstone. He says, "This is it here." I understand the cemetery's been restored now.

The old furniture store was long gone. He closed it when he left the area — he was in Tombstone for about four years, I would guess. He took me to the house they lived in. The house was on Toughnut Street. It was right across from the county building, where Wyatt Earp's office was. My grandfather and Wyatt Earp became good friends. After all, he was the marshal, and my grandfather was a businessman in Tombstone, right across the street from his office. My father used to tell the story about this particular gang that came through and shot up the city, shot up Tombstone. A bunch of the boys put on their guns and went out to get them. They never heard from the posse again. They don't know whether the gang got them or the Indians got them. Then he told of another incident, where they rounded up desperadoes. He said seven of them. And they took them over across the street — the gallows were still there when I was there with my father — and hung them all on the gallows. My father always told the story about the leader. Asked if he had any last words, he said, "Yes, boys. Please don't riddle my body with bullets," because evidently that was the habit in those days; when they hung somebody, the boys would all take a shot at the body after it was hung.

You know that Wyatt Earp had his two or three real good friends and Doc Holiday was one of them. Doc Holiday was a dentist. My grandmother always said, "Doc Holiday ruined your grandfather's teeth." But Doc Holiday could handle a gun as well as any of them. When Wyatt Earp needed a little help, he always called on him, along with two or three of his cronies. Evidently he had no money to pay deputies on a regular basis. My grandfather never packed a gun. He was just an ordinary citizen.

When I was in Tombstone with my father he showed me the Can-Can

Restaurant — you know, of course, the can-can girls — and I still remember on the roof there it was: CAN-CAN. This was 1932. CAN-CAN was still there but there was a broken part of the glass and the word RESTAURANT was almost obliterated. And the O.K. Corral. He showed me where it was and Fly's Photography Studio. I have, in my office, several pictures of my family taken at Fly's. I mean Fly's was so famous and all, and here I have pictures from Fly's.

The mines petered out in Tombstone. When my grandparents moved out, they then went to San Diego. Gold hadn't been discovered in Alaska yet, but evidently there was a big movement towards Alaska in the late 1880s. My grandfather and his oldest son came to Seattle and looked around and my grandfather opened a furniture store in Seattle in 1888. Then he sent to San Diego for the rest of the family.

The great fire of Seattle was June 6, 1889. The whole downtown burned down at the time, including my grandfather's furniture store. He operated out of a tent for six to eight months. I remember running across a packet of letters from furniture manufacturers and suppliers in the East, all writing him, saying, "Whatever we can do, please call on us and we'll send you whatever furniture you want to get started again." It was after the fire; a ship was on its way with a consignment for my grandfather. This is how he renewed his furniture and started the store again.

John Franco, seventy-seven, restaurateur, Seattle, Washington

I have been quite a few different things, but a large part of my life has been spent in the restaurant business here in Seattle. I also graduated from law school in 1933 and practiced law for two and a half years, so I have degrees in liberal arts and law. With the exception of one-quarter at Stanford, I spent the rest of the time here at the University of Washington.

My father had kicked around through the whole Levant as a jack-of-all-trades from the time he was eleven to the time he was twenty-one or twenty-two. He spent a lot of time in Istanbul and Smyrna, which was Izmir at that time, and Makri in Greece. Then, he returned to the Island of Rhodes and he established a grocery store. He was one of the few independent businessmen there at the time. That is nowhere near as great as it sounds, because business was sparse and earnings were low. At that time, Rhodes had a thriving Jewish population. In fact, the population of the island was almost equally divided then between the Sephardic Jews, the Greeks, and the Turks. The Turks and the Jews always got along fairly well, because in those days the Ottoman Empire was very protective of Jews. So the Turks would vent most of their fighting proclivities on the Greeks.

My father came to Seattle after the first ones of our Sephardic community in Rhodes had come in 1903. They had heard about Seattle because some-body they ran into on the boat or at some port advised them, so long as they were going to America, to just go farther west and that Seattle would be the greater land of opportunity for them.

I was born on the Island of Rhodes in 1909. A few months after I was born, my dad immigrated to this country with a first cousin of his. When he acquired enough funds he sent back to Rhodes for my mother and me. She came here in 1910 with me in her arms and her younger brother by the hand.

According to my mother, Ellis Island was all confusion. Don't forget, here you have a young mother with a year-old baby and an eight- or nine-year-old brother, not knowing a word of English, coming to a strange country. The people there at Ellis Island helped her. It's amazing. I have talked so often with other Jewish fellows at the Glendale Country Club, and a lot of them tell stories about how their parents and uncles and relatives had come through Ellis Island. Harry Brown, someone I know pretty well: man's coming through the immigration and the fellow says, "What's your name?" And the fellow says whatever it is in Russian. "What does that mean?" he asks him. "That's brown in Russian." "Okay, your name is Brown." Boom. Next one, see. And after all, what could these people tell you? They couldn't speak the language; they didn't know what people were saying.

My father's name was Marco, which biblically is Mordecai. My name is John Franco but my biblical names are Moses Jacob. My mother's maiden name was Mossafer. She was from Rhodes. Her father was a Hebrew teacher there. He had a private school. My dad was very fluent in Greek and Turkish and spoke some Arabic. As a matter of fact, voluntarily he was official interpreter for the Turkish and Greek consulates here. My dad never had a day of formal education until he had been in this country for some time and went to school for his naturalization papers. At home, I spoke Ladino.

Do I remember magic potions from Rhodes being used in Seattle? Oh, yes, vividly. My younger brother Albert, when he was about three years old, contracted diphtheria and he was near death. One night my maternal grandmother and I went a block and a half away to Collins Playground, near our house on Fifteenth and Yesler which was, at that time, the greatest concentration of the Orthodox people. By the light of a full moon, the two of us washed the whole sidewalk around there with what my grandmother said was consecrated water. They believed that you should scrub the area where something could have happened; in this case, that's why we were there, because my grandmother insisted that he got an infection from playing around the wading pool. Of course, we tried to tell her diphtheria is not that kind of an infection.

I remember that to this day just like it happened yesterday. I was about ten years old at the time, see, and my brother was miraculously healed. Of course, Dr. Houston was one of the finest doctors in Seattle.

There are practical things, too, like they believed that onion poultices could heal anything, and I could tell you a story that happened during the war where I saved a guy's life just with onion poultices, as laughable as it seems. Out in the middle of the Indian Ocean, and I was a pharmacist's mate, and I watched that poison just keep on coming up, coming up, coming up, until it got to his elbow, and I just had given him what I had. At that time, you only had sulfadiazine and sulfathiazol and a little bit of penicillin, which you didn't know how to use. In desperation we just happened to flag down a huge navy tug in the middle of the ocean that had a big bin up on its bridge full of onions — fresh onions. We traded them a bunch of magazines for onions, and I made a huge onion poultice for this Texan. I just took a great big huge dishtowel and these onions and bashed them good, and then wrapped them up — and it worked.

In the early 1900s it was very divided in the Seattle Jewish community. The so-called Reform Jews or the German Jews — let's put it that way; that's how they were referred to at that time — came here much earlier. They were established in both the social and economic community. Already, they were people of means. The next batch that started to come over were the people fleeing the pogroms, largely from Russia and Eastern Europe. Then the third and last were the Sephardic Jews.

Both groups looked down on us initially. But oddly enough, in 1915, when my father and others were going to build a synagogue, the people who were the most generous — as a matter of fact, they practically funded the whole thing — were the people in the German Jewish community. They were very helpful. They had it made and they were very helpful to the people that were coming up. Actually, this was really typical of all immigrants in those early days. I don't care whether it was the Norwegians or the Serbs or Germans, Estonians, whatever. The people that came here first and got established and made a couple of bucks always gave a hand up to the newer immigrants. This is something you don't find anymore. And I certainly criticize some very good friends in the black community just for that. I've told them, "The trouble with the black community is when you guys make it, as bankers and lawyers and doctors, then you forget all about the others." But what made this country great is that the people who were here first, and made a buck or two, helped the new people.

Considering the fact that most of these people were penniless, uneducated, it was amazing that they were able to bring so many vital things with them and develop them here. Certainly they didn't really have the Near East or Oriental cast to them. Gradually, you know, they worked away from it.

But in the earlier years, even the architecture of the synagogue reflected that Byzantine architecture. That's gone now. Eventually they built a new synagogue over by Seward Park, which is one of the wealthier areas. In fact, both Sephardic Bikur Cholim and Ezra Bessaroth are in the same area, three or four blocks from each other. The Sephardic Bikur Cholim is much more traditional. Ours is very *avant-garde* as far as the architecture is concerned.

We had two Sephardic communities, really. We had the Sephardic community that came from Rhodes and three or four of the close islands of that archipelago in the Aegean Sea. They are the Jews from the Island of Kos, from Leros, those islands. Those people and the people from Rhodes — call them Rhodesians, except that has an African connotation — those people actually considered themselves a cut above the ones that came from Marmara in Turkey and Makri in Greece and those places. In my lifetime, I've concluded that the worst anti-Semites are the Jews themselves.

Now we have quite a few synagogues here, and there are sects. So that brings me to a partial answer as to the division of the community. Year by year, as people got accustomed to each other, there was a little more cohesion in the Jewish community as a whole. But those thoughts persisted for a long time. In 1926, I entered university with Charlie Alhadeff. We were the first Sephardic Jews to be pledged to a Jewish fraternity — Zeta Beta Tau. There were other Jewish fraternities, and one had been formed just three, four years before — Sigma Alpha Mu — but this was considered the elite fraternity, because that's where all the German Jews were. Well, here is your great anti-Semitic story. I'll be damned if we weren't blackballed by a member or two in the Stanford chapter of the fraternity, so we were kicked out of the fraternity because we were Sephardic. They wouldn't stand for Sephardim. That made the national newspapers.

It was considered in those days almost as bad for a Sephardi to marry an Ashkenazi — more for an Ashkenazi to marry a Sephardi — as it was practically for one to marry a shiksa. But it did happen once in a while. In those days for someone in the Reform community who belonged to the Temple de Hirsch to marry either an Ashkenazi or Sephardi absolutely wasn't heard of. I would say that it wasn't until really in the late twenties here — because it was after I entered university in 1926; it must have been very close to the end of the third decade — we started to get a couple of marriages between Ashkenazim and Sephardim. That, I think, broke the ice enough so that then you started getting somebody from the temple marrying somebody from the other side of the tracks, you might say.

I married a Jewish girl and our marriage was annulled after two months. Well, then I turned around a year later and I married a Gentile girl. My dad and mother just wouldn't talk to me anymore. I'd see my dad every day in business, this and that. He would have nothing to do with my children, and it wasn't until after I went away during the war and came back in January of 1946 that things had softened up a little bit.

But that was 1935 when I got married the first time and it was annulled and it was in 1937 when I got married to the non-Jewish girl. At that time my family's attitude was the prevalent one, although, oddly enough, some of the most prominent Jews in the German Jewish community, at the Temple de Hirsch, were married to non-Jewish people. Many years later, as it started to become acceptable, then the rabbis got into the act with the conversion. At that time, they wouldn't even talk to me. Even if you asked them about a conversion — "Will you marry us if she agrees to convert?" — forget it.

We were Orthodox. We have an Orthodox Sephardic synagogue, the Ezra Bessaroth. And then, oddly enough, the other group still maintains their synagogue, which is called the Sephardic Bikur Cholim. Now, the Ashkenazim have a Bikur Cholim also. It's getting more and more difficult to keep these Orthodox communities afloat for financial reasons. The Sephardic community is shrinking in this regard — as far as its capital wealth is concerned, not numerically. But the synagogues are basically supported by really a handful of people of means. The younger people do not have the same commitment, as far as I'm concerned. I'm a Jew because I'm a Jew, and I would never have any thought about leaving Judaism, because what the hell for? If there is another Holocaust, they'll come for me just as they'll come for you. This is my attitude: I was born a Jew and I'll die a Jew. But a lot of the younger guys, they waver. It's so easy to slip out, see, when you are totally rejected by all the golf clubs and all the clubs and everything else.

I was in Port Said at the end of the war, and the commandant of the United States Coast Guard base there was a friend of mine from Seattle. He wanted to fly me over to the Island of Rhodes in a PBY, but I'd gotten very ill in leaving India and just didn't feel up to it. I'm very happy now that I didn't, because it would have been a very traumatic experience for me to go to Rhodes at that time, which would have been November 1945, and find out what happened to all my relatives. I didn't know anything about it until I got back to this country.

They all were rounded up and taken to Auschwitz and they died in the gas chambers there, every single one of them, with the exception of my first cousin Morris, who was in Uganda working for an Italian importer.

Stephen Anthony Zellerbach, fifty-nine, businessman,
San Francisco, California

I'm a fourth-generation Californian.

My great-grandfather's brother came to California in the latter part of

1848, and his younger brother, my great-grandfather, came about 1850 or 1851. Both of them were in New York, evidently with their parents. They were teenagers. The only documented whereabouts of a Zellerbach in that period were of an itinerant peddler named Zellerbach who was killed in a robbery outside of Philadelphia. This was in the 1840s. The chances are he was a relative. They were all from Bavaria.

My great-uncle came to California first and then sent for his younger brother. To the best of my knowledge, neither of them was in the gold-mining business. They lived in a town called Moores Flat, which is north of the Yuba River. My great-grandfather married Theresa Wolff, also reputedly Bavarian Jewish. They had two children up in the gold country — my grandfather and his older brother, Jake, obviously Jacob. My great-grandfather moved with his two children and his wife to San Francisco in the early 1860s. We have, again, documented evidence that he went into the stationery and paper business with a man named Adolph Falk. They officially opened an establishment on Commercial and Sansome streets in 1869. Adolph Falk committed suicide, and that left my great-grandfather with the business.

In the meantime, my great-grandparents, Anthony and Theresa, had seven children. One of them was my grandfather. His name was Isadore, and Janet Baruh was my grandmother. She was born in Nevada City, which is about forty miles from Moores Flat. Her parents were in the dry goods business. In fact, his yacht, the *Janadore,* was named after his wife Janet and himself. That was, and to this day is, the largest yacht that's ever been owned and berthed in San Francisco Bay — built during the 1930s by the Union Ironworks in the Great Lakes.

I never did tell you what Anthony and his brother Marks were doing in Moores Flat. Marks was a quote banker unquote. One says that with tongue in cheek. He was a usurious lender, obviously. He made a lot of money. Anthony obviously didn't, and Marks didn't share the wealth. He went back to Germany and left his nephew, who he'd imported from Germany, in charge of his business. His nephew robbed him royally, which left Marks with hardly a thing. Marks ended up living in San Francisco with his girl friend, very close to my grandfather. They used to play pinochle, et cetera.

Back to my line. Anthony started out as a paper peddler. He'd buy job lots of paper from the two major companies in San Francisco in those days and sell it to printers. Somewhere along the line he ran into Adolph Falk. All during this time he was having more children to support. They were ambitious people. After they'd been here about ten years, both Jake and my granddad went to work in the paper business with him. My granddad and Jake, I understand, both got out of high school, and that was the end of their education. One can reasonably assume that they started working when they were twelve or thirteen. My granddad signed, in essence, my great-grandfather's name in order to get a building built on the corner of Battery and Jackson streets, which was the first multistory building completed after the earthquake and fire. My great-grandfather would have never borrowed money to build the building. He and a fellow named Marvin Higgins — Irish, not Jewish at all, but a financial genius — ran a numbers game on the side, which was perfectly legal in those days. They did this in order to make a little extra money to help build this paper business.

They had actually built the foundation of the building prior to the earthquake. After the earthquake, my granddad went out and got an old California Street cable-car cable and had them wrap it around the foundation of that building to reinforce it even more in case there was another earthquake. Then they proceeded to make the biggest mistake, which was to build it out of brick. It was a six-story building. Originally it was A. Zellerbach and Sons. This was the period when my granddad took over running the business, right around the turn of the century, and built it into Crown Zellerbach Corporation.

There was a company called Crown Willamette Corporation, which had originally been formed by a merger of Crown Paper Company and Willamette Paper Company, both from the Northwest. They were having problems in the 1920s; my granddad needed more paper to sell, and a fellow named Louis Block, whose family is still in the area as well as in New York, was chairman of the board. He became chairman of the new corporation, called Crown Zellerbach Corporation, when they merged in 1928. So that's how they really got into the manufacturing business in a big way. They already had a couple of mills.

My granddad would lend money to everyone and his brother, but he wouldn't give money to charity — that type. When he died, Crown Zellerbach Corporation had to write off God knows how many thousands of dollars of debt.

My dad joined the business after graduating from the Wharton School. He graduated in 1918. He went to the University of California, too. He married my mother, who was from Cleveland and whom he met while he was back there. And there is today a Zellerbach Theater in the Annenberg Center at the University of Pennsylvania, thanks to my dad, as there is at the University of California, thanks to my dad and to my grandmother. He and my uncle J.D. took over from my granddad and really took it from a fairly substantial company to an international company, from 1941 through the beginning of the 1960s, really not that long a period of time. My uncle passed away in 'sixty-three; they'd both been retired from active management for a couple of years at that point. I worked there for thirteen years.

The corporation got split into two major parts a couple of months ago, the timber and corrugated-container business going to Sir James Goldsmith, a raider, and the paper-manufacturing business and distribution and packaging business to James River Corporation, Richmond, Virginia. My nephew still works for Zellerbach Paper Company. My brother retired last year when all this nonsense started; he was ready to retire anyway.

My granddad, of all of Anthony's children, was the only one to have male issue. He had two sons. All the rest had either girls or no children. Jake had no children. Henry had three daughters, all of whom are still living. Henry's final home was one block from here, across the street. They all lived in this area over the years — Pacific Heights — after they got money. Eugene, known as Barney, was the wild man in the family, who had numerous girl friends and evidently a number of illegitimate children, none of whom have surfaced with the name of Zellerbach. Isadore had two sons, my uncle James David, my dad, Harold, and one daughter, Claire: those were his three children. Bella Cross, her married name, had no children. She was the best of the three girls. She enjoyed the symphony, the opera, and the ballet. We used to always see her, and when she was a little old lady she'd come by herself and sit in the last row at the San Francisco Opera House. She was just a love. Hazel had one daughter, who lives in Los Angeles.

Then we have Lillian. Lily lived in Paris most of her life until World War II. She came back to San Francisco, lived in a suite at the Palace Hotel, had a big maroon Rolls-Royce. She used to go driving through the park every day. She would never talk to any of us in the family. I think there was probably a great deal of resentment over my grandfather, because he's the only one who ever made money, and he made them all rich. I actually met her once, and that was at Hazel's funeral. I said, "Aunt Lily, I'm Stephen," and she turned her head and wouldn't say anything to me. But at least I met her once in my lifetime. Curious woman. *Eccentric* is really a good word for her. She had no issue; left all her money to charity. She wouldn't be nice enough to give it back to the rest of the family, where it came from.

That was typical of my grandfather. He made every single one of his brothers and sisters wealthy in their lifetime, and he kept Jake and Henry working for him all their lives. In fact, Henry was still working at the Zellerbach Paper Company when I had my first job there, waiting to go into the service in 1945. I don't recall when he passed away, but it wasn't very long after that.

Isadore was the one who made the money and had the male issue. He was the business genius in the family. He was Jewish, but not a real practicing Jew. He never ducked his Jewishness. None of that generation ever ducked their Jewishness. His mother-in-law and father-in-law, his wife's family in Nevada City, kept a kosher household during the Gold Rush, if you can imagine. They had a separate kitchen in the basement. That house is now a California State historical landmark in Nevada City. They used to have services, but no synagogue, in Nevada City. To this day, it's not a very big town. One assumes they got their food from Sacramento, which, as you know, was "the city" in California for many years.

My grandfather probably belonged to Temple Emanu-El, which is typically German Jewish Reform. My father was very active here in the temple. He was president of it forever. In fact, I went rabbi hunting with him on one trip, which was rather fun. We went all over the country — New York, Cincinnati, Cleveland, you name it.

Did the others maintain their Jewishness at all — Bella, Hazel, and Lillian? I don't really know. I can't honestly answer that question. They may well have, but I don't know. Lily probably not; Barney probably not. My grandmother, very much so. I'm chairman of an organization called, rather grandly, the Commission for the Preservation of Pioneer Jewish Cemeteries and Landmarks. We own six cemeteries up in the mother lode — Jewish cemeteries which had been neglected for years and years. These are in the communities like Nevada City, Grass Valley, Mokelumne Hill, Sonora, Placerville.

The Jewish communities weren't big — maybe fifty, sixty, seventy headstones. Most of the headstones are gone. A good story is the Nevada City cemetery. An old fellow named Wanamake owns the property through which you have to go to even get to the cemetery. One day he went out and found this man with a pickup taking the headstones. The man said he was building a patio and he loved these marbles with hieroglyphics and he was going to use them for steppingstones. Mr. Wanamake said, "No, you're not, and put them back." Eventually, just in the last twenty years, we've put fences around the cemeteries. We take Sunday school classes up there every summer from various temple youth groups to keep them cleaned up. The cemeteries are open to the public, but people have to go to the local fire station, for example, to get a key. Almost all of the graves are of German Jews, as a matter of fact.

Growing up Jewish in San Francisco is so different, I suspect, from growing up Jewish anywhere else in the United States, because you don't have a real Jewish consciousness. I didn't realize what being Jewish was until I left the West Coast. My first realization . . . I'd read about and heard about anti-Semitism, if that's one of the things necessary to realize what being Jewish is. I guess it is, but never had I experienced it in San Francisco. There was no consciousness about Jews as such, certainly not in my world in San Francisco, not growing up here. It wasn't until I went in the navy, and subsequently to Swarthmore, outside of Philadelphia, that I realized what anti-Semitism really was; how pervasive it was in this country. Not in the

West. Probably because San Francisco was a very young, affluent community, a community that was very polyglot, which it still is, and hadn't
had time to form the necessary base to develop the bigotry needed for well-
established anti-Semitism, or anti-anything, other than Indian, of course. I
think it was true about Chinese, Japanese, everyone.

We had a Christmas tree and we had presents, but we also lighted a
menorah every year — the duality of it. Raising children here was very
difficult to do without recognizing that Christmas existed. I guess my parents
decided they didn't want us to feel that different. If you want to talk about
the religious aspects of living here, my real introduction to getting involved
with the religious aspects was when I got involved with the rabbi's daughter —
a Conservative rabbi's daughter, whom I married. Prior to that, I didn't
know what kosher was. Friday night was no different than any other night.
We used to have Passover service. We'd even have the rabbi over to conduct
Passover service at our home — the dinner and the whole number. We'd
all go to temple on the High Holidays. I went to Sunday school and was
Bar Mitzvahed in the temple; lots of penknives and pens. I almost flunked
Hebrew. I didn't know what Zionism was from Confucianism, not in the
1940s. It wasn't until the real momentum got going in Palestine to create
Israel that I was even cognizant of it.

I never knew what a bagel was until I went east. I never saw a bagel in
San Francisco. There was no such thing as a kosher-style delicatessen here.
I didn't know what pastrami was until I went to New York as a youngster
after the navy. I had my first pastrami sandwich, and it was love at first
sight. The first Yiddish I ever heard began with my in-laws. There were
words used, like he's a shnook, but no Yiddish. There was a ghetto in the
McAllister Street area of San Francisco where the Eastern European Orthodox kosher Jews lived. The German Jews were everywhere, mainly where
the nice people lived, if you know what I'm saying.

All my friends, many of them still very much alive, were a complete
mixture. East European Jews and German Jews and non-Jews, lots of non-
Jews, because those were the people I went to school with. In terms of family
image, I made the ideal marriage, my first marriage, marrying the rabbi's
daughter, German Jewish, born and raised in San Francisco. That was
definitely image. Going to work in the paper business was image — my
parents' image of what I should be. I'm now on my third wife, who's of
Italian extraction, and the best wife by far of all. I've told a lot of people
that. I'd even tell my first wife, who lives right over here. I have one son,
with my first wife, with a grandfather who's a rabbi. He should get away?
He gave thought to becoming a rabbi at one point. He's a very serious good
student, graduated magna cum laude and Phi Bete from Brandeis. He gets
his brains from his mother, obviously.

Is growing up a Zellerbach burdensome? Not really. It's only burdensome in that my family really didn't have any money until the 1930s. Income tax was very much in existence in those days. They built the business by selling stock to the public, so the family never had a substantial position in Crown Zellerbach Corporation. I don't think at any point, even when my granddad was alive, did the family own more than five percent of the company. That's during my lifetime. Because of a well-known name, people always assume that we were like the Hellmanns, the Haases, also German Jewish San Francisco families, who did have many millions of dollars. We've always been very comfortable. In San Francisco we've always been very obvious because of the name. You go into the bathroom and you can see "Zellerbach." A lot of propaganda. Even to this day, people just assume we have money coming out of our ears. I'm sure they assume I sold my vineyard — wine business — simply because I had a good sale and made a lot of money. I didn't sell the wine business because I had a good sale and made a lot of money. I was losing money — the first business in my life I ever lost money in, unfortunately. And I was unwilling to sell more assets to keep it going until we could turn the corner.

There are not that many Zellerbachs. My sister's two girls are married to Jewish men. My son is married to a Jewish girl, which would be natural. My brother has three sons, two of whom are married; neither of the girls is Jewish, but one converted, so the kids are being brought up Jewish. My cousins, one was married and hasn't been for years; that's J.D., who had two sons. He married a non-Jewish girl, and my other cousin married three non-Jewish girls. In terms of male Zellerbachs, there are my brother's three sons, my son, and my cousin Jimmy had two sons. That's the sum total of the male Zellerbachs.

11

Jews in the Middle

MOST JEWS in the small towns of the Midwest are gone or have assimilated to the point of no longer identifying as Jews. They, like other Americans, have migrated to the bigger population centers of the Midwest or have been washed away in the constant waves of opportunity that carry Midwesterners to the coasts. In Columbia, Missouri, for example, I had been told that the Barths were the pioneering Jewish family, so I wandered into Barth's Clothing Company, Incorporated, on the main street, only to learn that the Barths had sold the store in 1936 and that all known relatives had long since left Columbia. The then owner, Jimmy Hourigan, whose father had worked for the Barths, sent me "A Case Study of Pioneer Immigrant Merchants" by the historian Harvey A. Kantor.* I would have loved to interview a Barth.

The founding Barth merchant, wrote Kantor, had owned three female slaves before the Civil War. And as I was to learn several times over from the descendants of pioneer merchant families whom I did interview, the Barths were very typical of the German Jewish immigrant. They began as peddlers; accumulated capital and opened a store; married within the family, often by arrangement; and brought their seed from Europe to be sown in an ever-widening mercantile arc of the original establishment. Nephews and other relatives kept arriving from Germany; as Kantor wrote, "Soon there were clothing stores run by a member of the Barth family in Rocheport, Columbia, Boonville, Mexico, Lamar, and Trenton, Missouri, as well as Atchison, Kansas, and Oklahoma City, Oklahoma."

In describing his years growing up in a small midwestern community, Martin Bucksbaum, a shopping center developer, summed it up by noting:

*Missouri Historical Review 62, 4 (July 1968).

"The religion was the way it was. You had a small synagogue which, at one time, was up over our grocery store. We had a little neighborhood grocery store and you just thought that was the way it was every place. On the holidays they would rent the Eagles' Lodge or the Moose Hall or some large facility and that would become the synagogue for the holidays and that was just life in Marshalltown, Iowa."

The Bucksbaums had no trouble maintaining their Jewish identity. But Dr. Stanley Talpers, who grew up in Casper, Wyoming, said it was difficult, because there were very few Jewish families and no synagogue. For the High Holidays, however, they would get as a rabbi a student from the Hebrew Union Theological Seminary in Cincinnati. "The rabbis thought Casper was a terrific place to come," he remembered, "because Harry Yesness, who was the clothier, would give each rabbinical student a new suit and a cowboy hat and boots."

But this adoring view of Casper was not shared by Dr. Talpers's grandparents, who lived in Denver, almost three hundred miles away. They never traveled to Casper. "It was like going into foreign territory for them," he said. "They lived in a Jewish world, and we lived in a Gentile world, and they really didn't want to step out of their world into our world. We were always expected to go down to Denver."

One aspect of this "Gentile world," Dr. Talpers suggested, was the way Christmas impinged on him and his family. "Christmas," he said, "had a lot of emotional overtones for Jewish people in small towns. Christmastime is when you find out whether you are Jewish or not."

Louise Frankel Rosenfield Noun, seventy-seven, community activist, Des Moines, Iowa

My mother gave each of her three children Frankel as a middle name, because that was her maiden name. As we grew up, we scorned this. We thought she was being very silly about the thing, and then came the feminist movement and I became completely sympathetic with her view of keeping her birth name. Even before my grandfather's death, my uncles — at least one or two of them — had come to Des Moines and started a business. But they still had their business in Oskaloosa. They had a bank down there and a retail business. I guess my grandfather Frankel was pretty successful. As soon as my grandfather died, my grandmother scrammed out of Oskaloosa. She took my mother and my uncle Henry, who was still in his teens then, and they went to Europe for a year and traveled and then came back and settled in Des Moines, where I was born.

My father's family settled in Rock Island, Illinois. There were ten or eleven children in that family. I know my grandfather had a bank down there. I don't know what else he did. My grandparents on my father's side died before I was born or else before I had any memory of them.

The Des Moines Jewish community was very small when I was young — I'm no good at numbers — maybe a few thousand. The Reform Jewish congregation was established around 1885. I rather suspect my grandfather was a charter member of that, even though he lived in Oskaloosa. I have an account of his funeral and there were services, I think, by a Protestant minister in Oskaloosa and then he was buried in the Jewish cemetery by a rabbi here in Des Moines. My grandmother was devoutly Jewish, but not in an Orthodox way. My mother always claimed she was religious, but I'm sure she wasn't. She seldom went to temple, though she sent us all to Sunday school. I always felt she never went unless she thought she ought to. My father went only on the High Holidays.

Was I aware we were German Jewish rather than Russian Jewish? Oh, yes. They were "those" people. "Why were they kosher and why were they so uncouth and why were they so loud?" My mother — in terms of those days I'd call her a strong-minded woman — was on the board of the Jewish Settlement House. She would do for them but not with them. Of course, none of that generation of Russian Jews belonged to the Reform congregation. I suspect they'd have been let in, but they wouldn't give up their practices. It was just one of those things. I married an offspring of Russian Jewish immigrants.

I think my generation was an integrationist generation. If those "other" Jews were just a little nicer, maybe it would make it easier for us. Our friends were both Jewish and non-Jewish. Des Moines was better than Minneapolis. There was a lot more anti-Semitism in Minneapolis than there was in Des Moines. Des Moines was relatively free of anti-Semitism. As I look back now I get a different picture. In high school they had sororities and fraternities, and I longed to belong to a sorority, but there weren't enough Jews to make one and the others didn't accept Jews. There were two or three country clubs. One of them accepted Jews; the other two did not. The most prestigious one didn't, Wakonda.

We always felt as we grew older that this country club rule was — we had good friends that belonged — just a thing that they inherited and they didn't do anything about. Some time after World War II, in the early fifties, there was a move to let Jews into the country club. They had a secret vote on the thing, and all hell broke loose. They voted against letting Jews in. At this point, we knew pretty well which people were for and which were against. The Jews of Des Moines did not take it lying down, which surprised the Gentile community, I think. There were business connections that were severed; just a lot of hullabaloo about it. It was a terrible blow to us, because people that we thought were friends were not.

At that point, I wrote an open letter, which was published in the *Register,* on the Wakonda situation. I think it was the only letter written by a Jew. In general, I said, "What are they really doing, and why are Jews worse than anybody else? Aren't we contributing as much to this community? This is Christmastime, and you better look at your own conscience." After I sent the letter I thought, what have I done? The day that thing was published, my phone rang constantly from other Jews who thanked me for doing it. I heard from one Gentile, as I recall, and she was a woman of German extraction who had known my father and worked around these various houses as a waitress or a cateress. She said, "Mrs. Noun, you should hear what those people are saying at their dinner tables." It was a very interesting experience. My few Gentile friends who were standing on the right side were all right, but in general it just did something for the Jewish community that nothing else did.

I mean that there was a good deal of anti-Semitism here and we shouldn't have been so smug. You know, a lot of it is so subtle. My mother felt the social ostracism. There was a little club of educated women, and my mother really longed to belong to that club. They met and discussed high-minded things, and there was a blackball system and no Jews. That was really the bane of her existence.

We were talking about small towns the other night. At one point, I suppose, there were four or five little towns around Iowa where I had relatives living. I had cousins in Osceola who had a store. I had cousins in Ottumwa who had a store. Relatives in Creston who had a store. Those people, as you say, either assimilated or moved to bigger cities. That generation is all gone. I think probably if you go into those small communities, you might find other Jewish families there, but not those original ones.

It just amazes me about the Jewish families. For instance, my mother, who was born in 1875, wanted to go to Vassar from Oskaloosa. Her father wouldn't let her. He finally let her go to a boarding school in Chicago for a year, the Loring School, which was one of the better schools in Chicago. She remained friends with the people that ran that school for the rest of her life. She did say in later life that she liked Oskaloosa until she got to boarding school. My sister and I were registered at Vassar and Wellesley from the time we were born. Of my generation, my sister went to Vassar, my cousin Helen Frankel went to Wellesley, and another cousin went to Wellesley. They went off to the best schools. It's kind of interesting to me, this desire to really get there.

Now, the men in the family — my mother's brothers — none of them had any higher education. They went right into business. None excepting the youngest. My uncle Henry, who went to college after my grandfather died, went to Princeton in the 1890s, and he was looked down on by his brothers; they thought him effete and cultured. I used to feel sorry for him. He came back to Des Moines and was in business with his brothers.

My mother was a feminist. We pooh-poohed some of her efforts for women, but we always took for granted her support of women's suffrage. Her best friend was Flora Dunlap, who was the Jane Addams of Des Moines. I knew her as a personal friend and somebody who was around the house a lot. She was president of the Iowa Women's Suffrage Association. She was the first president of the Iowa League of Women Voters. Her main work was at a settlement house here. My mother was on that board for years. I asked Mother in later years when I began to be interested in the women's movement, "Did you ever march in a suffrage parade?" She said she wouldn't have had the courage to do that, but she gave Flora $10,000 for the suffrage referendum here in Iowa.

Flora Dunlap came here to head Roadside Settlement, which was not Jewish. But she was instrumental in organizing the first Jewish settlement house in Des Moines. She wasn't Jewish. I can remember vaguely the Jewish Settlement House was in just an ordinary house over in the East Side where the Russian Jewish immigrants were congregated at that time. Then the Jewish community raised money and bought another house and built a pretty good-sized complex, which was the Jewish Community Center for many, many years.

Do I relate feminism to Jewish women? There are two aspects of it. There are a lot of Jewish women who are feminists and who bring to the feminist movement a Jewish point of view. But there is a whole group of Jews who are in it to reform Judaism. They have gotten out a feminist Haggadah for Passover. It should be used more widely. I went to a seder last year and it ended with "now that all men have finished eating." The one this year was better, except that it did use the masculine pronoun all the way through. So I changed it when I did my reading. I changed it to "he or she." I'm not religious, so I'm not interested in that point of view, but I am interested in what these women are trying to do. To get a feminine lesbian group that's Jewish just blows my mind. I think it's wonderful. There are all those things going on within Judaism, as well as all the Jews working in the larger movement. Betty Friedan and Gloria Steinem are good examples of feminist leaders.

My father was a quiet, retiring person whose life was in his business. Mother ran the show with a firm hand. So when I say my family, I guess I mean my mother. She wasn't interested in Jewish affairs really, and so I guess none of us were particularly. As I say, we went through the motions.

We went to Sunday school, and we got confirmed. At that time, I'd never heard of a Bar Mitzvah or a Bas Mitzvah. We didn't have that. I'd never heard of a bris. We went to temple and celebrated seder at temple. We never had it at home. I never can remember lighting candles on Chanukah or doing any of that kind of thing. We had a playroom where we would string red and green streamers and we would hang our stockings, but we were never allowed to have a Christmas tree.

Ethelyn Swartz, eighty-nine, Des Moines, Iowa

I don't have much occupation unfortunately.

My father came as a seventeen-year-old boy by himself from Poland. He came to Des Moines and peddled outside of Des Moines, walking all the way to farms that might have been as far as ten, twenty miles. When he got a few dollars together, he bought a wagon and a horse and peddled that way for some time. He was peddling the items that housewives could use — utensils, needles, thread, yard goods, calico — just useful things. Oftentimes, in fact most of the time, he stayed at the homes of these people where he peddled. I know my family had many friends among these people who would later come to Des Moines and visit at their home. He saved a few more dollars and quit peddling and opened a little grocery store in Des Moines, which didn't last very long because he was inclined to do better than that. So he started in the real estate business, and that's what he continued all of his years.

My grandfather on my mother's side came to Des Moines in 1867. He came from Poland. He brought his family — he had five daughters and one son, but he didn't have enough money for the youngest daughter, so they left her with friends in England until they had enough to get her across. The reason he came to Des Moines was that they wanted a teacher of Hebrew for the young boys that needed to be Bar Mitzvah here in Des Moines. My grandfather got $300 a year in 1867.

The population at that time was very small. I have no idea what it was in the 1860s. By the beginning of the century, I think, there were more than five thousand Jews here in Des Moines. I think there are under three thousand today. I think that there had been some Jews here in the early 1830s. Iowa became a state in 1846. It's an agricultural state. I was asked to talk to, I think it was the Historical Society of Iowa, some fifteen years ago or so about the Jews of Iowa. So I did considerable research at the time plus what I could give them from family incidents. I could find only one Jewish family that was a farm family. There were many Jews that owned farms, but they were absentee farmers. There was one Jewish family that really farmed. I don't know now whether there are farmers there or not, but that was the only one at that time. That must have been around fifteen or more years ago in Iowa. It was the only one that I could locate. There may have been others.

My father was president of the Orthodox synagogue on the East Side where my grandfather went for many, many years. I can remember as a child coming and running down the aisle and jumping in my father's lap as he sat on the bema. But he also always had a membership in the temple from the time it was organized. His reason for it was, he could foresee the time that his children might want the Reform religion. While he never went to the temple himself, the ability of the children to go there was left. And all the children eventually did.

The temple group was made up of German Jews practically entirely. As I say, my father had a membership, but he did not go. I think that there was a sort of aloofness there. Although, you see, by the time I could remember, there was very good feeling between the two groups.

I have loved being Jewish. I really have, for the reason that I can make my Jewishness felt without rancor or anything. It's just that I feel Jewish. It isn't that I'm a particularly good Jew, although I observe the large holidays; it's all the little holidays I don't. I think that we've always been rather faithful members of the temple. I am not anymore, because within the last week I have given up driving. We rarely missed a Friday night going to temple. I enjoyed temple things. I was temple sisterhood president. My husband was brotherhood president. My son-in-law has been president of the present temple. My son is at present the president of the temple. We all feel Jewish.

The sisterhood in the past was really the right arm of the temple. Nothing was done in the temple that the temple sisterhood wasn't a part of. It is less busy, less important today, because of the change of women's work in the community. So it's very hard to even have a good temple sisterhood meeting now. We had a meeting the fourth Tuesday of every month, and generally that Tuesday was reserved by everybody that was a temple sisterhood member. They planned on being a part of it. They worked for it. They took responsibilities for it. We had a sewing group for more than twenty years. We made things that weren't exactly available in the department stores or shops. We sold from there. We made usually $1500, $1800 a year on those things. We gave it to the temple for use in the religious school. Finally, there too people stopped coming. They were too busy or wouldn't take the responsibility of certain areas in the group, and the price of things started rising so much that we could not make the money that we wanted to give to the temple. So it disbanded. We were all getting old anyway.

Simon Bourgin, seventy, writer and consultant,
Washington, D.C.

I was born and grew up in Ely, Minnesota, which today has a population of five thousand, almost the same population it had when I grew up. Ely is an exotic place. First of all, it's at the end of the line. The railway, when it went there, stopped and came back again. Ely is twenty miles from Canada, and all the way up to Hudson Bay there is no city its size. Thousands of Americans know Ely because they go up there to get into the canoe country. Ely is the jumping-off place for it. It's also a funny town. It has about two thousand Finns and another twenty-five hundred Slovenes, and then it has a few Swedes and a couple of Bulgarians. When I grew up there it had five Jewish families. Four of them had clothing stores, and one had a little rundown hotel.

There were two brothers, Mike and Louie Gordon, who each had separate stores. My father had a clothing store. The Rosenblums had another clothing store, and then there were the Bourgins, who had the little hotel and were distant cousins of mine. But the Jewish families did not consort much with the people in the town, who didn't consort with them. They saw each other almost only, and they played pinochle and poker endlessly. And at these poker games they quarreled endlessly. They would all come back again in a week because they had nothing else to do. They all had clothing stores and were competitive and watched who went into each other's store. Some-how they never quarreled about that.

Ely is an iron-mining town. It had among the deepest mines in the world and it was at the eastern end of the Mesabi Range. The Mesabi, of course, was the greatest ore-bearing deposit in the world, and built most of America — iron from Mesabi made U.S. Steel famous. The miners were Finns and Slovenes, and if you worked in the mine, it was known as "working in the hole." If you didn't go away to school, you just took it for granted you were going down into the hole. It was nothing that people looked forward to very much. Because I was middle class and belonged to a family that obviously was not going to send its son down into the hole, I was regarded as sort of special and elite.

My father was born in Lithuania, about twenty miles north of Vilna. He came to the United States, like a lot of others, to avoid military service in the Russian army. He left my mother there pregnant, and went first to Liverpool for a couple of months — the only trade he had was a tailor — then to Brooklyn for a couple of months or maybe a little bit longer. By good fortune — my good fortune — there were two people from his village who somehow had gotten up to northern Minnesota, and he wrote to them. My father took a look around Brooklyn and decided that really wasn't what he had come to America for, and so he went up, to a town called Tower, which is still there and is a tiny village. Ely was twenty miles farther up north.

He came in 1908 and he must have been about nineteen or twenty. My mother followed him about five years later. She said that she had heard nothing from him for several years and thought it was all over and he was undependable. Then came two tickets. I never discussed the emotional problems involved, but the thing I remember most vividly is my mother saying that when she came to Ellis Island she got on a train and she got on a train and she got on a train and she just went on and on and she finally got on the last train and it went obviously from Minneapolis up to Duluth. She couldn't understand what this husband of hers had done. It was the most godforsaken country; nothing but pine trees and boulders and a few lakes. Then when she got to Tower, that was godforsaken enough. In those days, Ely was just really a logging village. The mines had started about fifteen or twenty years before. Tower was a more sophisticated town, actually, even though today it has about two hundred people.

My father started out like a lot of other people. He became a peddler. But he was an unusual peddler in the sense that his customers were unusual. They were Indians who lived in the woods and on Indian reservations, and they were loggers and iron miners. When my father first started out on this, he used to hike between Tower and Ely, twenty miles. There was still no road then. He used to carry all this stuff on his back and sell it on the way, and eventually he made a grubstake enough to open a small clothing store in Ely.

My mother kept a kosher house until a certain event happened. We got our meat by railroad from Duluth, 120 miles away. Cohen, who was the kosher butcher in Duluth, used to send us the very worst meat. It came wrapped in paper and in a burlap sack. It wasn't very good when it started out, and it just got worse and worse. After all, he had a controlled consumer. I used to take my wagon and go down to the depot three blocks away and pick up this package which always was waiting for me with every other train. Even I began to understand that it smelled most of the time. My mother used to do everything but curse. She used to say, "I don't know what we're going to do." Finally, the meat came and it was really bad. So she took this meat and threw it into the garbage can, took off her apron, walked across the street to Grahek's, the butcher. The Grahek brothers had two butcher shops and they were marvelous people, Slovenes, and good friends of ours. My mother went in. He said, "What can I do for you, Mrs. Bourgin?" She said, "I'll have some meat." He looked, and his eyebrows went up. She took the meat back, prepared it, and served it to us. The heavens didn't fall in, nobody got sick, and from then on we ate good meat. The whole kosher thing collapsed.

I went to perhaps six synagogues until I was twenty. The nearest one was in Duluth. There was also one in Virginia, a much smaller town of twelve thousand, fifty miles from Ely. We used to go to Duluth for the High Holidays. We'd drive by car and stay with friends there.

I got a great deal of my Jewishness from my mother's sense of being Jewish. It was a question of having character. You were a Jew because you were different. And, by God, in Ely that was underlined. First of all, my mother wouldn't permit me to bring home any girl who wasn't Jewish. And the only girl in town who was Jewish was about five years younger than I. Because we were pushed together constantly, we despised each other. We were the wrong ages, anyhow. So I could never bring anybody home. That was a real problem for me, because it meant I grew up really with an exaggerated sense of what girls were. I didn't really consort with them. But also you were really made aware that you were Jewish. Kids at school treated me a little bit differently. They knew I was apart from them.

We lived a block from the Catholic church, which was the building that really dominated the whole city. The Slovenes were the largest population. The Yugoslavs were all Roman Catholic and the Catholic church was huge and Father Mahelsic was a real tough priest who ran the church and ran the local population. He made it his business periodically, during catechism, to point out what the Jews were because they killed Christ. I remember my brother Frank coming home once — he must have been twelve or fourteen — and saying, "Mother, they're calling me a Christ killer. What does all that mean?" So you got some of that kind of thing.

My best friend in high school later became a Lutheran minister. We were swimmers, and we went on canoe trips and swam five-mile lakes and that kind of thing. He came to me one day and announced that we couldn't see each other again because his parents decided he was going into the ministry and he couldn't associate with Jews. So that kind of thing shook you up periodically. Then my brother, very early in the game after he began to practice law, decided to run for mayor on an anti–mining company ticket. He felt the mines should do more for the people. There was a lot of populism in the family. During that little campaign in that small town, somebody strung up a banner at the main intersection, saying WATCH OUT FOR JEWS. It caused quite a stir in the town. Pete Schaeffer, who ran the local weekly, then the *Ely Miner* — the masthead of the *Ely Miner,* which still exists, says, "The only paper anywhere that cares about Ely" — ran this editorial saying we can't have that sort of thing in Ely.

I also got my sense of Jewishness from being apart from others, from the fact that everybody knew that I was going to go to the university, and from the fact that the five Jewish families spent time only with each other and not with townspeople. My father had this store, but that really wasn't enough. It really wasn't enough if he was going to save anything and put away some money to educate us. My father began very early to buy furs. The trappers used to bring in timberwolves, regular wolves, red fox, silver fox, martens, mink, weasel, muskrat, in very large amounts. As a matter of fact, I grew up watching my father, and I can still tell a good mink coat from a bad one. My father used snowshoes and he used to go out in the car to various places along the road and then he'd hike in to get furs from these trappers, or else they'd bring them in to our house sometimes. I used to sit in the car reading John Dos Passos, waiting for him to come back.

When the fur factor came in, that was the big time. My mother would get involved with my father then. She was much more aggressive than he was. My father was a very gentle man but firm. My father and mother would talk in Yiddish, and my mother would say, "Raise the price. What are you doing, giving it away?" I was always ashamed of their talking in Yiddish in other people's presence; that bothered me a lot. Sometimes I used to tell them to speak English. I recently saw a picture that opened on a scene with a young Hungarian in New York who answers a phone in a tenement and the first thing he says is "Mom, speak English." I thought I was right back in Ely.

We never had a Christmas tree. Wouldn't even hear of such a thing. As a matter of fact, one of the singular things I remember is how gloomy our home was at Christmas. I remember when I was still a boy, living at the other end of town, in the Slovenian section of town, a girl named Lucille Smith lived upstairs in our house and they had a Christmas tree. I remember she took me up there and it was a wonder of wonders. I wanted to know why we couldn't have one, and my parents just shut me up. I bore a resentment about it for a long, long time. We hardly even discussed Christmas at home. It was the opposite of joy, the mere fact that it occurred. My parents had this sense about Christians that they were no good, that sooner or later they would get you. My mother used to tell me, "You may think that they're all right, but sooner or later you'll learn that you're a Jew." It was that kind of thing. I never had real problems in that regard once I moved away from Ely. But I remember that stigma that stayed.

My father ran the store until he educated all of us, and then he moved away to Virginia, which is this town of twelve thousand, fifty miles north, where my brother David then practiced law. My brother the professor wasn't doing all that well at that point. So my father and my brother started another clothing store that my brother ran in Virginia. It had a big name on it: BOURGIN'S THE FAMILY STORE.

There are no Jews left in Ely. There are almost no Jews left on the iron range. The synagogue closed in Virginia. I think there's still a synagogue in Hibbing, where the singer Bob Dylan comes from. The Jews of Virginia were their own closed clique. The Jews of Eveleth were their own closed clique. Eveleth, another iron-mining town with a Jewish population, was three miles from Virginia. There were two other towns with considerable Jewish populations going northwest in another part of the Mesabi Range. One was Chisholm, and the biggest of all was Hibbing, which had about eighteen thousand and had the biggest open pit mine in the world.

But each community was really by itself. The most singular story that I can tell concerns the fact that all Jews on the iron range, including those in Hibbing, were buried in Duluth, which had the only consecrated Jewish cemetery. In Duluth there was a very large and ornate cemetery for the Reform Jews and then there were two for the Orthodox Jews. One was for the Lithuanian Jews and the other was for the Polish and Russian Jews. They were separated by a stone fence, and no Lithuanian was ever caught dead on the other side of the fence.

My brother Dave, who was a very bright and active lawyer, was a considerable figure in Virginia. My brother was a big contributor to the synagogue. But in time, synagogue activities became primarily social instead of religious. The whole attempt was to keep the kids there by having games and a lot of other folderol. My brother lost his sympathy and ended his contributions, but before that happened, there was this constant succession of funerals up to Duluth, and the same thing happened there that happened with meat from Cohen the butcher. The funeral parlors in Duluth, knowing that people from the range had no other recourse, would schedule them at the end of the day and sell them the worst plots at the most money, and this went on and on. Finally, we all came home from one of those funerals where we buried the person in the dark, and we came back to Virginia and my brother said, "This is enough. I'm going to start a cemetery in Virginia." Virginia had a very nice local cemetery. He went to the city and he got a plot of land and had it consecrated by a rabbi. Then he spread the word among the townspeople. They had a meeting at the synagogue, and everybody decided they would be buried there. The next person who died was buried there. But the next person who died, the family sent him to Duluth. After that, everybody went to Duluth. There was this one Jewish body in Virginia.

I would come home every couple of years and I would say to my brother Dave, "How's your cemetery coming?" He'd say, "I've still only got one Jew." This happened two or three times, and finally I came home and I said, "How's your cemetery?" And he said, "They took my only Jew." The family decided they couldn't afford to leave this poor dead Jew there all alone, so they took him up to Duluth.

One of my brother Dave's best friends was a very successful insurance man, Nate Keller, who was head of the local American Legion. He said to Dave, "Look, Dave, I know that when I die I'm going to have one of the biggest damn funerals this town has ever seen, and I'm going to be buried in your cemetery." Once Nate Keller was buried there, the other Jews fell in line. I was back there recently, and there is a big Jewish cemetery. All the notable Jews from Chisholm and Hibbing and Eveleth are buried there now. The ironic thing is that my brother Dave, who married a Lutheran in a second marriage, began going to the Lutheran church out of deference to his wife — no religious feeling. He was always fairly irreligious, anyhow. By her wish, he was buried in the Virginia cemetery with her mother, who died some time before, away from the Jews. So he's not in his own cemetery.

I told my wife that what I really want is to be cremated and I want my ashes spread by airplane over Burnside Lake, near Ely, which is the most beautiful lake in the world. I spent my youth there. I'll probably wind up at the cemetery in Washington, D.C., in Georgetown at Rock Creek. It's lovely, so we may wind up there. My father's buried in Los Angeles, and my mother in Duluth, and my brother in Virginia. Every time I go back there I shake my head and walk from his grave over to all those Jewish graves.

12

Jewish Mind of the South

THE JEWISH COMMUNITY of every major city I visited in the South seemed to be somewhat different from every other major city I went to in the South. Richmond and Atlanta, New Orleans and Savannah, Charleston and Miami — each different. Charleston's Jewish community, for example, is rooted in its pre-Revolutionary Portuguese and Spanish heritage, old and very proud. So, too, is Richmond's German Jewish community, tightly connected through marriage and a bit of snobbism. New Orleans's Jewish community appears to be more genteel, largely German Jewish, very insular. This was less true, I think, in the smaller communities that still have a Jewish presence.

I came away from interviewing in the South with a definite sense that Jews there enjoyed a celebrity and status in their communities — large and small — that was not true of Jews in the urban ghettoes of the Northeast. In part, this is the result of what the southern Jewish wit and writer Harry Golden once identified as the "philosemitism" that the Protestants of the South, especially the Baptists, had for the children of the Bible. In part too, I suggest, it is because there were far fewer of them, often only a family or two per town, and they rapidly learned to behave southern, so to speak.

There is no doubt that Jews were prominent in the civil rights movement. But there should be no doubt, either, that many southern Jews, particularly those in small towns who felt exposed, went along to get along and were mute. There even was a minority that was vocally segregationist. Charles F. Wittenstein, southern civil rights director for the Anti-Defamation League of B'nai B'rith in Atlanta, explained it:

"The Jewish community in the South felt very vulnerable. The charge was being made that integration was a Communist-Jewish conspiracy to mongrelize the races. Because the Jewish community in the South was so small, it lacked, it thought, the political clout with which to protect itself from the extremists who were selling that party line."

The Jewish community in the South, Wittenstein added, "wanted nothing said and nothing done that would publicly identify Jews with what was a monumentally unpopular cause in the 1950s and 1960s among the people in the South to whom southern Jews related, which is to say the white Anglo-Saxon Protestants."

In Atlanta, he said, he was fortunate in having a small group of Jewish leaders who saw the need to press for racial integration. But, said Wittenstein, "By and large if I went into communities of the South outside Atlanta, the Jewish leadership, including many affiliated with the American Jewish Committee, would say, 'Charles, we just have to stay away from it. It's too dangerous to dabble in desegregation, because if it comes out publicly that we're doing it, it would be a disaster for us.'"

There is a Jewish mind of the South, and it is different from the Jewish mind of the North, and it is intriguing and beguiling.

Cecil A. Alexander, sixty-eight, architect, Atlanta, Georgia

I think one thing that makes Atlanta different, and Jews different in their relationship with blacks, is the fact that most of us grew up with black nurses and black cooks, and there was real love between the two. The blacks don't like to have this recalled very much. It's such a paternalistic relationship, but it's there. I think that's one of the reasons why you did get change in the South; it was a more fundamental change than, say, in the northern or eastern cities or anywhere else, because there was no contact. I grew up in a very strange pattern, I guess. There was a new subdivision called Atkins Park. There were three streets: Saint Charles, Saint Augustine, and Saint Louis. It was a very saintly area. Behind the houses were servants' houses and garages and then there was an alley that went down the middle. In these servants' houses were black families, and they were almost never the blacks who worked for that particular family, because they didn't want to be on call. The man who lived behind me was a deliveryman and he had a magnificent motorcycle. We used to play catch together. He was a good ball player and I loved baseball. He used to take me out to ride on his motorcycle. So I grew up feeling very close to this man, very much a person. And yet I knew he was not "my equal."

When I went off to Yale, my father gave me all sorts of stern instructions about drinking and gambling. He stayed away from "women." I asked him about that to embarrass him. But I remember there was only one black man that I recall at Yale, and he was an art student and had played football, a tall handsome guy. I was out on the campus playing catch with him with a football, and I wrote this home. You would have thought I was going to marry a Hottentot from the kind of response I got from my father. He said that just won't go, that won't do. I went to Massachusetts Institute of Technology one year and there were no blacks there. I went into the marine corps. I was a pilot, and the few blacks I ran into in the service were in an inferior role.

A very telling experience for me was at Harvard. After the war, I came back and got my master's in architecture at the Graduate School of Design, and there was a black in my class who had been in that Tuskegee fighter group that had a spotty record in the beginning, then straightened out and had a very good war record in Italy. I found more in common with him over the fact that we were both pilots than differences over race. Remember, I'd been brought up in a segregated atmosphere. You'd walk the streets of downtown Atlanta; there were no blacks in downtown Atlanta. Their schooling was terrible. They were uneducated people, and they just were not equal to the whites, and that's the way I was brought up. Well, here I discovered a man who had had a similar experience to mine during the war, who was intelligent, who was a damn good architect. We became good friends. We did a problem together; it was an airport.

We lived in Cambridge, and my wife, who came from New Orleans and had studied sociology at Smith, was very encouraging to this sort of opening-up. I would say she had an awful lot to do with it, too, when we came back to Atlanta. She always took people as she found them. Race was at the bottom of her list for evaluating people. Back in the days when it just wasn't being done, we had mixed gatherings at my house and so on. I don't think I ever was or am pro-black. I think what got to me was that I really for the first time read the Constitution and the Declaration of Independence. Of course, I'd studied them. And felt that, damn it, as long as we had what we had in this country, it was a bunch of hypocrisy, and if they'd been any other group, I'd have felt the same way. I also had the strong feeling that when any minority group was being persecuted, it wasn't going to be long before the Jews were going to get it.

Those of us in Atlanta ran into a lot of strong feeling and anger from the Jews in the smaller communities. They said, "You're in Atlanta, you're in an atmosphere where you're protected, but you come out here to Montgomery or Selma or wherever, and we're exposed, and you bastards are putting us out front." Well, all of that stopped when the temple in Atlanta was bombed, because they realized then that we, too, were on the firing line. They never were as comfortable with it as some of the Jews who were in the forefront. The women in Atlanta, both Jewish and non-Jewish, were big catalysts in all of this, in keeping the schools open and seeing to it that Atlanta didn't go the way of Birmingham. They did and said things that their husbands might have felt but were afraid to do and say.

I think it was generally conceded that some Jewish leaders were very much into civil rights and for it. I think it was also known that there were a lot of them who were terribly opposed to the Jews exposing themselves.

The great thing about the 1960s was that those of us who were pro-integration just knew damn well we were right. There are only two times in my life I've absolutely known I was right. One was that period, and the other when I was fighting the Japanese in the Pacific. I only felt I would have been more right if I'd been fighting the Nazis. It was an exhilarating time, you know, and it was a dangerous time. I'd get threats and phone calls and all that stuff.

My father had an attitude, which I sure didn't subscribe to, that a Jew should keep a low profile because he was exposing the whole Jewish community if he had a high profile and did the kind of things I've done. You shouldn't do that. It wasn't safe. The only club he belonged to, that he was active in, was the Civitans, and something called the Bonehead Club. I came across a letter he wrote his mother saying that he'd been offered the presidency of the Civitans; he wrote, "But, of course, I didn't take it." This was because a Jew shouldn't be out front.

I think the Jewish mind of the South is in transition. I think the Jewish mind of the South, when I was growing up, was one that saw the South as a place of some danger, but also a place where if you went along, you got along, and where, particularly in the smaller communities, Jews became "our Jews." And they were different from the rest in a sense, but the Christians in the smaller communities were rather proud of them. I think that fundamentalism, which is nationally new but has been there in the South all this time, had a flip side to it in that the Christians saw the Jews as the keeper of the kingdom. After all, "Jesus was a Jew and this is where the ancient Hebrews might have been misguided at the time Jesus came along. But they were the source of our religion." When the temple here in Atlanta was bombed, one of the things that was very gratifying was this great outpouring of wrath in the Christian community over it. I remember seeing a letter on a dirty piece of paper, very laboriously written, and a crumpled dirty dollar bill from some woman in south Georgia, who said that "anyone who attacks the Hebrews is attacking me, too." It was a very moving little document.

I think the Jews in the South are becoming more and more conscious of themselves as a group, and less and less baseball—apple pie American. This is true all through. The Reform Jews have moved more toward the Conservative. I'm all for the continuation and even the resurrection of the forms of Judaism, because I think they make it alive.

I do have some problems. I think a lot of what passes for Judaism is really Eastern European custom overlaid on Judaism. I think the Jewish mind in the South now is split. There's one group that's intermarrying and wants to move away from Judaism, wants to forget it and all the problems and all the fund raising and Israel. There's another group that's probably got a lot more energy in it; it's heavily identified with Israel, heavily identified with Jewish charities and Jewish causes, and in a sense says, "Okay, so there's a Christian community out there. We'll participate when it serves us to do so." This is one guy's perception. In my own case, I think I've moved toward more concern and interest in Jewish affairs than I had when I was growing up.

Ralph L. Lowenstein, fifty-four, dean of the University of Florida College of Journalism and Communications, Gainesville, Florida

I was born in Danville, Virginia. My grandfather Jacob Berman, like so many people, became a peddler. But his territory was the South, so he would pack the pots and pans and the other stuff and a lot of hard-boiled eggs and borsht and whatever, and he would head south on a southern railroad train.

I look back over the years in perspective and I see my mother growing up in a totally different way from the way I grew up. My mother had no strong consciousness or sense of discrimination or inferiority, if you want to call it that, because of being Jewish. My mother considered herself an equal to everybody; did not ever sense a feeling of discrimination. And yet my mother, I think, was almost like a black growing up in a segregated society, because Jews accepted the discrimination as it existed. There were places that Jews couldn't live. In fact, when my mother wanted to move from Wilson Street when she and my dad got married, and get a little apartment in what could only be called a lower-middle-class section of Danville, they had to get the permission of neighbors to let a Jew move in then.

My uncle was also born in Danville and had the best clothing store in town and was in every activity; he founded the Red Cross there practically and was a community leader. When he got married in the 1930s, he moved into a very inexpensive house. But according to the zoning ordinances or whatever, he had to get the permission of neighbors for one hundred yards or three hundred yards, on either side, that it was okay for a Jew to move in.

These people accepted that. When I grew up I never accepted that kind
of bigotry, and I felt a certain kind of bitterness. I felt very different from
my Christian friends, although virtually all of my friends were Christian.
There was never more than one or two Jewish children in the same age
group. It was really a very unusual thing. My older brother, who is four
years older, became a nuclear physicist and worked on the atomic bomb
project and is now a pioneer in nuclear medicine. When he graduated from
high school, in about 1943, there were only two Jews in the class — one
was the valedictorian and he was the salutatorian. There was an incident.
One teacher, an elementary school teacher, said to her class, "Look, there
are two Jewish children who are going to be the valedictorian and the
salutatorian. We can't let the Jewish children get ahead of us like this."
There happened to be a Jewish child in that class, and the teacher was too
stupid to know it, and a delegation of parents went to see the superintendent.
There were always things like that.

A new development was started, right after World War II, and its sign
said RESTRICTED. They weren't high-class homes by any means. So one of
the members of the community called up and said, "What do you mean,
'restricted'?" They said, "Well, Negroes, Greeks, Syrians, and Jews" —
something like that. In fact, we had a lot in common with Catholics. There
were no more Catholics in town when I was growing up than there were
Jews. It was really Anglo-Irish-Scotch mostly. If you'd look, you wouldn't
see very many foreign names in the phonebook or anywhere else. You have
to keep in mind that at its peak Danville never had more than seventy-five
Jewish families, and maybe there are fewer than that now. In 1910 they
started an Orthodox synagogue called Aetz Chayim, Tree of Life. My mother
says, and I'm sure she's right about this, that she was a twelve-year-old girl
then and she gave the first dime for the first brick. The synagogue still stands
but is largely unused, because it's down in a poor section of town. None
of the Jews live there, but when I grew up on Wilson Street it was called
by the Jews "Kugel Avenue," because almost all the Jews lived along Wilson
Street. The synagogue was right across the street from our house.

The wealthier Reform Jews had moved, but the Orthodox mostly lived
on Kugel Avenue. In the 1930s they began moving away, but again, moving
up toward West Main Street, practically that whole side of the street was
Jewish. The Jews weren't scattered too much. They liked to live near other
Jews, but by then you could live anywhere.

I took an informal survey once of the second-generation children who
were born between 1925 and 1940, and it is fantastic. There are probably
two degrees for every child who grew up in that period of time. Every one
was college-educated; many have three degrees, like me. Why? Because of
the pressures they were under. Their parents never had a chance to break

out of this mold. I had one uncle who was a lawyer and two aunts who went to college, briefly. My mother even went to New York University Law School for one year. But it was more difficult; they tended to get married earlier; they tended to go into business.

All of my friends left. The only ones who returned, of all the Jews who were contemporaries of mine within ten years, were the ones who ran their fathers' stores or the ones who came back as physicians or attorneys. The others all left. There was really nothing there for them.

Jewish life was interesting because Jews really did not mix with Christians. Now they do, and certainly in my life today I do. I have two circles of friends. In Danville everything was centered around the synagogue, the temple, B'nai B'rith, Hadassah, or Helping Hand. The women had an organization called the Helping Hand Society, and it took in people from both the Reform and the Orthodox; so did Hadassah. It really cut across lines. Keep in mind that the largest the Orthodox congregation ever was was twenty to twenty-five members. Out of that they paid a rabbi some kind of pittance, but we were very lucky. When I was growing up, we had a rabbi with a Ph.D. from Heidelberg. He was an Orthodox rabbi who was a German refugee and he couldn't find anywhere else to go, so he came to Danville. This man spoke about five languages. He taught my brother Greek in return for baby sitting. He spoke Latin fluently, and this one man had a fantastic influence on all the children my age.

We did not mix with the Christian community socially. In business affairs, in club work — very few Jews were ever taken into Kiwanis. No Jews could join the country club, and there was only one golf club. My father loved to play golf, and he played every Sunday. For a time there was a municipal golf course where he would play. Then that closed down, and my dad would drive forty miles every Sunday to Greensboro, North Carolina, with a few of his friends to play golf.

Was there any overt anti-Semitism? Yes, always. The fact that you were a Jew meant that you were going to get into an occasional fight; that somebody was going to say something derogatory about Jews, though we had friends at school who were Christian, and all of my friends that I mixed with at school were Christian and we went out together at night. Some of the Jewish boys dated Christian girls; very few. I never dated a Christian girl when I was growing up, which is to say I never really had dates when I was growing up. I really didn't meet girls until I was eighteen years old and went off to college. I met girls, yes, but you'd have to go to Greensboro or Roanoke or Lynchburg or someplace like that to meet Jewish girls. During the war, when I was a teenager, there was very, very little travel between cities.

Now, when my mother was growing up, they used to pick up whole groups of Jewish kids and they would have dances. All the kids from Greens-boro and Lynchburg would come to Danville and they would stay in the houses of the people there and vice versa. So my mother had very close friends in Durham, Lynchburg, Greensboro; and her brothers and sisters did. But it wasn't true of my generation, partly because of the war, I think. The attitude when my mother was growing up was that the Jews all over that part of the South knew each other and had socials so boys and girls could meet each other. When we were growing up, I guess they figured we'd go off to college someday and meet other Jewish children there. It wasn't really the same problem. Back then, they didn't go off to college, so they had to have some way of meeting people from other towns.

The parents worked on Saturday. Because we children were needed so desperately for a minyan, we always had to go to shul for Friday night services. Saturday morning services were mostly children. We would go through services and then we would have Torah study afterwards. I went to Hebrew school from the age of five to the age of seventeen. I hated it and resisted it, but I always went. The other kids were going out for football and we were athletic and we liked to play. But the Jewish kids who were in the Orthodox congregation went to Hebrew school, and not until thirteen, but until they graduated from high school. That was the light at the end of the tunnel, graduation from high school.

Take this rabbi again. You have to consider that this rabbi was Orthodox and he was a Zionist. My mother joined Hadassah as a young woman, probably only three or four years after Henrietta Szold started Hadassah. My mother joined Hadassah around 1916, and my mother was either the president or the secretary of the Hadassah chapter in Danville for fifty years. So we believed very strongly in the establishment of the State of Israel. Again, in Danville there were always undercurrents of struggle. The Reform Jews had an American Council for Judaism chapter, an anti-Zionist group. So there was this struggle even among the members of the Reform congre-gation. A lot of people were unhappy with the rabbi; these Reform Jews who had Christmas trees and were already beginning to intermarry. We always felt that they were ashamed to be Jews, and then there was a struggle which erupted among the congregations themselves on this American Coun-cil for Judaism.

So I grew up very aware of the struggle and I always felt different. Unlike my mother, I grew up feeling very different, feeling very Jewish, feeling that Israel among the Arab nations was always me in Danville, Virginia. I had a tremendous empathy that always drew me to Israel, because I identified so completely with the Jews in Israel as being like the Jews in Danville. In fact, when I went off to Columbia as a freshman, the change was total; you can't imagine what a culture shock that was, to be surrounded by Jews.

You know, in a small town like Danville you always thought that if anybody was Jewish, it gave you an immediate bond. You were immediately close. In fact, the traveling salesmen who came through always stayed at our house. If they were jewelry salesmen or whatever, they came through, the ones that my dad dealt with, and they all stayed at our house and became members of the family. We've stayed close to them over the years. My mother stayed in touch by mail with hundreds of people all over the country. My mother was a very, very strong influence. She was really a matriarch in the community. My mother was a Zionist, also. However, when I joined the Israeli army, it crushed my mother. She went into shock and stayed there for a long time.

I went to Columbia College and Columbia University. It was amazing to me at Columbia College; half the college was Jewish, and actually they didn't feel anything for you especially. I'm sure the Jewish guys sort of recognized each other and things like that, but it was totally different from Danville. They didn't feel any special bond for you because you happened to be a Jew. As it happens, most of my friends at Columbia were Jewish, but I think it's because I selected them out. But that was surprising to me, you know, that Jews didn't necessarily feel any tremendous thing for each other because they were Jews.

This was June 1948 and I went over to a British farm camp to work. It was a cherry farm near Norwich, and I stayed there for about a month. I was supposed to travel through Europe for two or three weeks and then come back on the same ship; I had a return ticket. But I made up my mind that if I had a chance to join the Israeli army, I was going to do it. I really didn't know whether there was a good chance to do it. I knew it wasn't going to be easy, but I thought I would try anyway. Of course, I didn't say anything to anybody about it, certainly not my parents. I traveled through Europe and when I got to Paris I went to the Israeli embassy and told them that I wanted to join the Israeli army. This secretary looked at me and she wrote an address down on a piece of paper, a little slip of paper, and she gave it to me. I went to this address near the Arc de Triomphe and it was Haganah. It was just a bare room with a picture of a Haganah soldier on the wall. They sent me around to several doctors; one x-rayed me, one took my blood pressure, one did this, and the others did that.

Then they sent me to Marseilles. There were two other Americans. Three of us, as it happens, joined together. They were going through this same process. They were much older. When I say much older, I was eighteen and these others were all U.S. Army veterans. We were sent to a displaced persons' camp. They took away our passports. They gave us fake names. My name was Zarish Itzkovitch, something like that, because we had to go over as displaced persons. Only bona fide DP's were permitted to come into the country, although the Arabs were streaming in. That was kind of hypocrisy. Arabs were streaming in by the thousands and fighting, and Jews could only come in if they were bona fide DP's. We were in the DP camp in Marseilles for a couple of weeks. In fact, we were sent to two different camps, and then we were joined by other Americans, about twenty-five others who had been actually recruited. See, the three of us volunteered. Everybody volunteered, but the others had been recruited in America because some were pilots. They had special skills that Israel needed.

I never had really fired a rifle. I had fired .22's when I was in high school.

When I was there, there were only about two hundred Americans in the Israeli army. It was an amazingly small number. By the time the war was over, they say there were as many as a thousand or so. At the time I got there, there was only one American younger, and we still keep up with each other, Mort Levinson from San Francisco, who is now the owner of one of the larger insurance companies. Mort was a few months younger than I. We became good friends. He was on my half-track. Mort was an infantryman and I was the driver.

I went into combat ten days after I arrived in the country. Frankly, I never regretted doing it, but when we went into battle, I was very frightened. You know, the half-track is open on top, and the Galilee is hilly, and I could never understand why those bullets weren't coming inside the half-track. But the Israelis, many of them, were very brave or foolhardy. They would sit up on the end of the thing. It was a macho-type thing. The officers would go around without helmets. They had to show that they were really braver than the men. We had all Israeli officers, and they were very, very good.

I was there for about seven months. I left in January 1949. I was there a very short time, relatively. In fact, I only missed one semester of school. The war was essentially over, and they sent out a notice that everybody who was a student in America who wanted to return in time for the second semester could go back. So I came back on a ship called the *Marine Karp*, an American ship.

I became different, too. I would say, number one, fighting in an army for a war of independence — that was really something that everybody admired, except for Arabs. I mean, there was nobody who wouldn't say Israel should have fought for its own independence. It wasn't like Vietnam or anything like that. Most people have never met any American who served in the Israeli army. When people meet me and they find out about this, truthfully, I'm probably the only person they've ever met, not only American, who ever did that. As a young person it gave me a tremendous feeling, as I said, of confidence and of worth. You know, as if I could do anything; that nothing would scare me. It's hard to describe. I had a real feeling of worth. I had really done something interesting, important. I had really contributed. How many people help a country win its independence?

I served in the American army during the Korean War, but I didn't go overseas. I was stationed in Kentucky and El Paso, which is where I met my wife. When we went back to Israel to live for a year, from 1967 to 1968, the attitude of Israelis toward me was just totally different from their attitude toward any other American. They considered me like one of them. I'd served. We called it Machal. It stands for volunteers from outside Israel, or Eretz Yisrael. It's something that put me in essentially a different category.

I'm still a Zionist. I've always been a Zionist and I've been a leader in the United Jewish Appeal for twenty-five years. I'm adviser to the Jewish Student Union here at the University of Florida. Whenever there's an Arab on campus and they need someone to debate him, it's me. I'm not afraid to step in when others won't. There are a lot of Jewish professors who think it's going to hurt them when it comes to promotion or something like that, which is ridiculous. I'm the highest ranking Jew on this campus. For Christians it isn't anything that ever bothers them, for a Jew to be a Zionist.

Did the experience in Israel change my view of Danville, Virginia? Yes. I felt more comfortable in Danville, but I've never felt completely comfortable there. I never felt comfortable growing up in Danville, even though I have a lot of friends there. I don't feel comfortable in Danville today. I always felt that I was different, and it isn't fair to the Christians, because I don't think most of them ever took note of whether I was different or not or ever gave a damn. But it was a fact that I did feel different.

Solomon Blatt, ninety, attorney-at-law, Barnwell, South Carolina ("That's the only address you'll need. You don't have to put any box number or anything else. When it hits Barnwell, everybody will know where my office is and where I live.")

I live in Barnwell, South Carolina. I've been practicing law in Barnwell since 1917. It's going to be difficult for me to tell you the place where my parents were born. I can remember something of a place that sounded like Brest-Litovsk or something like that. I don't really know the correct name, but that's my recollection of where my father was born. My father and mother were married over there before he left and came to the United States.

He got enough money and got on a ship. Of course, he couldn't speak English. They tagged him for New York. My recollection of what happened is that a group of Jewish people met the ship and took him, and housed him somewhere and then they sent him on a boat that used to run between Jacksonville, Florida, and New York — it doesn't run anymore. They put him on that ship and tagged him for Charleston, South Carolina. There, another group of Jewish people met him. They took care of him for a few days and they decided he was going to peddle. A company by the name of M. Hornig and Sons operated in Charleston, a little wholesale place there, and they sold him a pack of merchandise without any down payment.

He started walking. He told me, many a time, that in the coldest of winter people wouldn't let him in the house. He had to sleep on the frozen ground, and he was very lucky if he got in a hay barn and they let him sleep out there under that hay, where he could keep warm.

He didn't know a nickel from a dollar. He carried a little merchandise like socks and ladies' stockings and handkerchiefs and whatnot. He trusted the honor of the people who bought from him to give him the correct amount that was owed on that merchandise. It was marked. They could have given him a dime and took a dollar and a half worth of merchandise. He wouldn't have known any different.

In those travels he came to Blackville. I understood this — sometimes he'd go down towards Savannah and go over to Augusta and maybe get some merchandise there and walk back to Charleston and load up again. From here to Charleston is a hundred miles.

My father had stopped peddling and got a little store not too much bigger than my office. I remember the store well, because when I came along I could see it there. It had a fireplace in the back and that's where he built a fire and cooked his meals. And then they had a counter about like this desk and the bottom of that counter was open and he would put a little mattress down there and sleep under that counter.

Then my mother came. They had one child that was born in Europe and his name was Jake. He was about three or four years old. She couldn't speak English, either. They got her off at New York and sent her on down to Charleston. At Charleston, they put her on a train and tagged her for Blackville. My father met her, of course. He had a little house rented. After my mother came to Blackville, he got into a little larger place. And he began to expand.

He was the best merchant I ever knew in my life. All these people that made millions out of the mercantile business — my father didn't, but he was the best merchant I ever saw.

Father and Mother could neither read nor write, and I remember a black postmaster at Blackville taught my father how to read a little bit and how to sign his name. But my father got into a little bit larger store and he wouldn't sell anybody anything on credit. You paid cash. My father stayed in business over fifty years, and when he sold out, he sold his business to his clerk, who had been with him fifty years. He sold that business for, I think it was for $500. It was worth several thousands of dollars.

My parents were religious to the extent that my father went to Charleston and they taught him how to kill chickens and all that. On the holidays, he closed and went to synogague, either in Charleston or Augusta. I can remember, of course, Saturday they had to keep open because that's the only day they did any business. Some days he wouldn't take in ten dollars. He wouldn't smoke on Saturday. I remember this: my mother would come to the store to help and she would not tear the paper off the paper rack on Saturday. She'd make the customer do it.

It was difficult to maintain our Jewishness. When I was a child, Blackville had about fifteen hundred to two thousand people. I'd say there were three or four Jewish families.

My mother and father tried their best to be kosher in everything that they did. They observed the holidays, sacred Jewish holidays. But it got to the point where they had to buy meat that wasn't kosher. My mother did the best she could under the circumstances. And I'll tell you one thing about it, there is one thing I am right proud of, and I'm that way, too: they didn't hesitate to let everybody know they were of the Jewish faith, and I think the public knew it generally, too.

I have proclaimed on many a stump and many times that I am of the Jewish faith and I'm proud of it, because I love my mother and daddy, and I couldn't love them unless I was proud to be a Jew.

My mother had loads and loads of friends. If she had an enemy, I never did know it. I don't think my father had many. He might have had one or two. Somebody asked me not long ago how I've lived so long and have so few enemies. Well, I said, I buried all my enemies.

Now, about whether or not my Jewishness helped or hurt my political career? It hurt.

You know, back yonder some years ago the Klan was very active over this state; well, everywhere. And it was very active in Barnwell County. I really didn't know who all belonged to it. But they were putting the squeeze on me in the practice of law. I paid a stiff penalty for being Jewish at that time. My clients got hurt and I lost business because they saw that I was running into difficulty. You'd have a jury made up of members of the Klan. The lawyer on the other side was a member of the Klan and the client on the other side — not my client, but the other fellow's client — was also a member. It was hard for me to win anything.

But I took the position that a man has as much right to join the Klan as I had to join the Masonic Lodge if he wanted to, if he felt that was in the best interest of himself and the state. That's his business. They tried to get me to talk against them. I never would. I just said, "Oh, no. I'm not going to have anything to say about this, other than a man has a right, as long as he doesn't violate the law, to do what he wants to do. And if he wants to join an organization, that's up to him."

I only lost one election, my first in 1930. Did my Jewishness have anything to do with it? It always did. It always did. It became more minor as the years went by. That resulted in part because the people began to accept the Jewish people. Then, I was not the kosher Jewish fellow that I should have been. So it began to break. But yet I don't think I ever ran a race that somebody didn't have something to say about the fact that I was a Jew. I remember that they put out a pamphlet in one race that I ran in which the fellow said, "I am a Christian," and all that sort of stuff, you know. I remember that he used that in the campaign against me — my being of the Jewish faith — but it didn't keep me from getting re-elected. I've gotten re-elected without too much difficulty.

But I wouldn't run for governor. I had, I'd say, about three of the most prominent businessmen in South Carolina call me and say they wanted to see me. When they came we sat and talked a few minutes and these business people asked me, "You know what we are doing down here?" I said, "No. I have no idea." They said, "We want you to run for governor," and said, "If you run, we'll put up every nickel of the money. You won't have to spend a nickel. We'll go out and fight for you. We'll get our organizations to do it." I said, "Nothing has pleased me more than to have you have that confidence in me that I could serve as governor of South Carolina, but I have no intention of running."

They wondered, "Why not? You've been a good representative. You've been a good speaker of the House. People respect you." I said, "Two reasons. The first is I can't get elected. And second is that I'm of the Jewish faith. And right now that would be a burden." They said, "Oh, no. They want you to run." Anyhow, we went to lunch and they asked my wife. Said, "You know what we been talking to Sol about?" And she said, "No." Said, "We want him to run for governor." I said, "Honey, don't you think about that, because I'm not going to run." So that quieted that off.

The next thing that happened to me, they wanted to put me on the Supreme Court. They offered me that without opposition twice. I thought very seriously about it.

I have never forgotten that I am of the Jewish faith. I never will. I may not be buried as Jewish people are buried. I'm not kosher in my eating; I've lost all of that. But I've never lost the love that I have for my Jewish faith and never will, whatever I do. I can eat a piece of hog meat tomorrow and still love being what I am.

Let me tell you what is happening to the Jews of South Carolina. They got a society in Charleston. It's made up of Jewish people. What is the organization's name? I got a speech I made there. It was a wonderful occasion. Hebrew Benevolent Society. They have a cemetery down there; old cemetery with a lot of famous Jewish people buried in it. They asked me to speak to that society. I agreed to go. I never will forget that Fritz Hollings, who is now United States senator, was there. He might have been governor at the time; I don't remember. General Mark Clark was there. People like that, a lot of them, way up there.

That was in the days when there was a lot of activity on the part of the blacks, and there is still, of course, a lot to get what they think is equal rights and whatnot and I wonder sometimes if they are not going too far. I think a man ought to earn what he gets rather than give it to him because of color. In that speech I begged the Jewish people to be careful how they dealt with this black problem. I said you are the ones who are going to suffer if you become active and I believe in fairness. But you are going to pay the penalty. They going to turn upon the Jewish people the first thing they do.

It's funny. I thought this because, as I walked the long road of life, I have seen fellows who made demands that jumped on those who tried to help them. Don't ask me specifically what I have in mind, because I can't tell you. It was something that was in you, in your brain or in your heart, and I told them. I said, You watch your stores and whatnot. And it wasn't six months after that before they began burning the Jewish stores, the merchants' stores in New York, and breaking the windows. It followed in line with what I said.

There was an effort to climb too fast and travel too far. I believe in fairness. I must treat them all right. Some of them may not think so. I got a cook's been with me thirty-five years. Right? I got an old man seventy-five years old who's been with me fifteen years; he drives me and takes care of the yard and cleans up the bathroom and whatnot. He comes every morning when I go to Columbia at five o'clock; he puts me in the bathtub and takes me out. Of course, there's been a terrible faster pace of demand in recent years than ever before. And they're expecting too much. For instance, if you got fifty percent of your people in Barnwell, say, black and fifty percent white — that isn't the exact correct figure, but I'm just using it — that doesn't necessarily mean that you got to have half of them black on the city council or half of them white.

The question is who is the best man for the job. I think that an individual is entitled to walk the long and treacherous road of life as far down that road as his character, his ability, his dedication, his integrity, and honesty will let him go. That's all. We must see to it that they have a right to walk that road and accomplish those aims, if they are better than the other man who seeks to do the same thing and wants the same thing. That's my philosophy.

Was I a segregationist in the 1960s? I remember that that question arose. I made a speech on the floor of the House, in which I said that I didn't want a so-and-so sitting next to my little daughter in school. They construed that to mean that I was confining that so-and-so to blacks, which wasn't true. It did include blacks, but it included certain white people, too. What I was trying to tell them, as they considered education and pulling everybody in together, was that they had to consider that little girl who couldn't take care of herself. That we had to protect her, both from whites and blacks.

As for anyone who would ask, "How could you have held the views you held and be Jewish, because Jews are supposed to care about social justice and equality?" my answer is "The same way that those minorities burned those stores in New York, broke the windows." If that indicated how they felt towards my people, I wasn't going to open the door and tell them to come in.

I've defended more black people, for which I got no money, no fees, than any man in lower South Carolina today. I've done it and I have no objection to having done it. I have no hesitation to say I am proud of the fact that the opportunity was mine to help somebody who was in trouble. I think that's one of the responsibilities I have as a lawyer.

Now let me tell you something interesting. Sumter, South Carolina, was one of the most intermarried communities in the South; that is, between Jews and Christians. I know about it because my wife came from Sumter. She was Jewish. She joined the Episcopal church. My son did. She was the organist at the Episcopal church; she was a wonderful organist. She played down there for them because they had a very small group, about twenty-five or thirty people, and they were looking for somebody to play and she offered to play. She played down there twenty-five or thirty years. They gave her a beautiful plaque; I say it was beautiful. It was a nice gesture and she was tickled to death. She organized a little choir for them. She did a good job. She loved her church.

She came to me one day and she told me she wanted to ask me something and hoped I wouldn't get mad with her about it. I said, "Honey, I'm not going to get mad with you; I don't know what you are going to ask me. What is it?"

She said, "I want to join the Episcopal church. Can I?"

I said, "Honey, let me tell you something. Anything that you want to do, that your heart tells you is something you should do that will benefit and help you as you walk the road of life and will bring happiness and pleasure to somebody else, you do it. Now, I want it understood, I'm not. But you do it if you want to and I'll still love you."

She joined. With much happiness she joined it. Now, some time after that my family joined the Episcopal church. The Episcopal minister came in to see me. When he came to the door, I said, "Now, preacher, you can come on in and I'm glad to have you, but let me tell you this is one Jew that you are not going to get."

Why is it that South Carolina seems very liberal when it comes to Jews in politics? People have become — white people — more broad-minded. They began, years ago, accepting us as citizens, as neighbors, as friends. Most of us have conducted ourselves on such a high plane that they couldn't thumb their nose at us. Before you know it, they were in there taking a drink with me and eating some of my rations. I can understand how a black man feels, because I can remember when I was a kid living in Blackville that I was never invited to the parties that the children had in school, my classmates or other people. I was never invited. I was a Jew. Just like a black is not invited because he is a black. And I tell these blacks; I say, "Don't tell me anything about minorities; I've been through it."

You know that sometimes the Jewish people bring on their own trouble. If you are a Jew, you got to be a Jew. But there's several ways of being one. One with honor, integrity, honesty. The other, telling lies, double-crossing people. A lot of people look upon Jewish people as a wringer where you put money up, everything they got it in, wring the money out of it, take it and put it in their pocket, and then tell you to go to hell.

You can't leave that impression. But a lot of them do. I heard a preacher on the television the other day said he loved Jews — I've forgotten the name now; he's very prominent on television. He said, "You know, Jews got money. And I don't blame them about that, because I like money myself." But he said, "I love Jews," and then he went on to talk about Christ being a Jew.

I think we bring on part of it ourselves. Of course, it's so easy. I've defended some pretty rough cases in my lifetime. Cases that were not popular for a lawyer to handle. Every now and then, families on the other side, families of the dead person say, "Damn Jew defending that man for killing my son or whatnot." It pops out sometimes. It never worried me.

I'll tell you. This is a little funny experience. I don't know if it has any value or not. There was this little town up the road, between here and Augusta, Georgia, called Dunbarton, and when the Savannah River Plant was constructed, it swallowed the town of Dunbarton. But every other year in the political campaign they had a meeting at Dunbarton and they spoke from the freight depot platform. Well, when they had the meetings then in those days — not like it is now — every country church would invite the candidates to come speak. Then they would go to each candidate and ask him for a contribution to buy the hogs to have a barbecue. Then, after you made the contribution to the purchase of the hogs, the church members would come and sell tickets. I had to buy ten tickets or whatnot.

I was at Dunbarton at a campaign meeting, and I spoke last. The fellow who was presiding at the meeting was a good friend of mine, this night's meeting. He introduced everybody else and they made their speeches and I was the last one and he was introducing me. So he told the audience, he said, "I regret that we are having something today that Mr. Blatt can't eat," referring to the barbecued hog. He said, "I just overlooked the fact of his religion, and I'm sorry and I regret it." He went on. He apologized. It was a very kind statement he made. But I didn't know exactly how that thing was going to go with people up there saying, "Well, we eat it. Why the devil can't that Jew eat it?" You know. But they didn't say that. When he got through introducing me, the first thing I told that crowd, I said, "Ladies and gentlemen, don't you worry about what you got here to eat today. Don't let it give you any concern, because I'm going to eat it, too, and call it goose." They applauded and I got a terrific vote up there.

Postscript: When Solomon Blatt died in mid May 1986, his record as a legislator was unparalleled: speaker of the South Carolina House of Representatives for thirty-three years, longer than anyone in the history of the United States; a state representative for fifty-four years, longer than any legislator in the United States; and, at the time of the interview in the spring of 1985, at age ninety, he was the oldest man serving in any legislative body in the United States.

13

Officers and Jewishmen

MY FATHER served in the United States Army during World War I, my brother during World War II, and I during the Korean War. When I was growing up, I often heard that Jews shirked military duty or, if forced into the service, angled for the quartermaster corps. When one looks at the figures, however, one finds that the percentage of American Jews who served in the military from the Revolution through the Korean War usually exceeded the percentage of Jews in the general population.

Claire Millhiser Rosenbaum is a college dean and a fourth-generation native of Richmond, Virginia. Her grandmother's uncle was with the cadet battalion of youngsters from the Virginia Military Institute that fought the Union Army at New Market. He later became a sculptor, and it is his memorial to the Confederate dead that honors his comrades in Arlington National Cemetery. He is buried beneath his monument. And Charles Wolf, a military, test, and commercial pilot from Texas, believes that one of his ancestors died at the Alamo: "His name was Alexander Wolf, which was my father's name also. My father was the one who said that he was probably a relative, because that branch of the Wolfs came to Texas so early. The original way I saw it spelled was 'Wolf,' although on the cenotaph at Alamo Square they've added an *e* to it, and whether the *e* was added at that time or later, I don't know."

Major General Robert Bailey Solomon, fifty-four, U.S. Army,
Fort Jackson, South Carolina

I was born on December 14, 1930 — a Depression baby. And I am a professional soldier.

In 1937, my parents bought a house across from a place that became central to who I am. That was the Petah Tiqva. Now, you may know that in Israel there's a town called Petah Tiqva. We lived within a hundred feet of the front door of the Petah Tiqva, which was one of those synagogues made from a large cottage. Instead of an upstairs we had a mechitzah, a screen which prevents the female from looking at the male and vice versa. Now, there's a rabbinic law as to the height of a mechitzah and the density of a mechitzah. But in our synagogue, since we had no upstairs, we actually had an alternate brick construction, constructed on the side so the women sat to the right of the men, and there were opaque glass windows which were opened up about an inch so that the women could hear the rabbi and the chazan. You could not see the women. And the women could not see the men. So the ability of the two groups to interrelate just didn't exist. Of course, the women's side became the hall for weddings and Oneg Shabbat and for Bar Mitzvahs.

Petah Tiqva did a number of things for me. It gave me an excellent foundation for understanding Jewish law, the Torah. Not as much for the Talmud; I picked that up in later life. I went to Hebrew school there four days a week. I was Bar Mitzvahed. I received sidurs as awards for perfect shul attendance. And I like to kid people and say, "What choice did I have? My mother could see me walk from my front door to the front door of the shul, and there wasn't any crossing my mother." You go to shul on Saturday. Then later on, in my teens, I joined Aleph Zadek Aleph and became very actively involved.

My high school was at least sixty to seventy percent Jewish. I wanted to be a singing truck driver. You laugh, but God blessed me with a little bit of a voice, so I went to Peabody Preparatory School and Peabody Conservatory for almost seven years. I wanted to be a concert or an opera singer. But I had a relatively thin tenor voice, although it has matured a lot over the years. Every choir has to have a boy with a high squeaky voice. I was it. As my voice changed, of course, I became first the second tenor and then the first tenor soloist.

My interest in the English language and journalism started while I was in that AZA chapter, because I started to put out a paper called the *Landsman*. AZA certainly had a profound effect on me, because the program was, of course, what they called the fivefold and full program — cultural, religious, charitable, social, and athletic, as I recall. I was the oratory champ for my chapter and for the region. So all of those are things which, I guess, formed a foundation that I didn't realize at the time would later be a tremendous help to me when I came in to the military. It also provided to me something that I lacked — some self-discipline.

I did not see making the military a career. Part of that is the basis of why Jews came to America — to escape military service in many cases, either in the Czar's army or somebody else's army. When I entered the service in November 1951, my grandfather broke down and sobbed uncontrollably, saying, "I'll never see you again. I'll never see you again." I didn't understand until years later what he was relating to was the fact that Jewish kids in Russia and Lithuania were drafted for twenty-five years and were baptized and were forced to eat pork, although many of them became like the Marranos — in effect, secret Jews. Many of them never saw their families again until they were old men, if they lived that long. So I think my grandfather related to that.

The Korean War began on June 25, 1950, and I enlisted. I had five days remaining in the marine corps reserve. I'd been in the reserve for three years, which was an experience in itself. I was the only Jew that I knew in Baltimore, Maryland, that was in the marine corps reserve. When it became known that I was Jewish, I never went beyond private first class in three years. Baltimore, as you know, has seventeen different ethnic communities, many of them extremely anti-Semitic. The Lithuanian, Polish, and Italian communities of Baltimore, when I grew up, were very, very anti-Semitic. Of course, being in a Jewish community, I didn't have to relate to them at all, except in high school. But like a lot of other Jews, I was a very good prizefighter. I was small then, and fast. And part of that was survival. To be honest, I am not a militarist in any sense of the word. I've never been a very combative person, never. I'm not today. But I was about to be drafted. I had gone to two years of pre-law at the University of Baltimore. I then entered law school, then switched to a couple of courses in advertising because I went to work for an advertising firm in Baltimore. Then, of course, the war started. Very happily, I was discharged five days later from the marine corps reserve.

Shortly after entering the army at Fort Knox, Kentucky, you were sort of quarantined for two weeks. You had to scrub the floors, the old wooden floors. It was the second Friday night I was there. I was with 220 individuals from Wisconsin, Minnesota; you know, the upper Midwest farming belt. Not many big-city kids in there. We had at least 150 to 200 Jewish kids in basic training at Fort Knox when I was there. So I went off to services.

Friday nights, you got down on the floor and cleaned up. That was a "GI party." Thank God we are a long way from that today. When I came back, there was a guy sitting on my bunk, and he says, "Hey, Solomon, where have you been?" I said, "I've been out." And he says, "Well, yeah, where were you?" I said, "Well, I went to religious services." He looked at me and said, "What are you, a Seventh Day Adventist?" I said, "No." He said, "Well, what are you?" With a little trepidation, I said, "I'm Jewish." He looked at me again. He said, "You're Jewish?" I said, "Yeah, I'm Jewish." He said, "Are your parents Jewish?" And he is looking at me very intently.

I said, "Yes, both my father and my mother and my grandparents are Jewish." And he said, "You don't look Jewish." And he is still looking at me. You remember the haircuts we had. Everybody looked alike. And so I finally said, "Well, why would you say I don't look Jewish?" because I always thought I did. He said, "Well," and he's looking at my head, he says, "You don't have horns." I said, "Pardon me!" You see, I had led a very sheltered life, and I said, "Are you kidding me?" He said, "Well, Jews have horns." I said, "How many Jews do you know who have horns?" He said, "I never met a Jew before." So I found out that of the probably 220 people in that company, there weren't more than five of them that ever met a Jew. The only ones that had were a couple of kids who had lived in Chicago, a couple in Milwaukee.

Now, the interesting phenomenon is that I spent sixteen weeks in basic training and had probably somewhere between twenty and thirty prizefights. Usually it was some fellow who wanted to beat my brains out because I was Jewish. I didn't lose a fight. I got knocked on my keester a few times, but I think the fact that I was willing to fight sort of let them know that I was not a spindly little Jew that they could walk up to and push over.

As opposed to making me more Christianized, the military service, if anything, has made me much more Jewish. I found nothing difficult about being in the army and I found nothing to compromise my faith in the army, from the first day. I did find a lot of people who were anti-Semitic. And I also found out that many of those were anti-Semitic because they didn't have the foggiest notion of what Jews were, where they came from, what they might be, what they believed. They simply believed popular myths about Jews.

And I have had, on a couple of occasions, a group of professedly Ku Klux Klan try to harm the best interests of the Solomons. I've never had a cross burned, although there were crosses burned on the lawns of black families in the area. But the KKK, of course, professes to hate both Jews and blacks. I became involved in letting a group of KKK know — this is over in Europe in the mid 1960s — that they couldn't intimidate me, nor would I permit them to intimidate the black soldiers who were in the 3rd Armored Division. But, no, I've had a number of things happen to me which I think, in some cases, were overtly anti-Semitic, and in others, very subtle.

But then I went off to advanced individual training and to leadership school, and it was during this period of time, of course, that I was selected to go to Officer Candidate School. I did it right at Fort Knox, so I spent a little bit more than a year at Fort Knox, and in the later part of 1952 I was commissioned a second lieutenant of armored cavalry, a tanker. I went off to Fort Carson, then Camp Carson, Colorado, the first time that I had been west of the Mississippi.

I went there and I went to Korea. I served in the 245th Tank Battalion, what they call the Two for a Nickel, which was a National Guard division up in the area of the Hwachon Reservoir and Chongchon and Yanggu, and I saw a very different culture for the first time in my life.

Originally, when I came back my fiancée and parents all were ready for me to get out of the army, and I said, "I'm sorry, I have another eighteen months to serve on my three-year commitment." I said, "We are going to be married, and we are going off to Fort Knox, Kentucky," where I was going to be an instructor at the armored school and a writer there. The ability to put words on paper has been an incredible asset. I owe a great deal to that one facility. Part of that results, I think, from my being Jewish. Part of it — unfortunately, I think my skills are sort of mediocre — is that I was literate and there were a lot of people in the army who were not.

Fran and I were married. We went off to Fort Knox. A year after we were married we had our first child, Sharon, who is now a captain in the army.

Frankly, we were poor as church mice. Lieutenants got a couple hundred bucks. I think as a first lieutenant with five years, I was making something like $316, so it was clear that I wasn't staying in for the money. I was challenged. I had an opportunity to exert some leadership. I had talents that were being used in the army. I was writing, I was speaking, I was teaching. I was able to be a very active member of a religious community. I was doing a lot of things that I enjoy doing. And, above all, I have to tell you, I think I may have an overdeveloped sense of patriotism. I love this country.

A lot of people will tell you you can't be a Jew outside of Israel. I've been to Israel. I think I have much more freedom to be a Jew in America.

When did I decide to stay? When we were in Germany. I think both of my parents were deeply disappointed, primarily because they felt that I would have no difficulty making it on the outside, and, frankly, I have a very close family. My wife is an only child and it was a much greater blow to her parents than it was to mine, who had three other children. I would say my mother above all expressed openly — not necessarily with hostility — her disappointment that I wasn't coming home to be a part of the Jewish community. Jewish mothers like mine, of my mother's generation and background, like to say "My son, the doctor," "My son, the president," "My son, the lawyer, the accountant." What Jewish mother wants to say "My son, the lieutenant"? When I was promoted to colonel I had twenty-two relatives up at the Pentagon, which almost blew the mind of the general who promoted me. I kiddingly say that my mother and father turned to me and said, "So, Bobby, I guess you are serious about being a soldier."

I extended for three years in order to go to Germany. Now, a very large part of my family said, "How can you go to Germany? How can you serve with those miserable Jew killers?" I had relatives — an aunt and uncle I loved dearly — who would never come to visit me. They were very wealthy people. Even when my son was Bar Mitzvahed there, they would never come to Germany.

I just had an amazing range of experiences, opportunities, experiences, and in each case I did, for example, what Jewish communities did here in South Carolina. You get a handful of Jews together. You seek out Jews to be with, people that you are extremely comfortable with. And I found that there are a great many people of the Jewish faith who had married out of the faith, who were not Jewish, because they didn't feel they could be Jewish. I, unlike them, felt it was important to have Jewish representation in the army, but I don't mean just a Jewish name. I mean real Jewish representation in the army. You see, I think I have a right to be in the army. There are a lot of people that don't think Jews ought to be in the army; people in the army and out.

When the Vietnam War started, I was called back from Germany to help establish a training center at Fort Bragg. I did so and I was selected for lieutenant colonel and for the Command and General Staff College. When we arrived at Fort Leavenworth, Kansas, in 1967, we immediately found a Jewish core there of about eight or ten people on the post, including Major Irv Jacobs, who was a member of the staff and faculty. He had two small children. I had three of roughly comparable ages. We got together and said, We are people of a similar mind; we want to conduct services here. So we found a chapel on the post and then, lo and behold, on the second Friday night there were a number of people from downtown who were present, who had heard there were services. These were Jewish businessmen and the widows of Jewish businessmen. They said, "My God, ten minutes outside the gates we have this absolutely magnificent temple! Won't you please conduct at least one of every two services down there and the High Holiday services?" I went down and I almost flipped out when I saw this place. It was gorgeous and unused. Up until three years prior to our arrival they had had music and services piped in via telephone line from Kansas City, the congregation had shrunk so much.

At one time, a hundred and some years before, during the days of the Indian wars, Jewish settlers and businessmen settled in Leavenworth, Kansas, because that's where the Oregon and Santa Fe trails separated. So people would cross the Missouri River. Jewish businessmen came and stayed. They were Orthodox. They founded the B'nai Jeshurun Synagogue. However, as the families assimilated — there was no Conservative then — they moved to Reform. Many of them that came in were Germans who were Reform. So, one time this place probably had three hundred to four hundred people for High Holiday services. But for roughly three or four years there had been no services at all. In checking around Fort Leavenworth, I found that there were thirty-seven Jews and quasi-Jews — people of Jewish faith who simply did not practice. Irv Jacobs and I went to all of them. These are commissioned officers — either majors or lieutenant colonels in grade and one colonel. We said, "This is a great opportunity." We had no idea whether anybody would show up, but we said we were going to have an organizational meeting for the Jewish community of Leavenworth and Fort Leavenworth at the B'nai Jeshurun, and we had a Sunday school going for roughly a hundred children. I was the president of the Sunday school and I was the chazan for the community. Irv Jacobs is very learned, much more learned in Torah than I am. So we were a good combination.

Leavenworth provided the first real opportunity to get into lay leadership. So from that point on, from 1967, 1968 on, I have been, in effect, a lay leader of every Jewish community I've been in.

Jacobs stayed in the service and he went his way. Fran and I went our way. I went to Vietnam. Irv had been there twice before; he was a Special Forces officer. But in Vietnam, I had another very moving experience as a Jew. I attended services at the Third Field Hospital every Friday night. I would see these bloody American youths come in during and after services. Unfortunately, one night they brought in a dead navy chaplain of the Jewish faith who was up in I Corps in the northern part of the country and his carryall went over a VC mine and he was killed. The chaplain at that time — a rabbi who was a Reform chaplain — came to me and said, "Could you and my chaplain's assistant conduct the High Holiday services?" — this is the High Holidays of 1968 — "I think I am needed up north." So we went into the largest of the halls of the theater and we conducted High Holiday services. There were six hundred Jews from all over the country, including some from the diplomatic corps and many others.

One of the things — as I think about it, it still chokes me up a little bit — I remember at the end of Rosh Hashonah looking out on six hundred Jewish faces as I was conducting the Rosh Hashonah service, and a fellow lieutenant colonel who had a good set of pipes on him, blowing the shofar as I said, "Tekiah, teruah, shevarim." What was going through my mind — I was saying the words — and I was thinking, "What in the world are we all doing here? What are we doing here? Six hundred Jews in this poor torn land." But the idea of six hundred Jews wanting to be together, coming from all over, flying in by helicopter, going down quite dangerous roads, to get to High Holiday services in Saigon . . .

And so again, that tells you something; that reinforces the way you feel about God and faith and about being Jewish.

We have a daughter who is a graduate in fine arts from the Maryland

Institute College of Fine Arts. She worked at the new East Wing of the National Gallery. In October of 1978 she came in and said, "Daddy, sit down; you'll never believe what I just did." My daughter, at that time, five-feet-one, maybe 115, 118, 120 pounds, had been an equestrian but did nothing athletic; never ran two steps in her life that I am aware of. Bright little girl, very assertive, from the age of twelve always telling me, "Daddy, you don't understand." Now she's having a chance to tell other people. But she shocked me by enlisting in the army. And certainly I would not dissuade her; that's what she wanted to do. Probably if I had attempted to dissuade her, it wouldn't have done a damn bit of good. But she enlisted in the army; she went to OCS; she was commissioned as a second lieutenant in the signal corps in 1979. She went off to Fort Benning, where, lo and behold, her stay there for OCS and jump school happened to coincide with that of Jeffrey Jacobs, Irv Jacobs's son, who had graduated from the Military Academy.

And where did they meet but at Friday night services, where the rabbi, this young then lieutenant, now captain, conducted a Reform service with a guitar. So when I went down to visit her, I said, "What's this mishegoss? What kind of service is this?" But it was beautiful and there were thirty or thirty-five, youngsters principally, who attended.

In any event, my daughter met, associated with, went to Fort Bragg with Jeffrey Jacobs to become a jumper. He was in the 82nd Airborne. My daughter was in an airborne signal and military intelligence unit. They fell in love, going to services on Friday night. In 1981 they married. I sang the blessings over their marriage ceremony, and much to my surprise, they have kept a totally Jewish kosher household since that time. As we moved around we sometimes kept a kosher house; sometimes we did not. Sometimes in Germany it was almost impossible — it's never impossible. That's a cop-out; we didn't do it.

They are both captains, and my daughter called me two weeks ago to tell me that she is pregnant. My son-in-law just came back from the Sinai. He said, "You know, Moses was a pretty tough guy to have climbed Mount Sinai." Both of them have considered getting out. Jeff is a light infantryman, airborne, airmobile all the way. Special Forces. His father was as well. He thought of going out and becoming a professor. He was accepted at four law schools. But now he's decided, probably because of the baby, to stay in the army for at least a while longer.

Soldiers in America were largely immigrants during the lengthy period of the expansion of America; they were Germans who couldn't speak English; they were Irishmen who were fleeing the potato famine; they were Italians and all sorts. But they were rarely Jews. Last year, 1984, there were seven Jewish general officers; none of them is as visible a Jew as I am.

The navy and the marine corps are, in my opinion, the ultra-conservatives of the services. The army is the most liberal. The air force is a very close second to that. Let me just say this: my personal belief, my philosophy, is that the armed forces of the country should be a mirror of the society of that country. Everybody, and I know a lot will disagree with this intellectually, everybody has an obligation in a country like this to give themselves to some public service of some sort. I don't care what level. But I believe that everybody ought to have a little bit of selflessness in them, like the ancient rabbinic saying: "If I am only for myself, what am I?" In order to be a whole person, you have to have self-love. But at the same time, in order to be totally complete, you have to be able to love others and to serve others and to do something for them.

It is unfortunate that the Vietnam War was the most divisive war in American history, including the Civil War. It created a separation, I think in many ways, in the way Jews perceive military service. After all, Jews served in World War I and World War II, far in excess of their numbers in the population. There was never any question; in Korea, there were more Jews, or the same number of Jews, in the United States Army equivalent to the percentage of Jews in the American population. You were expected to serve.

Not so Vietnam. The opposition was principally Episcopalian, Unitarian, and Jewish. The better-educated classes could not intellectually accept the fact that it was all right to assist a portion of a country that simply wanted to remain free from what they considered to be a totalitarian regime and an oppressive way of life. And I can fight the "just war" either way you want it. But in any event, my personal opinion is that it was a war doomed to failure. It was the wrong war at the wrong time at the wrong place. It was the height of America's arrogance to believe that we could support a war there unless we wanted to bomb that country into submission. But the application of ground troops, fighting a war in increments of six months to a year, was never a route to victory. In any event, that war polarized the attitude of American Jewry towards service, so when the volunteer era arrived there was no coercion whatsoever, and Jews simply did not flock to the colors.

The Israeli army has had a tremendous impact on the attitude of the American military towards Jews. People suddenly decided, "Hey, Jews will fight. Jews can fight." The ridiculous thing is that when I grew up I learned about Saul and I learned about Joshua and I learned about Solomon being a pretty good fighter and Bar Kochba and the Maccabees — these were people who in the field of battle were successful warriors, and these are the things we know. People know about Mickey Marcus but they really don't know that he was a graduate of the Military Academy and a very successful soldier, academically as well as in the field in World War II. They don't know about Maurice Rose, who was the son of a Polish rabbi and who commanded the 3rd Armored Division. He was easily the equal of Patton as an armor leader. And I can go on and tell you about others who serve and have served. I have books filled with their names, who have fought in defense of this country in wars that were understood and in wars that were not understood. But the average Jewish person, as a result of Vietnam and as a result of being in an era when it's not compulsory to serve, has simply placed military service as a non-option.

I've had a wonderful, wonderful thirty-four years in the army. I'm going to leave the army in a year with a host of memories, and I've met some wonderful people.

This is probably unfair and I have no right to have this attitude, but the only Jew who counts with me is one who is willing to stand up and be counted as a Jew, to profess "I am Jewish." I don't have to say "I am proud of being a Jew." I am Jewish; that's what I am, that's what I'm made of.

Colonel Jack Jacobs, forty-one, U.S. Army, Annandale, Virginia

I was born in Brooklyn in Crown Heights Hospital, which no longer exists. It's likely to be a parking lot or high-rise. My grandparents came here from Europe. My mother's side of the family are Ashkenazic. Her father was from Galicia. Her mother was from Bessarabia. My father's parents are Greek Jews, all of them. They are from Ioannina. My grandmother died just a few years ago, at ninety-six. She spoke and read Greek and Hebrew and spoke English, but not very well, even after being in this country seventy-some-odd years. Never became an American citizen; had a green card for her whole life.

My father's side of the family got here between the Balkan Wars and the First World War. It was in the order of 1912 to 1914. My father's grandfather, the old man, was a baker in Ioannina. He once heard that there was a dry goods business for sale in Albania and packed up the whole family on a bunch of donkeys and walked from Ioannina into Albania, only to discover that the business had been sold the day before. And, without a rest overnight, packed right back up and walked back to Ioannina. Most of my relatives lived in Brooklyn and on the Lower East Side and worked in the sweatshops. Both sides of the family.

I know it was probably a little bit difficult for my parents, who had to deal with two completely different cultures. For example, my father's side of the family spoke no Yiddish and ate Greek food. It seemed perfectly natural to me, but I guess it was difficult for my parents, whose own parents, as I understand it, were against the union in the first place, for obvious reasons. I don't think they went as far as starting to rend their clothes and so on, but I think it almost came to that.

Most of our religious focus was Sephardic and most of the cultural focus, at least partially because of the size of the Ashkenazic side of the family, was Ashkenazic. The Sephardic side of the family was more religious; more Orthodox. As a matter of fact, they were Orthodox. So we were kind of forced to be, too, because you couldn't make any concessions on that side. I didn't have an identity problem with that, though I suspect my parents probably had trouble with it. I can never remember the families being together, ever. They are completely different cultures, and I was at home with both of them. Strangely, though, my mother and the Greek side of the family did not get along all that well. Now that the Greek side of the family is all but gone, my mother, an Ashkenazic Jew, is the repository for all the Sephardic culture in the family.

On holidays we went to my grandmother's house and we did it Sephardic, and since the ritual is slightly different, we constantly got into arguments every year over the same issues of whether or not you make a Hillel sandwich; whether you put the karpas on the matzo or you don't, or you put the this on that. My grandmother never made any concessions to Ashkenazic culture whenever we had the Pesach meal, so it was all Greek food. You'd have the plate and all the ritual stuff. But for the actual food, you wouldn't have chicken soup. We'd have things like avgolemono soup — lemon and egg soup. We'd have lamb often; almost always have lamb. We wouldn't have chicken; we wouldn't have very much beef. It was just all Greek food.

On Friday nights, in my home, we had boiled chicken or boiled beef. It was an Ashkenazic dinner because my mother made it.

We didn't stay very long in Brooklyn. When my father came back from the Second World War, we moved to a low-cost housing project. First we moved to Quonset huts right about where LaGuardia Airport is currently located. I remember flying a kite at the end of the runway when LaGuardia was nothing but an airstrip. We had a kerosene space heater, as I recall. We used to take baths in the sink. It was a tin affair with a tin roof and all. In 1950 or 1951, we moved to low-cost housing in Queens, Long Island City. Then my father, who was an electrical engineer, bought a house in what was then the wilds of New Jersey, and he had to commute into the city. It's now at the junction of the turnpike, the parkway, Routes 1, 9, and Exit 10. And they still live there.

That's where I went to high school. It was a pretty well-mixed neighborhood. And it was that generation: the guys who would today pass for young professionals, who had served in the Second World War and were now doing fairly well in an exploding economy of post–World War America. They had a few bucks in their pocket. Interest rates were low and the economy was going strong, and so it was a mixed neighborhood. There were enough Jews to set up a bunch of synagogues in just about every community. There were a lot of Catholics. It's funny when you talk about religion. I grew up in a neighborhood in New York. I did not know what a Protestant was until I was about eleven or twelve years old, when I met a kid named Billy Something-or-other and asked if he was Jewish or Catholic and he said, "Neither," and it boggled my mind. I didn't know what else there was. If you weren't Italian or you weren't a Jew, you couldn't be anything, because that's all there was. My understanding of religion was that the world's religions were two — there were Jews and Catholics, and that was it.

I went to Rutgers University in New Jersey. I took ROTC when I was a student for a number of reasons, not the least significant of which is that I got married at a very early age and had two other mouths to feed besides myself and I got an extra twenty-seven dollars a month for being in ROTC. As much as that and more than that, it was a thing you did back in those days, 1962 to 1966. I had the perception — and a lot of people did — that everybody ought to serve. Everybody who was going to school at that time had parents who'd served in the Second World War. ROTC enrollment was very high, though there was no real enthusiasm for an army career. Very few people went into the military services as a career, especially from my background.

I went in initially with the intention of staying only three years. I was a regular army officer, but it was only an extra year; I was going to get out. I was going to go to law school and I was going to make something of myself. To this day, I can't articulate very well why it is I stayed. Part of it had to do with the fact that though I hated — funny, war is an abomination — I had the Hillel view to a great or lesser extent: "If not me, who?" That was part of it.

Also, part of it was I was pretty good at what I did for a living. I mean, I was a good soldier and I was a good officer. When you are fairly good at something, you enjoy it, even if you're doing something which to other people would be terrible. If you're no good at it, you are going to hate it. I was good at what I did. I enjoyed giving orders and instructions and determining what the objectives were and making sure that they got met. I thought that I was doing some work that was important. Third part of it is that it got to be a habit, like any habit. Habits are hard to break.

However, I always considered myself and still consider myself a citizen. I'm a citizen-soldier. I wasn't born to be a soldier and I am not going to be a soldier for my whole life. I sort of feel like the guys did during the Second

World War, I guess. I'm in for the duration. My duration happens to be twenty years.

Is it hard being Jewish and being in the military? No, not at all. I'm asked that from time to time. It's very easy, as a matter of fact. It is true that Jews often go into specialties which are not directly related to fighting, and so it is relatively unusual for a Jew to be in the infantry, for example, though I myself have fought with Jews in combat.

To the perception that Jews do not often end up in combat units, however, I would say it's a correct and an incorrect perception. It's a correct perception, but it is correct for the wrong reasons. There's a small number of Jews who served in the combat arms, I think at least partially, because of the Jews' insistence on education; a focus on education which almost forces people when they go to school into fairly narrow fields. There are a lot of Jewish scientists and a lot of Jewish specialists in the health fields. When those guys come into the army, they go into narrow fields. Being a combat arms officer — infantry, armor, artillery — you are a generalist. There are not that many Jewish generalists in American society. They are doctors and they are lawyers and they are scientists. So when they serve, they serve in narrow fields. That's just the way it is, I think. And I think you'd have that just about anywhere. You know, if the army has a guy with a brain the size of Yankee Stadium, whose entire developmental life is focused on a fairly narrow field, what the heck do they need him in the infantry for and the guy's interest is not there? He wants to do something which is commensurate with his education.

Is that a change? It is a change. It's a change since I've been in the service. It's a change in the last twelve to fifteen years. I can argue persuasively that you ought to go back to the old system of throwing people willy-nilly into jobs because we'd come up with a much more well-rounded officer corps. Not for enlisted men. Enlisted men are different. But officers, I think, need to have far broader capabilities and experience. And I think I can argue persuasively that the current army personnel management system is dysfunctional or certainly does not meet our long-term objectives. But that is a separate issue.

There are fewer Jews in combat arms than there are in specialties. That's because of what they are focusing on. People are not born and then immediately thrown into the service. They spend twenty-odd years getting educated first before coming into the service, so it is not surprising.

It is absolutely untrue that the services are anti-Semitic. The services are extremely tolerant, and the people are extremely tolerant. What anti-Semitism exists, exists on a personal level out of ignorance, and it is less so now than ever. Since I've been in the army, it's diminished from a very minuscule amount to almost nothing. I've been looking for it, because people tell me that there ought to be. You think it should be intuitively obvious to the casual observer that in American society there would be some anti-Semitism. I see it far less in the military than I do anywhere; than I have on the outside, for example. Certainly from what you read in the papers.

As a general rule do I think Jews do not want to enlist or to stay in the service? As a general rule they don't. I think a lot of it — some of it; the part about not staying — is kind of intriguing. One could argue that they don't stay because they're not patriotic or they're out for themselves. I can argue the opposite. That is, the mere act of coming into the service, with the intention of leaving it after two to four years, whatever the enlistment is now, is inherently patriotic. It bespeaks a commitment to some sort of service, that you must serve your time and then go about and make your contributions to society in other ways. So on a proportionate basis, Jews are much more patriotic — in that sense. Whereas among non-Jews, if you asked them why they're in the service, they are there to learn a trade. They are there because the money is good. They are there because they would have been thrown in jail. I don't believe we do that anymore. The explanations about why you are in the service are much more patriotic among Jewish enlistees than among Gentile enlistees, from my experience of twenty years. You ask a Jew why he is in. "I'm in because I want to serve; I ought to serve." The guy doesn't need to learn a trade — he's an educated man.

Now, enlisting in the first instance; that's much more complex, because you get enlistment for various motivations across the board in American society. Most of our enlistees are from lower socioeconomic groups because it is an opportunity for them without having been educated. Jews are educated. How many uneducated Jews do you know? I don't know very many. I took the student field studies trip to Israel and Egypt last year. It was a mind-boggling experience, being a Jew from America, where there are no or very few working-class Jews, and going to a society where they are all Jews, so there are Jewish garbage men and Jewish everything. A secular society. There are no or very few Jews that are not in the middle class or better in this country. So the motivation for coming into the service, which is the motivation for lower socioeconomic groups, is therefore the motivation for many Gentiles to be in the service; it's not the motivation for Jews. So it's not a question of Jews not being patriotic because they don't enlist. The middle class in America does not enlist. Most Jews are middle class, ergo, they don't enlist. So I think it's an American phenomenon; it's not a religious phenomenon. And until we have universal service, we are not going to have very many Jews in the service, because they are educated people.

Had I started out on the outside and never come into the service except to serve whatever I had to serve, I certainly would have been financially much better off than I am now.

I probably won't stay. I'll probably leave for a number of reasons. One is that — this sounds very self-serving — but I am starting to realize that maybe it's time for me to do something for myself. That's the first thing. It's really a minor point where I am concerned, but it's certainly a consideration. I see people with whom I was graduated from college and they are all doing very, very well. My wife and I have to save money so we can afford $700 to cover the kitchen floor with a new piece of linoleum. That's no way for a middle-aged Jewish man to live. It's just not.

I have two older children, one of whom was herself just graduated from Rutgers. She works as an assistant editor for an architectural trade publication in New York City. She paid her own way through college. It was a good idea. I mean, I did too. She cherishes the degree because it's all hers. But she did so out of necessity, because I couldn't afford to send her to school. I've got a son who is doing the same thing. He's a sophomore at Virginia Tech. He's doing it partially because his sister did it and he sees that it can be done. He'll have the same pride in ownership when his four years are up. But he is also doing it out of necessity. I can't afford $10,000, $12,000 a year. It's a significant portion of my income. It's okay to live like that — for a while. And it's okay to live that way if you can't live any other way. But I don't want to live like that anymore. I'm tired of living like that.

I was in Vietnam. I was graduated in June 1966 and I was in Vietnam by September 'sixty-seven, so I guess it was less than eighteen months. I was in Vietnam in September 1967 and again in July 'seventy-two. I went back again. I had two tours.

To answer your question, I may be the only Jew from Vietnam to win the Congressional Medal of Honor, although I don't know for sure.

14

Sweating It Out

IN EAST COAST Jewish folklore, certain names cry out: the Catskills, Miami Beach, the Lower East Side, Brooklyn, the Bronx, and the garment district. In the garment district a subset of evocative words would include sweatshops, the Triangle fire, the needle trade, the ILGWU, the Amalgamated Clothing Workers. For decades, the garment district embodied the soul of the great Jewish immigration of the late nineteenth and early twentieth centuries. It was entry work to a wider society. What the taxicab is to today's immigrant, the sewing machine was to yesterday's Jewish newcomer.

Leonard Garment, who served President Richard M. Nixon in the White House, is the son of a dress manufacturer who spent most of his life as a "contractor," doing work for the actual manufacturer. "I guess he started out stitching and sewing and then doing the various jobs that were done in the ready-to-wear business in New York. He worked in his father's factory and hated it. We all did, my brothers and my mother."

Here is Garment on the garment district:

"And then I would go into the garment district, running errands. That was another big part of my job. Also, with the pinking shears, I would work on — God, I still remember this, this vestigial memory of pain and suffering . . . And I would go on my endless trip back and forth on the Eighth Avenue subway to New York with packages; taking packages up there, bringing packages back — packages of buttons, packages of trimmings or passementeries, as they are known in the trade. It is a world full of strange businesses and odd nomenclature; technical descriptions of things. And the garment district — I suppose most people do not know what it was. It was a place full of hopes, dreams, borsht, bagels, hardening of the arteries, cirrhosis of the mind, a great deal of rushing back and forth, and a place of fantasy and fear; it was the lives of the way-out from the ghetto out of east New York into Flatbush, Eastern Parkway, Crown Heights, onward and upward, mobility for the parent and newbility for the child."

Gus Tyler, *seventy-four, union official, Great Neck, New York*

I am assistant president of the International Ladies Garment Workers Union. I was born in October 1911 in Williamsburg, a neighborhood in the heart of Brooklyn.

My mother had come over from Lithuania. First her father came over, and then she came over when she must have been about ten years old. By the age of eleven, she was at a sewing machine in the shop of Dudley Sicher, who had one of the more respectable firms because it didn't engage in home work and it was not one of these small contracting shops. He did white goods, underwear really, and he did his own manufacturing and he was a German Jew and a man who had achieved some status in the society. Meantime, my mother had three sisters who came over one at a time. As they came, they got off the boat and went into the factory. My mother taught them how to run the sewing machines. So at one point, four of the sisters were in the factory.

She never complained about it. She never said anything about it. She never felt that she was being oppressed or anything of the kind. It was a job. You came in; you did the job.

The four girls supported my grandfather, who was the perfect yeshiva bocher. He was one of twins. I think his twin went into the army and something happened to him. They never knew about him. My grandfather was a survivor, but he took life kind of easy. He felt that he had done his day's work if he went to the synagogue and if he talked to the other ancient boys there. To me, he was always ancient. He supported himself through the years that I knew him by a few weeks of work around Passover. He would rent a little wagon and a little horse and he had his circle of customers. He'd sell them matzos and wine. That was it. He had enough to pay his own rent.

My father came from Lithuania, too. I think he came from southern Lithuania, because he always confused *sh* with *s* — everything came out backwards when he spoke Yiddish. You ate "fiss" instead of "fish," et cetera. He came over about the same age and came into the industry — again the garment industry. He tried for many, many years to be a contractor. He wanted to be a businessman and make some money. He was very, very unsuccessful. He was unsuccessful all his life as a businessman. He was a very sweet man, good-looking, very sympathetic, and obviously for those reasons unfit to be a businessman where you had to exploit workers in order to live. He didn't fit. So he'd go bankrupt regularly, and then he'd get a job. Next thing you know, he was back in the industry. That's the way it was, really, to the end of his life. But the last ten years he ended up as a cutter. He was a skilled craftsman. In his last years, he'd pick up some extra money at a sewing machine doing bridal costumes and things.

My mother and father met through a shadchen, which I suppose was established procedure, because both of them had been married and both of them had lost their mates. My mother was married to a child of the family of court Jews. She was married to a Lieberman. They were Saint Petersburg Jews. They were terribly, terribly literate. They could all speak Yiddish and Hebrew and, of course, Russian and a little bit of Polish. They were educated people. The man to whom my mother was married — I was not born yet — was an actor. He was a Yiddish actor in the Second Avenue theater. You know how actors are; they can't make a living. So when he was "at liberty," like actors regularly are, he used to make his living as a silversmith, which he apparently was very good at. The way in which you got the silver to adhere before you put on the solder was to moisten it, and you moistened it with your tongue. He picked up metal poisoning and at a very, very early age he died. One of my sisters was already born; Anna was a child of that family. It was a very interesting kind of arrangement, because after my mother's husband died, there still remained a link with that branch of the family, partly because of my sister. My sister was a Lieberman; she was born as a Lieberman, which was the name of that family. There were two younger brothers. Anna's father was the oldest brother. One of the younger brothers was Elias Lieberman, who was the first Jewish high school principal in Brooklyn. He was principal of Thomas Jefferson High School, and he later became the associate superintendent of schools in New York City. He was the first Jew ever to be associated with high school administration. Up until that time, the succession in the New York City schools was Protestant, fundamentally Scandinavian and German. Then it went out of their hands and it really fell into the hands of the Irish Catholics, and then the Jews moved in and then the blacks and Hispanics. You could see the succession. His brother, Max Lieberman, was head of the English department at Bushwick High School.

It's very fascinating, because in a way they're not relatives of mine, but I always call them uncles. One of the wives in that group was a lawyer; another one was a schoolteacher. They were all well educated and well spoken, and for them the world of art and esthetics and literature and ideas was very important. They would come around to our house, not every day, but regularly. In my head, I was identified with that culture. You know, genealogically it doesn't stand up. It makes no difference; they were part of the family, and it was kind of a thing that you picked up. For a long time, my uncle Elias Lieberman was a kind of a role model. Over the course of a life, you pick up role models. He was one role model. At a later point, Morris Hillquit was a role model. He was head of the Socialist Party of the United States. I have to fill you in, because this is all part of the story, the way in which a life is formed.

Hillquit came here at the turn of the century — a frustrated European intellectual. He had to make a living, so he learned to run a sewing machine. But that was not what life was going to be for Morris Hillquit. He was an intellectual. He went to night school and became a lawyer, and became the intellectual leader of the American socialist movement from about 1895 to the day of his death, which must have been in the mid 1930s. He was an eloquent orator; spoke English, Yiddish, French, German, Italian. He would regularly go to international conventions as the representative of the American Socialist Party at a time when it was a significant movement — when Eugene Victor Debs was there and Victor Berger was there. Hillquit was a New York socialist, but he was recognized as the intellectual spokesman. People know Norman Thomas, who in my opinion never formulated policy for the movement.

I was very active in the Socialist Party as a kid. Williamsburg around 1915, 1916, elected a socialist to the New York State Assembly. That was the year, it must have been 1916, when New York City elected six or seven socialists to the New York State Assembly. I guess I know most of their names — Louis Waldman, Abraham Shiplacoff, Charles Solomon, Sam Orr, William Feigenbaum. When they got to the State Assembly they were promptly thrown out. There was a trial. They were traitors because they were not supporting World War I, and you do not allow a traitor to sit. There was a great debate — I forget now who was representing the state; a man of some distinction in later years. Morris Hillquit was busy defending these people. They said the men were traitors, and Morris Hillquit said, "Well, you know, today's traitors are tomorrow's heroes." This other guy who was arguing against Hillquit said, "Yes, today's traitors are tomorrow's heroes, if we allow the traitors to take over our government."

The neighborhood always had a high socialist ferment. I have very clear pictures of when I was seven or eight years old. In the summer days we'd go down to the street corner at Hart Street and Tompkins Avenue and right there at 167 Tompkins Avenue was a socialist headquarters. The Socialist Party had once been prosperous and they bought this building. It was five stories tall. Always on that street corner there would be meetings when the weather permitted. I remember George Kirkpatrick, who came out of the prairie states. He was one of these prairie preacher-type socialists. So far as I was concerned, he stood eight feet tall. He'd come out there with his red galluses and take his jacket off and he'd thunder away with these huge, dramatic gestures. He looked like a bird of prey about to descend upon you. The only way you could get a crowd was by overacting and by telling stories and jokes. You couldn't indulge in pure and simple oratory. You'd go no place. You had to stay with the narrative. If you didn't tell stories, you lost your audience. You couldn't explain about value and surplus value and moxie or any of that stuff. You could weave it into your line of argument. I'll never forget — Oscar Ameringer came out of Oklahoma. Oklahoma had two dozen socialists in the state legislature. That was at the height of the populist movement, when the Populist Party had merged with the Democrats. These people wouldn't go with it, so they were electing socialists. Ameringer had a daily paper out there.

Oscar Ameringer knew enough German and knew enough Jews to make his German sound like Yiddish if he had to. He was marvelous. And the way in which these people developed their line of talk — and this was also true of the Jewish agitators and orators at that time — they would work out little parables and examples. That was the one thing they knew. They were all intellectuals; that's the interesting thing about it. But they knew that their job was to educate the masses, and that you develop a speech that is meaningful to the masses. Oscar Ameringer would hold up his hand and he would say, "Here is the worker. Here is what the worker produces. In between you have profits; you have interest; and you have rent. Profits, interest, and rent cut into what the worker produces. Now look at it. There's no way for the worker ever to get to what the worker produces. Now," he said, "let's eliminate profits, interest, and rent. The worker can get to what he produces." Just like that. It was a kind of a genius. Most of these guys had it.

Apropos of the need to speak the language and the Jewish socialist and the Jewish labor movement of which the ILGW was part, it's all very fascinating to me. In the early years, the Jewish socialists in New York and the would-be leaders of the labor movement in New York refused to talk Yiddish. First of all, many of them couldn't. They did okay in German, Hungarian, and Russian, some Polish. Those were legitimate languages. They would not speak Yiddish to the workers, many of whom looked upon Yiddish as their first language. Most of them had another language, but they were sloppy in it. But Yiddish was the common language of the East and Central European Jews. The agitators would not speak to them in Yiddish. Why? Because they're talking about making a revolution. The Jews who spoke Yiddish and didn't know Russian and so on, they were Jews from the shtetl. The Jews from the shtetl were no material for making a revolution. They were peasants; they were backward; they were uneducated; they were docile. Too bad; they're brethren and landsleit and co-religionists, but they can't make a revolution. So what you had were these agitators who had their little intellectual circles, mutual admiration societies, where they'd gather. And really, they weren't organizing a damn thing; they couldn't organize. They came into the Socialist Party and they had a Russian-speaking branch and a German-speaking branch, the biggest branch in New York. Even when I got to touch the socialist movement, which was around 1924, 1925, the biggest group we had were the Finns. They had the Finnish Federation in New York. The Finns were it. They were powerful. The Finns and the Germans. The Jews were just coming up at that time.

The Jewish labor movement really was put together by two elements. First of all, they learned organization and strategy from the Germans. The German socialists said to the Jewish socialists, "Hey, come on. You're not serious people; you're just talking to one another. You're theorizing. You have to have an organization, discipline, dues, et cetera." It was the Germans who taught them. The Germans also taught them New York politics. They said, "You've got to get your people to vote; you've got to register them; get into this thing."

I mean Germans, not German Jews. The Germans were socialists. They had powerful organizations in New York. The Germans actually tutored the Jews.

The other one was Abraham Cahan. It wasn't just Abe Cahan, but Abe Cahan was an unusual guy. Abe was an intellectual. He was well educated. He came over here as an anarchist, and then he figured anarchism really didn't make much sense. He was a hell of a good writer. He started writing, and he said we ought to have a Yiddish press, and we should talk to the workers in Yiddish. It was a war. He was crazy. Not only do we talk to them in Yiddish, but we talk to them in the kind of Yiddish they talk in this country.

I was at the *Jewish Daily Forward* for a while, and I remember — I was told about it — this meeting where he was scolding the writers. He said, "You're writing about a war and you say we gained so many *viorst*. When you speak to your grandmother here in the United States, do you say *viorst*? No, you say *milen*. So why don't you write *milen*?" He decided that you just use the vernacular, and the intellectuals were outraged. Among other things, he was corrupting the Yiddish language. He was downgrading it. This was awful. He said, "This is the language they understand, and I'm talking with them." Then, of course, he set up this thing called "Bintel Brief," which has now become famous. It was advice to the lovelorn or advice to anybody. He ran these columns on how to blow your nose. "There's such a thing as the handkerchief, and this country uses handkerchiefs." He was asked, "You know, you're stooping?" He says, "You got a little infant, and you're standing up there and you want to elevate the infant. What do you say to the infant, jump up here where I am?" He said, "You bend down; you take the infant; you pick the infant up. That's the way you do it." He was marvelous. He had the common touch. The *Forward*, which is the publication he controlled, just did it.

The *Forward* really became the organizer, not of the unions alone. The *Forward* became the organizer, in my opinion, of the Jewish community, and not only here, because it went across the country. There are various ways in which you can look at the way in which the labor movement at various times springs forward and goes back. When you look at our labor history, what a guy is going to write about will be "this union was organized in this-and-this time." They may make a passing reference to the ethnic composition of the people in the trade and the leadership — even that you don't normally find in the labor histories. They'll say the machinists organized, blah blah. They go at it in a very mechanical kind of way. The truth of the matter is, by my reading, that the basis of the organization of apparel workers was the rise of the Jewish community in America, the rise of the working-class Jew.

I'm not talking about the Sephardic Jews, who had come over much earlier. I'm not talking about the German Jews, who went into business much earlier. I'm talking about the Jews who came here between 1880 and 1890 as immigrants from Eastern and Central Europe. Before they could do anything, they had to become a community. And they were not a community until they began to speak a common language, and that common language was not German, Austrian, Bulgarian, not Rumanian, not Russian, not Polish, or Lithuanian, which is where they came from. These were separate languages. Their *lingua franca* was Yiddish. Actually, the people who could speak the other languages didn't have to become involved with the proletarian movements. They were making it on their own. It's the workers who were stuck with the Yiddish. It isn't just the *Jewish Daily Forward*. Then there was the Workmen's Circle, which was a fraternal order.

The Workmen's Circle is a sickness-and-death society with social overtones and an ideological commitment. It was organized by Jews fundamentally on the East Coast and spread across the country. These were working-class people. Now, when you die, how do you get buried? When you get sick, where do you go for a doctor? Kind of like a workman's unemployment insurance thing, any kind of mutual aid. It was a mutual aid society. Was; it is. It still exists. They used to conduct their meetings in Yiddish. They set up an old age home. But it was also a social center, where you got together. You didn't go down to the lodge; you went down to the Workmen's Circle meeting. Lectures were all about economic and political matters, always with a working-class or a socialist slant. And they still are, at the present time.

Now it's another generation and it's not as big as it used to be. It used to be very big and very powerful and very, very rich, like an insurance company. Now it isn't, because that generation is not around; they don't want to go to meetings where they talk in Yiddish or talk about Yiddish culture. And then there were the Yiddish schools. The schools were not parochial schools, but they were parochial schools. They were not parochial because they didn't teach religion, but they taught you how to speak Yiddish and how to write Yiddish, not Hebrew, because you had the Talmud Torahs for the Hebrew. This was purely secular. All of this comes through at the same time, and the ILGWU comes into existence and you have the Jewish section of the United Garment Workers, which was the Amalgamated Clothing Workers ultimately. And the United Garment Workers didn't want them. They didn't want those "goddamn Jews." The interesting thing is if you read John R. Commons, who was a great and intelligent and very compassionate and sympathetic labor historian — there are a couple essays by him that said the Jews can never organize anything. They are too disputatious, too loose, too uneducated. He said of the Jews what later on I heard Jews say about the Italians. We don't have to worry about the Italians; they can't organize anything. And so they organized a good underworld; they organized an empire. Why the hell can't they organize a union? Well, they're Italians; they're ignorant. It just goes on and on and on. It keeps repeating itself in that respect. I lived through the damn thing. Basically, it was an uprising of the Jewish community.

The union was organized in 1900, and it was organized by cloakmakers. The cloakmakers were all Jewish. I think if you look at our charter, there may be one Irishman there at the head of the cutters' union. But it was basically Jewish. The cloak ranks are very highly skilled. They were European tailors, and they weren't looked upon as workers. They didn't look upon themselves as workers. They looked upon themselves as artisans. They organized as cloakmakers, and eleven of them got together from Newark and from Baltimore and they organized a union. Two years after they organized the union, they met in convention and said, "Maybe we ought to consider disbanding the union." There was nothing there; they were getting no place and there was a little bit of a recession. Nothing really happened, but they held on because they were ideologically committed. They were socialists and anarchists and a few others like that. We didn't have any communists around at that time.

The great push comes in 1909. Now we had the shirtwaist makers. The whole economy was changing, so that women now were buying their clothing in stores. Up to that time, if you were a lady you were part of the carriage trade, custom tailored. If you were not a lady, you made it yourself at home, either by hand or with a sewing machine. But the economy was changing; they were learning methods of producing it less expensively. Women in the United States were now able to buy things in the stores. The shirtwaist was a waist, but it was longer and could be used as a dress. That was mass production in New York City. They must have employed about thirty thousand people in New York City in 1909. The union was not much of a union, but there was a whole series of incidents. There was a grievance and there was much shouting and much yelling. They called a meeting down at Cooper Union. Cooper Union Auditorium can hold maybe three thousand people. That used to be the great meeting place. You didn't have to pay rent, because it was all in the tradition of Peter Cooper. You went to him and you gave him five dollars and you got it for a week.

They had the meeting and the story goes: "Yes, we have grievances and let's talk about a strike." The leadership of the union is intellectuals, and they're busy figuring out how can we conduct a strike. "We can't maintain a strike; we have no way of maintaining discipline. These poor immigrant girls are going to give up their jobs? We don't have money to give them for strike benefits. We don't have anything; we're bankrupt." So the leadership is up there saying, "Yes, we've got to strike; we have to find the right moment." What they were saying was "Don't strike." One crazy little girl, aged sixteen, Clara Lemlich, stands up there and she says, "We have to strike," and the place goes crazy.

They said yes, and the crazy kids went out on strike. The next morning they had twenty thousand of them on strike. This has nothing to do with unions or union leadership. If I had to explain it, I'd say the union leadership was opposed to the strike. Not because they were mean people. They were very responsible people who were going at this thing rationally. My final conclusion is the great historic movements are the irrational ones. If you want to go rational, it ain't going to happen. It became a *cause célèbre*. Mrs. August Belmont was very important and she organized all of her society ladies and expressed sympathy for these young girls. It was also a great moment. The feminist movement was picking up steam. "See how they rape these young girls and insult them and exploit them and underpay them, because they're girls?" They had these great parades marching down the streets where you had these workers, the right to vote, and these fancy ladies. Actually, this was an uprising of New York Jews.

It's interesting; that was in 1909. The following year, the cloakmakers go out. These were all men, and ten thousand of them walked out. You had the whole period in there where the Jewish ferment was very big.

Number one, Jews were tailors. It was a Jewish trade in many parts of the world, and in any little community even if you were not a tailor, if you were the woman, you learned to sew your own garments. What is it, in that little shtetl over there they went down to Bloomingdale's? You know how to sit there with a needle and thread, and when you had the sewing machine, you gravitated to it. It was a natural Jewish trade.

There were certain Jewish trades. Generally, they were the trades that were considered to be inferior. Why so many Jews in leather? Because you had to strip the beast. It was a stinking profession. It was a dangerous profession, and Jews went into leather. It was dumped on them. It was known as a "Jewish industry," and therefore fur, right next door to it, and shoes. In this country, this was not the exclusive trade. There were many jobs, and therefore it loomed large. The tobacco industry in the New York area was a hundred percent Jewish — German Jewish employers and Central and Eastern European Jews in the factories. Cigar makers, also. You have to remember who the head of the union was. It was Samuel Gompers, a Dutch Jew. The union was important enough so that he became the president of the American Federation of Labor, founder and president. You've got to ask yourself, How the hell did a Jew do that? I have my own theories on that. He was very smart, very gutsy, very able, married outside the religion. I think his wife was Catholic. He came in at a time when there was a great battle in the American labor movement as to who should run it, the Protestant church or the Catholic church? So they made a great compromise — this is my theory. He always wore a skullcap, always, while professing that he was a nonprofessing Jew. When asked why, he said, "If I don't wear it, I catch cold." There are all kinds of documents that someday will surface about his relationship with the so-called Jewish labor unions — very close, very understanding, and extremely sympathetic. He kept rejecting radicalism in public.

The Jewish labor unions were the apparel trades, the cigar makers, a number of the building trades, the plumbers in the New York area. In the Bronx, for instance, it was a Jewish business. There were carpenters' locals that were a hundred percent Jewish. The painters were a Jewish operation — Phil Zausner for many years was the great leader. The soft drinks, a spinoff from seltzer. Everything that was a spinoff from seltzer was Jewish. Needless to say, all of the Jewish foods, Jewish unions. The bakers were a Jewish union. I remember the day when you'd get a "steamer's" [Stuhmer's] pumpernickel and on it was the union label fastened there with egg white.

I don't remember the year now — it was probably before 1900 — when an organization was put together in New York called the United Hebrew Trades. I think the United Hebrew Trades may still exist. The United Hebrew Trades were very interesting. They declared at the very outset that they were not trying to set up a separate federation of labor, because they were not dual unionists. They said their function was to translate unionism for workers who were Yiddish-speaking or came of Jewish origin, whatever the language. They were really Yiddish. And so they had this little organization. At the present, there's a Jewish Labor Committee, which has a more extended function — civil rights and stuff like that. It's still around and it's still a force as a Jewish organization.

As for me, in 1924 when La Follette was running for President of the United States, I did what you were supposed to do. I was distributing leaflets for La Follette. The Socialist Party had gone along with the Progressive Party candidate. I was thirteen years old. This was kind of my Bar Mitzvah. When he lost, I couldn't understand it, because everybody on my block and everybody in my building and everybody who took my leaflets said they were going to vote for La Follette. He had to be elected. My view of the world was that it was divided between Socialists and Democrats. I knew there was a thing around called the Republican Party but I wasn't quite sure what that damn thing was, because that was three blocks away from me, where you still had some Swedes and Germans hanging around. The Irish, obviously not.

I went to Boys High School in Brooklyn, a great school. It was out of the classic tradition. I guess eighty percent of the student body had to take Latin — we didn't have to; we elected Latin, because we felt it was expected of us — and another language. I started my freshman year with Latin and German. Boys High School at that time was overwhelmingly Jewish. Not the faculty; the faculty wasn't. We didn't have many Jewish teachers, as a matter of fact, but they were good teachers. Many of them German, some Irish, and a few Jewish.

We took our studies very seriously; you were expected to. A lot of homework, and you had to get it done. But it was not a lopsided school. In 1925 we won the city high school football championship, a very inspiring moment. We had math teams and chess teams and debating teams, and we were expected to win. If you went to Boys High and you were on the debating team, you didn't lose a debate. We worked at it — a great, great education. Subsequently, I went to New York University at the Heights because I got a scholarship, and I felt it was a comedown.

Shortly after the New Deal, the ILGW began to sign up a lot of people, and I figured this was perfect. Here's a union that has a radical tradition. My family came out of the industry, and I knew some people in it. So I came down as a volunteer. My first job was not with the union, however. It was with the *Jewish Daily Forward,* where I was assistant labor editor.

David Dubinsky became president of the union in the late 1920s. When he came to the union, it was bankrupt. Number one, the union had lost membership during the twenties; then came the Great Depression. The industry was hard hit and nobody was able to organize anything, and the ILGW went bankrupt. It was still predominantly Jewish then but with a lot of Italians now coming in. The Italian leadership was left wing. Luigi Antonini, who was the Italian idol, was a very theatrical personality. He had this big black bow tie, the kind that hangs way over your shoulders and everything. He never spoke, he only thundered. A very authoritarian personality. He had come out, I think, of the anarchist movement, but in the 1920s he was one of the active communist leaders in the union. We had a number of active communist leaders. He was in the dress section. Sasha Zimmerman, who was Jewish, was one of the top leaders of the American Communist Party in our industry. In the cloakmakers they had their people.

The reason was these people had come from the Hapsburg and more of them from the Russian Empire. The word *Czar* was a dirty word. Here was a revolution in the name of the working class that toppled the Czar. You don't have to spend much time knowing where your sympathies are.

As for my union, the communists had it. They took the Dress Joint Board and the Cloak Joint Board. They didn't do very well in the areas outside of New York. They did not get the cutters' union. In 1926, there was a big strike in the industry. The strike was uncalled for. The union made its demands. Management was prepared to make concessions, but the communists had a theory that they had to get the masses out there and prove that they could get more. They had to work up a spirit of militancy. You know, dogma is dogma. The strike was catastrophic. They lost it. There were two reasons they lost. First, they were asking for impossible things. Secondly, the cutters would not go with them. The cutters were the key people then in the industry. If you don't have the cutters, you don't have muscle.

Dubinsky was heading the cutters, and he was not going to go with them. He also felt it was foolish. Anyhow, they lost, which in itself was not necessarily bad, but they had done something else. In order to run the strike, they tapped funds that were not theirs. We had contracts, and employers posted one week or one month of pay to guarantee they would live up to their contract. If you didn't, there was a period during which the workers still got paid out of the funds held in escrow. The communists used the escrow funds, and the union came out of that strike not only without money, but it owed the escrow fund several millions of dollars. The membership was angry. The membership was disillusioned, and the communists were thrown out.

Is it still predominantly a Jewish union? Jewish and Italian now predominantly in New York, probably in other centers as well. There are a few places around the country where we have Yankees. At one time, the International Union published a Yiddish newspaper, an Italian newspaper, and an English newspaper for its membership.

When you get into the 1960s, you have the organization now of the service sector, the white-collar people, heavily in government, and the teachers. Most of the teachers in America are not Jewish, but the American

Federation of Teachers is headed by Al Shanker. American Federation of State and County Municipal Employees is the same thing. You go into a number of these professional unions and you find Jews in a position of leadership even where the membership is not predominantly Jewish. By the way, a number of teamsters' locals were primarily Jewish.

In the Jewish community being a labor leader, or being involved with the labor movement, was an honorable career, in the same way that in many Irish communities joining the police force is an honorable career. Different people value different things. I don't know whether today in the Jewish community being in the labor movement in a position of leadership is looked upon as anything, but at one time it was one of the ways in which you would win respect.

If you look at the various ethnic movements in the United States, each one constructs its own ladder. At one time, even for Jews, prizefighting represented upward mobility. Another avenue of upward mobility for many groups has been entertainment. So at one time just about all of the comedians were Jewish. It's a channel through which you can move, and blacks have used the same channel, and most recently Italians, who are doing so well in Hollywood. For the Irish, the priesthood and politics, and for almost every group the underworld was a way to move up. It was a very respectable kind of thing to do, so long as you didn't get caught. But for the Jews, the world of social movements, it's always been something. And it is today. Sometimes it's different social movements — in civil rights you have a disproportionate number of Jews, in pacifists the same, in radicals, and also computer science, artificial intelligence, physics, abstractions, once all the fiddle players.

At one point, I don't know who it was who said it, the most proletarian nation on the earth are the Jews. Why? Because in medieval Europe they were denied property. So they were proletarians and they had to find a way to live. Well, they did not really in the first instance become employees. In the first instance, many of them became just luftmenshen, small merchants. You never knew quite how they managed to stay alive, but they did. Once you had a working-class movement, and many Jews were employees, they just moved in.

I think there's another factor in this, and that is the millennial tradition that's still there in Judaism, so that you find it easier to say "When I'm working for a union, I'm doing more than a nine-to-five job. I am now preparing the way for a new age." It's easy to absorb that tradition even when you're not part of it. Mortimer Adler is a perfect example. He's fundamentally a man who believes in absolute truths and lasting truths, and it's handed down, and the ethic is the backbone of all philosophy. He doesn't start with philosophy and go to ethics. He starts with ethics and invents a philosophy. It makes him a very rigid kind of a guy. Fundamentally you know — at the present time I think he's an Episcopalian — he's one of the prophets. He's a son of a daughter of the prophets.

It gets into your blood. It's in your bones. I think many Jews in the labor movement in some ways are unlike other ethnic groups in the same labor movement. I'm not saying other ethnic groups do not have people who have very, very high dedication. They do, and there's a long-run view for them beyond just holding the organization together, collecting dues, and signing the next contract. But it's very easy for Jews to say they're doing something more than organizing the union, getting a contract; they're part of a long tradition.

Fred Schwartz, fifty-five, furrier, New York, New York

My company is a wholesale and retail fur company, doing about a third of our business at wholesale selling to department and specialty stores and about two thirds of our business at retail.

My father was one of eleven sons, two of whom died in Europe as children, and two who died in World War I. So there were seven left. They came over singly over a long period of time, to the extent that my grandmother, when she subsequently came over finally with the youngest child, did not know or really much care to know her oldest sons, because they were so far removed from her, having become married men with families.

My father's family did the kind of work which was considered rather demeaning in a way: they took the animal skins which the peasants would cull from the sheep and goats and they would tan them in some process. Tanning historically was considered in the earliest civilizations to be sort of the lowest of any occupation. I was in a place in Egypt recently where they still do tanning by the most primitive methods, and the odor you could smell from five miles away. You could understand why it was such a vile profession, because anybody who works in that environment was just considered to be at the lowest level of human endeavor. My grandfather and his father before him, as far as I understand, were like these people who tanned and sewed together the skins and gave back garments to the peasants for warmth. That's about as close as you can get to fashion in a fur coat.

When they came here, I think there was a natural gravitation towards the fur trade. Of the seven sons, five ended up in the fur business. They lived in the Lower East Side at first and then they branched out to Brooklyn and the Bronx as the children got married. My father, I know, spent his first nights sleeping on flour sacks in a bakery when he came off the boat. He came here on his own when he was fourteen years old. He ventured out on a Friday night from his small Polish town, because the authorities would not be looking for Jewish children to travel on a Friday night. They were escaping conscription into the army. He went to Hamburg on his own; somehow or other got through that morass. He sailed on a ship that was a new ship in those days. If you took a maiden voyage, you went free of charge. But somebody took his money for the ticket from him anyway. When he came here he was apprenticed into the coat and suit trade. He got into sewing fur collars and then got into contracting and working and making the fur collars with one of his brothers.

I think they thought they were business people or were in business because they were sewing for their own labor. And they were getting paid for that. As far as being entrepreneurs, that was as close as they came. My father lived all of his life, I think, with the underlying idea that he couldn't believe people would pay him just because he worked for them — that he got money for just using his hands. He couldn't relate the two things: the effort and the compensation. He worked very much in fear of his job in the years that I remember him. Prior to that, when he was a very young man, because he was fairly skilled at what he was doing, he began to make a fair amount of money. My mother told me he was earning thirty-five dollars a week. I guess this would be somewhere around the First World War. I don't know why he was never in the army; perhaps he was too young. He came over around 1909. He dressed very well. His photos belie his later life, when I knew him, because he was photographed wearing spats, a homburg, a vest, and a gold watch fob. Totally unrecognizable to me, because when I knew him he was already slouched and indifferent to clothing and wore the same thing all the time.

All I remember about my father was that he was always very tired. He would work six days a week. He would get up on Sunday at about five or six in the morning, because that was his habit anyway. He would get all dressed up and put on a starched shirt and tie his tie — a very narrow tie — very tight, with a small knot at the neck. He would put on his Florsheim pointed wing-tip shoes, and he would go down to the bakery and buy us our Danish and bagels. He would come back upstairs, get the *Forward,* and I would read the color section — it was a sepia brown thing in an English language translation — which was the only thing I could read. He would proceed to go to sleep on the couch and sleep the rest of the afternoon, because he was just so tired. If it was a sunny afternoon, he would go down the street from where we lived in the Bronx. It was a major street with shops on it, and he would dress up in his best topcoat if it was spring or fall, and his winter coat if it was winter. Not really a shpatzir; they would stand in place in a doorway of a store that was closed because it was Sunday, and they would talk to their neighbors and friends. If it was summertime, they'd sit in the park or somebody's back yard and play cards — hearts and pinochle.

He spoke Yiddish to my mother mostly. They spoke Polish when they didn't want us to understand. "Pavolyva!" they'd say. That meant the children are listening; be careful. My brother and I were the only two children. We lived in a two-bedroom apartment on Monroe Avenue in the Bronx, one bedroom of which was rented out to a boarder, who paid us nine dollars a month. I think our rent was forty-eight dollars a month, which surprised me, because that was a relatively high rent. It was a nice apartment. It had the requisite cross-ventilation.

Phones were virtually unknown until after the war. Those who were "in business" had phones. We had a window washer above us who had a route, and he had to receive phone calls. We lived over a candy store, and all our phone calls, if we got any, were always by Mr. Friedman coming out in the alleyway and yelling up, "Schwartz!"

We slept on the fire escape in the summertime when it was very oppressive. My brother and I would put blankets and pillows out on the fire escape. The iceman would come, and if you were rich you'd get a twenty-cent block of ice; otherwise, you'd get a ten- or fifteen-cent block. You'd put it in the icebox and it would drain. We lived in a three-story building, so the drain-pipe — it was getting ultra-modern at that time — would drain down to the basement. We kids used to break off the drainpipe and have a kind of phone communication between the floors. We'd talk down the drainpipe. In the wintertime, Louie the iceman, who was an Italian, switched over to coal, and I used to ride in his truck. He would deliver coal in small quantities. There was penny candy, and I used to steal from the candy store, as did most of the kids. Sometimes we'd go to the five-and-ten and steal things, and then we'd go down the street somewhere and add up the amount of the things we stole just to see how much we could steal.

It was a totally Jewish neighborhood. The only Gentiles I knew were superintendents. I think it was very supportive. I think it was a very finite world. Around the corner was an alien area. Not that we didn't know the kids and everything else, but it was almost like another culture. You lived with the people whom you were proximate to. I still think to this day I can close my eyes and tell you practically everybody who lived in every apartment. But more important, I can tell you how to get a ball off the roof, and I know how to get into the basements. If the superintendent was there, he wouldn't let you get up to the roof, so you would go from an adjacent building onto the roof or whatever. I also knew where the sewers were, so you could pull off the cover and climb down into the sewer and find any balls that might have fallen into the sewer. We played on the streets. There were very few cars at that time, early prewar and subsequently during the war. Following the war, our stickball field was decimated by cars, because they were all over the place. Horses and wagons purveyed fruits and vegetables on the street daily.

Summers my family sometimes went to Rockaway. It was infrequent. We would take one room for the whole family, and my mother would always invite a couple of cousins along. We bathed in a steel tub that was really a very large pot that was brought into the center of the room. My mother would get the sand out of my hair at night. The kitchen, the bedroom, and the bathroom were all in one room. Sometimes we stayed home during summers. I did go to camp in later years when I was twelve, thirteen, and fourteen. One was a Workmen's Circle camp that turned out to be a communist camp, where we spoke in Yiddish and sang Russian army songs. My brother came up to visit me during that time at camp, and I left the camp to be with him for two days. When I came back, nobody knew I'd been gone. It's funny to recall all these things. The camp was called Gan Aden, Garden of Eden. I guess it was all right. It was very inexpensive and my mother was obsessed with the idea of air. She told me stories about the baby carriage, wheeling me to a park a block away because the air was better. This was a very important kind of consideration.

My parents were not active in social movements. I know many who were. My parents were not active in any of those areas. My father was much more social than my mother. It was really just a matter of sustaining life and getting along. My mother always told me she didn't care if I brought home C's on my report card. That was fine, just as long as I was normal. What would have happened if I'd brought home a non-Jewish girl? Probably it would have been a catastrophe. I don't know how I would have faced that. I don't think at that age, when I was going with my wife already, that I could have faced that. But they didn't like my wife either, because she came from a family that was almost antithetically Jewish. They had a Christmas tree. I went through a lot with that whole experience. It was almost as if I'd married a non-Jew. And I don't have a Christmas tree now.

I wasn't very conscious of my Jewishness. It wasn't very important, except the fact that we knew there were others. I experienced very little anti-Semitism, except I remember once during the war venturing a few blocks out of the neighborhood to what was a known non-Jewish area. Some girls said something about Jew bastard or something. I don't really remember, except it was the first insult that stuck in my mind. I sort of didn't know how to handle that and I felt very bad about it — about being called that which I didn't know how to respond to.

Or the time I made my first very big sale in the fur business. I made a $2000 profit on a sale and I was absolutely out of my mind. I was just a kid, working for a few years. I came home and told my mother we made $2000 on a single sale. Can you believe that? She listened to me and said, "So how often is that going to happen?" She's always there with the put-down. You never can rise too high.

My mother spent all her time on the Lower East Side until she got married. Her side of the family calls her Rifka, and my father's side calls her Molly. My mother's story was that her father came here before her. She had three brothers, one of whom died from measles in Europe at age four. His yahrzeit is on Rosh Hashonah. My mother tells the story that in the town they lived in this child developed this very high fever. She was about seven or eight years old. They didn't know what to do for the measles. There was no treatment. My mother's father and her two brothers were here sending money back. So this was a mother living alone with a daughter, my mother, who was seven or eight years old, and a sick boy. The child was dying, and they finally succeeded, after some days, in getting a Polish doctor to come along. My grandmother became frantic and hysterical, crying that the child was dying, and he didn't seem to be able to do anything. The doctor said to her in Polish, "Well, it'll be one less Jew in the world." That seared my mother's memory, and of course it was impressed upon me when she made that comment.

My grandfather stayed here, imagine, and shlepped coal up to people's houses. In apartments, in those days, you had to burn your own coal for heat. He'd shlep it on his back. He was really a scholar, but that's what he did to sustain himself. He made three dollars a week, and it was worthwhile for him to stay here and send money back home. Every three or four years he went back to Poland and made another baby, and then came back here.

He went back twice, I think, which tells you something about the cost of passage in those days, I guess. But he finally was able to bring them over here, and had an apartment for them, and brought them up. They lived on Clinton Street downtown. They lived on the fifth floor, and the toilet was down in the back yard. Finally, they got modern and put toilets into the hallway, one on every floor. And then they connected that plumbing into the house, so that you had running water in the sink, and they also put a toilet next to every sink. The toilet was always in the kitchen, because that was really the only access to plumbing. I remember seeing that. That was considered to be really an upscale thing.

My mother tells me the story that they used to have gaslights and you put a quarter in a meter in the apartment and the gas went on for a period of time. You lit the gas and the kids would do their homework and study by that. They used to have a next-door neighbor who had a lot of children and they were very poor. They would always ask if this little boy, Yankel, could come in and lie on the floor next to my mother and study by the gaslight. She told me this many years ago when he got elected. It was Jacob Javits. I told him the story when I met him some time ago. He loved the story. He remembered living on the Lower East Side.

I went to City College and I was a social science major, took some psychology courses, and I didn't know what I wanted to do with my life. My brother had formed a fur company. He was in business about five or six years when I came along. I told him the story about my job search, and he said, "You're an idiot. Look, nobody's going to hire you anyway; you might as well come to work with me." By that time he had built up an equity of about $20,000 in business, which was then an awful lot of money. He said, "You'll be my partner." Well, I came to work and I didn't know what to take. I was getting married and I had an apartment, so I decided I would draw forty dollars a week. It was like forty tons of guilt, because I never felt I earned a penny of it. I went on like that for a couple of years. My wife was earning fifty-five dollars a week and we had a little apartment in Mount Vernon. My father lived in fear that I would be on the streets one day and never be able to survive. That was the kind of encouragement I got. He really wanted us to live with him and my mother, which would have been the end of my life.

I can tell you stories about my father sleeping in the factory on the nailing boards. He'd be finished so late at night, it didn't pay to go home back to the Bronx. To save the nickel on the subway, he'd sleep on the nailing boards in the factory. My father had colitis. He'd be ashamed or afraid to go to the bathroom, because the boss would think he was goofing off too much. He lived in terrible fear of his job. That's the kind of environment I grew up in; it instilled that fear all the time. They had a chance to move to a better apartment; they were always afraid. It was sixty-two-dollars-a-month rent. Incidentally, it was exactly the apartment that Doctorow moved into in *The World's Fair*. It took place exactly in that spot, where he talks about the park and the ovals and the Bronx; that whole section where he deals with that. I was so surprised to read it.

It took very many years for me to get established in the fur business. I never liked it. I really hated the business. And it was only when I could really turn it to the interest that I had, which was more marketing- and less product-oriented, that I really started to develop.

As a very young salesman in 1954 — this will give you the flavor of the industry at the time — I would go around hopelessly to the buying offices, the uptown offices representing the department stores that had fur departments. It was hopeless for me to try to sell these guys, because they all had prior relationships with one or another furriers, and I had nothing special to offer other than somebody else's merchandise that I was trying to sell as a jobber. But there was one characteristic in the coat and suit industry and the fur market. Even though they're both in the apparel industry, they're worlds apart. And they never meet each other; one is below Thirtieth Street, one is above Thirty-fifth Street. There's almost no intercourse between them, but I had to go up to that market to meet the buyers.

In the fur market, if you're carrying samples, you carry them in a corrugated carton with white rope attached. If you're in the garment center, you put your samples in a black hard case with black straps around it and with wheels. You always knew somebody from the fur market because he carried a carton. I never knew why the distinction was there. Presumably the furriers couldn't afford the black case, I don't know. In any event, I got on line at one of the May Company buying offices, and there was a furrier by the name of Willie Elfenbein who also toured the offices. His firm name was Hacker, Simon, and Elfenbein — three names. There were at least two, but usually three partners. One was a skin man, one was a salesman, and one was a worker. It always worked out that way. Willie would see me there, and I'd be a nice-looking young man, fresh out of college, and he would say to me, "Look, you're a college graduate." He couldn't believe that I would ever be a college graduate and be in the fur market. "What are you doing here?" He would be after me all the time. This went on for a number of weeks, and finally he saw that I kept showing up anyway. So he gave me up as a hopeless dolt, and he stopped talking to me. One day I'm in line at the May Company and Willie Elfenbein is in front of me, and a young man who looks just like me wheels up a black case and stands behind me. Willie Elfenbein looks at me and looks at him and he sees this kid is totally in the wrong line, because he's not in the fur business. So he shouts across me to this young man, "By here, they sell furs." The young man looks at him, and looks at me, and stands there. He couldn't understand what he was talking about. So Willie decides to say it louder: "By here, they sell furs." I look at the young man, and I realize this is never going to translate, and I say to him, "This is where the fur buyer sees." So the young man thanks me and wheels his case away. Willie stands there and says to me, "So, Churchill I'm not."

A fur coat was an affirmation of femininity. It was always a male's decision whether a woman got a fur coat or not. It was almost never the woman's decision. I think it was obviously peer pressure. So whatever was in fashion; young women wore mouton coats during the war. First of all, it was more available than almost any other fur because it's an indigenous product. It required very little workmanship, so it was easy to make. They're very large skins. Persian lamb was just very prevalent, very popular, a European carryover from earlier periods. There were a lot of rabbit coats. They used to call them by all kinds of names — Hudson seal, cony — which today would be illegal, because now you have to describe a fur generically.

Fur was sold in a much more traditional European style. The Jewish woman, I think, to the extent that she could, would want to own a fur coat. It was a definite status symbol.

Why do I think Jews were attracted to the fur trade? Easy entry; equal opportunity for all; very little commitment to equipment; very little requirement for specific talent other than industriousness; facile minds could react and trade and interact quickly. Those who weren't, were horses. They just worked. There were both types. Usually every firm had an inside and an outside man. One who had the *savoir-faire* and the business abilities or at least some of them, and the other, who'd succeed at the factory by working, or do all the work himself. Very often the salesman himself, as soon as he finished selling, would run to the factory to earn his keep and make sure he was selling.

Very inefficient operators; generally the quality of skill was very poor. Contrary to a lot of people's opinions that the old craftsman who sits there and sews at the machine is a very skilled guy, mostly he does it because he doesn't know any better. There isn't a lot of skill that he needs. I see some of the young people today . . . especially if you go to the Orient and you see skilled work. You begin to appreciate the difference. It's not that some of them, of course, weren't very skilled, but a great many of them produced a very mediocre product, very inefficiently. The business methods were, with rare exception, not very great. As a result, we didn't have many major fur firms. There were several that arose during the period of time. Some of the owners ended up going into banking, some into real estate. The real money gravitated out of the industry. It could be made in the industry, but it never stayed in the industry. To this day, there is almost no reinvestment in our industry, in infrastructure.

There was a fairly decent equality of opportunity. I think the garment center and the apparel industries were of a similar nature at the time. Again, easy entry; you didn't have to know a lot or do a lot to be able to compete. Lots of failures; lots of lack of economic discipline. And then they'd be back in business the next day. People really didn't know what they were doing.

The brains in the fur trade went to the skin business — the buying and selling of the skins. From that evolved merchant bankers who not only traded in the product but also financed the purchasers. It was just a natural gravitation. The smartest people just went into that end of the business, because that's where the money was. In diminishing form, then, there were processors, then manufacturers, and then there were retailers and workers. It was a fairly accurate pecking order.

It was a totally Jewish industry with a Jewish union. Irving Potash and Gold and those people were the communist group who were subsequently indicted and were all leaders of the industry. I think very brilliant. But interestingly enough, and I'm not sure of my perspective because they pre-date my time, my sense is that they were also very good capitalists; that they really understood the workings of the system and that the boss had to make money to stay in business. So I think they were always available to negotiate. To my best knowledge, they were not terribly dishonest, but I know in the days of unions' forming, there were a lot of broken heads, a lot of action taking place along those lines. But subsequently, when the communists were thrown out, they were replaced by other Jews. But thieves, just rank thieves. The price of ever having a union shop was to pay them off.

I think the majority of the better or larger firms are still Jewish-controlled. Only up until the last couple of years, you didn't see anybody under fifty years old. Now that there has been growth within the industry, the economic factors are suddenly deciding to assert themselves and it's beginning to become attractive. People are bringing their sons into the business with some degree of pride, which is a total reversal. Because there's no greater curse that could have befallen a furrier in the 1940s or fifties or sixties than to have his children in the fur business. You only did that when there was just nothing left to do. When I told my father I was going to work with my brother, I can still see the look on his face. He became totally depressed. His face was wan. At least in my case, he saw that I had gone to college and he thought I would rise to some other area. He saw the fur business solely as a means of putting bread on the table. He never saw it in any other light. I remember telling my father, in the beginning, that I'd like to establish a brand; I'd like to get people to know the product. He looked at me like I was just dreaming pipe dreams. He didn't want to make me feel bad, but he thought it was something incapable of ever being fulfilled.

I think of the many regrets you have in life; with me, there was this whole pervasive idea of lack of encouragement towards opportunity. Lack of a vision, I think, of my parents, perhaps, to try to dream and think about things that could possibly be. They lived a lot in a terrible state of fear. I think maybe the Depression was the searing influence on their life, because they really had the fear at that time. They had two small children. I was born in 1931 and my brother in 1926, and the world sort of caved in on them. I think that fear never left them. Then it was replaced by the war, which threw their children into the war, which was more fear. There was this terrible feeling all the time of playing defense in life. I guess, also, it's a function of their personalities. Not everybody reacted the same way. But I know that was their feeling.

15

Mountains and Mountains of Food

THEY MOVED from the Lower East Side to the Bronx or Queens to breathe fresh air and then to the mountains. The phrase "fresh air" became a fugue. And the mountains usually meant the Catskills, the legendary playground and marriage-making summer home for countless Jews, most of them from New York's sweltering workshops and factories and sidewalks and streets. But there also were resort communities such as Saratoga and Schroon Lake, New York, and Atlantic City, New Jersey. If there was a characteristic of these resorts it was the amount of food demanded and provided. Of course, this food fetish was not confined to resorts. My own mother would place at least twenty-four dishes on the table and subject me to thunderbolts of guilt to get me to eat: "What you don't eat today, you'll eat tomorrow!" or the classic Yiddish importuning "Nehm, mein kind, nehm" — "Take, my child, take." It seemed as if overeating was part of every Jewish immigrant's survival kit. The late Leo Steiner, who owned the Carnegie Deli in New York City, remembered that when he was fourteen years old he lied about his age, passed for seventeen, and went to work in the "borsht belt," as the Catskill Mountain resorts were known collectively. Steiner was a bus boy and kitchen helper.

"They used to put tons and tons of food on the table," he said. "You name it, it was put there. Every day it was the same thing. It was a different menu every day, but every Monday it was the same thing; every Tuesday it was the same thing, and so on. Friday night's dinner, I don't know how you could ever walk away from the table. You got everything on God's green earth."

The Friday night menu? "They came in, and when they sat down there was challah galore on the tables, tons and tons. Then everybody had gefilte fish and lettuce and tomatoes and red horseradish and white horseradish.

Then next, we'd have chopped liver; bottles of seltzer were going like mad. After that they'd have chicken soup with matzo balls or kreplach or noodles or everything if you liked. Then would come a roast chicken platter with helzel and potatoes, either baked or pan-fried potatoes."

Leopold Steiner, forty-nine, delicatessen owner, New York, New York

I am the owner of the Carnegie Deli in New York City.

The Jewish waiter should never be a waiter; he should be your mother. He'll tell you what to eat, what don't eat. "Don't eat this, don't eat that. Listen to me, boychick; I know what you need." There used to be a place on the Lower East Side called Moscowitz and Lupowitz. They never had a menu. They had five menus in the deli. The waiter would walk over to you. "Hello, boychick, hello. Listen, boychick, take the mushroom barley soup today, it's good." "All right." Or, "He messed up on the soup; take the matzo ball today." "All right." Or, "Listen, he made a delicious lungen und miltz." "All right." Or, "Or else you like some stuffed cabbage?" "All right." And basically my waiters are the same thing. If the pastrami's too salty, they'll tell you, "Don't take pastrami today; take corned beef." If the tongue isn't right, "Don't take tongue."

What about the reputation of Jewish waiters for being cynical, sarcastic, brusque? Well, that's normal. You have to remember that ninety percent of your Jewish waiters feel that they should be on the other side of the table. They should be the doctors and the lawyers and the judges and the bosses. "What's the matter? You're sitting there and I'm waiting on you. Who the hell do you think you are? I'm just as good as you. All right, so you're lucky."

Joyce Wadler, thirty-seven, journalist, New York, New York

It was very important for my mother that we be Jewish. She said things like, When I went to the city and went to school, all the other kids would speak Hebrew fluently and I would feel terrible and feel very inadequate and left out if I wasn't fluent in Hebrew.

My family got to a very, very tiny part of the Catskills. Fleischmanns was the biggest town, but really what they grew up in was a tiny little dairy community called Halcott Center. When we're talking about these places, we're talking seriously rural. There was the Grange Hall, and most of our neighbors, at least in Halcott Center, were dairy farmers, Gentile dairy farmers. Their people had been there for generations — the Kellys, the Crosbys, and the Scutters. When I was growing up I sort of knew that not only

we were Jewish but the entire farm was Jewish. We had Jewish cows and
we had Jewish chickens. It wasn't a big hog place, but I knew that we had
definitely Jewish cows and Jewish chickens. I assumed that everybody's
grandmother spoke Yiddish until, I think, I was seven and realized that it
was a different language. It wasn't what grandmothers spoke. Also, our
neighbors had family graveyards, which was very weird and spooky to me,
because I didn't exactly know where Jews were buried, but I had a feeling
it was in the city in these massive places in Queens. I thought it was a little
barbaric to put relatives in the back yard, but they all did and they had
them dating back to the late 1700s, early 1800s. So there was an immediate
difference. You can turn around and say, Hey those people had roots there.
But when you're little, all you see is they have family that's buried in the
yard, and isn't that sort of weird?

The way the family got up there was that they all came over — all the
grandparents — in the big wave or the second big wave of immigration,
which I think was 1914. The grandfather I'm named for, Jake, was one of
seven brothers. They were all tailors. We're always confused about whether
he was Polish or Russian, because they were so close to the border, but I'm
pretty sure he was Polish. He came over with his brothers for two reasons:
to stay out of the army, and because you couldn't own land in Poland. He
knew two guys from the city and together they bought this little boarding
house with the farm. About ten years ago, I was doing a story on one of
our neighbors who was then in his late seventies, and he said, "I taught
your grandfather how to milk a cow."

I don't know what it was when it was bought, but I think it was probably
a farmhouse that took in some boarders. The way it was in the Catskills
then was there were lots of little dairy farms. Dairy farms were the going
business. I think at the turn of the century the farmers would take people
in, especially when influenza epidemics happened in the city and people
would come up. Also, it was different, if you remember: there were no jets;
only rich people had cars; and there was a railroad that was running.
Fleischmanns was on the other side of the mountains, where the Concord
and Grossinger's are, what people think of as *the* Catskills. But there was
a point around the 1900s where it was a very successful country resort. The
mountains were very much like Switzerland or the French Alps, and the
resorts were these big, old, rambling firetraps, with beautiful huge porches.
If you couldn't afford those, people had these farm boarding houses where
the farmers would take in a few people. That's what they ended up buying.
When they bought it, as far as I know, there was just a main house and a
barn and I don't know how many cows. The other two guys, I think, didn't
like country life especially, as they eventually gave it up.

My grandmother comes into the picture because she had come up with her sister during the influenza epidemic in New York. She said that she weighed ninety-eight pounds and was lying in a hammock when my grandfather saw her and liked her and started courting her. He first went to her older sister and said, "I like her." The sister's position was "Forget it," because there were still older ones who weren't married and so it was completely out of the question. Anyway, he was a farmer.

The other part of the story is that my grandmother had something like six or seven sisters and had come from Russia and wasn't too sophisticated. She worked at a sewing machine in a shop. Her sisters had come over in sections, kind of individually, and she was among the last. Her mother had died when she was very young.

Another weird story which took me a number of years to find out had to do with her father. I asked what her father had died of and she said, "He died of the cough." When I asked, "What cough?" she finally explained that he had taken some medicine to make him sick to stay out of the army, and the medicine had killed him. It worked, but it worked badly. Every time that he sent a daughter off, put her on the train, he knew that he'd never see her again, so he fainted. When he died, she came over with the last sister. There were always people bringing them over, which is why I think this family thing is so strong. We always depended upon family.

So she came over and wasn't sophisticated. They called her the "greena cousina." These Polish Jews were much more sophisticated than the Russians, at least they always looked down on them. She was in the sweatshop, and my grandfather, the farmer, just appeared, all dressed up, and she said to me, "He looked so good, I thought he was a boss." He told her to take the day off, and she took it off and they went to the opera that night. I think she saw Caruso. So he courted her and asked one of the sisters if it would be okay if she married before the older one did, and since the older one was engaged, they got married and moved up there. That was how that branch got up there. This was my father's family.

My Wadler grandfather never completely gave up tailoring, from what I can see. He was always back and forth to the city. That was another thing about the Catskills' Jews. We were very rooted in New York. All of the Catskills' Jews knew they were Jews, knew they were Europeans, and New York was very comfortable, whereas our Gentile neighbors had been to New York maybe once, when they were discharged from the navy. For us, it was the mother ship. My grandfather was killed when he was thirty-nine. He was out in a thunderstorm — he went out to bring the cows back, and the dog brought the cows back without him. My father went looking for him, and a tree had fallen on his head. That was it. My father was a freshman at NYU. It was June, and he was the oldest and the head of the household, so he quit and took over the farm. The boarding house by then was much bigger.

The boarding house was hysterical. I still laugh about it. The boarding house is something like five miles from the town of Fleischmanns, which is a real town with a main street and beautiful Victorian houses. By the time I was born, in 1948, the other side of the mountain was really taking off — the Concord and Grossinger's. They're really pushing it. Our poor side of the mountain is dying. When Molly Goldberg is buried in a Fleischmanns cemetery, that's it. That's the one celebrity. There are just hulks of grand hotels; they're remnants. These were fantastic grand hotels. We weren't a big hotel. We were a tiny little boarding house. I think they charged about twenty-four or twenty-nine dollars a week, which included everything. It included being picked up at the bus station and all your meals and just being taken into town whenever.

The boarding house was a big main house with a porch; then there was the dining room, which was actually two dining rooms — the main dining room for the adults, and the children's dining room; a huge kitchen; and a little pantry. Behind this main house and dining room in the back were various chicken coops, and next to the chicken coops was a place where the hired man lived. All of the boarding houses seemed to have some strange hired man. Ours was named Mike Syke and he wasn't Jewish; he was Russian, which again is a distinction that Jews make. Mike Syke wasn't his real name. He was very old and smelly. He had sort of come with the property and had partially brought us up. He always had stubble; he spit; he chewed tobacco; he cursed at my grandmother, and my grandmother cursed at him. As far as he was concerned, she was a Jew; and as far as she was concerned, he was a filthy Russian. But they worked with each other. There were some other buildings — maybe three other buildings. There was a barn, and I think there were about forty cows. There was a swimming pool. I think we finally got a public address system, but it was very scratchy and pathetic.

The season was from Memorial Day weekend to Labor Day weekend. I very vaguely remember that when things really got crazy, the family or parts of the family would move into a tent. If business was really cooking, they would do this number. I think sometimes even guests would end up in tents or they would double up.

Breakfast was at eight, and they had tremendous meals. Help was a little tricky in these situations. The family was my grandmother, who was the head of the family, my father, and my two uncles. My father's name was Bernie, then my uncle Artie, and then my youngest uncle, Hymie. When my mother married into the family — and she was in Fleischmanns and there just weren't that many Jewish people around — she definitely married into the family. My grandmother was still the head of the family and she came into the house, which has always been a problem. So the family worked in it, and my mother still calls them "those communists," because they shared everything. It was a communal situation.

For help you got it two ways. First of all because it was a dairy place you'd get farm cadets who worked on the farm. A farm cadet is just somebody who helps with the farming. The state or the county or the colleges would send a kid out and they would stay for the summer. For kitchen help, my father would take a car to the Bowery, where they had employment agencies that got drunks they would just pick up. Because there were stories that I'm sure are legendary, and not true, about people waking up and finding themselves in the mountains. They would just pick up a drunk and throw him in the truck, and that was how they got the kitchen help. They usually didn't pay them until the end of the summer, because if you paid them they'd go into Fleischmanns and get drunk. So that was the basic setup.

The family lived first in the main house, which, when my father was little, had been heated with a wood stove. I guess when I was five or seven they built our own house, which was a modern ranch house. But it was still the family and it was still a boarding house and a farm and everybody had something they did. My mother and father took care of the books until my mother rebelled and said, "Enough of this family," and went into Fleischmanns to work in her brother-in-law's bakery. My grandmother ran the kitchen and cooked. My uncle, who was briefly in the marines, cooked, and my youngest uncle, who is still a gardener, drove the tractor and milked the cows. They all did some of the milking, but it was basically my grandmother who ran the kitchen.

The food was terrible. Heavy East European stuff, except I really loved it because it was very nice, cozy home cooking. The main thing was heavy and plenty of it — I think so that you felt secure. Also, it was the way they cooked. Just tremendous portions of food. I think her gefilte fish was supposed to be very good, but I wasn't a gefilte fish person. They did their own sour cream, their own gefilte fish, and all that stuff. I remember the guests ate tremendous, tremendous amounts. It's what they came to the country to do — to eat and lie around and play cards. You just never mixed milk and meat. And I still cannot have a glass of milk with meat — you know, it's disgusting.

I ate at Gentiles' houses. When I saw that they would sit down and have milk with dinner, it was very peculiar. It was one way of knowing they were Gentile. I didn't have bacon until I was thirteen; I had it with some Jews, and it tasted exactly like forbidden food. I remember the first time I had shrimp it was also with some Jewish dentist. That it was very weird stuff we didn't grow up on.

Was I allowed to go out with non-Jewish boys? No, and that was the problem; that's why I had to wait until the summer for them to come up. When I was eleven my parents moved to another town so I could be in the school district for the Woodstock area. Even there, there definitely weren't any Jewish kids. In the summer, Jewish kids came up from the city. I waited for the summer and then I got my hands on whatever I could. And they were always these terrific, funny, dark, sexy, great Jewish guys from either CCNY, NYU, or Columbia.

I couldn't mess around until the summer, and then I'd try to do as much as I possibly could in two or three months, and then they'd go back to the city. I just felt terrible, because there went all my summer romances. There were some great guys up there; they were like the cream of the crop, because they were the hardest working guys who were going to put themselves through school. So you really got a great type of Jewish guy up there. But it was a very melancholy kind of resort. Remember the Jacques Tati movie *Monsieur Hulot's Holiday?* I wondered, when I saw it, if all summer resorts were melancholy because people go with such tremendous expectations. But Fleischmanns was particularly melancholy, because when I was born it was a resort that already had had its wonderful time. They were nostalgic about a Europe that really didn't exist anymore — with the little scraps of the Viennese stuff. But that Europe was gone.

These weren't rich Jews who were coming up, though they felt they were. In the morning, the staff always put out prune juice or prunes, and they had five-course breakfasts. For lunch, even though it was the summer in the middle of the day, I remember these boiled chickens and pots of potatoes. Enormous amounts of food went into these people. They were not athletic people and they were very demanding. My mother used to laugh and say, "How come everybody who comes up is a designer? Nobody works a machine in the city." They came up and they had bought their piece of the country and they felt they were lords. They sat around the pool with a maple leaf on their nose and all smeared up and loved the country. They lived to eat, and the men played cards. There were always traveling card games, and they moved along the shade. Once in a while a cousin of ours who wanted to be an entertainer came up from the city and taught them to dance on the front lawn. At night they went into Fleischmanns and went to a show. The shows moved from hotel to hotel because they were smaller hotels there. That was the scene.

By the time I was eight, the family started another business, the lumberyard. By the time I was ten, they were really phasing this out. First they phased out the dairy farm. Then the boarding house thing started to go, because by that time, 1958, people were flying to Europe. The railroad only existed until I was three, if even that long. It was another generation that was coming up, and they were not interested in the mountains as much. A lot of the big grand old hotels in our area had gone, anyway. It wasn't a viable thing. Dairy farms weren't viable, and these little boarding houses were just not winning propositions.

There were fewer and fewer people on Main Street. It was such an old gang of Jews; they were really the Europeans who came up there to remember Europe, and they were dying, literally dying. Their kids had moved to the suburbs and wanted to go to college. It was before this wave of people who liked country houses. They just found it very boring. What we were seeing up there were the European refugees and the people whose parents had been European refugees. It was the end of some kind of European connection.

Come the winter, how did life change? Well, you were a minority. You don't want to say "clung together," but the Jews really did. I didn't have a very Jewish family in the sense of a religious Jewish family. They kept kosher, but it was more of an ethnic thing. But they went to the synagogue. Yom Kippur was always after the season. Some Jews from the city would straggle up, but it was usually after the season. You were in the Orthodox synagogue, because as far as anybody knew that was the only kind there was. It was in Fleischmanns. We had an old guy named Meyer the butcher. He was an old man; he looked like God in these white robes. He had to be in his late seventies; white beard. He was the ritual slaughterer in Fleischmanns, and he ran the services because the community wasn't large enough to have a rabbi. Anyway, he behaved like a real rabbi. The women were separated from the men.

You didn't have music in the synagogue. What you had was Meyer the butcher. You had the thing on Yom Kippur where they have the period when you remember the dead. It was terrifying. The children were sent out and there was this whole thing of mourning and you were in winter clothes. I am sure it's when everybody's school starts, even though it's hot. There was a funny thing about being a Jewish female. I think it definitely affected me. When I sat in the women's section, I sat with my mother, between my two grandmothers. I mean, the other kids were my brothers, so they were with my father. Jewish women then were very girdled, very corseted, and very made up, and they wore a lot of heavy, clunky jewelry; and when you went to the synagogue, you really wore on your back everything that your husband earned. You wore a mink stole. I mean all these strong female smells and my mother — her father had had three diamonds, which he left to each of his three children. My mother had hers put on a Jewish star that she wore around her neck. And my father's mother used to reach into her blouse — she had it tucked in — reach into it, pull it out, and put it on the outside so people could see that she had a diamond.

These women really scared men. They were big, frightening. I remember one of them, a kind of massive lady, when I was eleven or twelve saying to me, "You are really developing quite a lovely figure," and I was terrified. I thought I was going to get huge boobs, a mink, all this jewelry, and that that was what being a Jewish adult female was. I didn't want all this paraphernalia. They were such a terrifying, opinionated bunch. That was the synagogue. That was our basic tribe.

You could look around the synagogue and see the Jewish community, like the dentist, the grocer, the doctor. It's hard to explain. Even when you went out, the teachers would say things like "Jewish kids are so bright." I was remembering it this morning. How could you have a Jewish stupid kid? We did actually have one or two who weren't so terrific, but we were convinced that Jewish kids were good students. It was like Jewish kids had souped-up brains.

You knew that you were different, because my friends' grandmothers didn't speak Yiddish. We went to New York two or three times a year, and the way it went was in the morning we split up. My mother and I went to Thirty-fourth Street to Franklin Simon, to Ohrbach's, which did knock-offs and had mezzanine dresses for $8.98. We went to Altman's; we had lunch at Schrafft's. My father went downtown to the Lower East Side to get supplies, like salami and kosher pickles and that sort of stuff. Then we got tickets to a show and then we came home. It was very much a part of the Jewish Catskills thing. With the Gentiles, it wasn't. So in the summer, there was a large Jewish community and you saw that the Jewish kids from New York were very different. They were talking about city blocks and you had no idea what they were talking about. We didn't have blocks. The rest of the time there were maybe two Jewish kids in my class, and it was absolute farmers. They had things like shivarees, which you'll see sometimes in the West. They are kind of a pioneer thing; on the wedding night they kidnap the bride and the groom. If you look at *Oklahoma!* you'll see that they do something, I think, like a shivaree.

We were definitely Jews; that was the main thing. I could see we were Jews and we were a family. When I was little, like when I was in kindergarten, I remember somebody asking me what religion I was. I said "Jewish Democrat." That's what we absolutely were. There was no separation. It was like FDR had made it, I was going to say, so Jews didn't lose their farms; you didn't lose your farm during the Depression. Jews were Democrats.

We were very definitely dairy farmers, much more than the people in Fleischmanns, because our neighbors were such good and neat and nice people; I mean, just lovely people. They would go deer hunting and bring us a part of the deer. Even my father and uncle, though it was extremely non-Jewish, hunted when I was very little, before my mother decided no guns in the house.

My father was the mayor of Halcott Center, and he was not only a Jew but a Democrat. Halcott Center wasn't even a town. There was a combination general store and post office and a crossroads and maybe three dozen farms scattered through there.

We were upstate, rural people who were very connected to our neighbors because of things like the Grange. The Grange was — I hate to say grass roots — but it was a part of the populist grass-roots world coming-together thing and they had state fairs and at the Grange Hall they sang "We Will Gather Round," you know, and they sang songs with Jesus in them which Jewish kids never mentioned. We definitely belonged to the Grange, absolutely. When my mother was pregnant, she had a shower at the Grange. I was in the Christmas shows at the Grange and in Girl Scouts.

We were European, we were American, we were Jews, and we were upstaters. And, I think, Norman Rockwell. The things I think about, I'm sort of realizing now that he keeps coming back, but it's probably from Rockwell and those *Saturday Evening Post* things that there was this tremendous pro-America feeling. People when they got snowed in dug each other out. It wasn't like there were barn raisings but people did baskets when other people were in the hospital. It was a farm community. But we were also European Jews who knew that if we hadn't been here, we'd be dead.

Did I ever find out where Jews were buried? All were buried in Queens. I was right. Except my grandmother. There's a little Jewish cemetery in Fleischmanns; she was buried there, and my uncle was buried there. It was astonishing to me, because when I was growing up, she belonged to the burial society and I knew that was another reason I thought Jews were buried somewhere in New York. I guess there were reasons for all of this. She paid the dues on this. I think when they came over one of the first things they did, I don't know why, was join the goddamn burial society. It was only a few dollars a month, and my grandfather was buried out there and my other grandmother and other grandfather, so it was always agreed that she wanted to be, too. Then she surprised my father by saying she wanted to be buried in Fleischmanns, and was, and that was a small funeral.

But when my uncle died, he died very unexpectedly: heart attack in the business. The cemetery was tiny and there was a little hill and the immediate family was in a horseshoe around the grave. But when I looked up, there was all of Fleischmanns stretched out for my uncle. It was very lovely. The Methodist minister and everybody was there, all of the workers. It was the Rockwell thing again. It was a very small town. He knew everyone. Even though the rabbi who said the eulogy didn't know him, it was to me what being an upstate Jew was. The family was around, Jews were a little closer, and the Gentiles were all there. They'd all come, even though it was different. Everybody was respectful and they knew — it was that old thing. They watched the family put the dirt on the coffin and they just knew.

So it's why finally I'm very glad that I grew up there, because I think I have a very different feeling one, about being a person growing up and two, about being an American. I went through the whole thing with the 1960s and people saying I hate America; I never felt that. I still felt that America was where you didn't turn into a lampshade. You could have anything you wanted if you worked for it. And where people didn't discriminate, because in Fleischmanns they absolutely, even though I heard occasional stories, didn't discriminate. A worker like a farmer was a farmer was a farmer. We were Jewish farmers and they were Gentile farmers, but we were all farmers and we were all connected.

Alan M. Gelb, forty-eight, lawyer, New York, New York

My mother's parents came in the early 1900s, my grandmother from a little town called Siget, outside Budapest. It's the same town where Elie Wiesel was born. My grandfather was from a Polish town called Borislav, which became ultimately part of Russia, as so much of Poland did. My father's parents, with whom I was not as close, were both born here.

My father's father fought in the Spanish-American War in the Philippines. He boxed there under the name Kid Gelp, I understand. He used to work at the Brooklyn Navy Yard and then was in the venetian blind business in Brighton Beach. Grandpa was very cold and quiet, as was his wife. Uncommunicative, basically. But the influences on me were from my mother's parents, who spent lots of time with us. My mother's father was a member of the hatters' union — made ladies' hats out of straw. He and my grandmother told me what America was all about — I guess the kind of things that are now clichés but were life and death to them. America is the land of opportunity. America is a land where you're able to accomplish in the most extraordinary way. The "goldene land," Grandpa said, and I suppose that was true. I don't think Grandpa ever made more than $5000 or $6000 a year in his life. He used to get up at four o'clock in the morning and travel for hours to get a job; walked picket lines; denied his family the benefits of whatever earnings that he might have had because he felt strongly about the union movement. He spoke English with an accent; with a wonderful, charming accent that I can hear today.

Grandpa was not formally religious nor formally political. There was just a thing about him. They put the highest premium on education. Not in an assertive way; it was just something that was expected. This was carried directly through to my mother and into our house, all of it. Mother went to high school. She was the eldest of three and had to leave to work. Her younger brother was able to go to law school, became a lawyer. And I then got the chance to attend Columbia Law School, which was pretty extraordinary. I don't mean unique; just extraordinary in the promptness of the move from the early 1900s, in fifty years, to the finest schools in the country — less than fifty years.

When I was a child we had gone to bungalow colonies in the Catskills. A bungalow colony was a series of bungalows, a country community, in which people from the city resided during the course of the summer. The owner provided organization and certain services and facilities: the handball court, the baseball field, generally a little lake for swimming. Nothing very ambitious, but it filled my parents' concept of what country was and was an important place for my sister and myself. It was kind of an extension of the Brighton Beach crowd — the handball players, very aggressive softball players, all the men loving to do that, lots of gin rummy, mahjongg for the women, linoleum floors with the newspaper on it on Friday after my mother had scrubbed them and mopped them, and an oilcloth top to the kitchen table. We played baseball, we hit a tennis ball on the handball court; there were no tennis courts there. We swam. Ran around.

As best as I can recall the bungalow colony was totally Jewish. We went to different communities in different years. But the feeling was always the same; the surroundings a little different. My grandparents — my mother's parents — were always with us. Yiddish was spoken as a secret language, something I regret deeply. I had to catch on despite attempts to keep it from me. I now regard it as one of the rich parts of my heritage that I was exposed to it at all.

We went for an extended period — whether it was a month or two months, I can't tell you. It was not just a very brief period. Dad would come up on weekends. Friday night was special because Dad was there. That was the special thing. He would stay a portion of the time, I suppose a week, but he worked for all the years we grew up. He was first a salesman for Beech-Nut, then went into the jewelry business: became sales manager for a company that made ladies' earrings.

The Catskills was country. The Catskills, I guess, was Jewish country. It was a comfortable community. I think my parents felt more uncomfortable in a Gentile world than I grew up feeling. A Gentile world became an ordinary part of my existence, something I frequently did not even notice. I think, though we never spoke of it a lot, I think they had a heightened consciousness of that and wanted to be in a comfortable place.

We lived in Brooklyn; in Flatbush. We were part of the Jewish community.

What that meant was that I had to go to Hebrew school. My father had not received such training; it was very important to him. He had no Jewish education. Very important to him that I do that. And I excelled at that. I led services and such, and that brought my father into the synagogue and made him a very happy participant.

The public school — P.S. 238 on Avenue P and Ninth Street — was not all Jewish by any means, but there were a substantial number of Jews in the place. But there were non-Jewish people there, too. And they were different. The Italians were tougher. The Irish kids were very, very tough; very tough. The Irish kids . . . one of those kids had a grandmother who drank. We didn't know anybody who did that. Kathleen's grandmother. Her father was a fireman. They were very different. I learned at an early stage that they didn't want Kathleen to play with me because I was Jewish. That came as a great shock to me. It's the first time that I ever learned the difference; that there was a difference of this sort between Jews and non-Jews. The Irish kids who used to go to Saint Brendan's — we'd throw snowballs at them — and if they'd catch one of us — *the girls* — they would beat the hell out of us. They were just as tough as could be. And they clustered around their church as an educational institution, which was interesting; they went to Catholic school. Some of them did not go to public school at all but went to this Catholic school. That was the line of demarcation that you began to notice. When they beat you up, you certainly noticed. But the kids in public school were very different. They did not dress as well, with such care; I don't mean finery, but with such care. They tended to be more rough, sometimes more athletic, although some of the Jewish kids were fabulous — basketball players, baseball players. The Jews were a quieter group, I thought; that's my memory. But very good and always at the top of the school academically.

The sense of Jewishness is in the home and in the cooking and the dishes that I miss today because Grandma is not around.

I spent one summer in camp in the Poconos. The Jewish camp gave off the same feelers as the bungalow colony, except for the fact that the adults were not around. Same kind of bunch. By that time, by the time you were twelve or thirteen or fourteen, you knew that you were Jewish and that there was another world and it was different, sometimes hostile, but different, and that there were expectations that your family and community had of you to which you had to respond.

Has it changed? Well, it changed and then it changed back. It changed away, but I get a sense that the young people, for example, who are coming into this law firm have a heightened sense of their Jewishness and want to find a place for themselves as Jews as well as professionals. Men and women. We are coming back to some traditional values in that. You hear some talk about it. Sometimes especially from the women, because they are struggling to make a place for themselves without role models in history and structure, as men have had. I think that Jewishness gives them a hold on who they are and how to conduct themselves.

In 1955 I went up to Morningside Heights. I thought Columbia would be something out of English literature, with old retainers there taking care of the kids, instead of the Puerto Rican elevator man and the dreadful dorms. And it was the great experience of my life — being at Columbia. That was a move of thousands of miles away from all the rest of this stuff, but with the anchor that this business gave me.

One of my fraternity brothers in my junior year had worked for several years in the mountains. I worked every summer. Many of us worked every summer. It was expected. The jobs were not particularly wonderful, but it was your obligation to pitch in, because parents made sacrifices and you needed to help. I was supposed to have gotten a job working on a freighter, and I had my seaman's card, but that year was very bad for the shipping industry. Old-line people were being laid off, so there of course was no room for me. I got a job throwing around exhaust pipes in a warehouse in the West Forties. I wasn't thrilled with that job. It was a job. Then I got a call from my fraternity brother, Stanley Mandel, saying they needed some help at his hotel; would I like to do it? I called home right away. I told my mother I wanted to quit what I was doing. And I did. We did some shopping that night; I bought some shorts and shoes and such, and I was on the bus the next morning. I told her I might be on the return bus, because I had never really done this before.

I took a bus to Ellenville. It was the New Alpine Hotel. I had spoken with the boss. I told him I had worked at the Columbia University Club. Had I? No. I went to work that next morning. My first experience was breakfast, serving forty people.

It was a legendary experience. First, there was an aura about it. So many others had done it. It was hard work. But it was, number one, country; number two, remunerative. You could really make money there. This was an aspiration, because it was generally considered one of the best jobs you could get. I saved a thousand dollars or twelve hundred dollars. I started after the season began and that was a great deal of money at that time.

While I didn't feel in any way prepared for it, I was committed to give it a shot. So off I went. I picked up a tray and went off to work. It was obvious from the outset that I did not really know what I was doing. On the other hand, I like people. I was pleasant enough to the people I served to make up for my lack of mechanical proficiency, even though the tray teetered on my hand as I carried various hot dishes or piled-up plates. It was obvious to my employer that I was not experienced in this, but my attitude with his guests was sufficiently pleasing that after a stern lecture, he expressed a willingness to keep me on if I did a proper job. So off we went. We had breakfast.

Breakfast was a particularly difficult meal in that it was not a single sitting. People could come over an extended period, and the menu was very varied. It was huge. All the possibilities of breakfast were explored there. I have a memory of a dreadfully thin woman, quite birdlike, who would come in at the very, very end of the breakfast sitting, and first she would apologize for being late. She'd tell me she was not well and she'd been in her room. And then could she have some prune juice? And then some prunes? And then some bran flakes? I thought that she was going to blow herself up. Then she wanted oatmeal. Then she —

"Do you have some pancakes, waiter?"

"Yes, we can get you pancakes."

"With an egg on them?"

And she went through the entire menu with this most prodigious appetite. All of this was what they got for whatever they paid to be there. And it was a major part, obviously, of the event, of being at this place. But it was difficult because of the variety, and you had to run back and forth as people came in. Lunches and dinners, single sittings with fixed menus, were a lot easier. We would, after we cleared the breakfast, set up for lunch, go rest for a few minutes, and come back to prepare for lunch.

Lunch was heavy but not varied. There was soup and there was salad and there may have been noodles and there were accessory dishes and then there was a main course and perhaps a second main course. And they could eat as much as they wanted, and they did. Eating was an enormous part of the experience. Then dinner was the same. No formality. All quite informal, except for Sunday lunch, which was steak, where we figured out that some people would not stay and the owner could save money.

It was a very Jewish crowd. Very Jewish. I remember one woman at breakfast: "Vaiter, I vant a ricekrips mitot milk," she said. "Ricekrips" I understood. "Mitot milk" threw me. So I said, "Lady, do you mean with hot milk or without milk?" and she says, "That's right, mitot milk." So I brought the milk on the side. These were people who liked to drink very hot beverages. I don't know why, but people who come from some parts of the world appear to enjoy very hot things. I remember the one who asked for tea. I put boiling water in the little carafe and brought the carafe and a cup and saucer and teabag and she said, "Not hot." "Lady, I just took it out of the cauldron." "It's not hot enough." I pick it up. I go back in the kitchen. I leave the carafe as it is, but I open the spigot and run the steaming water over the handle of the cup. I bring it back. It's the same water. She pours it in. "That's hot."

They were wonderful. The accented English is something I recall. The lady who wanted a "linkesveal." "Excuse me?" "A linkesveal." I don't wish to be rude. I go into the kitchen. I shout out to the Chinese chef, "One linkesveal," and out it comes — a lean piece of veal.

We had a separate dining room for the children. Mitchell Mitursky was the children's waiter. A separate tip was to be given to him. It was very important. The children's waiters had to protect their turf. The tip that they gave us in the main dining room went for the bus boy and the waiter. But the children's waiter was separately compensated.

There is much to be learned about protecting yourself. Mitchell told me about the woman who would come in: "What's mine son eating?" "He's having lamb chops, lady." "Take them away; he wouldn't eat them. He doesn't like those." "Twice he's asked for more."

It was that kind of conflict that we lived with that made it a fabulous experience.

All the waiters were Jewish students.

If we got paid, it was minimal. So little that I don't even remember it. It was tips. They gave us modest accommodations. Chicken-coop kind of accommodations. We all lived in one great big room: waiters, bus boys. What distinguished the waiters from the bus boys? The luck of the draw, I suppose. Nothing more than that. Different functions to perform, but if you were just lucky enough to be a waiter, you got bigger tips. The son of the owner got the best station and the biggest tippers. My memory is the split was fifteen and five a week. That was a good tip. Fifteen for the waiter and five for the bus boy. I remember my friend Stanley; at the end of the session he gets this tip and he asks, "Was the service all right?" "Yes, why do you ask?" "Well, your tip was somewhat below the average," and a great fight ensued in the middle of the dining room with the entire guest group assembled. Great dispute between the two, and this fellow said, "Well, when I was your age, I was a waiter," and Stanley yelled, "Where, in a whorehouse?" It was kind of dramatic, somewhat tasteless, but you were fighting for something that you really thought yours.

We got leftovers, if there were any, or second-rate kind of stuff. Sometimes you could get a decent piece of meat, a steak perhaps if the cook was your friend. There was the Chinese chef. He was quite proficient, I suppose. He knew all this stuff — he certainly knew the lingo — and out it came. The food came out in enormous quantities. He was just part of the scenery. Midnight snacks and raids were a regular course. It was a constant struggle to see if we could outwit the owner. We were also hungry. There was food there and we wanted to get it. Not at all easy. But we managed, we managed. Yet there was a clear distinction between what the guests ate and what we ate.

The owner was a very aggressive little man with sallow skin who was certainly tolerant enough to permit me to continue there. Served steak only once a week. Very tight. Very cheap. Something that was obvious from the poor accommodations we had, the poor food we had. If he found you sneaking in at the end of the day to grab a peach, that was cause for a great dressing-down and lots of threats about losing your job. We also knew life was unfair, since he gave his son preferential treatment with the best-tipping guests. But I think we all had respect for him because he ran a good hotel. We knew that, because we were pretty good at what we did. There was a kind of pride — a great pride — in what we did. Great camaraderie. The waiters hung together. We kind of liked each other. It was a struggle that we pursued together.

There was great striving. Great striving by the waiters. To maximize what you did, you ran a lot. There was always a great outpouring of energy. Marvelous training for practicing law, in my case. Great discipline. You really had to press yourself to get this thing done. I found I did because I was starting so far behind the line. You had to bite your tongue with guests. The same thing with clients; adversaries you can lose your temper with. Dealing with the public is a dreadful thing. So many people whose conduct you do not wish to accommodate. You had to learn to swallow it or at least to ameliorate it and get along. But we were allowed to be more intrusive than at many of the other places, where waiters got fired in the regular course for speaking up to protect themselves. We were fortunate about that.

Free time was mostly in the evening, although you were expected to spend some time with the guests. There always has been a legend about sex and the Catskills. I was thinking about that while walking to the office this morning. I never saw it. I heard about it. I heard people tell stories about it, but not that they had participated. Certainly there was never anything like that at our hotel. You were expected to talk to these people, to put on shows — this was not one of the great meccas for entertainment. During the week we waiters were expected to play the piano if we could, or a guitar or whatever, and entertain the guests in the evening. On the weekend, they had a comedian, a singer who was part of the entertainment as well.

Sometimes you'd get off in the evening. Sometimes you could take a couple of hours to go to town in the afternoon. Ellenville was like all the other communities — Nyack, Spring Valley, Swan Lake. They were small towns, what I would think of today as something in the Midwest with the little taxpayer stores. It was all very local and very rural. Not a lot to do, but colorful. It was a different world. It certainly wasn't Brooklyn. A million miles from Manhattan. It was nice to visit. I don't recall anything other than that.

Social life was mainly with the guys going into town; no big thing with women. Sometimes we would go to another hotel. This was exhausting work, as I think of it. We really worked like crazy. We got up at six. We were in the dining room before seven, setting up for breakfast. We each had stations that accommodated no less than forty — that's a lot. Sometimes more, depending on how crowded it was. Then you had to clear. The bus boy would clear. We would set up for lunch. You'd rest a bit and then come back for this next experience and then dinner and then whatever your obligations were to entertain the guests at the end of the day. It was very full.

As for the guests, there was a turnover. Sometimes they stayed for a week; sometimes for two. Others stayed longer. Those were the ones with whom you entered into stronger relationships. That was better for tipping. Better for talking. They carried it with them to this place and all the other places. If you were at the Nevele, which was down the road, that was a fancier place, a much bigger place, but it was a Jewish community. While we saw broader aspects of what a Jewish community might be like — different kinds of people, jobs, values, conduct — it was a place that all of us were comfortable with.

I would say it was the bungalow crowd that would rather *be* served than serve themselves. That was the main difference. You went to the hotel, there were services. You went to the bungalow, the mother cooked, Grandma cooked, and we went shopping. The guy with the best jelly doughnuts I ever ate used to come with a little cart every day to the bungalow colony. I just remembered those jelly doughnuts — nothing like them. In the hotel it was the same kind of group, although there were a substantial number of older people.

They did the same things that they did in the bungalow colony. They played gin. They played mahjongg. They swam. They sat at the pool. They bossed around their children — "Tatela, don't do this." "Tatela, don't do that." It was very family. It was a great feeling of community. I remember one of the old guys, he reminded me of my grandfather and he gave me a very poor tip. I had this little conversation with him at the end of the week. He looked at me with these sorrowful eyes and told me, "I'm sorry, I can't afford anymore." And I was stricken. I had taken this wonderful man, who no doubt had endured a dreadful life, and made him feel ashamed, and that was just the worst thing I could possibly have done. I thought it over, how badly I had performed, and I wanted to find him so that I could apologize. I walked in and found him sitting in the card room. I looked, and the money was flying and this guy was playing — he was a demon. I remember transfixing him with an angry stare. The next week I got a very good tip.

Did any of the mothers try to fix up any of us with their daughters? That happened to friends of mine at other hotels. One of my partners met his first wife when he was a bus boy at, I think it was Grossinger's. Her family had come from Shaker Heights. Stayed there. He met the daughter. They got married. Quite extraordinary. That was terrific. Now, there weren't too many young daughters, certainly not attractive. A different group from the ones that we would have seen socially at college. Not a lesser group, just a different group. While the people were interesting to talk to because they had business and real world experience, it wasn't where any of us was hoping to go. We were hoping never to have to go back there as a guest. We were trying to use that as a platform to go elsewhere.

Alvin Fertel, forty-nine, junior high school assistant principal, New York, New York

I went to Hunter College. I didn't train to be a teacher; I majored in political science and I minored in psychology. In my last year, I took nine credits of education as a lark. I went into the army for six months, and when I came out there was a depression; to me it was a depression. It was a recession — 1958. It was very difficult to get a job. I don't know what my great rush was, but I felt I had to have a job. So I got out of the army in December and I was teaching in February. I got an emergency license. I remember the principal squeezing my arm, my biceps, patting me on the back, saying, "You'll do okay." That's how I entered the school system.

I was born in the Bronx. My older brother was born in the Bronx. And my younger brother was born in the Bronx. We were all educated in the Bronx. I lived in the same neighborhood and the same apartment from my earliest recollection until I was married. That was in a Jewish neighborhood. Not an affluent Jewish neighborhood, more of a working-class Jewish neighborhood. We were unusual in the fact that my father had a business and we owned a car.

I went to elementary school through high school in the Bronx. It was truly a community. Everyone knew each other. On the holidays you knew the neighborhood was Jewish; everyone was dressed in finery. Whether or not they went to synagogue, they appeared to be respectful of it.

Growing up was really being encased in a very protective world. Everything had its place: where you played ball, where you sat on the stoop, where you sat in a little triangle with benches on it. There were certain people who would sit in certain windows and watch the streets — yentas, we called them. The only experience we had with police was if they came to take away our stick for playing stickball.

There were three or four stores on the street; all did a good business — a drug store, two grocery stores, and a candy store. Everybody would hang out in front of the candy store and look at the girls or talk about the girls.

Then there were the regulars, who got there for the early edition of the newspaper, late at night, the *Daily News* or the *Mirror*. It was an experience, growing up there as an older teenager. There would be a place where you'd meet. There was a cafeteria in a different part of the Bronx that everybody would go to after dates — the 167th Street Cafeteria, out of business now — and there was a whole atmosphere that I think people don't have today. My children don't have it in the suburbs. I think the people still living in the Bronx do have it.

We all knew we were Jewish. As a matter of fact, growing up, I thought most of the world was Jewish; I thought President Roosevelt was Jewish. I thought Gentiles were definitely in a minority and I couldn't understand how we could be persecuted when we were the majority, although I would have the experience of going to my grandmother's neighborhood, which was at that point already a changing neighborhood, where the shul was and running the gauntlet. We had to wear yarmulkas because my grandmother was religious. But we couldn't wear them in the street, because we'd surely have a fight and probably be beaten up if we went into that neighborhood wearing them. So we'd keep them in our pocket, and just before we got to my grandmother's house we'd put them on and go in. We were brought up, for whatever reason, at least by my mother, not to fight. If somebody bothered you, you avoided the fight. It was a mistake. My father felt otherwise, but apparently my mother prevailed, because we were always afraid to fight these Gentile guys; they were going to beat us up.

I remember the shock of my life when I went to camp — I had this stomach operation and I went to a rehabilitation camp — and I saw all these Gentile guys who I thought were so tough, and when we all got undressed and took our physical, I could see that I was bigger and stronger, even being sick. And that was my first revelation — since I had never seen any Gentile kids up close — that these were not people to be afraid of by themselves. The first time I had a fight with a Gentile guy, I just let him hit me. I never even hit him back. I remember it now; it must be forty years ago and still sticks in my mind. A year or two after that I went to this convalescent camp, and I was determined to not let that happen again, and I didn't. At that point, whatever fights I had, I wouldn't run away. So I think that was a change in my attitude.

In the summer, I went away. Not too many of the other kids went away. They remained and they played their games. We went up to a bungalow colony in the Catskills, which was even a smaller cocoon. I think most of the people were Jewish. Occasionally, an Italian family. And occasionally what was then considered intermarriage, which would be an Italian and a Jew. People got along pretty well.

It was about a four- or five-acre square, all cleared. Bungalows all around the perimeter. Cochaleyns would be the best way to describe them. I went back about twenty-five or thirty years later to show it to my children. The building was still standing, even though it was abandoned. They couldn't get over the smallness of it, I mean the actual tininess of it. The entire bungalow wouldn't fit into a normal-size living room. The bedrooms were just big enough to accommodate two double beds with a space for one person to stand between them. The living room — there was no living room. There was just a very tiny kitchen, a three-burner stove, a wooden icebox, cold water. No shower. You took your shower in a community shower. The women washed their clothing in a community washtub. There was a tremendous spirit of camaraderie. Plenty of kids my age. We had enough to have a baseball team and every kind of team. Everybody seemed to be very nice.

We played ball. There was a swimming hole. We went swimming. I learned how to swim up there. I started to go out with girls up there. Again, Jewish girls. It was, oh, taboo to go out with a shiksa. My mother would have died. She drummed it in to us from early on that this is something that's definitely expected of you. We all married Jewish girls.

There was a "casino," they called it — more like a social center — where they had a band on Saturday night and people would dance and have parties. Nothing on the intellectual side. The only time you would see anything resembling that would be when they had a Jewish fund raiser. At that time — this was the forties, when Israel was establishing itself — I particularly remember a fund raiser where men came to raise funds and one of the men was black and he spoke perfect Yiddish. It stands out in my mind, all these years later, and he was raising money to buy guns for Israel, and people were being reasonably generous.

We would drive up. It wasn't too far; about a two-hour drive. The fathers would come up on the weekend. My mom would be there the whole week. There are three of us, three sons. My mother would stay with the three of us. Then my father would come up. He had a bagel bakery in the Bronx. He would come up alone after the weekend, because he was busy on the weekend. He would come up Sunday morning and go right to sleep, usually, because he had worked a thirty-hour shift, and he'd stay as long as he possibly could. He would take a couple of extra days when he could, when business was slow. We had his company quite a bit. He and my mother seemed to get along pretty well, and it was a pretty good situation.

The men would come up to the country and there would be pinochle games; it was a source of pride that my father was a good pinochle player. He never bragged about how much he won but he would have a Yiddish expression about this so-and-so being a kalyeka who would make mistakes in pinochle. He kind of felt sorry for him rather than looking down, because being able to play a good game of pinochle was considered an important attribute.

The women were in different groups. And this was an eye opener to me, growing up. There were women like my mother who were very devoted to the children and would cook meals on this little three-burner gas stove without an oven — you'd have to put the oven on top of the burner — and always be chasing after us to feed us and whatnot. And then there would be other women, who I guess were more Americanized and who had never experienced being hungry themselves, and their kids were more or less given a lot more freedom and not chased after. My mother keeps telling a story about me: she was always chasing after me trying to feed me and I would never eat and I came running into the house one day and I said, "Ma, quick, get me some bread! Get me some bread!" So she cut a big piece of pumpernickel, brought up from the Bronx, and buttered it, and I ran outside and fed it to the chickens.

There were, let's say, a dozen families out of maybe thirty that came year after year until I was about sixteen. I went there until there was really nothing for me to do as a teenager. Then we went to a similar place, bigger and with a swimming pool and more teenagers, where we went for a number of years. Same type of situation; same type of people. Maybe a little more affluent at the second place. Again, very safe. I can't get over that because of the contrast with today.

Primarily, we went because, the reasoning was, the children had to get out of the city and get fresh air. All sorts of healthful things were attributed to fresh air. We would be taken out in the coldest weather, bundled up. I recall my younger brother in a carriage, bundled, with his nose sticking out in the winter to get fresh air. Somebody once told my mother, "Fresh air!"

It was just a nice experience. I haven't thought about it for a while. I just look back on it and it was very pleasant. I'm sorry that we didn't maintain a relationship with the kids I grew up with; it was a transient kind of thing for many of the families. Even the ones who kept repeating, we didn't keep contact with over the years, which was a mistake.

Al Thomas, fifty-one, hotel manager, Atlantic City, New Jersey

As it happens, I speak Yiddish. It was my first language. I was a Yiddish comic, and I still do that. I work now for Israel Bonds and for the Federation of Jewish Agencies and for Jewish organizations. Boris Thomashefsky was my father's, ohav shalom, uncle. He was the Barrymore of the Yiddish theater.

I am general manager, the operations manager, of this hotel, which is now called the International Hotel, which was formerly Teplitzsky's Olde

English House. In 1944, Mr. Teplitzsky, who was a kosher butcher, decided that he wanted to be in the kosher hotel business and he purchased a hotel called the Olde English House. From the Olde English House, Mr. Teplitzsky then purchased the next-door property, which was called Shulson's Cottage, and following that, the Hirsch-Carlton Hotel, which was a much larger hotel. Mr. Teplitzsky put those three places together and called them Teplitzsky's Olde English House. Then, perhaps twenty-five years ago, Mr. Teplitzsky built this present building, which he called Teplitzsky's Hotel.

In those days, there were perhaps thirty operating kosher hotels in Atlantic City, each of which had its own clientele and each of which was an extremely busy place. One by one these hotels fell away; they dwindled. The people interested in kosher facilities stopped coming to Atlantic City, for whatever reason. Today, we are the only remaining kosher hotel in this area. We cater, for the most part, to people who are interested in living in a Jewish atmosphere. Many of our guests are not particularly interested in kashruth. But they are, in fact, interested in being in a kosher atmosphere, rather than in just kosher food. They are interested in a synagogue on the premises, which we, of course, have, certainly. We have daily minyanim. We have shachrith every morning; we have mincha and mayrev every evening; we have Shabbes service; kavalat Shabbes services; we have memorial services.

We have the licht benching, which is very beautiful. We have a public licht benching. All of the ladies bench licht in one public area. Then, we have kavalat service and then we have our Friday evening dinner, which is the regular dinner people are used to eating at home. We serve gefilte fish, we serve matzo ball soup with mandelin, and we serve stuffed roast chicken, with carrot tsimmes. The regular Friday night dinner; it's a beautiful, beautiful meal, with a cup of tea. Then the people sit around and sing z'mires at the table. Friday night's beautiful; Friday night's very beautiful.

Many of our people only have this Yiddishkeit when they come to this place. They come from areas where they can't experience this kind of Yiddishkeit. We have people from Virginia, we have people from Long Island, living in Conservative Jewish areas where they don't have daily minyanim, and they come here for that.

My children are observant Jews. But Yiddishkeit they don't have. The kind of Yiddishkeit that you are finding, they will never have. Now, my children observe all the yom tovim. They observe Shabbes. They keep a strictly kosher home, just as we do, and they are devout Jews. But the Yiddishkeit that our parents brought to this country and some of our grandparents brought to this country, our kids will never see that, because it's lost.

Of course, the dining room here is classic. The reason people come to this place, in many cases, is because of the dining room. It's a compendium of Jewish menus from all over the world — these things that they get here. They get homemade kishka; it's a great dish. Baked herring, fried herring for breakfast. These are things that you can't get anyplace else. You must come to a place like this to get them. The younger people that come to us — and we have many of those — come because, in many cases, they remember their bubbe making these dishes, they remember their parents making these dishes, and they can't make them. So they come here to enjoy them. Most interesting.

We have a complete kosher regimen here. Our dining room is milchik for breakfast, and for the evening meal, it's a meat meal. People are interested in kashruth. People are interested in these dishes that you can't get anyplace else, like fried kreplach and boiled kreplach and kasha varnishkes, things that we specialize in in a dairy restaurant.

We have a very fine chef. We have had some interesting chefs here. We've had an American Indian, whose name was Frank Halfhide, and on "Hollywood Squares" they used the question "Is it true that a kosher hotel named Teplitzsky's in Atlantic City has an American Indian named Frank Halfhide as the chef?" This is fact.

Our dining facilities are available to anybody that wants them. And we have, interestingly enough, many non-Jewish people that come here for our food. We recently entertained an Armenian group of two hundred persons that spent five days with us. They liked our physical facility and they thought it would be interesting to have this kosher food. They have never before booked the same place twice. But they have already booked for another year.

We eat breakfast from nine until eleven A.M. and we dine from six to eight in the evening. Our coffee shop, which serves a full-course dairy meal, is open from eight A.M. until midnight. We have entertainment every evening, which most hotels no longer provide, generally ethnically oriented entertainment. We have Yiddish comics; we have Yiddish musicians.

My aunt was the Rumanian in the family. My uncle had married this Rumanian woman and went into the Rumanian restaurant business. And he sent for my dad. My dad came here from Russia in 1915; he was a very young man. For some reason, my uncle took the name Tomback from Thomashefsky. He told my father, "When you get off the boat and they ask you your name, tell them 'Tomback.'" I have a cousin who used that name. In any case, somehow my father got confused and he didn't know what to say, so he ended up with Thomas.

My family were in the Rumanian food business; kosher Rumanian restaurants. My folks came here to Atlantic City in 1934 or 1935 and opened a restaurant on the corner of Mississippi and Pacific and it was called Thomas's Rumanian Restaurant. To this day, I remember the smells that came out of the kitchen. My aunt, who was my father's sister-in-law, was a cook and she made her own pastrami, gefilte fish, and mamaligge. It was a real Rumanian restaurant. They even made their own raisin wine.

We left there, probably in 1940. We moved to Philadelphia, where my dad went to work with his brother, who had a restaurant on Fortieth and Girard, a Jewish cafeteria — another classic example of early Jewish life. I don't know if you recall what they were like. But they were regular stand-up, walk-in cafeterias. They had a hot section and a sandwich section and a cold section. They sold things like kreplach and hot vegetables, kasha varnishkes, kishka with gravy. It was open twenty-four hours except for Shabbes. They closed on Shabbes. They closed Friday afternoon and they opened again Saturday night no matter how late Shabbes was. They were very well known in this area — Jewish cafeterias. The most famous cafeteria in Philadelphia in those days was Grossman's at Fortieth and Girard. Philadelphia had many of those. My dad subsequently went to work for Gimbel Brothers as a restaurant manager and he spent the rest of his working years there.

Teplitzsky's became an institution in Atlantic City; it really did. We now have the third generation coming here. I was here for years with the Teplitzsky family and I married one of the girls in the Teplitzsky family. She was a Philadelphia girl. My father-in-law was a kosher butcher. His uncle, Mr. Teplitzsky, owned this hotel. All the Teplitzskys, at one time, worked here. Mrs. Teplitzsky passed on a couple of years ago, but Mr. Teplitzsky is living in Florida.

When the Teplitzskys took over this hotel, as I said, there were thirty or thirty-five kosher hotels in Atlantic City. This one was immediately well known, because he was a well-known butcher in this area. People started coming here and the remnants of the guests that came to the hotel of the Hirsch-Carlton, when it was the Olde English House. Mr. Teplitzsky was the host incarnate. He was a super, super host. He walked around the dining room with a bottle of schnapps and everybody got a schnappsel. There was no liquor license in those days. Who had a liquor license in a kosher hotel? But the schnappsel was always there. Everybody drank "L'chayim" together and it was a very familial kind of thing. It was like one big mishpocha. And over the years, people came and they brought children and their children brought children. And we now have guests in this hotel whose grandparents started coming here forty-five years ago. Very, very interesting people and very interesting stories.

Teplitzsky's today is no longer the same place it was. You ask if gaming made a change? It did make it change. It created a need for rooms, for sleeping rooms, because the way Atlantic City is today, there are not enough rooms outside the casinos where people can stay. It created a demand for our rooms; not our meals particularly, but our rooms. We still get all the Jewish people, but in addition to those people, we get many guests who are not particularly interested in the fact that it is a kosher hotel. It is a nice, clean, comfortable hotel, with nice facilities. We have a shvitz and a sauna and we have a lovely swimming pool. We have a nice restaurant on premises, and these people don't even realize it's kosher.

I have an interesting thing. Some of the girls who work for me — none of them are Jewish — never realized that they could eat kosher food until they started getting things in our coffee shop. When I told them it was kosher, I thought they were going to die at first. They didn't realize that many things that people eat are kosher. You go into a supermarket and you'll find thousands of products with OU on them or K on them. And you are taking something kosher home. Many non-Jews think that kosher food is gefilte fish and that's kosher food. They don't realize that much of what they eat is kosher.

Let me tell you about Passover. Three meals a day. Super story. At seven o'clock in the morning we have juice for those people who are so disposed and little cakes, mizonos, before prayer. We don't eat bread; we eat cake. So people come in at seven o'clock in the morning for their prune juice and cake, and then the prune juice works, and then they wait until eight o'clock for the opening of the breakfast. The dining room opens at eight and the first question they ask the waiters: "What's for lunch?" The reason for "What's for lunch?" is "I wonder how much to eat for breakfast, should I leave room?" Of course they get their menus for lunch and then they eat their regular breakfast. Or they'll come in at eight o'clock and say, "I'm not going to eat a full breakfast now. Just give me a little lox, and a little bit of prune juice, and give me a piece of grapefruit, and give me two pieces of matzo and maybe a egg, and I'll be back later for breakfast." Then five minutes to ten, just before the close of the dining room, they come in: "Duh! Now, it's time for our breakfast. Give me fried matzo and give me two pieces of baked herring." That's breakfast. Then these people run outside to wait in the lobby because lunch is at one o'clock. They sit and wait for lunch. This is emes; this is the truth. The lobby fills up at a quarter after ten, waiting for lunch. And at one o'clock the dining room doors are thrown open: mad charge; the people run into the dining room for lunch; they sit down, fill the dining room for lunch, and "What's for dinner? Because I've got to know how much to eat for lunch." This is the truth. Sounds funny; it's true.

Once again, a gourmet meal. It's a milk, dairy meal. It's soup — a milchik with soups, a cold soup and a hot soup. And always a fresh vegetable dish —

eggplant parmigiana, some type of noodle dish, a Passover noodle dish with cheese, Passover blintzes and cheese kreplach, potato kreplach. These things are served for lunchtime.

Then, the interesting thing to see is the packages. Making up packages, because dinner is not until seven o'clock. So from two to seven you could starve to death, God forbid, so we have to take a package back to the room, you see. Now we come back to the dining room at six o'clock. The dining room will open at seven. At six, the lobby is filled because we have to be ready for the seven o'clock dining room opening. At seven o'clock the dining room opens. The people — once again, it's a herd of elephants — run into the dining room and, once again, a full-course meal, and our Passover meals are delightful. All of our evening meals. It's a meat meal, so many great things to eat.

Following all these great things to eat, once again packages go out of the room because now we have to wait until tomorrow morning, tomorrow morning, so we have to take home a pear and a banana and an apple. Because you have to have a piece of fruit. Fruit is very important, very important part of our diet. And we've got to take a little matzo, because you don't know, God forbid, in the middle of the night you could get hungry and you've got to have something to eat. So you take a piece of matzo, a couple of macaroons, and a piece of honey cake, a piece of sponge cake.

This is a typical Passover day so far as the dining room is concerned. And it is a standard thing. Most comics who work the kosher hotels, the Jewish hotels, are familiar with this routine and make a very funny shtick out of it. And the people laugh, and why do we laugh? We are laughing at ourselves, because it's emes, true. It's how we are.

Unfortunately, we have never had a Passover in this hotel where we haven't lost somebody. I know of no kosher hotel that has not had someone leave. In most cases, it is just that these people, their system is not used to ingesting the kind of food that they eat; the amount of food, the quantities; huge quantities of food.

"Ich hub zu viel gegessen" is our biggest complaint. Our biggest single complaint in this hotel. "Oy, I ate too much. I can just about walk. How come you give so much food?" Very standard.

But we have gotten a new clientele in the hotel who are primarily interested in sleeping rooms, because they come here to play, they come here to gamble. They come on one-day, or two-day, or three-day bus trips from all over the country. We are now seeing people who have not been to Atlantic City ever before in their lives. And for those people we are a motel — we are a place to sleep, to rest in between their gaming junkets. What happens when some of them find they are in the middle of this Jewish atmosphere? Some of them immediately get their hackles up: "I didn't know it was *that* kind of hotel." Some of them come because they're "my best friend is Jewish" kind of people. We get those as well. "Oh, I'm glad I'm here because my best friend in Shamokin, Pennsylvania, is a Jew." The token Jew in Shamokin is everybody's best friend. That's funny. They later become very condescending in many cases. And some of them just take it, you know; it just happens to be that kind of place. It just doesn't make any difference to them.

Interesting enough, the Armenians that I mentioned, they came in here not realizing it was kosher. When they came and we discussed menus with them, then they realized it was kosher. They didn't mind at all because the facility is nice; the physical plant is nice. Then after they spent their five days with us, as I said, they arranged to come back because they really loved it. They didn't miss bacon at breakfast. They ate lox. Many of them had never eaten lox or smoked fish before, especially for breakfast. To the non-Jew or to the non-Easterner, particularly Jews, this is alien food.

Who eats fish in the morning? Jews eat fish in the morning! I think it's wonderful to eat fish in the morning and I'm sure you agree. It's expensive, there's no doubt about that, it's very expensive, but it's great to eat fish in the morning. Who can eat it? "Look at that lox. It's raw fish!" "It's not raw fish!" But to many non-Jews, people who don't know lox: "Who eats raw fish in the morning? It's bad enough eating fish at all, but raw fish?" These are comments we get — "Ooh, how can you eat that?" It's great.

Many of our foods, of course, have become accepted on the American scene. You go into great restaurants and they serve borsht. Borsht wasn't traditionally Jewish; borsht of course came from Russia. We serve cabbage soup. We don't make stchav; we buy bottled stchav. Rokeach makes a great bottled stchav, which is very good.

A lot of these dishes are falling by the wayside because there's nobody here to make them anymore. Petcha, for example, which is a Rumanian dish, by the way. It was originally made from calves' hoof jelly. It was made with calves' feet, but when you can't get them, you know you can make great petcha with chicken feet, but chicken feet you are not allowed to ship anymore. They don't sell chicken feet. You remember you walked into a butcher shop and the chicken hung and you bought it with the feet? Do you ever see chicken feet today? Think of it! You no longer see chicken feet. Do your kids know what petcha is? My kids don't know what petcha is. Never heard of it. But it's great. I love it with knobel. A super dish. And cholent. Cholent was a dish devised by Orthodox people. You cook it for twenty-four hours with beans and potatoes and a piece of meat. We put kishka in our cholent. It was the hot meal. We were commanded to eat a hot meal but you were not allowed to cook on Shabbes. So what do you do? We had to get around it. There were two commands coming at us from both directions, so we came up with cholent. You could cook it for hours and hours. You used to cook it on a small fire in a heavy pot. You put the beans and meat and a layer of shmaltz in there and throw some bones in there and it cooked for twenty-four hours on a very small fire. You throw potatoes in. They get nice and crispy, and this was a Shabbes meal. It satisfied the sholesh sudos commandment, you know, the second meal commandment. It's a great dish.

Jewish food, of course, is a world unto itself. Jewish food is a great world. It's possibly not the healthiest food. It's tough. It's high in calories. It's high in cholesterol, very high in cholesterol. But it tastes good. That's what it was all about. People that come here for this week, for the Passover ten days especially, or the High Holidays in the fall, it's the same story all over again: three meals a day and the orgy of eating from early morning until late in the evening. We have sort of a magnificent steak. But on steak night, we also have veal dishes, stuffed breast of veal — it's a great Jewish dish. The bones, you'd chew them until nothing's left. Certainly. Steaks they can get anyplace. But where can you get a real Jewish-style stuffed breast where you can chew the bones? You can't. We make cutlettin. You know, cutlettin are hamburgers. Baked cutlettin, broiled cutlettin. It's chopped meat with knobel and garlic in it and onion in it and you broil it. It's better than a steak. It's so filled with flavor.

We serve seltzer in a spritz bottle. This is the last batch of spritz bottles in Atlantic City. Nobody else uses them. We use the siphon bottle. Even in our coffee shop, you see them there. Oh, yeah, we serve the spritz bottles. And baked herring, another thing. You take a shmaltz herring and you bread it a little bit and throw it in the oven and bake it with onions. It's not the greatest thing in the world for you, but it tastes good. It tastes good.

Aaron Brenner, seventy-two, semiretired attorney; and
Helen Brenner, sixty-eight, Saratoga Springs, New York

AARON: In New York my father was in business with his brother. For years and years, they ran the dining rooms during the school year at Yeshiva University and the Jewish Theological Seminary. My uncle heard about a hotel in Saratoga and talked my father into joining him. That was 1922. My uncle was a rabbi but had never exercised his profession. He bought the hotel from people named Heller. The hotel was built, I would say, about 1870, the front part. The latter part was probably built ten or twelve years later. It was originally, let's call it, a Gentile hotel until about 1890, when it was bought by some people named Suarez. He had a Cuban clientele. Heller bought it from Suarez and only ran it for a few years; then we came along. For a number of years after we started we had quite a Cuban clientele and they would come with their nursemaids and maids and with the whole retinue behind them. They were the wealthy Cuban class who would escape the heat of Cuba during the summer months. They loved it here, loved the Jewish food, the kosher food and all.

But let's get back to Saratoga first. Saratoga's never been a big Jewish community. It's always been a small Jewish community. In permanent residency, we had no more than about forty families in 1940. The first Jews arrived here about 1860 or so. The Goldsmiths and the Starbucks were the first two families here. There are probably others we don't know about. They found a paper that a synagogue was organized here in 1898, and then we don't know what happened to it, because we don't recognize any of the names on there. Nobody knows the names. The next time, the same organization is being reorganized in 1911. So actually the Jewish community of 1911 up until about 1920 was very, very small. I doubt whether there were ten families. Between 1920 and 1924 about twenty-five more Jewish families came into town. But Saratoga was never a big Jewish community until about 1950, when the influx of Jews came with Saratoga Industries, which is an electronics plant. Skidmore College began to employ more Jewish instructors and professors and staff. So that we had an influx, they say, of 200, 250 families. Now, we are not sure how many there are. We think there are approximately 300, but we don't know. Every once in a while when an unfortunate thing happens, they come out of the woodwork. Then they come to us. They want a rabbi, they want a plot, or they want something like that.

There was a lot of anti-Semitism in Saratoga right up until 1940. There were many signs that appeared on the hotels, actually on the outside: NO JEWS ALLOWED. We had a doctor on Broadway, his sign on the window said NO JEWS TREATED. It was an anti-Semitic town.

Do you remember Saratoga in its heyday, from 1922 to about 1940? What happened was that the Europeans — the German and Hungarian and Rumanian Jews — were great believers in the spas. They came out here in droves at that time. Between the entrance to Saratoga to, let's say, the middle of Broadway, you probably had fifteen Jewish hotels alone. We had maybe thirty-five total outside of the rooming houses and we had dozens of rooming houses for the less fortunate people. Saratoga was wonderful in those days. It was a wide-open community — I'm not talking about gambling or racing. I'm talking about the Jewish community.

The better-class Jew came. For example, you couldn't go into a dining room without being formally dressed. I'm talking about a tie and shirt and jacket. There was music during the mealtimes. Each hotel had a band and they played luncheon music, dinner music, and then they played dance music in the evening. When the meals were over, the women would stroll up and down Broadway in their finery with the men; the sidewalks were crowded with Jewish people and prominent Jewish people. There were rocking chairs on the porch. Everybody was sitting on the porch and watching people and their friends parade up and down Broadway, and they'd greet each other.

After the evening meal, we had dancing, too. An orchestra actually played at the place, and people would dance. Most of these people were older people, and they enjoyed watching rather than dancing. But they enjoyed having outsiders walk in and they'd watch them dance; it was very popular.

After the war, a different form of entertainment came in. The hotels began to realize that they didn't want this noise in the hotel. A lot of people were complaining about the acoustics upstairs, like there's too much noise — the dances, the music, and so forth. So what they did — you know where the synagogue is now — that used to be Masonic Temple, and they leased it from a bank and they turned one of the rooms into a theater. They hired a standard company of about seven or eight actors and paid them; each hotel paid a certain sum to the fund. All of the hotels that belonged to the association could send their guests to this Jewish theater.

HELEN: Guests from hotels that did not belong to the association could come, but they had to pay for their tickets. Our guests got tickets from the hotel. They'd come over to the desk and they'd say to me, "Helen, I need a ticket. I want to go to the show." And I'd give them one. What happened was a lot of people came in for the meal, just for the meal, to get the ticket. They'd have the meal and ask for a ticket and I'd say, "Sorry. Guests of the hotel only." You know, they'd try to pull that sort of thing. But the guests went free. And not only did we pay the actors, but we'd also have to house them. So each hotel had one actor or one actress.

AARON: It was vaudeville, Yiddish vaudeville. And it was very popular with the guests. They loved it. That lasted, I'd say, from 1950 to 1970, about twenty years.

Let's say back in the 1930s, if you got thirty-five dollars a week with three meals a day, it was very good. You'd make money on it. Then later, you know, times changed, money values changed. You got a room. You got three meals a day. Some had bathrooms; that was more money. We had rooms with private baths, with a bath and a shower overhead, you know, and that sort of thing. Then we had rooms with a lavatory. Of course, people took their baths and showers at the bathhouse all day. They felt they didn't need a bath, and some of the rooms just had a sink.

When people came to Saratoga in the early 1920s to the 1940s or fifties, they came with tremendous trunks — four or five big trunks. They stayed for three or four weeks. They took a complete set of baths. Twenty-one was the magic number. I don't know why twenty-one was selected; don't ask me. But the doctors recommended twenty-one baths. Both kinds of bath: some mud, some mineral. You couldn't get into the mineral bath, it was so busy at the time. It was extremely popular at one time. But Americans don't believe in baths or therapeutic waters.

In fact, the waters are wonderful. I have personal experience. I can tell you many experiences of people who could not walk. Whether the water, whether the rest did it, we don't know; something did it for them. And they believed in it and they came back year after year. On the typical day, most of them got up in the morning early and went down to the Number Three water, where they used very oversize glasses. The reason for the oversize glasses was that they were supposed to take two or three glasses a day. So instead of going through the line twice — and you might stand in line for an hour before you got to the well — they would take an oversize glass so they could go once and fill it up. Or else the hotels would send taxicabs down to the wells and they would fill up the water, let's say, two or three in the morning, and bring it back to the hotels. Guests would come down in the morning and have their Number Three water.

Immediately after, they would have a hot drink, either tea or hot water or hot lemonade or something, and then would relax until breakfast. Breakfast was served and then they went to the bathhouses. By the time you got into the room, got your tickets, it was an hour's treatment. About twenty minutes was given over to the bath itself. The length of the bath depended upon your health, upon your heart condition. The heat depended upon it, too. If you were stronger and had a good heart, you got a higher temperature. If you were less fortunate, you had a lower temperature and less time in the bathtub.

You came into a private room with a tub. The water was pumped in there at a certain temperature, depending on what the doctor recommended. You sat there, did nothing but sit there. Let's say you sat for twenty minutes. The attendant boy helped you out of the tub; you had a sheet over you. You went to a restroom and lay there for about thirty minutes, because it's a very, very tiring effect after the baths. In Europe, they use a common pool. Here, they use private tubs.

Mud baths were different. Mud baths were privately owned, not state-owned. There's a law in New York State — Charles Evans Hughes was governor when it was enacted — that there could be no privately owned mineral wells. When Franklin D. Roosevelt came in a number of years later, they created this reservation with a park and the bathhouses, the Gideon Putnam Hotel and the recreational facilities and whatnot. But primarily because of Roosevelt's interest — he was a great believer in hot springs — he and Governor Lehman made this thing. It was during the Depression days. They had some general contracts, but most of the park was developed by the WPA.

People went to the baths, came back, let's say, for lunchtime. It was a very leisurely lunch, music. Then they retired for the afternoon. They either took a stroll or went to their rooms. At dinnertime, they came down with more or less semiformal clothes or dress. Dinner was served very leisurely. We ran a kosher hotel, strictly kosher. We had three kosher butchers, two Jewish grocery stores, two fish markets, two bakeries.

Our food was not heavy. The meals were very bland because of the different type of people we had. This one had diabetes, that one had stomach trouble, this one had God knows what. I went to the Catskill Mountains once and I took my first spoonful of food in my mouth and I nearly died. How could they cook that way? We had diabetic people, sugar-free cakes, sugar-free this, nothing in this, no fats. It was a very bland — I wouldn't say bland; bland compared to other places.

We always served dairy at noon and meat at night, because it was easier. But they changed that about thirty years ago. You had dairy breakfast, meat lunch, and dairy supper, but that was too much trouble. We had all sorts of things. We made all sorts of food. We had a complete meal. We'd have a fruit. You have a salad. You have soup. You have a main dish — main dish might be fish or might be any sort of vegetable loaves or vegetable dishes; there's a dozen. Blintzes were not a very popular thing with us. It was a little too heavy for most people. So we had to watch ourselves.

HELEN: They didn't go for fried stuff.

AARON: Fried stuff we had very little. And of course we had a baker who baked and we had dessert, mostly plain cakes. They didn't prefer anything fancy. No coverings to it, you know. You could put a drop of whipped cream on it; that was the furthest they would go.

We had a nice clientele. In the 1920s they came up by train. Some came up in limousines and so forth. Their own cars.

HELEN: My mother came up by the night boat to Albany and then took a taxi from Albany to Saratoga. I was this big. All I remember is coming up on a boat at night. My mother was staying at his place. That's how I met him.

AARON: Mostly people came by train or bus, later by bus. Thirty-odd years ago. Older people met. Many a time they met. Widows and widowers came up and they met. We never had a young crowd in that sense. The men played pinochle, the women played poker, the men and women played poker too. Mahjongg wasn't popular. People went to the races once in a while.

HELEN: You had half a dozen through the summer who went.

AARON: And all those gambling places? We had no crowd like that. We had primarily a middle-class or upper-middle-class Jewish clientele who in the evening sat around. Prohibition didn't bother us. None of the Jewish hotels had bars. The Jew liked his Kiddush and liked his shot of whiskey every once and a while. At evening time, we would send the bellhops to the Number One water, bring back gallons of Number One water we'd serve to the guests. Three is a very strong laxative. Number One water is like a tonic. My grandchildren love it. They call it the bubbly water. I've got three or four grandchildren who refuse to leave town unless I take them, must take them, down to the bubbly water, and they love it, they love it.

HELEN: I have a son and a daughter-in-law who are crazy about that water. I have another son who loves the water. His wife won't go near it. Her parents won't go near it.

AARON: What was the kind that used to smell like rotten eggs? Number One. That's still there. It's right at the park.

HELEN: It didn't smell so bad.

AARON: We got used to the odor. It didn't bother us. We drank it and we knew that it was terrible.

Brenner's was the last Jewish hotel that operated here. My father died. My family and I didn't want it. We hated it. We closed it in 1973.

HELEN: We had to deal with sick Jewish people. How obnoxious they can be!

AARON: Oh God, that was a tough life.

HELEN: I'll tell you, there's one family that I felt sorry for when we closed down the hotel, because they were very kind people — they were refugees. Both of them had lost their families in Germany, and the man and the woman got married, with no family. When they came up, you didn't know those people were in the house. Whatever they got, whatever rest, was fine with them. They were the only ones I felt sorry for. Other than that, the guests came up and they'd brag about how much they paid in Florida, but when you raised rates from one year to the next — five dollars a week — you'd think, God knows, we were robbing them. And you know how prices had been mounting.

AARON: It wasn't that so much.

HELEN: My kids hated it. We depended on them.

AARON: I didn't need it. I used to go to work in the morning early and work until three o'clock, come back and work until eleven o'clock at my hotel. The problem became help. That's what killed them in the Catskill Mountains, which had at least three hundred hotels at one time, maybe more. Have you been through there lately? It's pitiful. But just take a drive around — we were there about a year ago — and see the number of closed hotels. Some were very, very big. They just couldn't take it anymore.

What happened was the State of New York came along with its rules. For example, the State of New York said that if you employed a person for three hours a day, you had to pay them for eight. Now in what business, if I worked for you and you knew that I did three hours of legal work and

I handed you a bill for eight, what would you say to me? Not in the State of New York. They drove me mad.

In the hotel's heyday, we used to have 150, 200 people.

The season, primarily, up until about 1940, started June tenth or so. After that, it usually started immediately after the Fourth of July weekend until about the twentieth of August. About 1955, we opened for Passover and stayed open until after all the holidays were over, and that went over to Simchas Torah, which goes into October. So we were open about nine, ten months a year.

HELEN: We didn't make money.

AARON: Well, for the amount of work, it really didn't pay. We made money, but not for the amount of work . . .

HELEN: It didn't warrant.

AARON: It didn't warrant it. It was too much work to make a hotel kosher.

HELEN: The stories — most of the stories were hair-raising. See, I knew most of them who were the refugees, the people on reparations, and the stories that they told and what they went through was unbelievable. We had one woman came in and wore gloves all the time, and it was not my business to ask "What's the matter?" I never did. The only thing I did do, after they stayed a week or so, I said, "How do you feel? Are the baths helping you?" This woman said to me, "I think I'm a little better." She took her gloves off and I was ready to pass out. There was no skin; it was all raw flesh. They had split the fingers — in the concentration camp — they had split every one of her fingers so that there was no skin and she had poisoning and she couldn't lift a spoon on her raw flesh there. We had one couple who told me — well, the woman did — that she was carrying her baby and they were marching to one of the camps and the baby started to cry and the trooper or whatever said, "Shut him up!" She said, "I can't. How can I? He's hungry." He said, "I'll show you how." He took the baby by the legs and smashed his head against the tree, and that was the end. I get goose pimples to this day. And I'll tell you, those are the stories I can tell. I can tell you the abuse that some of the children put their parents through.

AARON: Some were so pitiful, the children used to dump them on us. They'd come and dump them on us. Some of them were very unfortunate. The way the children treated their folks, it's something very puzzling to me.

Sometimes families came back for thirty or forty years. Second generations, no. Second generations came up to visit their folks. They'd drop in to say hello. But they were not believers, the second generation. They became Americanized.

HELEN: Some children were very good to their parents, like we had Mr. Goldberg. The daughter and her husband, the son-in-law, would say, "Helen, I'm leaving Pop with you. Anything, call me."

My daughter was a waitress in the hotel, and she came in to me at the end of one summer and she said to me, "Mama, please, I'll be a chambermaid. I'll work in the pantry. I'll work in the kitchen. Please don't make me go out to wait on the people anymore."

AARON: Dining room is a tough place to be. We had some very nice people.

HELEN: You have to operate with cooks who are very temperamental. We had a cook who threatened a waitress with a big heavy frypan.

AARON: They work in a hot kitchen; it's tough.

HELEN: Yeah, but they're temperamental people.

AARON: This is a story about a man they called Rabbi Chernowitz, and this man was about six-one, six-two. He was the chief rabbi of Odessa until the Bolsheviks came in, and they tossed him out. One day he calls up my father and says to my father he is bringing a lady with him but take it easy on her price. In walked a short woman, I doubt whether she's five-two, five-one, wearing a plain black dress and she registers "Mrs. Rabinowitz." After I get talking to her, she was Sholem Aleichem's widow. His name was Rabinowitz. Very pleasant woman. She used to tell me he sold his own stories for a dollar, a dollar and a half. Poor. Poor as a church mouse. Particularly him. Just think of *Fiddler on the Roof;* could have made him a multimillionaire.

We used to run a Night of Stars. We were the only one outside of New York City that used to do the Night of Stars here, because we had the entertainers at the gambling houses. For example, one year we had Harry Richmond, Sophie Tucker, Bing Crosby, and so forth. Have you ever been to a Night of Stars performance in New York? I don't know if they run them anymore, but they used to run them, one vaudeville act after another. Sing a song, tell some jokes, and so forth, and used to make them a lot of money for the United Jewish Appeal. We did the work. We used to get the convention hall, which is next to the synagogue here. We used to run taxicab services between these night clubs so we could get these people here on time. All sorts of orchestras came. It was very entertaining. We made $5000 or $6000 in those days.

Brenner's now is called the Inn at Saratoga. It's owned by some people from Albany. They put a tremendous amount into it.

HELEN: If you remember the hotel at all, I suggest you walk in there now. We went there to have dinner last night and, I want to tell you something, we were amazed. The lobbies have been changed. Where we had the dining room and the kitchens, it was all made into rooms. And they added on. They enclosed the porch, the side porch, and they made a dining room out of that and the lobbies. They took us in to see a suite. They made one room out of two — it's two rooms but they made a suite out of it. Whoever did their interior decorating did a beautiful job. We understand that the man put a million dollars in that place. It's on Main Street, right next to Saint Peter's Church.

AARON: We had a writing room. We had what we called like a television room, where people would sit around and watch television. It was a large room. In fact, it's a dining room now.

HELEN: One-armed bandits we had in the writing room.

AARON: Years ago.

HELEN: We had a woman, her name was Kaminsky, the old lady, do you know what she used to do? She used to play the one-armed bandit from the time breakfast was over. She would go in there and start playing it and when lunchtime rolled around, she'd put a slug in it to jam it so nobody could play. Then, after, we had to call the repair man — this happened every day — and he'd get the slug out and she'd stand there and wait for him to get it out because she'd stopped playing. The day she had to leave, her chauffeur was having a fit because he was all packed, he was ready to go. She wouldn't go away until she hit the jackpot. You know, of course, the one-armed bandits were illegal, and so when the police were coming, we'd get the word and those things disappeared.

AARON: Today, we have three synagogues. We got one in the summertime run by a rabbi [HELEN: Whatever], very Orthodox [HELEN: The Chasidic group], and then we have the regular synagogue on Broadway, which now is split between Orthodox and Conservative, and then we have the Reform.

HELEN: The Reform was just born, what, about ten years ago?

AARON: About ten, twelve. See, we — the Orthodox — had a rule that we couldn't take any mixed marriages in our organization. We had no mixed marriages. And there were a lot of mixed marriages, particularly the Skidmore faculty that came in. So they couldn't join. So they made their own. I don't know how well they're doing.

HELEN: I understand they are doing very well. They've got a lot of people.

AARON: A lot of transients. A lot of transients there. They are here and they are gone the next day. You don't see them.

HELEN: No. But a lot of locals are in it.

AARON: Not too many. Where do the young go? We don't know. Nobody knows. Nobody can find them.

HELEN: Most are in the Reform. Most of the younger couples are in the Reform.

AARON: When you talk, they are in their fifties, you want to call them young?

Do any Jews come here now for the baths or for anything? There's a few. But very, very few. They all died out — that generation is gone.

16

Butcher, Baker, Coffin Maker

THE FATHER of my friend and neighbor Harry Sanders was a plumber. Freddie Wolinsky's dad was an upholsterer. Charlotte Danto's father was our butcher. And every Saturday night, ritualistically after sundown, we — my mother, father, brother, and I — would walk the several blocks to South Pearl Street, then the heart of the Jewish neighborhood, to buy the week's food supply, stopping at Danto's butcher shop and Zuckerman's bakery and Fishman's delicatessen. The parents of most of my childhood friends were such tradespeople, hard-working people, poor people. My grandfather, as I said, was a shoemaker. And my uncle Sam was a baker.

Pearl Worman Leibowitz's father was a baker, too, in Jacksonville, Florida, where she is the co-owner of a Jewish delicatessen. "Oh, let me tell you what he used to say when we would get a little impatient with the customer," she told me. "He would say, 'Do you know how lucky you are that the customer comes to you? Let me tell you, I used to go up three flights of steps. The lady would yell down to me, "I want three rolls!" I'd take up three rolls. She would take out two rolls and say, "That one is too brown. I don't want that one." And nothing would please her. Down the steps I would go to get some more rolls to see if I could find one more roll to please her.'"

Roughly fifteen hundred miles away, in Burlington, Vermont, Bernard Cohen made deliveries for his baker father. "Oh, we always delivered to almost every Jewish family," he told me. "We used to deliver two rolls to this one and go up three flights of stairs to deliver it and we used to deliver half a loaf of rye bread, and if it wasn't well baked they'd send it back down for a different half a loaf."

On June 1, 1949, Maxwell Dane joined up with Ned Doyle and Bill Bernbach to found Doyle, Dane, Bernbach, Incorporated. Dane recalled that one of the accounts that came to the advertising agency at that time was Levy's bread. "Most of the population of the New York area is non-Jewish. How do you get them to buy a rye bread bearing the name of Levy's Jewish Rye? So we felt from a marketing point of view we had to appeal to the rest of the population, and that led to the development of the campaign 'I love Levy's.' So it caught on. Our principal medium was subway station advertising, where we could get color and penetration for a relatively modest expenditure.

"We faced it frontally," he said. "It would have been kind of stupid to try to duck it. The only way to duck it, we could call it Smith's or Mc-Pherson's Jewish Rye Bread." The campaign used different and obvious ethnic groups to say "You don't have to be Jewish to love Levy's real Jewish Rye Bread" — a Chinese waiter, an Italian woman, a black youngster, and an American Indian.

So much for rye bread and rolls. I knew that the bagel, which, along with matzo ball and chicken soup, as the quintessential Jewish food, had arrived when one day, while I was traveling with my wife to an interview in South Carolina, we passed a huge building with this sign prominently displayed: IT'S BAGEL TIME AT THE KITCHENS OF SARA LEE GREENVILLE.

And later on I knew the bagel had totally assimilated when Burger King announced the sale of "bacon, ham, or sausage on a bagel."

Jack Becker, seventy-nine, retired butcher, Jacksonville, Florida

I left Warsaw when I was about fourteen years old. My parents were afraid I was going to be taken into the army, so I left by myself. I came through Ellis Island. It was like a dungeon. My elder brother was there waiting for me. And he took me out right away. I spoke no English whatsoever. My name was Becher. But they couldn't pronounce *ch,* so they pronounced it with a *k,* and that's the way it remained. I had to learn English while waiting on the trade. I went to night school only. I worked. Ever since I came to this country, I have been working.

My father wasn't feeling well. He had a job as a shochet. His employer was very mean; used to get him up six o'clock in the morning to travel in the woods to buy a calf and kill it in the woods. In those days the roads were rough and the trucks were old and he couldn't take it. So he decided he would try and go in business for himself so he wouldn't have to work so hard. Well, since I didn't have anything to do right offhand, I said, "Daddy, I'll help you out for a month or so." Well, that "month or so" lasted thirty-nine years.

I'll tell you what a kosher butcher is. In those days, we used to go and buy cattle at farms; we used to pay a dollar, a dollar and a half for a calf;

seven, eight dollars for a cow. Meat was sold cheap, nineteen cents a pound, twenty-five cents a pound. Times were very hard. Many a time the city used to come and cut off the electricity because I didn't have enough to pay the electric bill. I didn't have the dollar to pay for the calf. I used to ask from a customer would he please loan me a dollar. So those were hard days. I have worn shoes with tired soles.

The butcher shop was in an old store. I stayed in the same place for thirty-nine years. Certain things we gave away. Heart we used to sell for a cent a pound, two cents a pound. Five cents was an outrageous price. Liver we used to sell fifteen, nineteen cents a pound. Then during the days when they had the NRA we used to sell steaks for twenty-five cents, nineteen cents. Those were hard days, but during the years I have worked, I built up a wonderful trade, and my customers, ninety-nine percent of my customers, became personal friends. The mutual relationship and trust was beyond doubt, and ninety-nine percent of our business was on credit. We used to have three or four bicycle boys to deliver the merchandise. We opened the store at six o'clock in the morning — every morning, rain or shine. We used to close at eight, nine, and Thursday we used to close at eleven o'clock at night. Saturday night, after sunset, we used to be there and start to cook corned beef. Later on, people waited for hot corned beef. People used to keep the stores open until eleven, twelve o'clock at night. After they closed, they came to our store to buy their meats.

There are no more kosher butcher shops in Jacksonville. We were the last one. Two of them went out of business before. One, I helped to keep him in business as long as I could. He didn't have a shochet, so I sold him my kosher meat, and somehow I was the last. I stayed in business not so much for the profit, but as a matter of service to the community. I had a moral obligation. Finally, I got someone to take it over. He stayed about a year, a year and a half, and then he closed up.

Now they get kosher meat from all over, from Atlanta, from Orlando, from Miami, from Chicago. A group gets together and they order one shipment that comes in by refrigerator truck. I think one man has 100 or 150 customers give him orders, and he sends the orders into Sinai in Chicago, ordered into one place, a hundred packages, and they call them up and each one comes and takes it and each one has a separate bill and that's the way it's handled.

During World War II meat was rationed and all the people that had licenses were allowed to butcher cows. You couldn't buy a license for any money. We fortunately had a license naturally, so we were in good shape. We bought cattle and we sold it. Ninety-nine percent of the business was under the table. I used to go at four o'clock in the morning to farmers and buy cattle, come back to open the store on time, and send out our group, white and black, to kill the cattle for trade and some for kosher. We used to sell five-hundred-pound barrels of corned beef for seven cents a pound, eight cents a pound. Do you believe it? We used to sell them for that.

We used to buy shmaltz — paid a cent and a half a pound, two cents a pound; people used to handle it. They used to sell it; I don't know what they did; they used to use it for explosives. Bones, I guess, used to be in hundred-pound bags, a penny a pound. So we made a great business that year. Those years would be good business. During the Second World War when we had to sell meat, the price list had to be posted, but you couldn't do the business, so what did they do, the government, just to give us a rebate? They knew how much cattle sells for, so they knew we couldn't sell it for the price that they wanted to sell, so we had to give them a report how many cattle we slaughtered, how much we paid for it, and they used to give us a rebate. It was a lot of work; used to stay up nights and count points. We did a good business. That was one year that you could get rich quick. So I decided that was the year for me not to get rich; I left my business and went to study for a year in New York. I went to Columbia and we went to Jewish Theological Seminary. Two colleges. My wife and I went up. People think I was crazy. What would you think?

The disappearance of people keeping kosher is because no Jewish young man wants to go into a slimy business. He wants to be a lawyer, a CPA, a dentist. The younger generation doesn't want to be in this kind of business. There's about 200 or 250 people in Jacksonville that are buying kosher meat — all imported. If a man wants to open up a place, he couldn't get rich, but he could make a nice living. It's just that nobody wants to be a butcher. There's an easier way to make a living. You see, he wouldn't work like I did. Times were hard. We used to sell on credit. Every Monday I'd have to go and collect from various customers. There was never a doubt about how much you are owing. Whatever I said, people didn't hesitate for a minute whether the count was right or wrong.

Most knew what they wanted when they came into the store. First of all, there was no cut meat. There was no such thing as cut meat. We used to have live chickens in the store, sure, live chickens, and we used to pluck them. We used to charge a nickel for killing and a nickel for picking. Some rich women didn't want to pay a nickel for picking, so they picked the chicken themselves and got all messy, but they saved a nickel. And lamb and veal and poultry. The margin of poultry was so small it's pathetic, but competition was keen. Three butchers in a small Jewish community, and everybody tried to outdo the other.

The margin of profit was so insignificant — make two cents a pound and delivery and credit and whatnot. They called up six o'clock in the morning.

They wanted to have meat in time for lunch. They had to kosher it, don't forget.

Mostly people would kosher the meat themselves in those days. Later on, we started to kosher it in the store for them. Koshering at home was simple. You soak it for a half an hour in cold water and you take it out and salt it from all sides for an hour and then you wash it off good and then it's ready to be cooked. Object in koshering. We human beings don't like to eat meat generally because it's not moral to eat life, but what can we do? You have to exist. So the Torah told us the least you can do — eliminate the blood. The blood is the essence of life, so you wouldn't become a cannibal. Show that much respect for life by not consuming blood; by soaking it and soaking it, that removes the blood.

The only prayer is when you slaughter the cattle. It has to be a special and unusually sharp knife, without any spot whatsoever. It has to be absolutely perfect, so when the animal is killed, it is so swift that she becomes unconscious in split seconds. There's no pain whatsoever. That's the only time we make a prayer, but as far as koshering —

My father's role as a shochet was naturally to go and slaughter the animal and when he killed it to open up the animal and take a look at the lungs and see that the lungs are perfect. If there's any spot on the lungs, then it is not kosher unless he can quickly remove it; it had to be taken out, the lung, carefully. If it is removed, the animal is kosher. If it isn't removed, then it's treyf, because it is a sign that the animal is not in good health. The difference, you see, is between glat kosher and not glat kosher. Glat kosher, they advertise it in the kosher restaurant. When a shochet kills an animal and looks at the lungs and there is no spot on it at all, that's perfect, that's glat kosher. Glat is smooth. If there is a pimple on it, it has to be removed; if it is removed, that means the animal is not diseased and it is kosher; but it is not a perfect glat, as smooth as it is. So that was his job. His job was to supervise that the animal was healthy, was killed kosher. Also, if meat is over three days old, it gets too hard and the blood could not be soaked out well enough. It had to be washed off in three days' time to keep it soft and moist. Then they put it in the water or in the salt. The salt was able to draw the blood.

There is a difference with poultry. With the chicken, it is not as strict as with the calf. With the chicken, normally, that's up to the women. Every Jewish woman knew when they opened the chicken they would find sometimes this nail or something, and they used to come to my father or to the rabbi with what they call a shayla. A question. In the gizzard mostly you find something; that's already a point of law. Or the chicken's leg was broken. It depends where it was broken. Above the knee it's treyf, because this interferes with the circulation of the blood. The Jewish dietary laws are very strict about the health of an animal. Many a time when my father condemned cattle, it wasn't healthy enough, the government inspector okayed it. So, that's the kosher meat.

Blood spot on the egg is the same thing; has the symbol of blood. Blood is forbidden. You are not allowed to eat it. That's the reason all the eggs generally, you know, go through a light and you can tell whether they are clear. Whenever you open up an egg and see a little drop of blood, you throw it away. There's no other way to do it.

Alvin Fertel, forty-nine, junior high school assistant principal, New York, New York

My grandfather was a bagel baker in Europe. He came to America and he worked as a bagel baker.

My father left school at nine years old and went to work at a variety of jobs. He was the oldest of ten, eleven; ten surviving. He worked in a variety of jobs, as I said, and he was laid off one time for something that was the fault of the business. It had such a traumatic effect on him that he swore he would never work for anyone again. He would only work for himself. He opened the bagel bakery on a string in the Bronx with two bags or three bags of flour and a rented basement. My father went into partnership with his father. He would do the outside work; that is, get customers, see the deliveries were made, pay the bills. My grandfather couldn't do any of that stuff. My grandfather would make the bagels and so on. Just bagels and it was all wholesale. There was no retail. It was a different era. Water bagels, salted and plain, at that time, and that's what it was for many, many years.

My father told the experience of opening the bakery and having kerosene thrown on his bagels when he delivered them, because in order to have customers he had to take somebody else's customers. He said he was hit on the head one time; he had a scar over his eyebrow from being hit by some hired hooligans.

He built up what was a reasonable business, and that was my experience growing up as a kid. All my friends would go to the movie on Saturday. I would go to the bagel bakery on Saturday. I worked in the bagel bakery with my father from the time I was about thirteen until I was in my thirties. I was an assistant principal, already, and I didn't want to work there anymore and he didn't force me, but he appealed to me. He wanted me. He trusted me. He knew he could go away and the place would be watched and so forth. I did it for many, many, many years, long after I felt I needed the income anyway. I put in almost twenty years.

Today, you make a bagel with a bagel machine. In those days there was no bagel machine. You made the dough in a machine. It was a formula. Water, flour, a certain amount of salt, yeast. You mixed it up in a machine, and the machines were capable of holding five to six hundred pounds at one time. It would mix a certain amount. It would come out of the machine into a receptacle and then you would put it on a wooden bench. The bench would be ten, twelve, maybe fifteen feet long. You'd put this big piece of dough on it — and then you would slice strips out of it. You'd roll it into what looked like a rope. Originally, there were two men working on making them and one man baking them.

They would be rolled out and then you would take your index finger, your middle finger, and your ring finger, wrap the bagel around it. You'd take your pinky and your thumb, snap it off, and roll it forward and back in one motion, and as you rolled it back, you'd hold it in your hand and put it down on a board that had crumbs. From stale bagels we would grind up our own crumbs to use on top of the board so that the bagel wouldn't stick to it. And the bagel would have to proof a certain amount of time, thrown into boiling water — proof means to rise. There's a whole separate vocabulary. You'd take it and put it on a board; you'd put the board on a box which was called a stoysh — I guess that was the Jewish word for it — and it would be allowed to sit. The box had a lip on it of about three inches.

Now, depending on the weather, you would either close the box to keep it airtight or you'd open it a certain amount to let the air through. Warm weather, you would open the box so that the bagel wouldn't proof too much — what they call overproof, or blow up. Then you'd get a bagel without a hole and it blows up into a ball. If it gets too overproofed, you'd have to throw it away. There was no air conditioning; you worked, like I said, in a basement with a coal-fed oven. These fellows were really, truly bakers, not like the guys today. They were bakers!

There was no freezer. There was no refrigerator. It had to be made just so. You had to look at the humidity, the temperature, and you had to make adjustments as you went along so that it would come out just right.

These two fellows made the bagels, and then a separate man came in; he was a baker. He would bake the bagels. He had a man assisting him who would throw them into this boiling kettle of water, stir them up. Take them out and put them on long boards, maybe twelve feet. And they would take the board and put them all the way into the oven. They would stay in the oven for a minute or two until they dried up. Then he would bring them out, take a piece of string, run it under the bagels, and then put them in and turn them upside down. So the dry side would now be touching the oven. And once they were in and they were dry, he had a long peel — it was a pole. Again, the peel is almost as long, I'd say half as long, as the board. It was a long, thin board and narrow. You really had to be skilled.

Not like today. Today they use a wide board, maybe three feet. This thing must have been four inches wide. You'd slide it underneath and you'd have to really be able to manipulate and turn them over according to how they bake.

The oven was set at about five to six hundred degrees. That stayed the same. Bagels baked better in those days because the ovens were brick and lined and they were really a different construction. The modern ovens are not made as well. The luster comes automatically from boiling them first. That's why a water bagel looks different from any other thing. There is no oil or anything put on it, like they do with a bread to make it look pretty. No, this is natural. They boil it. That's what gives it a unique taste and its look and its crispiness on both sides. It was — I keep saying the same expression — a whole other world. The bagel bakery.

I never even thought of going to college when I was a kid. I wanted to become a bagel baker; that was it. Although I could probably never have become a union man, because my father was a boss. So my father had a bakery, but I couldn't work in it in any of the union jobs. That was the type of union — it was a very strong union. Or very weak bosses; either way you want to look at it. It was Bagel Bakers Local 338, I believe.

The New York City experience with the bagel business was almost all Jewish, with an occasional black and Gentile. These people would get into it because they had been working as a kettleman, which is the fellow who mixed them, and learned how to bake for the baker, who, let's say, would be lazy and let the guy finish up for him or do the last three lines or whatnot. Then when someone would be sick and there would be no union man to send in, these fellows would be called in in an emergency by the delegate, who was like the czar of the bagel industry. Everybody would sit down and applaud. You were made. You were now "being used." Once he marked you kosher, you were going to become a union man, and being a union man meant you'd have a life of prosperity, because they were the best paid of all the bakers — better paid than the fancy cake bakers, because it was a small industry and they were able to exact a pretty good salary.

I grew up in awe of unions and in disgust of unions, because I could see what they were doing in that small business to my father; in a sense, in a lot of things he had no say-so. They would send us incompetent workers. The bagels would be ruined. There would be no hiding it. We were forced to eat it. And we had workers delivering bagels for us who couldn't drive a truck and missed customers, who did the same route every night and did it wrong. We were stuck with them.

We would get plenty of stale bagels then, because the terms of the delivery were you only pay for what you use and whatever you don't use you give back. We give you full credit. So we would always be getting the stale bagels back and using them. Now we don't do that — my brother has the business now.

Some years later there was a strike, and this strike occurred at a point when my father and several other bagel bakers were not in a position any longer to give out any more raises. They were really squeezed. This was the first time the union had really squeezed them. There was no more money to give. And so this was the first time that they fought a strike.

My father made bagels and he taught me how to make bagels. He taught me how to make bagels in one day. This was this big production that I had been waiting for my whole life. I was already an adult; I may have been married. I know I was teaching in a high school. I must have been twenty-four, twenty-five, twenty-six, and I would come in in the morning — this was a great source of pride to me and to my father — come in the morning, by myself, open the bakery, take a hundred pounds of flour, throw it into the machine, mix it up according to the formula, whatever it was that he had taught me, which was not a big deal, and then make, all by myself, whatever it was, whether it came out to be twenty-five or thirty boards of bagels from a hundred pounds. We didn't have any facilities, freezers or refrigerators, for getting ready ahead of time. Then my father would come in, let's say, around seven-thirty, eight in the morning. I would be all finished, and the bagels would be baked. And this was great. I look back on this as a fulfillment of something that I was able to do for my father. A tremendous amount of pride. I think this meant more to him than whatever other accomplishments I did. Not so much that I could do it, but when he needed me, I was there. We beat them on that strike, and since then we have not had a union.

Not all bagels are made by machine today. There are both kinds. It doesn't make as much difference as you think in the taste of the bagel, whether it's made by machine or made by hand. There's not much of a difference. The difference is in the way it's baked and in the way it's allowed to proof. And a lot of the new people really don't do it right.

Bagel making's no longer a Jewish industry, either for customers or for producers. It's becoming simplified. Mainly, it's not union much anymore. So anybody can really open up a small place with his family and do it.

I would say bagels became no longer the sole interest of Jews when Lender's Bagels opened up a bagel bakery in Connecticut somewhere and started mass-producing them and freezing them and shipping them all over the place. They are very, very big. They started out small and went into this. Now, to the real bagel eater, that's not a bagel. But I guess to a real pizza eater, frozen pizza is not a pizza either. It's that type of thing. And that was able to go around the whole country. There were always jokes about bagels and advertisements about bagels and things like that. But not by the bagel industry. By the cream cheese people. By other people.

Egg bagel is not a bagel. Egg bagel is a piece of bread shaped like a bagel. A bagel is a water bagel. I say it with authority, because we used to scoff at these other things. These things would come out flat on the bottom. We knew they weren't bagels. Bagels are round on both sides. These other things, such as cinnamon bagels and the like, came out some time, I think, around the late 1950s or early sixties. All these varieties started to come out, and whoever it was that started one thing, everybody would see it and would copy it. These things came to be when the bagel bakeries were forced to look for additional revenue, and since they could no longer make it on the wholesale, they were forced into retail. They didn't go into retail to make a lot of money. Most of them went into retail to survive. And many of them turned out to be very prosperous because of it. You would find a bagel bakery in a shopping neighborhood, no longer in a basement where rent was cheap. You'd go into a prime neighborhood, pay the rent, have a counter setup. It turned out to be better than anybody dreamed it would be. Then, again, it got flooded. Competition came in and so forth. Now it's an industry. I guess what happened was as the neighborhoods changed, the people who moved in started buying the bagels. It was in the neighborhood. My brother's in a neighborhood that I don't think is five percent Jewish. When we went there in 1960, it was ninety-five percent Jewish. So now it's five percent Jewish, but he's doing business. The people eat bagels. They don't think of it as a Jewish food anymore.

I ate bagels every day. I never got tired of them. I don't eat them today every single day, because I don't want to gain the weight. But it's a taste I never got tired of; I never thought it was too much. My father would bring them home. We'd always eat them. Today, if I'm passing by a bagel bakery, I'll buy a bagel or two.

I only eat water bagels. The other things aren't bagels. They just look like bagels. Bagels are water bagels.

Mark Stoler, forty, history professor, Burlington, Vermont

My grandparents came from Russia, somewhere in the pale of settlement. They came to the United States — I don't know the exact year; my guess is the 1890s. My father was born in 1909, the last of nine children, and to my knowledge all the children were born in the United States. My grandfather was a coffin maker in the old country. He brought the trade with him and practiced it in New York. He died in 1912 or 1913, and my grandmother took over the business. Either my grandfather or my grandmother hired one assistant, and that was the business until the 1930s. What happened then was that my father and his brother began to work the family business and gradually began to expand it.

I worked with him for a summer, so I know a little bit about it. In fact, he had wanted me to take over the business after I finished college. His belief was that by the time I took over, the owners would not have to do any physical labor anymore, and that it would be appropriate for a college-educated son of his to do. I said I'd rather stay in academia.

So my father, and his father before him, and his mother made coffins for the Jewish community in New York. To be appropriate by Jewish law, it had to be made out of all wood, no metal, because it has to be totally of organic materials, and the shop had to be closed on the Sabbath and all Jewish holidays . . . Essentially that's where it comes from, in fact; the name Stoler means carpenter in Russian.

Primarily, their material was only wood. They also made some with some metal in them for the non-Jewish community or for those who wanted it. My father would go so far as to make wooden pegs so that nails would not be used. For those who wanted a hinge, he made wooden hinges, which he virtually invented on his own. When my grandfather did it, it was the plain pine box. My father and his brother began making these really beautiful pieces of furniture. In addition to the standard pine, they'd use a very heavy pine; they'd use cherry. I believe they used some oak. The fanciest thing they used was mahogany.

Had my father not grown up during the Depression, he told me, he might have been a forester. He loved wood his whole life, and loved to work with wood. His favorite wood was, of course, the carpenter's wood — pine, which is what I chose to bury him in for that reason, though obviously not the plain pine box. He could make coffins as simple or as fancy as was called for. The one that my mother was buried in, for example, was solid mahogany, all wood with an incredible silk lining.

Ironically, even though the business had to do with death, you never knew that. You never saw that while working, because all there was was a group of carpenters working. It was the funeral directors who dealt with the bodies. And my father delivered straight to them.

There were special orders in terms of size, things that he didn't have in stock. The most special "special," and I remember this very well, was what he would have to do for the Chasidic community. They did not believe in coffins. They believed only in shrouds, but the State of New York required a coffin. So what he would do was provide them with a plain pine box and loosen the wooden pegs before it went out. Then the minute that thing hit the ground, it collapsed. He also drilled a hole under where the back of the head or the back of the neck would be so that earth would get in immediately. All of this — the need for wood in the Orthodox community, the need for this in the Chasidic community — stems from the literal interpretation of man's being but dust and ashes, and a prohibition against using anything that would prevent that from happening.

My father really began to prosper during the 1960s. First of all, he bought out his brother. There had been problems there. He took a new partner and really went into high gear. He expanded the factory, which was located exactly where my grandmother and grandfather had had their shop on the Lower East Side of New York. It stayed there until 1978 or 1979, when the city finally condemned it to put up a project. It was called C. Stoler and Company. The company is still in existence. It has been bought by a lumber firm in North Carolina, but it still exists, still doing that service, still on the same basis.

My father would not deal with the individuals. He only dealt with the funeral homes, unless he was dealing with the Chasidic community, in which case he had to deal with them semidirectly. When he would get calls from individuals, he'd say, "I do not deal that way." The bulk of the business was in New York. He began to branch out to Montreal, Florida, and those areas. Basically, what I remember are the names of all the funeral homes and all the funeral chains, because that's what was on the sales slips. I also remember, in terms of his roots, that he really couldn't stand office work. Any time he'd get frustrated, he'd go down to the mill room and just start throwing lumber for a couple of hours.

He used to kid that he could go on "What's My Line," but he didn't want to. It was strange; most people did associate the business with death, but he had nothing to do with that. All the men who worked for him were in the carpenters' union. Was there a requirement that they be Jewish? No, not at all. Inside the coffin was, and still is, a stamp. What the stamp essentially said is the name of the company, that this product has been created to rabbinical standards, it contains nothing but wood, the shop has been closed on the Sabbath and all Jewish holidays. It was in English and in either Hebrew or Yiddish; I'm not sure which. When I came back a year or so ago, my uncle told me a funny story. One of the large corporations that had gone into this didn't know what they were doing, essentially. So they took that label and said, Okay, we'll redo the English part. But nobody there read Hebrew or Yiddish, so they duplicated the rest. What went into whatever company coffin it was, said in Hebrew or Yiddish, This is a C. Stoler and Company casket.

When was my first realization that I was the child of a family that made coffins? Not until late. I remember in the fifth or sixth grade the teacher asked us to write down what our parents did. I thought my father was a lawyer; I didn't know what he did. So I would say not until the sixth grade, which would have made me about ten or eleven. I was eighteen when I worked for him for a summer. It was strange, but it never embarrassed me to say my father was a coffin maker. Not at all.

I have seen what this stuff looks like. You hire everybody, from the totally unskilled worker who's just throwing lumber around, to craftsmen who were really artisans who sculpted wood, and men who were experts at varnishing and lacquering, and a seamstress. I am not talking about crude boxes thrown together. That's what it started as. They kept that up for the few who wanted it, but that's a very small part of the business. What we're talking about here is a wood box that is a work of art, absolutely beautiful. There's very little furniture I've seen made that well. And it always occurred to me that there's something crazy here, in such a beautiful piece of work, throwing it into the ground. Though when I was in Egypt this last year, I saw what the Egyptians threw into the ground. So I guess all societies do it. When I said I buried my father in pine, I buried him in pine that was this thick with a rounded top and curves; a beautiful piece of wood, not the plain pine box. For myself, I think a plain pine box would be fine.

Samuel Hyams Jacobs, eighty, insurance agency executive, Charleston, South Carolina

At the present time I'm still involved with Triest and Sholk Insurance Agency. My father-in-law, Montague Triest, founded the agency in 1903 and we're still in business.

We don't need another story on the Coming Street Cemetery. There are many stories written about the cemetery, but if I were to write a saga about that old Coming Street Cemetery, I would have to say it is steeped in history. It's bordered with the usual sadness you'll find in a cemetery, unfilled dreams, infant mortality primarily, and it's tinged with a lot of humor — the epitaphs on the tombstones in this historic old cemetery.

The earliest grave in there is 1762. That's the Right Reverend Moses Cohen, D.D. Of course, there were no ordained rabbis in America at that time. He died April 19, 1762, aged fifty-three years. He was the first rabbi of Beth Elohim, and his friend Isaac DaCosta permitted him to be buried in that cemetery. Strangely enough, Isaac DaCosta was the owner of that cemetery and in 1764 he sold it to Congregation Beth Elohim. I have the deed to the land, and how it's worded to bury all the Sephardic Jews in the whole South or anywhere, even in Barbados in the West Indies, to bury them in this cemetery. You couldn't possibly. The cemetery is just under an acre of land.

What is, I would think, the most important thing is that there are ten Jewish men that were soldiers of the Revolution buried in this cemetery. I doubt if there's another cemetery of less than an acre of land with ten Jewish men who were soldiers of the Revolution. You have plenty in New York City, but I don't think they have the names, and we have documentary evidence of this. It's fascinating. The stonecutting in there is fascinating.

I think this is the greatest epitaph. There is a Rachel Lazarus, Marks Lazarus's wife. I smile every time I quote this or read it: "Died on the 27th of Heshvon A.M. 5608 corresponding with the 6th of November 1847, age 85 years, two months, 15 days. Fifty-five of her descendants preceded her to the grave and 121 survived her. Our mother, she taught us how to live and how to die." And Marks Lazarus, the husband, who was a sergeant major in the Revolutionary War: "A native of this city, born 22nd of February 1757, died the 1st of November 1835 in the sudden 79th year of his age. This tomb is erected by his bereaved widow with whom he had counted the 86th descendant and enjoyed 59 years of conjugal happiness." Well, they didn't have television in those days; they didn't have football games; they didn't have movies; but they had a lot of descendants, a lot of children.

The history in this old cemetery, there's so much history that very few people know about. For instance, there's the Jewish dentist who made the first palate for false teeth, a lightweight palate. Very few people know about this little fellow. His name was Rodriques.

The sad epitaphs, like the Hilzheim boy who was killed in the Civil War, and the Goldsmith brothers. "Alexander M. Hilzheim, a victim at 18 years to the horrors of war. Wounded at Kennesaw Mountain, Georgia, he filled an unknown grave. We do not mourn his loss, as God gave and God hath taken away. Truly the works of God are incomprehensible." It's a cenotaph, actually, just a monument to his memory. There are no remains there. That's one of the many young boys that were killed at the age of seventeen, eighteen, nineteen. Another stone is for the Goldsmith brothers. They were killed in action in the Civil War. We have one man that died on a prison ship just as the war ended. He was still on board the ship going to some prison probably up north somewhere.

That's some of the sadness in there, and it goes on and on. We have men in there, soldiers of the Revolutionary War, the War of 1812, and then the Civil War. Our men that were killed in World War I and World War II are not buried in this cemetery. A few of the Spanish-American War, yes.

How many bodies are there in the Coming Street cemetery? I would say there are approximately six hundred graves in the cemetery. I would say that at least 350 are infants. These little people died from whooping cough, measles, diphtheria, yellow fever, primarily. They are all the diseases today that they have cures for. These little people died, most of them, at birth, some of them in their early years, three and five years old.

The cemetery is full now. There'll be four of us buried in there. My wife Adelaide's sister Caroline, who has never married. Caroline Triest will be buried in the Triest plot, where Adelaide's mother, her father, and her brother are interred. Her late brother, Meier Triest, is buried in there. He died at the age of sixty-nine, sixteen years ago now, and his widow, our sister-in-law Miriam, will be buried next to him in the Triest plot. Adelaide's great-grandfather is buried in there, and her great-grandmother. The board of trustees gave us a plot, right across the pathway from her great-grandparents' grave, so Adelaide and I will be interred in that plot. And that's the end. Four more graves in there, and they will close it, I imagine. The problem is the maintenance, the upkeep. I can get, frankly, no one. Young people or newcomers here, most of them are not interested in who's buried in this old cemetery.

I've talked to thousands of young kids from the various churches and schools in the city of Charleston. I think it's important to let these young people know that Jews were here since 1695. As I mentioned before, these early Jews didn't cross the Rockies in a covered wagon, but they brought a culture to this community, to the province of South Carolina, going back to provincial days. Some of them were doctors; some of them were lawyers; some of them owned vessels; some of them were slave dealers, that's true. But they brought a certain culture.

This cemetery is something we cannot let go. You see, there were other cemeteries, and there the mistake was made. There was a cemetery at Hanover Street. This was a private Jewish cemetery for the Harby family. Isaac Harby was the founder of the Reform Society of Israelites. That was the start of the Reform or liberal worship in this congregation in 1824. Isaac and forty-seven of his friends petitioned the board of trustees at Beth Elohim to make the services more meaningful, particularly to the younger people; that the minister — they didn't refer to the rabbi — should give a sermon in the mother tongue, which was English. By that time, the second and third generation of young Jewish men and women born in Charleston couldn't follow the fast-moving Sephardic Hebrew service, and they petitioned the board, but were refused. So these forty-seven men and women, men primarily, resigned from Beth Elohim and started the Reform Society of Israelites.

The family of the Harbys had their own cemetery. That cemetery, along with the cemetery that the Robinson boys, Irving Robinson and all, talk about where their family was buried, is another story. I won't dispute them, but that cemetery was called the Jew Portuguese Cemetery, not Jewish Portuguese, and that was on another street. That was the DaCosta Cemetery. The same Isaac DaCosta who owned the Coming Street Cemetery started the Portuguese Jewish cemetery between Amherst and Hanover streets. There's nothing there anymore, not even a tombstone. It later became a cemetery to bury indigent Jews who couldn't afford to have a cemetery plot in the Coming Street Cemetery — they probably weren't members of Beth Elohim, and they wouldn't permit them to be buried in that cemetery. You know how Jewish congregations are.

What happened to the cemetery on Nassau Street, the Jew Portuguese cemetery, and the Hanover Street cemetery, was that in 1931 they paved the center of the streets there and the sidewalks. We were assessed abutment taxes. I say we; Beth Elohim owned those cemeteries, you see. There was no other synagogue in Charleston, and these very early cemeteries were owned by Congregation Beth Elohim. These abutment taxes were more than the congregation could pay in those days. The city of Charleston took those two cemeteries over; the land for the taxes. Beth Elohim couldn't afford it. Actually those cemeteries might have been owned by Beth Elohim, but they belonged to the Jews of the city of Charleston. Every tombstone was moved. Many of its tombstones are in pieces. I've searched and searched, trying to find some fragment with a Jewish name on it. The ground is still there. There's a black church on the ground.

Why the former Rabbi Dr. Barnett A. Elzas, when he found these valuable stones and graves, didn't get Beth Elohim to move these tombstones, just the stones? There were no remains; they would have been cenotaphs, in other words. But move those memorials to the old Coming Street Cemetery. Put them on the brick walls if necessary to keep these early stones. Every one is gone.

Arthur Bloomberg, seventy-two, retired state tax auditor and legislator, Burlington, Vermont

The chevra kedisha, the burial society, is still going. We still prepare bodies. They wash bodies and prepare bodies. We use a goyisha funeral director, but we still use a kosher box. Everybody has the same box. There was a story I heard of a Burlington boy who died in Chicago — he'd been in business there — and came back in a fancy box. The chevra kedisha said everybody in our cemetery has to have the same box. So they forced the widow to buy another. The undertaker here bought her box. Everybody is buried alike. There was a time here when we would bury without boxes, in a shroud with boards on each side, something like that. Then, it seems there was a nisht gedugedocht. A woman died a short time after her husband, four or five months, and they buried her next to him and the ground was soft and he rolled in. So then they decided to get boxes.

There was a time when they used to talk to a dead person. The chevra kedisha would talk to him and say, "Now you're being buried according to the ritual of law." And they had a watchman to stay up at night with the body. Yeah, I've done that, not very often, but they used to take turns doing that. Everybody in the community was a member of the chevra kedisha if they belonged to the synagogue, and they had to take turns. If not, they would pay somebody to sit up for the night. That goes back to the old days. The reason for that goes back to the desert, to watch the body so that the animals wouldn't get to it. There was a time when the bodies were kept in the home overnight, too. They weren't left in the mortuary. Sure, I remember my parents. We had the bodies at home, and the funeral was from the house.

17

Bar Mitzvah

I HAVE TWO IMPRESSIONS of my own Bar Mitzvah. The first is the joke "Today I am a fountain pen," because that item seemed to be the gift of choice in the early 1940s. The second is the frenzy after the ceremony, at which the Saturday morning regulars at our small Orthodox shul devoured the pickled herring that had been set out on newspaper, and drowned the fish with shots of schnapps — cheap rye with names like PM and Four Roses.

Stuart Lewengrub, forty-seven, Anti-Defamation League
regional director, Atlanta, Georgia

I remember the reception much more than I remember the ceremony. It was in the back of a delicatessen. I think it was called Topper's Delicatessen on Second Avenue and Twelfth or Fourteenth Street in Manhattan. We lived in the Bronx, but we had it in Manhattan, because that's where my grandparents lived. And the other thing I remember is we weren't allowed to have any music, because my grandfather, on the paternal side, had just passed away within the month. So we couldn't have any music, and the festivity of the Bar Mitzvah was somewhat hampered.

My family didn't have a great deal of money. In fact, I won't say we lived from hand to mouth, but it was kind of a struggle. I remember offering to chip in to pay for the reception with what I collected from my Bar Mitzvah gifts. My parents rejected that idea, and they let me keep it. When I was about eighteen I think I blew it at the track.

Lena Rosenzweig, eighty, housewife, Savannah, Georgia

We didn't have a Hebrew school. That was another thing when the European parents came over; they had to prepare the boys for Bar Mitzvahs. The girls . . . they felt it wasn't too important for them to know. All that was necessary for a Jewish girl to know was the important baruchas that she would have to make as a Jewish wife and a Jewish mother. So they had a little fellow by the name of Shavinsky. Charged twenty-five cents for a lesson. I can see him now, a little fellow with a sack on his back. He'd come into the house, put the little thing down, take a little box of snuff, stick it in one nostril, stick it in the other nostril; and he smelled like a tobacco factory. And he'd sit down and teach my brother for the Bar Mitzvah.

The Bar Mitzvahs were a little different then than they are today. When a boy got Bar Mitzvahed, they took a bottle of vishna, a bottle of whiskey, a honey cake and a sponge cake, and after the Haftarah they cut it up and everybody made L'chayim and mazel tov, and people went home. There was no hullabaloo like they do today. But people took the Bar Mitzvahs very seriously then. As I said, I don't know how my mother did it.

Abraham Chasanow, seventy-three, retired businessman, Silver Spring, Maryland

I remember we had a very tough teacher who thought nothing of throwing kids down the stairs if they didn't behave or didn't know their lessons. Apparently he was a very frustrated old man who eked out a bare existence, and he used to take it out on the kids, to the point where I hated it. I learned enough to get through my Bar Mitzvah, and from that time on I wanted nothing to do with it. Later I had an uncle I was very fond of; in fact, he was my father's employer for a while. He used to go to Reform temple, which I enjoyed. But I had a mental block as far as the Hebrew was concerned, to the point where today I can only understand or read a few words of Hebrew. But I enjoy the Reform synagogue.

Edward Elliott Elson, fifty-one, business executive, Atlanta, Georgia

My father was a most unusual man, and he wanted me Bar Mitzvahed, and I was Bar Mitzvahed. At my Bar Mitzvah, and at the celebration after at our home, was the crew of the *Exodus*. What had happened was that the ship, the *Exodus*, was an old Bay Line steamer that went between Norfolk, Virginia, and Baltimore, Maryland, on the Chesapeake Bay. It had been purchased by the Haganah to transport refugees to Israel. It was brought into Norfolk, where it was purchased, for refurbishing and for getting the food supplies and the linen on board. My father was then the chief of the community, so to speak, and he was involved in the refurbishing. Literally, the meeting to get the *Exodus* going was at our home. I know the date. It was my Bar Mitzvah date, March 15, 1947. So the crew was there.

Stanley Talpers, fifty-nine, physician, Washington, D.C.

The only Hebrew instruction I had was in Denver. I would go to Hebrew school in Denver in the summer. I got a strange Jewish education, because I would start in June. As soon as school was out, I would go down there. I would be in class with my friends in Denver in the West Side in the shtetl, and then in September I would disappear and return to Casper, Wyoming. I got a few months each year of Jewish education. But when I was twelve, my parents realized they had to do something different, so they left me with my grandmother the whole year. I was Bar Mitzvahed in Denver.

It was hard to have a yahrzeit service in Casper. When I was Bar Mitzvahed, I suddenly had a great value. I made it easier to find a minyan for yahrzeit services.

Shirley Povich, seventy-eight, sportswriter, Washington, D.C.

What I remember is the Poviches being the focal point of everything. When the peddlers or the drummers came to Bar Harbor, Maine, and they needed yahrzeit minyans, they were always directed to the Poviches. We did our best. We went knocking on doors. We were going to collect a minyan somehow. We needed a tenth man? One of my duties to find the tenth man, as a little boy, was to go down to the wharf, meet the Boston boat at six o'clock, and anybody that looked Jewish, I would ask if they would come to the minyan.

18

What Makes Sammy Run
or Not Run

I WAS NEVER very athletic. But had I been, I guess I would have resented going to Hebrew school every day after regular school. It deprived me and those of my friends who also went to Hebrew school from developing whatever athletic skills we might have had. The alternative, of course, was to defy one's parents and not go, an almost unthinkable act when I was a youngster. Perhaps this explains the fascination many Jewish men seem to have with sports; not as active players, but as seat and box holders, fanatic fans, passionate statistics mavens, managers, owners, and sportswriters. Shirley Povich, who for fifty years was the most distinguished sportswriter at *The Washington Post*, has the view that back in the 1920s and 1930s "when all the other kids were out playing ball, we had to go home to help Papa in the store to keep down the overhead. Time wasn't as free as for the others. You know what the disposition is of Jewish boys toward study. I don't think that being physical is quite as important to them as it might have been to others."

Boxing was an exception. The common wisdom was that because young Jews had to fight their way to and from the ghetto, they became good boxers. Povich said: "It was an escape from the ghetto for so many. The earliest group of boxers were the Irish. Then because the Jewish kids in the ghetto were thrust among these tough elements, they had to learn to defend themselves. They could move into boxing because it was inexpensive. All you needed was a pair of trunks; you needed no other paraphernalia. You could get boxing shoes, and they would give you boxing gloves, and the cost was small. You couldn't tell the Jewish fighter, because it was fashionable then to adopt the Irish name — popular because that was supposed to denote a little more ferocity in the ring, so-called Irish temper."

If one considers gambling a sport, consider this conversation with Abraham Chasanow, a former government employee who was unfairly hounded from his job by the McCarthy scourge of the 1950s, later fully exonerated, and reinstated:

Q: Do you think Jewish men gamble more than do others?

A: Yes, I think so.

Q: Why?

A: I think every Jew feels somehow that he leads a somewhat precarious existence. Life itself being a gamble, he's attracted to other forms of gambling. Of course, I'm influenced by the fact that the club I belong to is predominantly Jewish, and we're all poker players or gin players or gamblers. These are the guys who go to Las Vegas and Atlantic City and go to the track and just enjoy it. I don't know whether this is a reaction to our having been so poor; I never had the money to gamble with when I was little. I guess you get two kinds of poor people: those who become parsimonious, and those who gamble in later years.

As a final note about my own relationship with sports when I was a youngster, let the record show that my aunt Hilda, my mother's sister, was the best-known Brooklyn Dodgers fan in the history of that celebrated ball club. It was Hilda who, at every Dodger home game, rang her famous cowbell.

Herman Neugass, seventy, retired businessman,
Washington, D.C.

I married in 1940, came up to Washington, D.C., in 1942, and worked for Lansburgh's Department Store, and from there I left in 1968 or 1969 and became involved in government — economic activity.

My family came from Germany. Both my grandfathers, neither of whom I really knew, had come over as young men and both of them married New Orleans women. One was a commission broker and the other one imported hats. Incidentally, my father was the youngest man ever to graduate from Tulane University. He graduated when he was sixteen. He then went into the mercantile business and had two stores and two gins in small towns in Mississippi. Then he got into the moss business, ginning moss in a small place across the river from New Orleans. The moss was used for stuffing furniture, primarily, mattresses and furniture.

I began my athletic career in high school. I was one of the top tennis players and also participated in baseball, basketball, football, and track. All in a minor way. In fact, when I went to Tulane, and I went there on a scholastic scholarship, I had decided to go out for tennis, which I happened to believe to be my best sport. I was small. I didn't hit the ball hard, but I could get it back all the time and very consistently. So I went out for tennis, and we had a very interesting coach at the time named Mercer Beasley. He was one of the top coaches of his day, coaching such players as Frankie Parker and others of that caliber. He decided that the best thing for his athletes was to go out for the track team for a period of three weeks as conditioning.

So, like all the rest of the tennis possibilities, I went out for track. The last day I ran a hundred-yard dash — I don't know what the time or the conditions were, except that I no longer was on the tennis team and I became a track man.

Because I was so small, the coach very wisely worked on building me up in form and endurance and things of that nature, so while I was a freshman I did practically no running. But in my sophomore year I ran as a first-ranked sprinter, won a number of races, and finished in the conference championships. In fact, in one of my races in my sophomore year I beat the man who had run in the 1932 Olympics, Glenn ("Slats") Harden. He was really a hurdler, but he was very fast anyhow. We ran 220 yards in those days. I beat him in that race. Then I went on to win my conference championship and went to the national intercollegiates.

I had finished third in the 220 and fourth in the 100 in 1935 in the intercollegiates. Two of the three men who beat me — one was Jesse Owens and the other two were Anderson from California and Peacock from Temple. Both of them had pulled legs and no longer were running, so I moved up in the ranking. A point of interest was that I was the youngest of all those men who ran. When I graduated, I was only twenty, and hypothetically you improve as you get older. Owens was several years older than I was, as were most of the other runners. So, on conjecture, I was destined to improve both with age and experience. But that's purely conjecture.

I quit running after that race in California. I graduated in June of 1935. During the latter part of 1935 this questionnaire came out. It was sent out by the Olympic Committee to all American athletes who had placed first, second, or third in the national track and field events or held Olympic records. I answered that I would not participate myself. I did not comment on any other aspect of the American participation, because it was not asked. These questionnaires were sent out to some five hundred of the top athletes in the country at that time. I just said that I would not participate and that was the last thing I did.

I gave no reason. That was all I said at that point. I never really discussed it with any other athlete. There was no one of Olympic caliber in New Orleans who participated at that time. The closest ones were athletes from

Baton Rouge who attended Louisiana State, and several of them qualified. I knew them very well, but we just never discussed it. I was out of school by that time.

My coach and I had several discussions about it. He was very disappointed, of course, because I was his hope. He had never coached an Olympic runner before. He was a very, very fine coach, and I felt very bad. We stayed friends for many, many years.

Some time later, and this was after the Nuremberg laws were made public, I decided I was going to make some kind of statement, and that opportunity was presented to me when one of the local athletes said that he was going and why shouldn't he, since "Neugass is Jewish and he's going." I don't know where he got that idea, but that was his statement, whereupon I wrote a letter to the local paper, which was then picked up throughout the country and republished.

I basically said that I didn't believe that the early German pledges of nondiscrimination were being kept. Of course, we didn't know about any of the atrocities or anything of that nature. We just knew, by virtue of the Nuremberg laws and other things that I had heard, that there was not an equal opportunity for people to participate and that there was discrimination against Jews and others — other minorities. So with that in mind I said that, as an American who believes in the tenets of freedom of expression and action, I would not participate in any country where this had occurred. I said I'd made my position known to the Olympic Committee and I would not myself participate, although I didn't speak for the rest of the athletes.

The letter was dated December 10, 1935. It said:

> My attention has just been directed to a press-association dispatch, recently appearing, in which I, a Jewish athlete, am quoted as wanting to participate in the Olympic Games to be held in Germany next year.
>
> As a matter of fact, because I felt that any expression from me might have been misconstrued, I have consistently refrained from making any statement whatever in the controversy which has been going on relative to the American participation in the Berlin Games. Since, however, my name has been mentioned in that connection, I felt constrained to state my position.
>
> I had hoped that early German pledges of nondiscrimination among the athletes of that country would be kept, and, if they had been I would never have opposed American participation in Olympic contests in Germany, although I, personally, would not have participated in such games in any country in which the fundamental principle of religious liberty is violated as flagrantly and as inhumanely as it has been in Germany.

I have been advised on what I believe to be unimpeachable authority that the German pledges have not been kept. Under these circumstances, as an American citizen who believes sincerely in the cardinal tenet of freedom of religious worship imbedded in the Constitution of the United States, I feel it to be my duty to express my unequivocal opinion that this country should not participate in the Olympic contests, if they are held in Germany.

In response to an inquiry from the committee in charge, I have already notified it that I will not participate in the Olympic Games next year.

And I signed my name.

A very interesting thing — when this letter was published, I received letters from people all over the country, including people such as Rabbi Stephen Wise from New York and the Auxiliary Bishop of Boston, who later became Cardinal Spellman of New York, and from places all over the United States. I guess a couple of thousand letters came in. What interested me at the time was nobody said, "Who do you think you are?" There were no negative letters. I guess people who thought negatively wouldn't have written anyhow. But they were all very wonderful letters. Unfortunately, those letters got lost when I moved from New Orleans to Washington. I've never been able to find them, but they were carefully kept until that time. They were wonderful expressions that made me feel that I was very right.

I know I was right at the time, remembering that I was twenty and was looking at the alternatives: Do you go and show them what a Jewish athlete can do? Or do you refuse to participate and stand on a principle? Well, I chose the latter. I never regretted it. No. I think I would do the same today. But today's conditions are very different.

I gave up running, as I said. In those days there was very little to do besides the Olympics. They had the local American Amateur Union and a few other minor things, but if you weren't in college in those days, there was very little. Things like the Maccabean Games I never even heard about, because I think I would have participated in those had I qualified, and I think I would have.

To answer your question about the two Jewish sprinters from the United States at the 1936 games, I only know that they didn't run. When I talked to one of them, Sam Stoller, who I knew here in Washington, and asked him about it, he told me that he was told by one of the coaches on the way back that the reason they were withdrawn was that the German authorities had come to the coaches and advised them that they were not in a position to protect any athletes in case there was a riot or something of that nature. That's what he told me. I don't know anything more than just what he said.

Postscript: In the book *While Six Million Died,* by Arthur D. Morse,* there is this note about the querying of potential Olympic American athletes in 1936: "Of the hundred and forty replies only one opposed participation. It was from a Tulane University sprinter named Herman Neugass."

Marty Glickman, sixty-six, sportscaster, New York, New York

Back in 1936, I was a freshman at Syracuse University. I was eighteen years old, having been brought up in New York City — in the Bronx, where I was born, and in Brooklyn, where I really became interested in athletics and became a fairly well-known athlete.

I made the U.S. Olympic team, which is to say, I was one of the seven sprinters who made the team by finishing in the first seven in the Olympic final trials. I had won the Eastern Sectionals up at Harvard at a hundred meters. Jesse Owens won the Near Middle West in Ohio, Ralph Metcalfe had won the Far Middle West in Minnesota, and Frank Wykoff had won the hundred meters on the West Coast. We all qualified with the second- and third-place finishers for the semifinals and the finals at Randalls Island on July Fourth.

In that final race I was placed fifth, and I say that advisedly. Jesse Owens won the race; Ralph Metcalfe was second. There was no question about their order of finish. Jesse was winner by at least a full yard, and Ralph was second by at least a full yard. Then the rest of us were strung across the track. The race was so close that Ted Husing, who was broadcasting the race, called me over as he was interviewing the finishers, and said, "Here's Marty Glickman, who finished third." He started to talk with me and just then he was interrupted, and he said, "I'm sorry, Marty was placed fourth. Here's Frank Wykoff, who finished third." And they talked with Frank and then he said, "Here's Marty, who finished fourth — oh, just a second, here's Foy Draper, who finished fourth. Marty was placed fifth." So Foy Draper was placed fourth, I was placed fifth, Sam Stoller, the other Jewish boy on the team, was sixth, and Mack Robinson, who was Jackie Robinson's older brother, was placed seventh.

Mack later qualified for the two-hundred-meter run as well, and he won the silver medal in Berlin in 1936, back of Jesse. Sam was one of the great starters, perhaps the best starter amongst the group of us. Ordinarily, amongst Wykoff, Draper, Stoller, and me, if we ran four races, four different individuals might win every one of the four races. We were that tight. I beat Wykoff, for example, in Paris after the games. Wykoff beat me in Hamburg

*New York: Overlook Press, 1985, p. 184.

after the games. Stoller beat both Draper and me in the Olympic Village as a warm-up race for the relay. So that amongst the four of us, you could pay your money and take your choice. It was that close. And we were supposed to be the relay. The relay was supposed to be composed of Wykoff, who finished third, Draper, who finished fourth, Glickman, who finished fifth, and Stoller, who finished sixth. We were the relay team.

We went to Germany, and Sam and I and Frank and Floyd practiced passing the baton. There was no question that we were the relay team. We had our set order and we'd worked at it for about two weeks, getting there approximately a week before the games began, and then our event was to take place about ten days into the Olympic Games, all the relays coming late in the games. Owens and Metcalfe never touched the baton in the course of that period of time.

The morning of the day we were supposed to run, the morning of the trials in the four-hundred-meter relay, we were called into a meeting by Lawson Robinson. He was the head coach of the University of Pennsylvania and the head coach of the U.S. Olympic team. The assistant head track coach was Dean Cromwell, head coach of Southern California. In the meeting were the two coaches and the seven sprinters. We sat in this small room on the chairs and the desks and the beds. Robinson announced that, because of the threat from the German track team — they were hiding their best sprinters and saving them for the relay — he was going to make substitutions on the four-hundred-meter relay team. He was going to substitute Owens and Metcalfe for Glickman and Stoller, and that shocked the hell out of us.

Being a brash eighteen-year-old, I objected. There was no way the Germans could hide their best sprinters, because in order to be a world-class sprinter you had to run in world-class competition. Their best sprinter, who finished fifth in the hundred-meter final, was Erich Borchmeyer. Frank Wykoff finished fourth. So Wykoff could beat Borchmeyer. In a later post-Olympic meet, I beat Borchmeyer in Hamburg. But this was all after the fact. I said there was no way you could hide German sprinters, because it wasn't possible.

Sam Stoller was a senior at Michigan, and he was stunned. This was the culmination of his track career, and he'd been a fine track athlete. In those days, at the end of four years of collegiate competition, that was about it. Most athletes went on to work and to get married and things like that. They didn't have the careers in sports that they have now. Sam was hurt very badly.

I, on the other hand, was only a freshman at Syracuse. I had 1940 to look forward to. I could win it all in 1940, win the hundred as well as run on the relay, if I was to do that. Of course, 1940 never came. Plus the fact that I was a football player at Syracuse, and I had a football season to look forward to. I was angry; Sam was completely saddened, upset, shocked. Fortunately, I gave vent to my frustration and disappointment through anger.

At that point, Jesse Owens did what I still consider a wonderful, marvelous thing, and he was my friend all his life and mine. He said, "Coach, I've won three gold medals already. I've had enough. I'm tired. Let Marty and Sam run; they deserve it." Cromwell pointed his finger at Jesse: "You'll do as you're told." Remember, this is 1936, and blacks did not have the level of accessibility they do now. There are other side stories I could tell you about Jesse, how he was not allowed to live in any hotel in New York above the second floor in midtown Manhattan, how he had to use the freight elevator at the Hotel Paramount where he stayed. He couldn't use the regular elevator. This is Jesse Owens, mind you. So Jesse volunteered not to run, and he was told to do as he was told.

There's no question that Ralph and Jesse were the best two sprinters on the team. Jesse was a yard better than anybody, and Ralph was also, perhaps, a yard better than anybody. They finished one, two in the hundred-meter run. Frank Wykoff said later that even though they set a world's record in the four-hundred-meter relay final, we probably would have run faster had Sam and I run because of our superior baton passing.

That was the end of the meeting. They ran, and Robinson at least had the decency to come over to me afterwards and say, "Marty, I made a terrible mistake, and I apologize." Dean Cromwell didn't say a word. Avery Brundage didn't say a word. In retrospect — I didn't think this at the time — I think anti-Semitism was involved. I mentioned it at the meeting. "Hey, coach, there'll be a terrific furor back in the States about the only two Jewish guys on the team not running."

We were the only two athletes on the entire U.S. Olympic team, track and field team, who did not compete. To the best of my knowledge, I know of no American athlete in the history of American participation in the Olympic Games, 1896 to the present — who was physically able — who did not compete in the games, except Sam Stoller and me. Everyone else who was on the team competed. After all, that's the key to the games: not winning, but taking part, participation. I don't know of any other athlete who ever was substituted for.

It is my belief, and has been for many years now, that we were replaced to save Hitler and his entourage and the Nazis generally from further embarrassment by having Jews compete and stand on the winning podium in the Olympic Stadium, just as the blacks had done. There were ten American blacks on the team, and they were world-class athletes, world record holders. You couldn't keep the American blacks off the team. If you'd tried to keep

Jesse Owens and Ralph Metcalfe and Cornelius Johnson and Archie Williams, and people like that who were record holders and who were very prominent international athletes, from competing in Berlin, you'd have no American team. But you could keep two obscure American sprinters off the team, giving that kind of an excuse to save, I think, the Nazis from the embarrassment of having Jews standing on that winning podium, as we would have.

I had gone to the Olympic Games for two reasons, and I think probably Sam felt the same way. One for the very selfish purpose of being on the team and hopefully winning the gold medal, and secondly to show that Jewish athletes are just as good as any other athletes. Jews are as good as anybody else, if not better. And I wanted to show the world that was true. There was some talk in 1936 about boycotting those 'thirty-six games, but it was a minority group. Jeremiah Mahoney, a judge in New York, led some of that opposition. I have to explain to younger people that 'thirty-six was different than 'forty-four or 'forty-five or any of the later years. Nineteen thirty-six was still two years before Kristallnacht. It was three years before the outbreak of the war and five years before we got in the war.

I was affected by Jewishness in other ways, which didn't come from me but from outside. There were two situations in particular. One had to do with my playing football at Syracuse. We had just beaten Cornell and we were undefeated. We beat them fourteen to six, and I scored both touchdowns. It got me into the broadcast business. I was the first jock. I intercepted a couple of passes, made some key tackles. It was the best day I ever had by far. We went down to play Maryland, in Baltimore, and I was the star of the ball club. We're getting dressed for this football game. It's maybe eleven-thirty before the one o'clock game and we're in our jocks and T-shirts, and the coach and the athletic director walk into the room and ask for our attention. The fullback, the fellow who played alongside me in this box single wing, was Wilmeth Sidat-Singh, a Hindu name. He was actually black. His mother had married a Hindu physician and they had adopted the name of Sidat-Singh, his stepfather's name. The coach and the athletic director said that Will will not be allowed to play today because they've just learned here in Baltimore, Maryland, that he is black. Here we are getting dressed for the game, and he's a regular, a star on the team. Will is my teammate and during the football season my roommate. We slept side by side; went to class together. This was 1937, after the Olympics.

I'm sitting there alongside my friend Will, and I'm saying to myself, "Marty, stand up and say if Will doesn't play, I don't play." I'm torn about standing up and doing it, and I'm saying to myself, "But, Jesus, if you do that, they'll point the finger at you as being one of those troublemaking

Jews. After all, you had that trouble in Berlin in 1936; you'll be making more trouble by standing up and objecting to this thing and not playing, and maybe the whole team will walk out." This is what we should have done in the first place. The stupid athletic director and coach . . . we should have canceled the game. Now I know that. Here I am sitting alongside my friend and thinking I should stand up and say, "He doesn't play, I don't play." And I'm the star, and I could have had something to say. And I don't, because of what happened in 1936, just a year before, and because I'm Jewish and I don't want to make trouble.

To this day, I'm sorry about it. Will got killed in World War II. He was good enough to get killed, but he wasn't good ᵉnough to play in this silly game. Of all the things in my life that I'm unhappy about, that's number one. Of all the things. I wish I'd have done it.

The second thing was that after the games I was invited down to participate in the Sugar Bowl track meet, around the New Year. They used to have a track meet in conjunction with the Sugar Bowl football game. I had no place to train for the outdoor meet, and I'm training on the boardwalk at Coney Island. It's awfully cold out there, and I encounter a friend of mine I used to run against, Eddie O'Sullivan, who ran for the New York Athletic Club. He said, "Hey, Marty, why don't you come down to the A.C. and work out with me?" I told him that would be terrific. I take my little satchel and get on the subway and go to the New York A.C. and I walk into the lobby. There's Paul Pilgrim, now gone, who was director of athletics for the New York A.C. He says, "Hello, Marty, what are you doing here?" I said I came by to work out with Eddie in the indoor track. He said, "I'm afraid you can't do that." I told him Eddie invited me down and I'd like to go up and work out with him. He said, "You can't, Marty; there's no room for you." I said I'd use Eddie's locker. I've just got my track clothes, that's all. I told Mr. Pilgrim I was sorry and I walked out and got on the subway, and suddenly it dawned on me that I couldn't go in because I'm Jewish. Since that time I've never gone back to the New York A.C. for any activity. I don't even mention them on the air. That was one of the few times in my life that being Jewish and an athlete . . . after all, I had already been on the Olympic team. I was no stranger.

Red Auerbach, sixty-nine, basketball executive, Boston, Massachusetts

My mother was born here. My father came from Minsk in Russia. The last business he had was a couple of dry cleaning stores. Prior to that he was in the restaurant business.

I was born in Brooklyn and lived in the Williamsburg section, which was sort of mixed. There were a lot of Jewish people and there were a lot of other kinds, too. For example, the guys we played ball with, on our team, you had three Jewish kids, an Italian kid, an Irish kid, a Polish kid; you know, that type of thing.

In those days, you didn't have the sophisticated Boys Clubs and Jewish Community Centers and big playgrounds. And when you lived in the city, you had to improvise. In New York, everybody in every different area had their own type game, whether it was a kind of punchball or whether it was stickball on the East Side or whatever it was. But the one thing that was constant was basketball, because you didn't need a great deal of room. People would say to me, "Why didn't you play baseball?" Well, for us to get nine people together and get the carfare and the equipment and find a field, we had to go all the way out to near Prospect Park. You had to kill a day, and who the hell had the dime to do it? As a result, very few of us played baseball in that particular area. Matter of fact, my high school didn't even have a baseball team or a football team. And if a guy had some talent in that direction, he went to Boys High or Hamilton, which was not too far.

So in my school we concentrated primarily on basketball and some handball; and incidentally, the former world champions, two of them, are around — Jimmy Jacobs and Vic Hershkowitz. They're both Jewish. They were two of the greatest that ever lived or ever played the game. The 92nd Street YMHA was very famous for handball. Nationwide, everybody played it, Jews and non-Jews. But the Jews seemed to dominate with Hershkowitz and Jimmy Jacobs. Hershkowitz started out as a one-wall player. Again the improvisation, where it was the only area where they played one-wall handball, like on the beaches in New York. Then he went into four-wall; won the national four-wall. Jacobs won it for many years. He's still a great, great player.

I played basketball at Eastern District High School in Williamsburg. After that I got a scholarship to Seth Low Junior College, Columbia University. I stayed there a year and a half and they dissolved the school. Then I got a basketball scholarship to George Washington University. Graduated from there. Got a master's. Coached on a high school level, about three years. Went into the service. After the service, went right into the pros.

The Jews dominated basketball, as I said, because of facilities. They used to talk, even then, about Indiana, but they really were not as good as the New York players, because you had the original Celtics, before the establishment of the National Basketball Association, the NBA, you know, way, way back. This goes back to the 1920s with Nat Holman, Davey Banks, and some other guys who weren't Jewish. Then you had the Saint John's Wonder Five, which was a great college team, where you had Posnack,

Schuckman, Rip Gerson. Most of those guys were Jewish playing for Saint John's. Later Boykoff and Gotkin. Oh, there were so many of them who were Jewish that played for Saint John's. Of course, City College had their amount, and LIU with Torgoff and Shechtman and all those guys. Torgoff was a great All-American. He played for me later on in the pros. Hertzberg played for City College for Nat Holman. This was in the thirties. Hertzberg was a little later. But Torgoff and Shechtman, they are about my age. Moe Spahn, he's about seventy-two.

Do I think Jewish kids saw this as a way to go to college, the scholarship thing? So did the non-Jews. But, see, then you had the Eastern League, which was in the thirties and the early forties — the Philadelphia Spars, that South Philadelphia Hebrew Association. They had a league run primarily by Eddie Gottlieb, who used to own the Philadelphia 76ers. And that league was predominantly Jewish. They played at the Broadwood Hotel in Philadelphia. They had games and dances. Then you had the old Rochester — I forget the name of the league — where you had Fort Wayne, Sheboygan, Oshkosh, Rochester. Still Jewish? No. The Rochester team was owned by Les Harrison. He's still with them. In fact, he made the Hall of Fame. He had Red Holzman, who later coached the Knicks. They were kind of mixed, but there were enough Jews around, even then.

Then it started to die down after the war when the pros started; a lot of these Jewish ball players went into the BAA, which was the Basketball Association of America, which was later changed to the NBA. See, I've been fortunate. I've been in the BAA, NBA, since its inception. The first day. I think I'm the only guy around left. Incidentally, from the Saint John's Wonder Five, I forgot Kinsbrunner, Mac Kinsbrunner. A very great player. But after the first year or so they found out there were other great players, other than the Jews, who could play the game. So little by little they were displaced by these non-Jews. And in 1950, the blacks came in. Before that they used to play just exhibition games with the old Renaissance and the Washington Bears and the Globe Trotters and things of that sort.

Oh, of course, you had Dolph Shayes, and his son is now playing in the league, and Dave Wohl coaches the Nets and he's Jewish, but there are very few of them. I think the reason — now this is the key point, I think — was due to the affluence of the Jews. In other words, when the kid growing up outside New York was sixteen, he'd get a car and then belong to the beach clubs and to the country club and they'd go to Florida and they'd go here and they'd go there. The Jewish kids were told that it's good for business to take up golf and play tennis. You found out that most of your athletes who were Jewish could afford to go to college, those that were athletic, and they didn't kill themselves to get the scholarships.

Then they started moving out of the densely populated areas because you had an influx of blacks, Puerto Ricans, Koreans — all the ethnic groups that came in and displaced them. They moved out to the suburbs, and in the suburbs, even though you had basketball courts on your playgrounds, for some reason or other they'd go to the beaches, they'd go sailing, and they'd play golf. All of a sudden they found out that there were other things than being a "gym rat." And I think basically that's been the cause of the decline of the Jewish basketball player.

I was at the time of Sid Luckman — a year or so behind — and the same time as Marty Glickman, and there were other fine athletes, but that was it. That was the density at that time, within a ten-year span. Then later on, as I said, it started to decrease. I think the period after the war was the end of the Jewish athlete, per se. All you had were exceptions; see what I mean? Do I remember Mark Spitz? Yeah. But Mark Spitz, you see . . . I don't know whether he was affluent or what, but to be a champion swimmer you have to live in a climate conducive to it, number one. Number two, you've got to take lots of lessons and you've got to spend five, six, seven hours a day in the pool. The discipline is tremendous. Now you have a few tennis players that are around. Boxing was a Jewish sport because of economics — a way to get out of the ghetto quick. Football, being a team game, was tough.

There were a lot of schools where they did not know what a Jew was. They thought of a guy with horns or whatever, you know. I know even down at George Washington a lot of kids we recruited from Texas and so forth didn't even know what a Jew was. We had a few Jewish players on a football team. But on our George Washington basketball team, five or six out of eleven were Jewish. That was from 1937 to 1940.

But the thing is this. In my whole career, I never focused — and tried very, very hard not to focus — on religion, either as a player or as a coach. To me, a player is a player, and that's it. I didn't care about his color or his religion, and I can tell you a story. I had a guy come over from Israel and he sold the owner a bill of goods he was a great player. He was a stiff. He couldn't even have made a good high school team. And he wanted a tryout and the boss promised him the tryout. He was a real stiff, so I sent him home. I got rid of him. He calls me up a couple of days later — he had all this chutzpah. He says why don't I give him a green card so he can extend his stay here as a member of the Celtics. I said, "You are not a member of the Celtics, no way." Then he calls me up another day and he says, "Oh, I heard you was Jewish. Imagine, you are Jewish, I'm Jewish. What a drawing card" — this and that. I said, "Would you get the hell out of here?" Those are the things sometimes you put up with rather than ability.

A lot of people during the course of time would say, "So-and-so is anti-

Semitic and my son doesn't have a chance. He won't get it." It's a lot of crap. Just like Adolph Rupp. He had a rap in New York because he didn't like New York, you know the city thing, and that he was anti-Semitic. Now, he was just a Southerner that didn't come into contact with many Jewish people. He knew I was Jewish and we were good friends. We went over to Germany to do some clinics for the air force, and while he was there he spotted a Jewish kid from my high school by the name of Sid Cohen. He recruited him for Kentucky and later Cohen was captain of the University of Kentucky. So you know he wasn't anti-Semitic at all. It was a terrible rap.

Did I experience any anti-Semitism as a basketball player? No. I can honestly say no. Once in a while, you'd get a snide remark; you just don't pay any attention to it because it is an individual thing rather than a common thing. Sports is your common denominator, where I think talent overrides the majority of prejudices.

Do you still find Jewish kids playing basketball? It's like the older people, the older Jewish people. They feel it's part of their roots. That's what they were noted for. They used to have a cliché many years ago: If you want a smart, ball-handling guard, you'd get a Jewish kid from the New York area. But that was dispelled very quickly, because you found out that there were non-Jews who were smart, too, with as much talent and more talent.

Did I contribute to the cliché? Oh, yeah, like when I organized the Washington Capitols in 1946 I believed in a heterogeneous group. You see, the Knicks got all their players from New York. Pittsburgh got all their players from Pittsburgh. A lot of Jewish players. A lot of Jewish players in New York. When I organized the team here, I got Feerick and Scolari and "Bones" McKinney and Norlander and Mahnken, and none of them Jewish, but I had to have a Jewish smart ball player, so-called, because I didn't know how great these guys would have been. So I had Irv Torgoff and I had Sonny Hertzberg, so I had mine, you know.

What did my parents think about my playing basketball? That's a good point. My father thought it was a waste of time, because my older brother was more of a student, my younger brother was brilliant, and I was just an average student but the best athlete. It turned out that I was the one who went to college, because we couldn't afford to go to college. My older brother tried it at night and it was just too much for him in those days. But I had everything paid for when I was in school.

It didn't bother my mother that much. But my father — I finally took him to a game when I was playing at junior college. We were playing against a team that had a zone and I was the ball-handling smart guard, you know, moving it. And at the end of the game I only had about two or three points, because I was in the back. He says, "No wonder you don't score"; he says, "You are in the living room and all the action's in the kitchen." I never forgot that. It was a good bit of coaching.

19

Courting Jews in Washington

MARSHALL RAUCH of Gastonia, North Carolina, remembers that when he first decided to run for public office, thirty-five years ago, "the older Jewish people came to me and said, 'Don't do it, don't rock the boat.'" Nonetheless, he ran first for city council and won, and subsequently, in the mid 1960s, became the first Jew to serve in the North Carolina Senate. Parenthetically, Rauch and State Representative Ted Kaplan from Winston-Salem were co-sponsors of a bill that has made Yom Kippur a state holiday in North Carolina; not a paid holiday, but on a par with Robert E. Lee's birthday.

The "don't run" attitude of Gastonia's older Jews toward Jews seeking political office was widespread, especially before World War II and in places where Jews were a distinct minority. It was the general Jewish notion at the time that if you were very quiet you would not be noticed, and if you were not noticed you were safe. Of course, there were Jewish mayors, legislators, and governors throughout American history. I delivered the evening newspaper to Governor Herbert H. Lehman in Albany in the early 1940s. But for much of their time in America, Jews played a more prominent political role offstage than on. That has changed. For example, Jews now serve out of proportion to their numbers in the population in both the United States Senate and the House of Representatives. Jews now run unabashedly for all major city, state, and national offices, both where there are significant Jewish populations and where there are not.

And many Jewish citizens, no longer believing silence is golden, actively and aggressively employ the democratic process to lobby for things they believe to be important, such as Israel's security, freedom for Russia's Jewry, civil and human rights, continued separation of church and state. Most of this lobbying has been directed at the Congress, but some of it in more recent years has involved the White House.

"There are really two types of Jews in the White House," said Stuart E. Eizenstat, who served as President Jimmy Carter's chief domestic adviser from 1977 to 1981. "First of all," he noted, "there aren't a lot of Jews in the White House in most administrations. In the Reagan administration, there are none who have really any significant policymaking responsibilities."

One type, Eizenstat explained, is the Jewish liaison. Every modern administration, he said, has had its Jewish liaison, just as there is a black liaison, a labor liaison, a Hispanic liaison. "Because the very nature of their position as liaisons makes them in the eyes of the rest of the government advocates for their constituency," he said, "Jewish liaisons are generally, in fact I would say almost exclusively, not in the policy loop. They become advocates for the community to the administration as much as they communicate the administration's views to the Jewish community.

"The second type," according to Eizenstat, "is someone like Leonard Garment or myself, who is at a senior level in the White House and who happens to be Jewish. Our portfolios do not designate us as Jewish representatives. We're not Jewish advocates; our role is not to communicate with the Jewish community. Leonard was counsel to the President, and I was the domestic affairs adviser, but by virtue of being Jewish, we have a special sensitivity to issues that influence the Jewish community."

Richard Peele, forty-two, government official, Chevy Chase, Maryland

I am the Assistant Secretary of Defense for International Security Policy.

It started with the imposition, I believe in the late spring of 1972, of the education tax, as it was known, where the Soviets began imposing a levy on would-be emigrants that varied according to the amount of formal education they had received. It went as high as 35,000 rubles, which was clearly prohibitive. This created a sense of crisis in the Jewish community and among others who had been watching the gyrations of Soviet emigration policy. There were a series of meetings, with people on the Hill and elsewhere sitting down to think about how to respond. It seemed to me that the meetings were directionless. Everybody knew how they felt about it. They didn't like it, but nobody had a very clear idea of what to do about it.

At about that time, the Nixon administration was asking for authority to conclude a Most Favored Nation — MFN — status agreement with the Soviet Union, which would have opened the U.S. to Soviet imports at the lowest existing tariff level, the same tariff level that applied to other nations with which we had MFN agreements, which were principally friendly countries — most countries of the world. Most Favored Nation status with a non-market economy poses special problems. We have those problems with most of the non-market economy countries with which we have MFN agreements, because when two countries open their markets entirely to one another, the terms of trade are affected in part by whether the exporter is exporting at fair market value or not.

So there was a strong economic case against extending MFN to the Soviets to begin with. There was a bit of controversy in the Senate; not a lot. I can recall one meeting that was held in the basement of the Senate Office Building with a number of Senate aides present. It was yet another discussion of what to do about it. I got on the idea of conditioning Most Favored Nation status on a liberalization of Soviet emigration practices, but in the first instance a repeal of the exit tax, the education tax. Curiously enough, in talking about it, one of the Senate aides present, who didn't much like the idea, said, "If you really want to do something, you'd prohibit their receiving any credits." I said, "That's fine. Let's do both." And that's, in fact, what the Jackson-Vanik amendment does.* It prohibits credits for the Soviet Union directly or indirectly and it makes Most Favored Nation status contingent upon the liberalization of emigration policy.

The idea was to introduce the amendment, which was done not long thereafter. I took this to Scoop Jackson. He thought it was a dandy idea and set about securing the co-sponsors necessary to introduce it. It wasn't hard for him. It might have been hard for somebody else. He was just very good at grabbing his colleagues, mostly in the gym at six or six-thirty in the evening, or off in the cloakroom, and explaining things in such a simple, clear, and direct way. It never ceased to amaze me how he could go out and come back with support from even unlikely senators. We pulled a group together of eight or a dozen, and he made a speech on the floor of the Senate, introducing the amendment. But we knew, because it was late enough in the session that it wasn't going to be voted on, and you had the presidential elections, that we'd have to start all over again in the next Congress.

In the meantime, Kissinger, who was negotiating intensively with the Soviets, could point to this legislation hanging like a sword of Damocles over the economic relationship the Soviets wanted with us, and say to them, "Look, you'd better clean up your act and get rid of the education tax, because they've shown they can introduce this legislation and gather a lot of support for it and reintroduce it." There were in fact some discussions,

*Senator Henry Jackson, Democrat of Washington, and Representative Charles Vanik, Democrat of Ohio.

and the Russians strongly implied that they were dropping the education tax; that they would no longer collect it. They didn't remove it from the books, but they indicated they would no longer collect it.

The Congress, ever distrustful of the Executive Branch, worried that, once MFN and access to credits was granted, the Soviets could find some other device for stopping the flow. The emigration tax was understood, not as a way of recovering the investment of the state in the education of Jews, but as a way of stopping the emigration of anybody but the most menial émigrés. Even bus drivers had to pay the tax, but it was prohibitive for anybody with any serious education. So when the subsequent Congress opened, in January 1973, we reintroduced it. There followed a lot of discussion with Kissinger and the State Department, and we said to Kissinger, "Go out and use this." By this time, Mark Talisman had introduced Vanik to this. So when we reintroduced it in 1973, it now had sponsorship on the House side.

The amendment grew in the Senate, in the sense that having started with a few co-sponsors, we got a very solid number against it. As a matter of fact, we had some help from Nixon himself. In 1972, Nixon knew the election was coming. He knew that the legislation would die at the end of the Congress and would have to be reintroduced. He wasn't anxious for the administration to be opposed to this thing. So we got Nixon to agree not to discourage Republican senators from joining the amendment. This, from Nixon's point of view, was a dreadful tactical error, but he was a great maneuverer and in this case was simply outmaneuvered. Jackson made the case that it would die at the end of the session and there was no point discouraging members from joining the amendment, which they wanted to do anyway. It would hurt him politically. It was 1972, and it was an election year. But once they joined, it was difficult or impossible not to join up the second time.

So in 1973, when we reintroduced the amendment, it was with something like sixty-eight co-sponsors. I don't remember the number, but a clear majority. In the meantime, Mark was working very hard in the House with Congressman Vanik. The biggest problem they had in the House was with Wilbur Mills, who was at the height of his powers then. It was before the Fanne Foxe incident. He was chairman of the Ways and Means Committee and this legislation went to the Ways and Means Committee. We were very anxious to get Wilbur Mills to support this thing.

A man named David Herman, who was Jewish and in his seventies and hard of hearing and who had made a small fortune in the footwear business and was widely respected in the industry, had met Wilbur Mills some years earlier. He and Mills had struck up a friendship. I can't remember how we met David Herman, but we did. We asked David if he would intervene with

Wilbur Mills. He agreed to do so, and he came to Washington for that purpose. I went to see him at his hotel to brief him on exactly what we needed from Mills — all the details.

Mills in those days was a very capable, thoughtful man, and David wanted to be able to answer all the questions. We spent three hours, I think, going over all the details of this thing. David came down with his secretary, who'd been his secretary for years, always traveled with him. The two of them went off to see Wilbur Mills. Tony Solomon was at the time on Mills's staff. I think Tony had been telling the business community not to worry, that Mills was going to bottle this thing up in the Ways and Means Committee, and Vanik was just an upstart and it would never go anywhere. The structure of the House being what it is, the chairman of the Ways and Means Committee probably could have. So this very important meeting took place — David, his secretary, and Mills. I don't think Tony was there or anybody else was there. Tony was dead set against this amendment and remained opposed to it all along, and I'm sure is still opposed to it.

David Herman, who had been coached to the last detail, went into the meeting prepared to answer any questions. But his basic pitch to Mills, as he described it to me after the meeting, was that once before in history people had failed to act when Jews were in jeopardy. This was another such occasion. Nobody knew what would happen to the Jews of Russia if they slammed the door. This was not part of the briefing. This was pure David Herman, seventy-two years old, a man of great charm. A very decent man, heavily involved in charitable activity, who wanted nothing for himself. He made this presentation to Mills, at the end of which Mills called his secretary into the office and dictated on the spot a statement of support for the amendment. Before Tony Solomon or anybody else could intervene to stop it, Mills had issued a public statement. And that was that. There were repeated efforts to pull him off it, but they never succeeded, and from that day on the amendment was safe in the House.

It still took a lot of hard work to keep that coalition together, and to keep it together in the face of Soviet statements that were intended to dislodge the votes. In fact, it took a very long time. The amendment was first introduced in, I think, June 1972, and didn't actually come to a vote until late in 1974. It came to a vote in 'seventy-four. There's one whole side of this that has never, as far as I know, been carefully enough written. In its most compressed form, we were engaged through virtually the whole of 'seventy-three in a negotiation with Kissinger, who in turn, we believed, was talking directly with the Soviets, I'd say the whole of 'seventy-three. It really picked up in intensity after the House vote.

The House voted before the Senate, as it happened. The House vote was a shock to Kissinger, who I believe had been telling the Russians that this legislation was under control. I don't know whether he'll remember that or acknowledge that. In any case, it was a real shock when it passed the House. The Russians were stunned by it, because clearly the votes were there in the Senate, and the House was always more difficult to read. Both before, but especially following, the vote in the House, there was an intensive negotiation in which we said to Kissinger, in effect, "You go and negotiate a decent deal with the Soviets quietly" — he was a great exponent of quiet diplomacy — "and on the basis of a satisfactory negotiated settlement with the Soviets, we'll amend the amendment so as to give the President authority to set the amendment aside." If you look at the Jackson-Vanik amendment as it finally passed, it does indeed contain authority for the President to set it aside if he declares to the Congress certain things.

The things he is asked in the final amendment to declare to the Congress are the things that Kissinger had told us the Soviets had agreed to. The essence of the agreement is contained in a letter from Kissinger to Jackson on October 18, 1973, when an exchange of correspondence took place — a letter from Kissinger to Jackson, a letter back from Jackson to Kissinger clarifying certain points, and a third letter from Kissinger to Jackson saying that he agreed with Jackson's clarifications. Every comma in those three letters had been negotiated, we believed, with the Russians. In effect, Henry was shuttling between Jackson and Dobrynin and various other Soviet leaders whom he met with on his various travels.

In fact, an announcement was made at the White House on October 18, I think, or the next day, and these letters were released. We had been accused from time to time of having undermined the deal that was struck by the public announcement at the White House. The public announcement at the White House was Jake Javits's idea. Javits was a supporter of the amendment, but the most difficult battles that were fought were keeping the coalition together and not settling prematurely for unsatisfactory terms. Javits had a tendency to want to get a quick deal.

Much of the negotiation was handled by respective staffs, with Hal Sonnenfeldt handling it for Henry. I have, or there existed in the Jackson office, not only the final exchange of correspondence, but the earlier drafts. I would give a draft to Sonnenfeldt, and Sonnenfeldt would come back three days later with some revisions which the Russians insisted upon, and we would accept in some cases and in other cases we would modify the Russian revisions. It was, we thought, a serious negotiation that led up to the exchange of correspondence on October 18, and Kissinger subsequently testified that the deal struck on October 18 had been confirmed by Brezhnev directly to President Ford at Vladivostok, which was in November 1973.

So we thought we had a deal with the Russians with Kissinger as their ambassador, and under the deal the number was to rise. In fact, the letter from Kissinger to Jackson reads, "On the basis of discussions with the Soviet authorities, I am pleased to inform you that . . ." or words to that effect. We insisted that that sentence be in there; that this not be simply a commitment from Kissinger, but that the letter reflect his discussions with the Soviets. Under the terms of that letter, the Soviets were to remove obstacles to emigration, not just the education tax, but other obstacles, and were to end the practice of harassing people and firing them from their jobs. They were to grant visa applications in the order in which the applications were received, because they had a practice of saying no to the leaders and yes to the bus drivers.

I think we thought of everything. We thought of all of the various ways in which an agreement with them could be defeated, and drafted the commitment broadly enough so that if we could get the Russians to accept it, it would really pave the way toward much freer emigration. In addition to that, we had early on asked for a minimum number of émigrés, and I think this was the principal sticking point. We started out asking for 100,000 a year. We didn't think we could get 100,000 a year, but it was a good place to start. In the end, we settled for sixty thousand a year, which was a lot more than we were getting at the time. At sixty thousand a year, with the other commitments to end the harassment, et cetera, it simply meant it would take longer for the population we believed wanted to go. But it was an acceptable outcome.

Because the sixty thousand a year was such a sticking point, we stated it in an odd way, as I recall in the Jackson letter to Kissinger in response to the Kissinger letter to Jackson: "We will take, as an initial benchmark of good faith, visas at the rate of 60,000 a year." The third letter from Kissinger back to Jackson that confirms his understanding was really the key letter, because the way the correspondence as a whole reads, it is Jackson who identifies the sixty-thousand level and Kissinger who agrees with it. So the sixty thousand is not mentioned in the initial letter.

In any case, we thought we had a satisfactory settlement, and on the basis of that we negotiated a revision to the amendment that gave the President authority, if he made certain certifications, to go ahead and grant Most Favored Nation status and to grant credits. The details of that were worked out in a series of meetings, with the administration represented by a senior official from either Commerce or Treasury. So on October 18 we thought we had a deal. Henry subsequently testified that he thought he had a deal, that moreover even Brezhnev had confirmed the agreement with Ford. From October 18 until January that deal was in effect.

It was never repudiated until January 10, 1974, which I think significantly confirms the existence of a deal, because the Russians would have denounced it immediately. But they didn't. Why did they repudiate this agreement in

January? I don't think we'll ever know the answer to that, but one thing that happened that I think bears on it is that in passing the legislation that included the revised Jackson-Vanik amendment with this authority for the President to set aside the restrictions, other amendments were added to the bill. One was an amendment added by Senator Adlai Stevenson that limited the credits that could be extended to the Soviets to $300 million. The legislation was a four-year authorization, and it was wrongly interpreted to mean $75 million a year. What the Senate said in adopting that $300 million ceiling was a matter of congressional control over expenditures: "Come back to us after you've exhausted $300 million in credit, because we want to see what sort of deals you're supporting."

There was a lot of nervousness at that time. It was in the immediate aftermath of the oil embargo, of massive energy loans to yet another un-reliable supplier. So there was another amendment, which I think Senator Frank Church had introduced, that prohibited these credits from being used for energy projects in the Soviet Union, and that was one of the major areas where the Soviets had expected American capital to flow. My reading of it — and as I say, I don't think we'll ever know, because they don't open the archives in the Soviet Union after fifty years — is that the Stevenson amendment was a disappointment to the Soviets, and even humiliation, because after all of this, after having made these really unprecedented conces-sions, the Congress then turned around. The carrot that we were dangling in front of them shriveled up and became insignificant in financial terms.

I sat in on a meeting when Senator Stevenson came down to propose this $300 million ceiling, with Senator Stevenson and Senator Jackson and the fellow who was Stevenson's principal aide on this, Stan Marcus, who later went to the Commerce Department and is now a lawyer in town. I can remember, as if it were yesterday, saying, "But why do we need that?" Stevenson said, "That is all the administration has in mind now anyway, and if they want more they can always come back to the Congress for more, and besides I'm disgusted with Kissinger." And Kissinger said, "This is fine. This will not inhibit the program that he has in mind anyway." We were in an awkward position to oppose something that Stevenson and Kissinger had discussed between themselves, especially after the history of the legis-lation. I think it was a terrible mistake, and I've never forgiven myself for not probing further into it. But it was immediately before the bill was coming to the floor and the meeting was in the morning and the bill was up in the afternoon, and it passed.

The Russian Jews themselves have never for a moment lost faith or confidence in the amendment, even when there were crackdowns and the emigration was minimal. To a man they believe that it was probably the only thing that kept them going in that period. There was another element to this that isn't well understood. The amendment had the effect of enormously elevating the morale of the Russian Jews themselves in very difficult periods. It was an indication that the Congress of the United States was prepared by an overwhelming vote to make economic benefits for the Soviets contingent upon their freedom.

Probably the most moving experiences I had in connection with this, and I know it was the same for Scoop, were the occasions where we were together with Russian Jews; it was an extraordinary thing. They would come up to him in groups, singly, and embrace him. He was a hero for them, and still is in the Soviet Union. In fact, many Russian Jews thought he was Jewish. They just couldn't believe that a non-Jew would have taken on that long legislative battle. In trips to Israel and in meetings with Russian Jews who visited the U.S. subsequently, he's a great hero. So it kept the movement going at a time when there was a risk it was going to be snuffed out. If you look at the numbers, this simple and incorrect impression that everything was fine until the amendment came along is really quite wrong. If you look at the numbers, you find that the highest level ever attained was attained while the Jackson amendment was pending in the period after it was introduced, when the education tax was eventually dropped in practice and the numbers soared. Then immediately after the passage of the amendment, and its repudiation by the Soviets in January 1974, the numbers dropped, and then they grew again. They actually reached fifty thousand a year in 'seventy-seven, 'seventy-eight, around there.

It proved something we've known all along, which is that the Soviet story that the number of visas corresponds to the number of applications is a monstrous lie. Some bureaucrat sits in Moscow and decides how many people will be given their freedom, and for whatever complex of reasons — to send a signal, to express displeasure, to relieve the pressure that builds up as the backlog increases, for whatever manipulatory reasons — they are prepared to let people out sometimes and not to let them out at other times. To this day, a decade later, the amendment is there on the books, and the Soviets will never get Most Favored Nation status or credits until they come to terms with it somehow.

For those who doubt the efficacy of the amendment, I suppose the simple response is: What was the alternative? The alternative was to do nothing and leave it entirely in the hands of the Soviets, to associate no cost at all with beastly behavior and no benefits with doing the right thing. *The Economist* had a cover story after the amendment passed. There was a picture of a Russian émigré, and the caption was "Buying People Is Right." And that's what it was. We were buying people out.

There's the Rumanian side. The amendment applies to Rumania as well. It applied to all non-market economies. And there's China, which was swept up in this. We had to find a way to deal with the China problem. On the Rumanian side, I would say only that the amendment permits the President to set it aside every year. Every year the Rumanians come up for renewal, and every year in the final weeks before the Congress has to vote on renewal, they let a lot of people out. It applies not only to Jews, by the way, because there is no reference to Jews in the amendment, and there never has been, although it became widely reported as affecting only Jews.

Scoop Jackson carried on an annual negotiation with the Rumanians in which we would give them lists of people who we knew wanted to leave. Until those lists were disposed of, we made it clear that we would oppose extending MFN for the following year. Thousands of Rumanians came out, Jews and non-Jews alike. In fact, we had a woman on the staff in Jackson's office full time who did nothing but handle Rumanian cases. She was an outpost of the State Department. I don't know what the State Department has done since Scoop's death. They probably had to hire somebody to do it. Our little office in the corner of the Old Senate Office Building, on any given day, was filled with Rumanians coming to say "My cousin in Bucharest can't get out, and what can I do?"

It's still true today that every year it comes up for renewal, and it is the principal source of leverage we have. Last year, the Rumanians introduced an education tax and it became a small crisis in the U.S.-Rumanian relationship. I had some conversations with Lawrence Eagleburger at the time and reminded Larry, although Larry needed no reminding, that under the law, they were going to have to withdraw if they didn't get rid of the tax. And they did. So it's still alive and well and affecting Rumanians.

Mark Talisman, forty-two, organization official, Chevy Chase, Maryland

The Jackson-Vanik bill is an interesting story. It came about mainly because of the anger that Congressman Vanik felt, and I did too, with a travel tax that was being imposed by the Soviets in late 1971 and early 'seventy-two, before the Nixon trip. It's a little different than the public history or the belief about it.

By late 1972, we had devised an amendment that was being put on in Ways and Means, separate and apart from anything else. That was too late in the session. It was in October and it wasn't working. It was an election year, and it was all screwed up. The purpose of the amendment was, in essence, to restrict trade specifically with the Soviet Union because of restrictions on emigration. What developed later was much different.

By late 'seventy-two, early 'seventy-three, the Jackson folks had come to talk to us, to me specifically, about how to refine the amendment, because

Scoop Jackson had been messing around in the same field but totally separately and without our knowledge. We didn't know what each other was
doing at that point. There was an enormous uproar in our district and
everywhere else from both Baptists and Jews about what was considered
to be this enormous pressure building up. And it was; it was just awful.
But it was really the first public recognition of any kind of dilemma for
Soviet Jews in emigration. It was really right at the beginning of that era.

There was, by that time, the existence of the Conference on Soviet Jewry
nationally, which was a consortium of thirty-some Jewish and related groups.
But the notion of using governmental instruments to do this was beyond
anyone's understanding. I did a lot of research at that time, and found what
still is not believed but happens to be true. And that is that this mechanism
was used twice before for the very same reasons.

In 1863, Abraham Lincoln unilaterally enforced a trade embargo against
Russia because of mistreatment of American Jews who were working in
our consular office in Moscow, and because of Russian Jewish people being
subject to pogroms. It was about $1.5 billion in our dollar terms that was
eliminated at that time and it was not restored during his term. It happened
again in the election campaign between Taft and Wilson, in which this was
a dominant foreign policy issue, because of the terrible reports of pogroms
against the Jewish community. The issue was: What should the United States
do about it? One of Wilson's first foreign policy acts was to implement, in
essence, what was later the Jackson-Vanik amendment. He imposed trade
sanctions against the Soviet Union until they stopped the mistreatment of
Jews.

Did they stop? They did. At least they said they did. The sanctions were
lifted temporarily. So it was something that was not only in a general
philosophical way not new, but in a very specific way was not new. I was
astonished. Those portions of the speeches that were put in the *Congressional Record* never made the light of day. A lot of people were very troubled.
Some people are more troubled now; they feel that this activity has no place
in American economic and foreign policy. I believe strongly to the contrary
even today. Congressman Vanik did obviously. He was the principal, and
I was pushing hard, but he was very, very much his own person on matters
of this sort. We felt that a basket existed on each side of the table, and that
there were items that could be taken out of the basket and put on the table
or left in the basket as regards a list of trade activities. Some could be
straight economic, commercial; some could be philosophical.

In the voluntary acts of trade between two nations, the imposition of a
mix of items was perfectly logical, not only in history, but in fact. We had
a right to do those things. We had the capability of doing those things, and,
in fact, in this day it would be nice to think that we would want to, that

we would elevate some of these things above pure commercialism, especially since the stories coming out of the Soviet Union were so terrible. Vanik is a Slav. He by nature understands the Soviets better than I do.

When it came time to be serious about this, we started coordinating with Senator Jackson's office and glommed onto the Trade Reform Act of 1973–1974 as the vehicle for what would be an amendment. The irony is the Senate folks didn't realize, as they never do, that it is the House's prerogative to start these matters, because Ways and Means starts these matters first. So it came to us, and it came to me, and it came to an incredible number of people. I. L. (Si) Kenen, by the way, who founded AIPAC (American Israel Public Affairs Committee) and singlehandedly formed the Jewish lobby, was one of the stalwarts. He started developing outside interest in the bill, in what would be known as the Jackson-Vanik amendment.

What the bill would do would be to deal with non-market economies, meaning communist-socialist countries. It would relate trade activities directly to the ability of people's rights to emigrate. It does not mention Jew in the title, nor in the body of the language at all. It relates to everybody. It relates to China. It relates to Russia. It relates to a lot of countries.

It was an astonishing series of things that happened. The Russians were directly interested. Kissinger was directly interested, but didn't appear to be. He never once testified in the House side on the matter. He finally testified in the Senate side. He felt, and he had said in newspapers, that he could take care of the Parliament. That was the phrase he used. He did indeed.

Wilbur Mills was brought into the picture by us intentionally. This is a very interesting story that has never been talked about. Charlie Vanik felt very strongly that as co-sponsorship was developing on this incredible bill, which was having an enormous impact all over the country, the chairman of the committee should be the sponsor. Once that happened the whole nut would crack open, because any bill coming out of Ways and Means during his heyday had to be Wilbur Mills's. It was no one else's. Vanik was willing to take a second seat to the chairman. I'm convinced, I believe I'm right, that Wilbur Mills at that point felt he had to take it over to control it and kill it. It was his desire to kill it. A series of events happened that no one can believe as we went around for co-sponsorship. Since the Russians and Kissinger were so interested, it was our task to keep it as quiet as possible. So there were contacts being made personally, word of mouth, no pieces of paper traveling anywhere.

There was enormous constituency interest both in the Protestant churches and among the Jewish groups, as well as others. Members were being educated about it. The questions that were being asked were phenomenal. "Will I have blood on my hands if I don't help on this?" was the question that I got more times than I can tell you from people I knew very well in the House. One third of the co-sponsors came on as anti-communists, not a majority, but one third. The labor movement was very much involved in it, but most people wanted in on it in remembrance of the Holocaust, because at that time there was an awakening. You know, so many people did so little or nothing, and look what happened. Is this one of those repeats?

The Russians were made to believe, as Kissinger's office was, that we had no more than fifty people. Somewhere around February 7, 1973, we held a press conference — Jackson, Vanik, and Mills in the old Ways and Means Room in the Capitol, right off the Capitol floor — to announce the introduction of the bill with 263 co-sponsors, which just sent shock waves everywhere. It's just hard to believe the pressure that developed. Kissinger was outraged. The Russians were incensed.

By the fall, when the vote came, Kissinger's folks let it be known they did not want the bill passed; that a deal had been cut with the Soviets; that there would be emigration of thirty thousand guaranteed, but nothing in writing. I was asked specifically by parties unknown to me to this day, through intermediaries, the weekend before the bill was to come to the floor, literally to remove the bill from the calendar, which I refused to do. The disputes that started from that point forward, the recriminations that still go on about the mistake that was made in going forward with Jackson-Vanik, are premised upon the notion that this was an imposition on the trade posture. It was said that it was an insult to the Soviets, and was meddling in their internal affairs, and that emigration from that point forward diminished because of that act.

I have made a case, which I think is strong, that, in fact, in America we had the right — had we had a unified Congress and Executive Branch, which we did not — to have the Russians understand that under their own laws they could have done what we were asking them to do. And that the level of hurt that was going on to people, so soon after the levels of hurt that had gone on under the Nazis, was ungodly, unwarranted, and had to be dealt with, and literally the only tool we had was this. So had there been a unified force, it would have been fine. I think one thing that was disastrous was the imposition of the Stevenson amendment thereafter, restricting credit. I think that was the real reason, and the Jackson-Vanik became the coverup for what was a withdrawal of permissions to leave the Soviet Union. On the other hand, to be fair, from that time forward emigration rose as high as 54,000. I wanted desperately for our Jewish community to agree with the notion, at that point when there was response going on, to allow the President to waive Jackson-Vanik, as he has a right to in the law, based upon the finding that 54,000-plus dissidents were coming out and so on, and have a trial period of nine months to a year of trade to see if the system worked. Jackson and his staff went crazy. It was disallowed. That never happened.

The answer to me now is, well, after all, Afghanistan happened shortly thereafter. And my position is, that would have made no difference if Jimmy Carter had lifted Jackson-Vanik as a presidential mandate. But as part of the Jewish community, I think it was important for us to allow the amendment to work, if, in fact, the facts warranted it. In any event, it was passed in October 1973 by 319 votes on the floor — something like that; overwhelming. The Senate took it up the next year. Richard Perle and all of those folks with Jackson passed it by over eighty votes. (He lives across the street, by the way.) So it was an overwhelming passage. It was Gerald Ford's presidency that signed it into law.

I do not believe it is by any means a failure. I think the amendment is very instructive. It is being complied with by several countries — Hungary, Rumania. In Rumania's case, while it needs an evening out, in fact it's demonstrably successful. And I think the level of insult that the Soviets feel really can be diminished significantly if the right Executive Branch is dealing with them.

Mark Siegel, thirty-nine, lobbyist and political consultant,
Chevy Chase, Maryland

I'm a first-generation American. My parents are still living and are quite old. My father's eighty-three and my mother is eighty. They both came to this country as teenagers.

My mother is from Odessa and my father is from a town in Bessarabia. They lived through some pretty bad pogroms. My mother survived the famous Kishinev pogrom, and her travel to get to this country was particularly bad. My grandfather left three years before the rest of the family to come to Canada, actually. All he put together was enough money to pay for the family to go from The Hague by boat to New York. It was up to them to get from Odessa to The Hague. They actually walked from Odessa, across Europe, to The Hague. They started out being four children, my uncle Sam and three daughters. They only traveled at night. One night, crossing a lake while they were still in Russia, my little aunt, who was two years old, fell through the ice and was lost. It was such a painful memory that it was only as an adult in talking about what was it like did I even learn that there was another child. It was something that the family never spoke about.

My mother came in 1917. My father came in 1916, I believe, and he came directly to New York. His family was here. My father was an apprentice floor scraper and ultimately became a "seltzer man." I don't know

if you know what a soda and seltzer man is. He made home delivery of
soda and seltzer. He didn't run a seltzer plant. He had a truck. He would
deliver it like a milkman would deliver milk. He delivered seltzer, soda,
beer, and Fox's U-Bet syrup, the classic chocolate syrup used in the making
of egg creams. This was very important. Why is it called an "egg cream"?
It only makes sense if you make it right.

You put the milk in first and then you spritz in the seltzer, and it makes
a very, very white, foamy mess. Then, very carefully, you dribble the chocolate syrup down the side and mix it up so that you have a chocolate soda
with a beautiful white head — an egg cream. Now you know the secret
recipe. There is no egg. It's just called egg cream. It's like a meringue top.

My mother and father stayed in New York and had three children. I grew
up in New York, in Brooklyn, in East Flatbush. I was born when my parents
were quite old. My mother was forty and my father was forty-four. I have
a sister who is twenty years older than I am and a brother who is sixteen
years older. I was an accident of sorts. My parents spoke Yiddish at home,
so my first language was Yiddish. But typical, I guess, of first-generation
Americans, I wanted to be Americanized, so once I started to go to school,
I wouldn't respond to them unless they spoke to me in English, which is
kind of too bad. Growing up in that neighborhood, in East Flatbush, it was
a totally Jewish environment. I mean, there were two Gentile kids in my
elementary school. You could literally sleep on the street during Yom Kippur. We were Orthodox, but not Chasidic, but we were very, very observant.

I went to Brooklyn College, so I stayed in that environment for a long
time and slowly saw the neighborhood changing. It wasn't until I actually
left New York that I understood what it was to be a Jew. People don't quite
know what that means. For me, growing up in New York, there was no
discrimination, no sense of isolation. I lived in a totally Jewish environment.
It was my own shtetl, basically. Only when I went to graduate school at
Northwestern University did I go through a terrible period of culture shock;
women with blue hair and white gloves, and churchbells and serene people
and no one shouting. It was very, very different. And I didn't have any
incidents of anti-Semitism until I got into the army, where for the first time
in my life I really confronted anti-Semitism. I didn't like it one bit, either.

When I was thirteen, I became enamored of politics because of John
Kennedy, and from that moment on it sort of enveloped my life. I worked
for Bobby Kennedy in 1964 in New York and was very active in politics
from that point on. I decided to be a political scientist. I went to graduate
school, hoping to get a Ph.D. Got a master's degree, then was interrupted
by the army experience. Army service was six months, and I went back,
finished my Ph.D. with a thesis on political parties, and specifically on
Democratic delegate selection procedures and the reforms in the Democratic

Party. That same year, I won an American Political Science Association Congressional Fellowship to come to Washington to work in a Senate office for a year. I selected the office of Senator Hubert Humphrey. I had a very good experience. Because of my expertise in delegate selection, an expertise in demand in 1972, in addition to being a legislative assistant I was in charge of delegate selection in the Humphrey campaign. And I was ultimately the person who was in charge of the credentials committee and was the person who wrote the California challenge in a last-ditch effort to stop McGovern.

There was a great coalescence of anti-McGovern forces. We won in the credentials committee and lost on the floor of the convention. But after the election, the same basic group, the same political coalition, coalesced once again, throwing Jean Westwood out of the Democratic National Committee and replacing her with Bob Strauss. At that point, I was an assistant professor of political science at Loyola University in Chicago, but came back to work on the Strauss election. When he won — that was December of 1972 — he asked me to come back to Washington to direct the reform effort in the party. There were three reform commissions that he wanted me to supervise. We went to Washington in January of 1973. I have been there ever since, and a year after I came to work for Strauss, I was made the executive director of the Democratic National Committee, which was especially exciting for me, because only a year before I was working on a doctorate on political parties. Suddenly, a year later, I am the executive director of the oldest and greatest and blah blah blah.

During that time, when I was executive director, we appointed Jimmy Carter as our national campaign chairman for the congressional campaigns in 1973 and 1974, and he asked that one of his staff people be put on my staff to coordinate. That person, who worked for me, was Hamilton Jordan. I certainly did not hide the fact that from 1973 to 1976 I was totally devoted to Hubert Humphrey. There was nothing that I wanted more than for him to be drafted by that convention. But I maintained a nice relationship with Jimmy Carter and Hamilton all during that time. After he received the nomination, I was given some responsibilities, staying on as the executive director of the DNC. After we won, Hamilton asked me what I wanted. I said, "Well, something I always really dreamed of; I really would like the Assistant Secretary of State position for congressional affairs." And he said, "You can have that, but we would much prefer that you come to the White House as my deputy, because you have strengths where we have weaknesses."

My initial responsibility as deputy assistant to the President for political affairs, as Jordan's political deputy, was to be in charge of all party matters, in charge of the Equal Rights Amendment and its passage in the state legislatures, delegate selection rules for the next national convention, and things like that. But after two months, Carter made that speech in Clinton, Massachusetts. His first town meeting was in Clinton, and in response to a question about the Middle East, he openly proclaimed the need for a Palestinian homeland. At that point the shit really hit the fan, in terms of the Jewish community.

Carter had never been close to the Jewish community in Atlanta. The community was far more liberal than he was, and they were associated with Carl Sanders, and God knows during the 1976 campaign the Jewish community was strongly lined up behind either Scoop Jackson or Moe Udall, depending upon the ideology of the Jews — but not behind Jimmy Carter. There was some concern that this important constituency might, in fact, not break Democratic in 1976. We had a few incidents at the platform committee which were problematic, at best. We had in our 1972 platform a declaration that the U.S. embassy should be moved from Tel Aviv to Jerusalem as a symbol of the unity of the city. That was in the McGovern platform, and he was not particularly close to the community. Carter did not want it in the 1976 platform. I was working on the platform committee. Moynihan was one of the drafters. Moynihan said to me, "I don't care if he wants it or doesn't want it. I am going to move it and we'll take a vote on the floor of the convention." So I went to Stu Eizenstat and said I think we should tell the governor that this is going to be done. I spoke to Carter. And he said, "Look, you can go ahead and tell him to do it. We are not going to fight it, but I want you to understand this is not my position and I will not endorse it and I will not campaign on it." I said, "Well, I don't think it's going to be raised, so I don't think we have to go out of our way for you to say all of those things. This will just defuse the issue." That's just sort of an anecdote. He was up-front and honest about it.

Going back to Clinton, Massachusetts — Hamilton came to me and said, "You know, we never wanted a Jewish liaison or any liaison in the White House." And I said, "I agree with that." He said, "Well, we finally realize what you've been telling us for a while, that the Middle East issue is a domestic as well as a foreign policy issue. In light of your responsibilities to us in terms of political affairs, would you agree to assume an additional responsibility, to work with the Jewish community on issues that relate to the Middle East?" I said, "I am very uncomfortable with this." I said, "I have very strongly held views on this." I had already been exposed, at this point, to a few months of Zbig, Dr. Brzezinski, and I knew there was a potential there for problems. But I said, basically, that I like the President and trust the President. We met, the three of us, and I said, "I will do it as long as you understand that I see this as sort of a dual role. I will be liaison from you to the Jewish community, but I want to be able to have access to you and let you know what the community thinks on given issues. If I have that assurance, I will do it." I got the assurance.

I would go out and speak a great deal around the country for Jewish activist organizations, Jewish charities. Every couple of weeks I would go out for a day or two and do that. Sometimes it was very difficult, because things started to develop.

Ultimately, the arms sales to Saudi Arabia developed and it was a very unfortunate period; it was a very difficult position to be in. I would inform the Jewish community regularly through Mailgrams and letters of anything the President was doing that was relevant to them, either in terms of human rights, Soviet Jewry, anything of interest to the Jewish community, as well as the Middle East. I would send out copies of all of his speeches. I would ask them if they were going to be in town to come and see me. I set up four meetings with Jewish leadership with the President, Zbig, Vance, others in the White House. Two of them were luncheons. President Carter was very accessible. There were many things wrong, but accessibility is nothing I would fault him on.

The first real crisis that occurred in my job was on October 1, 1977. That was the day the Soviet-American communiqué on the Geneva conference was issued. I had been making a speech for the President in Minneapolis. Hamilton was in southern Virginia making a speech. I found out about this driving back from National Airport with the radio on, and I swear I almost swerved off the George Washington Parkway. They read the agreement, and I was flabbergasted. One, I hadn't known about it, and two, I thought the contents were a disaster. This was the Soviet Union and the United States calling for reconvening a joint Geneva Peace Conference with the Syrians and the Soviets and Palestinian representation. This was sort of antithetical to everything that we had been trying to do with Egypt or with the moderates. They were very concerned about Soviet involvement. And procedurally — in terms of process — my God, this was my subject area, and I'm hearing about it on the radio.

I thought to myself, There is going to be a terrible reaction in the Jewish community. At the very least, they should have given me a little bit of warning so I could call up a few of the leaders and say there is going to be this announcement in a few hours. Even that courtesy would have taken away a lot of the sting, and that's the way you should deal with human beings. If you are courteous, people appreciate it. I tracked Hamilton down through the White House switchboard and I told him, and it was the first time that he knew of it. This was something that had been kept from Jordan. Brzezinski said he didn't know. We never believed him. They blamed it on poor Marshall Shulman in the State Department, but there were meetings

that Hamilton and I convened in the White House. Dinitz, the Israeli ambassador, was brought in. Brzezinski was brought in. Shulman was brought
in for these meetings in the Roosevelt Room, and I must say, Hamilton was
wonderful. He was very, very tough in terms of content and process. He
was very good at substance and procedure here. Finally, three days after
that communiqué, a joint Israeli-American communiqué was issued. I was
working on this with Hamilton. This is political now. This is the political
staff involved in a foreign policy issue. I thought it was a very good development.

It was a very unchallenging kind of atmosphere in the White House and
I saw what was happening in terms of the President — a very decent man,
and I think of very good instincts. But it was a tabula rasa on the Middle
East. It was totally blank. And Zbig was filling it in, and it was getting
worse and worse. He had this very simplistic view — I think it's simplistic —
that he had convinced the President about, and I saw it as a very dangerous
view. It basically suggested that there were inevitable social and political
forces in this world that will ultimately prevail, that are beyond our control.

He talked about the situation in Vietnam in this context, which flabbergasted me, because he was one of the principal hawk-academic supporters.
On the campuses it was very hard to find a hawk. Zbig was the principal
hawk, and I thought it was outrageous for him now to say this was really
a war of national liberation and Ho Chi Minh was a nationalist. We pushed
him into being a communist. This was rewriting history . . . his own history.
In fact, that may all be true but this is something quite new. And then he
convinced, sort of convinced, Carter that there are other social forces working in this world that will ultimately prevail and we should get on the right
side of those issues and not on the wrong side like we did in Indochina.

To Zbig's credit, Iran was one. He never exactly said what we should be
doing. He didn't talk about developing a moderate democratic base like the
Philippines or anything. But he knew that inevitably the Shah would not
prevail. South Africa was another. There were seven, and I must say I don't
remember the seven, but the last one — the one I remember that jumped
out — was Palestinian nationalism; that the Palestinian people will ultimately have their own homeland with us or without us, and it will be much
better if they didn't do it fighting us, if we embrace them. That, I thought,
is a very, very simplistic world view. Saudi Arabia was another one, by the
way: the inevitability of the fall of the Saudi royal family. He didn't talk
about Muslim fundamentalism so much as a radical insurgency. Just remember this was many years ago, and I am trying to reconstruct it for you.

There was a rub there and we did not hit it off. Possibly I was not suitably
deferential, which may be a character fault of mine. But I, from this envi-

ronment in New York of screaming and hollering, believed in open dialogue and questioning and challenging. Dr. Brzezinski was different.

This all came to a head. I was sent to the Middle East by Hamilton in November of 1977 to find out basically what the Israeli government and the Israeli people really thought of Jimmy Carter; thought of the peace initiatives; thought of the Clinton problem, the October 1 thing. You know, to do a real hands-on there. Coincidentally, it was arranged that I would go with a congressional delegation that was going to Spain, to Egypt, to Israel, and then on to Portugal. But I would stay on in Israel for several weeks. It was a delegation led by Jim Wright and Danny Rostenkowski. It was a leadership delegation of Democrats.

We flew to Cairo and we met with Sadat and it was at that point that Sadat announced that he would go to Jerusalem. It was in the context of how upset he was by the October 1, 1977, Soviet-American communiqué; that this undermined everything he had tried to do by throwing the Soviets out of Egypt; trying to develop a process where no one had a veto power. He was very eloquent about the Soviets and the Palestinians and the Iraqis and all of these groups pushing Egypt every few years into a war where the blood and the pride of Egypt was spilled for no reason but Arab pride, and he was not going to be held hostage to these kinds of vetoes and he would even go to Jerusalem. He was serious about that, and this started the process, which I became deeply involved in by coincidence, though no one ever believed that it was by coincidence that I was there. Let them believe what they want, but it was a coincidence.

I wasn't the messenger. Sadat said to us he would go to Jerusalem when he got a proper invitation. He was a very protocol-oriented kind of guy. So was Begin. We met with Ambassador Eilts at the time and they cabled Sam Lewis, the ambassador in Tel Aviv, to see if a proper invitation could be arranged. There was all kinds of speculation around the world. Was it going to happen? When will it happen? In the interim, we fly to Jerusalem, which was our next stop. I go with Sam Lewis to our consulate in Jerusalem to wait for the cable, which would be the official invitation. I was feeling somewhat awkward.

The cable was going to come from the U.S. embassy in Cairo to the U.S. embassy in Tel Aviv to the U.S. consulate in Jerusalem, where Sam Lewis and I were waiting for it so we could bring it to Begin. We finally get it.

It was a cable from Eilts to Lewis and it said that President Sadat has indicated that if there was an invitation forthcoming from the government of Israel, he would come to Jerusalem at the earliest possible moment we could set up.

We were literally alone. I wasn't experienced in this, but I had taped the

whole Sadat meeting and I transcribed it myself and it was very long; it
was a twelve- or thirteen-page, single-spaced cable that was sent. I believe
I sent the cable to Zbig. What I did do was speak on clear lines to Hamilton
several times each day, telling him what was going on, especially in Jerusalem
when things were really breaking. I spoke to Hamilton two times each day,
I would say. I spoke to Eizenstat once. I spoke to Zbig twice. I spoke to
Bill Quandt a couple of times. I later learned from Hamilton that as soon
as the Sadat trip was agreed to, Brzezinski wanted me called back. He wanted
someone who was engaged in foreign policy to be there to represent the
President. Hamilton absolutely refused, and in the Knesset, when Sadat did
speak, I was the representative. I mean, I was there.

We get the cable. We bring it to the Prime Minister's office. There is a
press conference called. The Prime Minister, with Sam Lewis and me standing there, had this press conference — there was some American press at
this point and all the Israeli national press. Mr. Begin said we have received
word from Mr. Sadat that he would come when he received a proper invitation. It is an honor on behalf of the people of Israel to extend an
invitation for the President to come, and he gave a time and a date; that
all had been arranged in advance. A few hours later Sadat agreed. I don't
remember the sequence. This may have been a Monday and we are talking
about Sadat coming on a Thursday. It was that close.

I had three days and I got my wife to come over. She too was in the
Knesset for that historic moment. I stayed in Israel for a week afterward,
doing what I had meant to do, but to be in Israel during the Sadat visit,
and to stay at the King David Hotel with Sadat, is another extraordinary
thing. They emptied the King David out completely, but they let me and
the members of Congress stay there.

Did they regard me as a representative of the White House? Yes. Absolutely. I had a relationship with Begin. What can I say? I can still almost
not talk about it — it was an emotional experience. But I spent a week to
ten days more in Israel, doing what I was supposed to be doing. It was a
wonderful time to be in Israel, because I was getting the people's reaction
to all of this. I decided not to go to the airport when Sadat came, because
I wanted — and this is again part of the reason I was there — to be with
an Israeli family who had lost a child in the 'seventy-three war. I was with
them for dinner when Sadat arrived. He arrived at night. It was on television.
They played "Hatikvah." They played the Egyptian national anthem. The
parents were crying, openly crying. I said to the father and the mother, but
it was directed to the father, "Your son died in the 'seventy-three war. This
man caused the war and caused your son's death." I almost couldn't talk,
and I said, "I sort of know what you might feel. How do you feel right
now?"

He said, "If I was there I would hug him and kiss him, because I have two other sons." That was what it was like to be in Israel at that point. It was great.

Well, when I came back, there were all kinds of problems. There was a meeting of the staff. The Vice-President was there. Zbig was there. Hamilton had me there. I wouldn't normally report at a meeting like this, but I was to report on what happened. Before I was to report what happened, they announced that Sadat had asked Begin to come to Ismailia and for the White House to send a representative. Zbig said the purpose of this meeting was not only to hear Siegel's report but to determine whether we would favorably respond to this request from Sadat. This is called the "shit hitting the fan" for me. Zbig began by saying that the Carter plan for peace in the Middle East always envisioned a comprehensive peace in the Middle East between Israel and her Arab neighbors; between the United States and the Soviet Union, and involving a Geneva conference, where this would all be worked out in a comprehensive package. And he was terribly concerned that what was developing now was, in fact, a separate peace between Egypt and Israel. You may think that is a positive development, but from his perspective it could be a tremendous setback to the comprehensive peace that we all want and that President Carter is committed to. A few other people spoke.

Then it was my turn to speak, and I said, as is my way — I am very sort of candid — I said, "I am stunned to listen to this. The most dramatic diplomatic event in thirty years has just occurred, and we are talking about whether we are going to embrace it and let it continue or whether we are going to nip it in the bud and not allow this opportunity."

I talked about what Sadat had said about the October 1 communiqué, and I said, "There may be, in fact, a difference between a separate peace and a first peace. But we should take what we can get, and if there can be peace between Israel and her principal Arab enemy and military threat, with any hope and with our good offices, it could lead to a comprehensive peace. This could be the model for it." Again I said, "I am flabbergasted. I cannot understand what you just said, Zbig. It's as if we are in a different world. I mean, I was just there. I wish you could have been there to see a miracle take place. Talk to Sam Lewis; bring him back here. If you don't trust me, because I am not a diplomat, bring your ambassador back and confront him with all of this." Hamilton, after the meeting, told me that I had done a fine job. Zbig told the President, apparently, that it was an emotional tirade. Believe me, it wasn't. It wasn't. I didn't get into any of the things that could be emotional like we just talked about. It was just real politics. This is happening. We could play a major role in bringing it to fruition.

I think from that point on I basically was frozen out of the White House decision-making loop on the Middle East, although Hamilton and I, who remain very friendly by the way, never really talked about it. It probably just became too much of a heavy weight for Hamilton to make sure that I continued to be involved, because it was such a clearly adversarial relationship and Zbig was so insistent that his foreign policy could not be politicized and this was political staff and all of that. But from that time — November 26 is when I came back — through the time I left the White House, it was a most unpleasant experience.

And the deal — quote deal — that I cut with Hamilton and the President in March of 1977 — that dual relationship — that disappeared. What developed is always the danger to the role of a Jew in the White House. Suddenly, I was expected to go out and sell the policy and do all the things that were part of the job of liaison with the Jewish community. But there was no longer any opportunity for me to access back in. Okay. So it was only half the job. It became all but impossible over the Saudi Arabian arms sale, because I did not agree with the logic of the sale. Hamilton and I had talked about it at great length. I tried to make them understand what the Israeli pysche was like. If they are going to make leaps of faith in the direction of peace, the Israelis can't do it if they are going to feel threatened, and this was a threatening development. I was speaking almost psychically. In any case, the decision was made. The President went to Saudi Arabia in December. We had New Year's Eve with the Shah — that awful exchange of toasts: "The greatest democrat, America's greatest friend." But first the President was in Saudi Arabia. Whatever arrangement was cut, was cut then. I wasn't there at all.

Hamilton made it clear that this was the policy and I was expected to get in line and to sell it. What can I say? The notion of a lead Jew, a Jewish liaison — that role. We all know from Jewish history that there have always been court Jews; Jews that are in courts and have been advisers to Presidents and Prime Ministers and Kings, and often they have been used against their own people. Did I feel I was a court Jew? Yes. After the dual role. After it was gone. After I came back and it was January and the arms sale was going through and I was being told to go out because I had some credibility — people knew who I was — and I was being asked to peddle things I didn't believe in. I was being exploited. I think I understand the difficulty of that role and how sensitive we all have to be, wherever we are, that we do what we think is appropriate but are not used or exploited or allow ourselves to be.

I did make a couple of speeches around the country. One was in Los Angeles. One was in Detroit. I was going to appear before the Young Leadership Council of the United Jewish Appeal. It's sort of the next generation; I would say thirty- to forty-year-olds, very rich but very activist, very well informed. There were about a thousand of them. I had drafted a speech which I thought really expressed what I saw as Jimmy Carter's views on the Middle East. It was sent to the State Department for clearance and they totally redrafted it. There was nothing left of my speech, and I was told by Vance's office, and I don't remember who it was, that I had to deliver their speech and not deviate from it. The speech also defended the arms sale. They said, "Don't go off the cuff. This is the speech. Be very careful. This is very sensitive. We are not sure you should be doing this." All this kind of stuff.

It was a ringing defense of the arms sale; the sale of F-15's to Saudi Arabia and a good deal of very technical information about the capabilities of the F-15 — stuff that I didn't have any particular expertise in. But it was very technical information about distances and bomb racks and all kinds of things. That it's the best defensive interceptor in the world, with little or no offensive capability, and on and on. I delivered that speech as I was supposed to. From the audience . . . bad reaction wasn't the word for it. They were hissing, booing. It was very difficult for me, because I didn't believe in all of this. I was being denied access. I thought I was being exploited and all of that. And these people, whom I basically agreed with, were hissing and booing, and I was thinking to myself that if I were sitting out there, I would be hissing and booing. How did I ever get into this kind of box?

The first question was "Your information was all wrong." It was someone who had an ad from the builder of the plane promoting the F-15 as a great strike plane, offensive strike plane, and talking about the offensive capability of it. He said, "That speech is wrong. You just lied to us." And I said, "I don't believe I did, but if I did I certainly will apologize to you." I went back to the White House and I called up the Pentagon and I just probed. I didn't say that I had this problem and someone questioned the data. I just probed to find out what they were going to say, and it was someone on a very high level. But they went into some detail and it sounded like this was a hell of an offensive weapon. So I said, "What would you think of a characterization that this is really a defensive weapons system, lacking offensive capability?" He started to laugh and he said, "That's bullshit."

I said, "Thank you, I think I understand." That was February 27 or 28, and I wrote my letter of resignation March 1, 1978. It was a very good letter of resignation, I think. It was not the typical bullshit — "It was an honor to serve you and I wish you well" and things like that — although it was very positive about the President. It was four pages, single-spaced. Hamilton did ask me to take out a paragraph, and I did it. I don't know if I should have, in retrospect, but it was the paragraph about my conversations with Brzezinski and one incident with Brzezinski where he appeared a few weeks before, before one of those luncheons at the White House that

I put together. He said to the ten presidents of the largest Jewish federations in the country, when asked about this arms sale, "You people better stop interfering in our foreign policy" and "you people" and "you people." I wrote that there was a tone and a hostility that was picked up by everyone in the room. And Hamilton said, "I think you should take this paragraph out. We would appreciate it. The President would appreciate it."

The letter itself was rather specific about my objections to the policy and access and things like that. I wished the President well and at the very end I put in the Hillel quote, which I wanted to do. It was so apt in terms of that. I said: "During my life and especially during the last few weeks I've been guided by the words of Rabbi Hillel, which I want to share with you today" — and this was to the President, and the quote was — " 'If I am not for myself, who will be for me? If I am only for myself, what am I? If not now, when?' " It was perfect. Hillel wrote it for these circumstances, you know.

When I left under these conditions, I was something of a hero in the Jewish community, and certainly in Israel for doing this, although I didn't know it at the time. The first time I made a speech and got a hero's welcome, this was beyond me. I didn't understand this kind of reaction, because it seemed like the appropriate thing to do and I was embarrassed that I hadn't done it two months earlier and I had made all these speeches and things like that. Apparently there was some comment from someone in the Israeli Defense Ministry that it was better for them to have me there to argue and to fight than not having a strong advocate.

Let me say about Jews and politics — you just assume the worst. You assume you are going to get screwed. We have thirty-eight hundred years of good case studies. It takes a very long time of people being put to the test and passing to finally get the seal of approval, as Hubert Humphrey or Scoop Jackson or Frank Church did. I remember Gary Hart said to me last year, when he was getting such a low percentage of the Jewish vote, "I've always voted right. I have a perfect voting record. Why am I not getting the Jewish vote?" And, of course, it wasn't enough that he voted right. You had to feel that he believed it and when push came to shove would really go to the end.

With Jimmy Carter there was no track record at all. He'd never been put to the test on any foreign policy issue, never having been in the Senate. He had no relationship with the Jewish community in Atlanta or in Georgia. This was really rolling the dice. This fundamentalism thing I think made people also very, very nervous.

For a long time in this country, Jews were behind the scenes as power brokers. Within the last x number of years — and it has only been recently — you have eight senators. You have congressmen — they are out front. They no longer hide. Something new is happening. Jews were afraid to be up-front. They talk about Jewish influence, and Jewish money, and Jewish this, and Jewish that. So they were always behind the scenes. Although the numbers were there in terms of Jewish activists in the Democratic Party and Jewish campaign managers and media experts, they would never run for office themselves. That is changing fundamentally. We have the development of Jewish political action committees in this country. Mine was the first. My PAC was created in 1978, right after the Saudi Arabian vote, because so many people who had been close to the Jewish community had voted the wrong way and had broken commitments and things like that. There are now seventy-two PAC's modeled after it.

Now, whether you think PAC's are a good or a bad thing, the notion that you would create a PAC committed to the election of candidates who understood the special relationship between the United States and Israel, promote candidacies of friends of Jews or Israel, and you would state this? Twenty years ago you would actually say something like that? Even now, with these PAC's — the title — the fear is still there. Mine is the National Bipartisan Political Action Committee. There is one called the Committee of Eighteen, another the Committee to Preserve Our Heritage; there's one called Joint Action Committee. They all have names that still show the fear.

They all have the same aim. Now some are more multi-issued than others. Mine is clearly a liberal, Jewish PAC. The separation of church and state is almost as important as support for Israel. We would never give money to a Paula Hawkins even if she voted for foreign aid for the rest of her life. But there are some that are single issue. This is a new development. The political maturation of the Jewish electorate.

Chic Hecht, fifty-seven, United States senator (Republican of Nevada), Washington, D.C.

From all the accounts of history that I was able to determine, I was the first Jewish state senator from Nevada, and, of course, I'm the first Jewish U.S. senator from Nevada. There are very, very few western Jewish senators. In fact, offhand I can't think of any.

The Hecht family started with Grandpa Hecht, who came over from Poland, arrived in New York, was given a few bolts, some thimbles, some threads, and piece goods, and became a peddler on the streets of New York City. Later on, he moved to Saint Louis, Missouri, and then to Poplar Bluff, Missouri. There were ten children in the family. All the children were born here, and all entered into the retail business. Some joined up as partners originally, but later branched out on their own in the men's and women's business. Many of their children, my first cousins, are still in the business, as is my brother. My father, Louis Hecht, was born in Saint Louis and right before World War I went to Cape Girardeau, Missouri, and opened up a store. The war came and he went in. He came back, reopened the store, and married my mother, who was living at that time in Saint Louis. My mother and her family were immigrants from Russia. Her home was Kiev. I love to add this to every interview. What a great country this is, that the son of an immigrant can rise to the position of a United States senator!

The Hecht store that my father started after World War I is still in existence. My brother runs it and has added several other stores in surrounding areas. The latest is a store in Saint Louis. My father is still alive and is ninety-seven years old. After World War II, my mother passed away and my brother came back from the army. Within a short time he went in business with my father and took over the business. My father then decided to semiretire and move to Nevada, which he did in 1947. The next year he opened up a business, and when I graduated from Washington University in Saint Louis, the School of Retailing — I've been in retailing all my life — I moved out to Nevada and worked with my father in his clothing business. That was 1949. In 1950, the Korean War broke out, and in 1951 I was drafted into the armed services. I entered infantry basic training. Then I was assigned to intelligence school at Fort Holabird, Maryland. After that I was sent to Europe and served as a special agent undercover in Berlin for eighteen months. Returning to Nevada, I joined my father for just a few months in business, but my independence got the best of me, and on a friendly basis I opened up my own business in 1954. I kept it until the month after I was elected to the U.S. Senate.

I grew up in Cape Girardeau. It was certainly a Waspy community. There was one country club we were not permitted in. There was a surrounding Jewish community. We had a synagogue which my father and a few others built. On Friday night, we would have services, and for the High Holidays we always had services and would bring rabbis in from other areas to conduct them. On Friday night, different laymen would conduct the services. Cape Girardeau itself maybe had ten or twelve Jewish families; with the surrounding areas maybe we had another twenty families. It was a farming area, very small. The main industry was the shoe factory. As I was growing up, the population was probably eighteen to twenty thousand people.

We maintained our Jewish identity the same way it's been maintained for nearly four thousand years: in the family — your mother, your father. We were raised in a semi-Orthodox house, never any bacon or ham. We did not keep kosher. My father had someone from Saint Louis drive down every weekend to teach my brother and me for our Bar Mitzvah. We did not have a Hebrew teacher then. When we were younger, we had a Hebrew teacher; much younger. Probably a couple of families moved away. They couldn't afford it. At the time I got Bar Mitzvahed, my father had the man drive down every weekend and stay at our house. That was 125 miles. He would stay over, and all weekend I would study with him. I davened for many years after that.

My brother is very Orthodox, davens every morning, keeps the Sabbath, and will not answer the telephone on the Sabbath. His son is a doctor, a radiologist in Chicago, and is a Lubavitcher. He has nine children. My brother is very active in Jewish day schools. He has eleven grandchildren in Jewish day schools at the moment. He's been very active in Jewish affairs. He built the Hecht Synagogue on Mount Scopus at the Hebrew University. He's on the board of the Hebrew University. At one of the dedications, my brother and his wife, my wife and myself, took Senator and Mrs. Helms over. That was Jesse Helms's first visit to Israel. We toured the country extensively for eight days. The motivating factor for this was the dedication of the Hecht Synagogue, which Jesse attended.

In Nevada, we have certainly led a Jewish life. We never had a Christmas tree when our kids were growing up. My wife is Jewish but was never raised as religious as I was. She was born in San Diego. As long as I had my store, I closed every Yom Kippur and Rosh Hashonah. I'd put an ad in the paper that we were closed. It has not been a negative factor, and you always hear certain people are surprised that Nevada, one of the most conservative states, would elect a Jew. It's not been a factor at all. I just don't think religion makes any difference for public office one way or another. I think it's definitely changed.

In the United States Senate we've got eight Jewish senators. That's a tremendous proportion relative to our population. The younger generation made the change. The older generation . . . my father always said, "Never get involved in politics. You run your business; don't ever get involved in politics." I didn't listen. In 1966, I ran for the state senate. That was the year Paul Laxalt ran for governor, and a guy by the name of Ronald Reagan ran for governor of California. So our paths have been intertwined since then. I served as a state senator for eight years.

Last year or the year before, I was rated by *Roll Call* the most conservative senator. So I'm either number one, two, or three, depending on who's doing the ratings. I'm probably the only — I won't say the only — without a doubt the most conservative Jew in the United States Senate. Everyone will acknowledge that, Jew or non-Jew. Probably my thinking, my philosophy, is that of Orthodoxy. What does that mean? You talk about the social issues. I feel strongly against abortion, which is certainly the Orthodox thinking. School prayer — there's a picture over there of Lubavitcher rebbe, and he's talking to me in that picture. He's telling me that the moral caliber of America in the cities has deteriorated so badly that we must have a prayer in the morning so the students will know there is a Supreme Being, and we should have school prayer. This is strictly an Orthodox bill. I'm talking about Jewish Orthodox. And tuition tax credits for school — I told you my brother has eleven grandchildren in Jewish day schools. I favor tuition tax credits. So these are probably three of the social issues that the liberal Jewish community is against.

I think the evangelical movement — they've been some of the greatest friends of Israel, some of the biggest backers of Israel — and I don't see that as a threat, as a lot of people see it as a threat. I think they have been outspoken in their support of Israel, of Judaism. I know that troubled a lot of the people in the East in the last election, between President Reagan and Mondale. I do not see that at all. Some of my best friends are in that area, because they are all conservative. I think they respect me because of my religion. There is certainly no hatred, any which way.

I've been a small-business man working very hard. I point out this one little anecdote. Our kids were in college — we have two daughters — when we got here. They came the first summer and worked here, and we had lunch in Georgetown one Saturday. They said, "Daddy, this is the first time in our life we've ever been with you on a Saturday," because every Saturday I had to work. I was in retailing. When you have to work so hard to meet that payroll every week, it does make you a conservative.

I think what you hit on is a true conservative Jewish senator in the Senate. I'm with the conservatives all the time. We meet — the Republican senators — every Tuesday, all of us together, with the Vice-President. Then on Wednesday we divide up into two groups, the conservatives and the moderates, and I'm always with the conservatives.

I think as far as Israel, this President has been the best friend the State of Israel has ever had. I just don't think there is any question about it. I voted against the arms sale to Saudi Arabia, but then when it came forth with a presidential veto, I had several sessions with him. It was something more than that. It was the prestige of the presidency, and I supported his veto. First of all, he took the Stinger missiles out, which made it more palatable. Many organizations said they would not oppose it. I think the best interests of the State of Israel, the United States, and the free world are served by being friends with the moderates. Egypt has been proven. I think Saudi Arabia, Jordan, will come around.

Because I tend to be a conservative, because I am, I'm probably not as much sought out for support as some of the other people, the liberals, because most of the eastern Jewish organizations are very Democratic-liberal oriented. I don't fall into that mold. I feel very comfortable with them, but sometimes they don't feel comfortable with me. Anyone who wants to walk in and see me from any Jewish organization, I'm here.

A lot of people told me, when I first decided to run for office in 1966 in Las Vegas, that I would encounter some opposition because of my religion and the fact that I served on the temple board and I closed the store, and everyone knew I was Jewish and I lived as a Jew. Probably the biggest community in Las Vegas is the Mormon community. The bishops invite different candidates to come over and talk to them. So I went over one day to tell the Mormons that I was running. They didn't know me from Adam. I brought out the similarities in the Mormon religion and the Jewish religion — very, very strong family ties, living a good clean life, working hard, the work ethic, saving so much time for prayer. Then at the end — this was during the period where there was a lot of trying to break down many, many barriers in the middle 1960s — I brought out this point to the Mormon bishops: I said, "I'm Jewish; I do not believe in assimilation; I have two daughters; I do not want my daughters marrying your sons." And they liked that, and they supported me. I meant it. I was right up-front with them. I said, "I do not want my daughters marrying your sons."

20

In and Out and In Again

"MARRYING OUT." That's the pejorative phrase I heard in my youth to mark the person who decided to marry someone who was not Jewish. I think it is fair to say that before World War II particularly, marrying out was severely frowned on in many Jewish communities. Less so, apparently, in areas of the country where eligible Jews were few and far between.

The phrase carried with it a connotation not just of mixed religion but of mixed Judaism, a fruit just as forbidden. This meant that Sephardic Jews, those from Southern Europe and the Mediterranean, were not to mix their seed with that of the Ashkenazic or Northern European Jews. With even more specificity, this translated into the inbred desire of the German Jews to keep their progeny from marrying Jews from Eastern Europe.

As odd as it may seem today, interviewee after interviewee told of the religious, parental, and even community barriers to their dating outside the religion. Stanley J. Talpers, age fifty-nine, a practicing internist in Washington, D.C., recalled this about his older sister growing up in Casper, Wyoming: "My sister was popular and she was in a pep club and she had dates. There were no Jewish boys and I don't know what my father expected. He would get very angry with her, almost irrational. That part was painful for her. I didn't realize how painful until we talked about it a few years ago."

Stories were told of parents who would declare a child dead for marrying out of the faith and sit shiva, a mourning time for the dead, for the "lost" child. Some persons recounted how they waited years to marry out, often postponing their marriage until a surviving parent, usually a mother, died.

Keeping the faith was a vital aspect of maintaining identity and vitality and critical mass, so it was important to be Jewish and to be with other

Jews. Rose Wexler Jacobs, sixty-seven, whose parents were born in Rumania, recalled:

"I was born in Bowling Green, Ohio. I must have been two or three years old when this took place, because we left there when I was three. My sister could not have been nine years old yet. We were the only Jewish family in Bowling Green, and one Sunday, one of my sister's Gentile friends came and asked my father if she, Dorothy, could go with her to church. And that's when my father decided it was time to move on. He was not staying in Bowling Green, where his children could not have any Jewish friends. That was it. And we left and moved down to Savannah, Georgia."

And Rosetta C. Elmer, of Shreveport, Louisiana, whose family arrived there in the mid 1800s from Alsace, remarked:

"Many of the prominent Shreveport families are descended from Jews who came to this country at the same time my grandfather Henry Levy did and with whom he was friendly all of his life, but who married planters' daughters. This has always amused me. I call us the stubborn ones. We wanted to retain our Judaism. It was through choice, because living in Louisiana we could easily have walked to another church, and that would have been it. It's been a wonderful world to grow up in. We've been Jewish because we wanted to be Jewish."

In recent years, the success of Jewish acculturation in America has been, ironically, potentially damaging. This is because intermarriage and abandonment of the Jewish religion and heritage have grown at a rate that alarms some Jewish leaders. Essentially, their concern is that near total acceptability will sap the American Jewish community of its being, even though numbers of fallen Jews are finding their way back to Judaism and many of the children of "mixed marriages" are being raised as Jews.

Julian Hennig, sixty-three, a retired banker and attorney from Columbia, South Carolina, is descended on his mother's side from a family named Goldsmith that arrived in Rhode Island before the American Revolution. His paternal grandfather's family were Kohns, who came to New York from Germany in 1848. His great-grandfather, Theodore Kohn, joined the Confederate Army and became a member of the Edisto Rifles. He was a corporal who served for four years and was wounded in the Battle of Drewry's Bluff, just below Richmond, Virginia.

"Do my children ask about the family at all? Yes, they do, and they're interested. I very occasionally take them to services, usually on my mother's or father's yahrzeit. I've taken them on the High Holidays. But they're members of the First Presbyterian Church.

"Is the line beginning to assimilate out? I would say definitely. I'm probably the last of my generation. I'm Jewish, but my wife and children are not. I have a sister who has no children. She's Jewish; her husband is not. Yes, we may be the last Jewish generation."

Reuben Greenberg, forty-two, police chief, Charleston, South Carolina

I am fairly certain my Jewish ancestors came in through New York, as there were other relatives who remained in New York; this indicates to me that they all must have come there. But they were wheat farmers, not merchants. In Texas they were wheat farmers as well.

Jewish ancestry comes from my father's side of the family. His grandfather came to the United States in about 1896, 1897; that period. From what I can find out, it was after a pogrom in the area of the Ukraine where he was living. He came to the U.S. and settled in Texas around the San Marcos area, which was a cattle-raising and wheat-farming section. They had been active in wheat farming in the Ukraine, and there were a number of other Jews from the Ukraine who were also wheat farmers and had settled in that section of Texas at that time. He met my grandmother not in that particular area, but in another part of Texas.

I was born and raised in Houston. I knew of the Caucasian background in the family because my father himself was at least as white-skinned as you are. My mother, of course, was dark-skinned on her side of the family. So I knew that there was Caucasian or European blood in the family from that side, and his relatives, his sister, for example, was very, very light-skinned like my father was. Unfortunately, my grandparents, both maternal and paternal, died before I was born.

My father's mother was black and not Jewish. I don't recall what religion she was. Nobody ever mentioned. She was a Christian of some sort, but which particular branch I have no idea. When I grew up in Houston, could I be Jewish? Well, it never occurred to me. There were people who went to jail for attempting to go to Baptist churches who were Baptists. But the churches were all-white churches. And the synagogues were all-white. We have many synagogues, for instance, now that are all-white, but they are all-white for different reasons. They are not all-white because they would refuse to accept blacks. But the synagogues in Houston, at that time, were all-white because they would refuse to accept blacks; they didn't accept blacks in any of their other activities — nonreligious activities. There was no reason to assume that they would accept them in religious activities.

People would say that we had all of the vices of the Negro, which was the term used to describe blacks at that time, along with the cunning of the Jews, which made my father, for example, much more dangerous than he would have been otherwise to many people. He was very active in the

NAACP and the Progressive Youth Association, against discrimination in housing and employment, police brutality, that type of thing. He was in the insurance business, which made it possible for him to be active. There was no way he could be economically impacted by the white establishment, like fired from his job. He worked for a black insurance company, a debit company where he had a lot of small nickel-and-dime policyholders. They couldn't put pressure on all that number of people to have any impact on him, so therefore he was in an ideal position to engage in these activities, to make statements, and upset people, with no economic consequences. He was never unemployed, never laid off or anything like that.

One of the things that was interesting, the reason why whites did not frighten my father as much as they did many other blacks when I was coming up, and the reason he was able to speak out, is that he never looked upon whites as being anything special. That was due to his background, his Jewish background. They were in his family. He saw them at their worst moments and at their very best moments, as well. So he had no basis for assuming that he was racially inferior. He managed somehow to impart that to his children.

Did he identify at all as being Jewish? Not really. Among my brothers and sisters — I'm the oldest of the six kids in my family — only the two oldest identified as being Jewish. When we grew up I became affiliated with various synagogues, converted, and so forth. My brother did also. Unfortunately, he was killed in Vietnam. Also, it is very important for you to understand that during the time that I was growing up my father's name was Greenberg, but he dropped the *berg* from his last name and became Green.

He was married twice. He had six children with my mother, who was his last wife, and three children with his prior wife. They were Greenbergs, because that was at an earlier point in his life. At a later part of his life they were Greens.

My name was legally changed. That was the original name anyway. Two groups of kids from the same father, normally you would find them with the same name. One of the old jokes is "Hey, your name is Smith now, but what was it before?" I guess in this case it was going back the other way. All of them pretty much had Jewish names to start with: Reuben Morris Greenberg, that's me, and Joshua, and pretty readily identifiable Jewish names, particularly in his first family. But that was not the case so much with his later children. The reason I was named Reuben was because, I think, in Hebrew it means "first seed," firstborn son, and that is what I was.

Do I ever get tired of answering why Reuben Greenberg who is black is also Jewish? I get tired of it, yes. I am not tired of it now, because nobody has asked me in a long time. I have met a number of other black Jews. I knew a number of kids — younger kids — in San Francisco whose mothers were Jewish and fathers were black. I also knew Jewish men who married black women. Speaking of marriage, by the way, my grandfather never married my grandmother. The reason is because it was not legally possible for blacks and whites to marry or even to cohabitate as man and wife until 1967, which would have been twenty-two to twenty-four years after they were dead, let alone when they had first met. That didn't prevent them, in fact, from living together as man and wife for about thirty-two years. He had left that area where his family had brought him from the Ukraine to be a wheat farmer and had moved to the Houston area. Apparently she worked for him as a housemaid, a laborer type of thing. At that time, he had learned tailoring, and was Greenberg Tailors.

Are there any Greenbergs or Jewish wheat farmers or children of Jewish wheat farmers left in the San Marcos region? Oh, no. I suspect there's some wheat there still, but it's pretty much cattle area. There were relatives of ours there, but they never wanted anything to do with me or us or with my father because he was black.

I was attracted back, you might say, to Judaism in a secular sense when I was sixteen years old by the tremendous effort Jews were making in Texas and elsewhere in the civil rights movement. That's what got me thinking, "Hey, you are Reuben Morris Greenberg, you know, right?" It was a name, you know. But the Jewish community to me was just different. There were whites and then there were blacks and then there were Jews. And Jews were different than other persons. They seemed to get better treatment. There is no question about that; I mean as a human being. They may not have treated you any better so far as work, but so far as on a person-to-person basis, or human-being basis, you got better treatment.

I left Houston in 1962. George Wallace had not yet stood in the school-house door. He did not do that until 1963, and so things were pretty segregated in Houston at that time, but I think we had gained the right to sit in the front of the bus. But that was about it. I was about eighteen years old in San Francisco then, where it was possible to go to a synagogue, while in Houston it was not. In San Francisco, I went to Temple Emanu-El. That was my first experience. Naturally, in school I met a lot of students, Jewish and otherwise, and I became very active in the civil rights movement. With the exception of blacks, Jews dominated the civil rights movement. Most of the Caucasians involved in the civil rights movement on the grass-roots level were Jewish. We worked very, very closely together and they would ask me about my background and all that. Naturally, I told them. But I became affiliated with formal Jewish organizations like Hillel when I was at San Francisco State University.

The rabbi at Temple Emanu-El, which is a great, huge religious place, was very active. He taught on campus at San Francisco State, was very active in the civil rights movement, a very prominent Jewish religious official, and so he had a tremendous impact upon all of us really.

Jewish law is reasonably specific on who is Jewish: the lineage comes through the mother. At first, I didn't convert because Temple Emanu-El is a Reform synagogue. But that policy, even at that point — San Francisco is a very liberal city — was very controversial. So I felt it was in my best interests and I converted to Reform and then later I converted to Conservative. The only Reform synagogue I ever belonged to was Temple Emanu-El in San Francisco. Then, when I moved to Savannah, Georgia, I was at Agudas Achim Synagogue. I went there in 1976. That's a Conservative synagogue. Then, when I was in Miami at Hialeah, I was a member of Tifereth Jacob Synagogue. When I was in Orlando, I was at Temple Israel, which is also a Conservative synagogue. And then in Tallahassee it was Shomrei Torah and then here at Synagogue Emanuel, where I am an officer of the synagogue. I've held posts in other synagogues as well. Just before I came here I was elected to the board of Shomrei Torah, which is a Conservative synagogue. But I left there about a month later. Strangely enough, the president of that shul at that time, in Tallahassee, was from Charleston. So it is interesting that I would wind up here.

Things have happened to me over the years. I'd go to the dentist. I'd make an appointment and they'd say, "Excuse me, Mr. Greenberg, the dentist will see you now." I'd stand forward. And they'd say, "Excuse me" — looking past me — "Mr. Greenberg." I'd say, "Excuse me, young lady . . ." "Mr. Greenberg. Mr. Greenberg." And I'd say, "*I* am Mr. Greenberg." They look at you — you can always tell when they are Jewish. The ones it has the most effect on are either Jewish or black, because it hits them like a wet towel. They say, "Oh?" I was shown in then.

Plus you are often in a very interesting position, a lot of times, to hear a lot of anti-Semitic things, both from blacks and from whites. I've never heard anything anti-black from Jews without them knowing that I was Jewish. In other words, you've got Jewish racists like you have other kinds of racists, and they make anti-black statements in the public sense or whatever. But there were people — who are blacks — who assumed that I wasn't Jewish, which I felt was a reasonable assumption on their part, who made anti-Jewish statements.

There were many Caucasians who were not Jews who made anti-Jewish statements in front of me. They knew I wasn't white and they just assume all Jews are whites; therefore, whatever I say against Jews to this guy will fall upon fertile ground or welcome ears or something. As a matter of fact, people have even said how Jews "exploit you all," and gone into great detail on how they thought Jews were exploiting us blacks, and had no idea that I was Jewish.

One of the things that amazes me is the amount of anti-Semitic feeling there is in certain branches of government, even in the academic community. You'd be surprised. When I was teaching in California, the department chairmanship opened and we had to decide who was going to be the new chairman: somebody inside, or were we going to get somebody from the outside. We decided to get somebody from the outside, and during the discussion someone said, "What about so-and-so?" And he was pretty good. And they said, "No." Very candidly, right in front of me: "We already have too many Jews." They knew I was Greenberg; they knew I was Jewish. It didn't register. It didn't count, somehow. This was just a faculty search committee which I was on. I guess they put me on for the affirmative action aspect of the thing. They said, "Oh, yes, we also had a member of the minority community on the search board." There were no other Jews on that search committee. It was 1970. That person was cast out. It was amazing.

When I was in North Carolina in 1973, during the Arab oil embargo, I heard people on the faculty say, "Well, I'm not going to let my kids go cold this winter just to save a handful of Jews." I mean literally. You know, they would make statements like that, and these were guys who you really respected. If there was anybody enlightened in America, this would be it, at a fine university like that. I'm not naming the university; it could have been anywhere. One was in the South; the other was in the Far West. One was in a political science faculty; the other one was on a sociology faculty. But the point is that these intelligent people, well known in their fields and so forth, would make such a ridiculous statement. They just didn't care. It is hard for me, even at this point, to think that they were actually anti-Semitic. It's just that they didn't care.

This is an unusual perch. I have had people here call on the phone, even on this job, as well known as I am in town, and complain about some police practice, and I say this is the policy and so forth, and they say, "What I should have expected from a goddamned kike," or "fucking Jew," or something like this. Both blacks and whites. It certainly happened much more frequently on other jobs that I had where I was the number two man and consequently didn't have as much public exposure. They didn't know who they were speaking with. They made all kinds of anti-Semitic remarks. As I say, both blacks and whites have made those comments, not knowing — I didn't say not caring — not knowing.

I wish, in many ways, many blacks could be in a similar position to what I have been. What many blacks are convinced of is that Jews are just another kind of white person who is accepted fully by all whites and so forth. Your people say blacks, Jews, and whites. And so you say, "Don't you equate Jews with being white people?" They say, "Oh, no. They are different." They are neither black nor white. But from their level of experience, when they say they are neither black nor white, that's not saying it in the positive sense. It's said in a negative sense, because they want you to know that they're white.

But it's amazing. If they could look at all this hullabaloo between blacks and Jews, for example, the disaffection would be a lot less if they really knew the true story. I have never met a person in my life who was anti-black who was not also anti-Semitic, unless he was Semitic himself. I have never found one, never found one yet. If they hated blacks, they also hated Jews, unless that person was Jewish himself.

There are certain professions where I think being Jewish has helped people — in law, for example, because you have a whole network. Unfortunately, there is no such network among Jews in law enforcement, because there are very few Jews in law enforcement, period. I think New York City, that one department alone, has more than all the others put together. For example, in this department, there are only three Jews as officers. I just hired a person as an attorney who is Jewish. She'll be the fourth person. In Atlanta, there's only two. In Opalaca there were none, and in the Florida Department of Law Enforcement there were only about five or six. In San Francisco, there were maybe, out of two thousand police officers, maybe fifteen. There are very few chiefs that are Jewish; very, very few. In some tiny departments somewhere there might be some Jews. I am talking about major departments. There's less than six or seven.

People always told me, "If you want to be in the law, why can't you be a lawyer, because that is respectable. But to be a policeman, that's for the goyim." So there is no network. The long and the short of it is, I have never found being Jewish to be a benefit as a police officer. It's only been a minor hindrance, mainly coming from people who are anti-Semitic to start with. For example, a guy made a statement on the radio in Orlando when I was there — this was a black fellow, a preacher, of all things, a fundamentalist preacher — that "we wanted a black" to be the chief deputy sheriff in Orange County, Florida. That's the number two man in the department. "And what did the sheriff do? He goes out and he brings in a black, all right, but of all the things to bring in — a Jew." He said it in a tone that was obviously "anti." There was no question about it. As a matter of fact, I got numerous calls on it asking me what I was going to do about it; telling me that I should report it to B'nai B'rith and the ADL. By the way, at that time I also was on the regional board of the Anti-Defamation League out of Miami.

From the viewpoint of southern law enforcement people in earlier days,

ADL was a communist organization. Why was it a communist organization? Because it was a Jewish organization. I've cooperated with them, very much so. I've worked on antiterrorism conferences, which obviously dealt with the whole question of terrorism, the Holocaust, and so forth. I was very active in Holocaust commemoration types of programs. Law enforcement people, first of all, are more intelligent today. You are getting away from the redneck style. Forty percent of our people in this department are college graduates. That's a contrast to what we had when I came here three years ago; there were five people who couldn't even read and write. Now we have none.

We have certain types of crime, such as certain white-collar crimes, where you will find Jews. But even today armed robbery is not a Jewish-type crime. Homicide, rape, crimes of this kind are not typically Jewish crimes. They are very heavily involved in drug sales, smuggling, this type of thing, which, after all, is a kind of business. But to find people just common thieves and so forth is not the case.

There are certain types of ethnic-oriented crimes. For example, certain types of sexual perversion–type crimes, you would find very few blacks involved, such as indecent exposure, that type of thing; you know, flashers. We get very few calls on that and I think I am qualified to make that point, having worked in six police departments. You get much more of that with whites, in general, than you do with blacks. On the other hand, income tax evasion obviously would not be a primary crime problem in the black community. Driving under the influence; very few blacks are arrested. It's very discretionary. This is one of the curious things about law enforcement. It's that very few blacks are arrested for driving under the influence. It's not because they do not have cars. They have a lot of cars in ghetto areas. But they don't drive while intoxicated. And I think it has to do with the culture. The intoxication takes place on foot in a social-type group rather than an individual situation, and in the neighborhood, where driving isn't important.

Latinos almost never attack the elderly, whereas white thugs and black thugs will attack an elderly person, snatch their purse, knock them to the ground, and apparently have no pangs of conscience about it. But elderly people in the Latino culture are very revered and important, and they simply aren't attacked. They find another victim, a younger one. In certain kinds of crimes that take place, we can tell from the crime the probable racial background of the person that committed that crime.

Bernard Stolboff, fifty-six, distillery vice-president, Syosset,
New York

I left Albany pretty quickly after high school. On balance, I also have to
say that personally my experiences in Albany were affected by the fact that
I lost my parents when I was young. I was fifteen when my mother passed
away and sixteen when my father passed away. So I was affected by this
personal experience, although right now I feel warmly about many of the
experiences that I had then.

It's important that you recognize where I'm coming from, living on the
periphery of a Jewish ghetto area, then totally surrounded by Gentiles. My
father was a tailor in a Gentile area about six blocks from the core of the
Jewish ghetto area. This was on South Pearl Street in Albany. We experienced a great deal of anti-Semitism. We lived a block from a Catholic church.
The immediate community was largely Catholic. The persecution was fairly
intense. I remember passing the church, and the kids would insist that I
bow my head out of respect to their religion, which I refused. There were
fights. We got into fistfights. I also went to a Hebrew school on Ferry Street.
We would get involved frequently in fights. We would play, basically, handball in between classes, and the kids in the neighborhood would come out
and attack us. So there was that kind of experience.

Here we were living in this segment of the community where we were
subjected to a lot of persecution. The family insisted that we cling together
and socially we only meet with other Jewish people. So we separated ourselves from the non-Jewish community. My brother was a member of this
high school fraternity — ABG, or Alpha Beta Gamma. It was sort of a
natural thing that I followed my brother in joining the fraternity, which
had tremendous significance. Not only did it help me prolong my association
and my identity as a Jew, but it helped me to separate myself from this
persecution, from the anti-Semitism, and bridge the Jewish social gap between downtown and uptown Albany. The fraternity was a blend of people
representing both the downtown or the poorer segment of the community
and the upper-scale members of the Jewish community. So this represented
a tremendous opportunity from many social points of view. The fraternity
itself at the time represented all kinds of potential, in terms of socializing.
We did this with dances and with sporting events. There were all kinds of
avenues that were developed because of the fraternity. It helped us, of course,
to maintain our Jewish identity.

The fraternity met Monday nights weekly at the Jewish Y in Albany. This
was not the only fraternity. I believe that there were two others, a total of
three — Mu Sigma, and I don't remember the other. But ABG was the most

popular. It had a wider membership. It was a fraternity in the real sense in that it employed the blackball system, which in retrospect is horrendous. I can't recall anyone actually being blackballed. But the fact that it had the system is ridiculous.

There were other chapters primarily in upstate New York but reaching down as far south as New Jersey. Periodically, the chapters would host social events . . . I haven't thought about this in many, many moons.

I was elected president of this thing. This was the high point in my young life, to become a president of this chapter. It was quite an experience.

There also were sororities. We were involved with the sororities. It gave us an opportunity to meet females outside of the high school situation. The high school that I went to, which was Schuyler, didn't provide the same social opportunities that the other high school provided, Albany High School. There were fewer Jewish girls at Schuyler than at Albany. I was keenly sensitive to a social difference. The uptown-downtown syndrome was extremely strong. That was Jewish. So the sororities represented an opportunity to meet more girls at a higher level also from a social point of view.

My family came from Russia and settled in Albany. My grandmother lived with us and she was a very strong factor in terms of maintaining the old traditions. She was the Orthodox influence in the family. We went to the Orthodox synagogue, and I went to the Hebrew school.

Hebrew school was the worst — a very exacting, bad experience. I think the teachers in the Hebrew school perpetuated separation. They really didn't want us to integrate with the community, which was an attitude that my grandmother had also. She wanted total separation; she wanted to maintain this because she felt the supremacy of the Jewish race. I think she also felt threatened by integration. You can see today. I married a Gentile wife. We have four kids. Our kids specifically don't make much reference to that at all. They don't feel uncomfortable and are not intimidated by the fact that they're neither fish nor fowl in a religious sense or a social sense either. I think they're more non-Jewish, however, than they are Jewish. We don't talk about that. I think my marrying a Gentile is in part a reaction to my experiences when I was a kid, because there was this dogma. There was the dogma that existed at the Hebrew school, at synagogue, where everything was done in such a way that made no sense to me. People involved in the synagogue didn't relate to us at all — to the kids. They didn't explain things; they didn't want to develop things. They wanted to perpetuate, but they didn't take the time to develop things properly with us. This strict Orthodox dogma eventually turned me off. I'm not in the traditional sense religious at all.

I look back fondly at Albany now. I wasn't involved in the community, so I can separate myself from some problems that existed. But I remember very distinctly the downtown Jewish area. I had to get the daily *Forward* for my father every afternoon after school. I had to stop there and stop at Zuckerman's bakery and sometimes stop at Smith's chicken place to pick up our chickens and get the meat, et cetera, and travel this whole route from school to the shopping area to home. I look back fondly at some of these experiences. It's not all bad. I go into an area similar to it in a city, such as Toronto, and see a resemblance, a similarity, and it brings back warm memories.

William S. Cohen, forty-five, United States senator (Republican of Maine), Washington, D.C.

My dad followed me all over the State of Maine. He would come directly to wherever we were playing basketball, Presque Isle way up at the top of the state, no matter where. And he would get back by three in the morning and go directly to work. He was just a fanatic about it.

For me, at least, the fact that I am and I am not Jewish begins with Hebrew school. I started that when I was six; it was actually prior to Hebrew school. They had one year of a kind of kindergarten. This was in Bangor, Maine. It was there that I first became aware of the difference, that I was not "one of them." That was principally because my mother was Irish and had not converted. When I was eight years old, the difference really started to become more evident. I was at that time an aspiring athlete, and I joined the Young Men's Christian Association in Bangor solely to play basketball. I think I lied about my age at the time. I was supposed to have been either nine or ten and I was big for my age, so I just signed and went in and started playing basketball.

I had worked out a deal with my father and mother, but mostly my father, because of Saturday services and going to shul. Of course, the YMCA was open Saturday mornings, so I made a deal that I would go one week a month to the YMCA and then I'd go the rest to the synagogue. Then it became two and two, then it became three and one, and then, finally, I stopped going to the services altogether and just played basketball. This really was my love at that time. It caused some very hard feelings, because they used to take class attendance every Saturday at the synagogue, and the class that had the best attendance for Saturday services always got not only the gold stars but they got an award at the end of the year. I proceeded to mess it up for my classmates, and it led to fisticuffs and a lot of brawling, as young kids would do at that time.

There was also a good deal of pressure placed on me in the classroom. The rabbi would say, "How many here keep a kosher house?" and everybody's hand goes up but mine. Mine stayed down. Or he would say, "Zev, why is there a Christmas tree in your window?" During the winter months, my mother would have a tree. And it would be embarrassing to me to have to explain this. Of course, I reacted to it in a fairly adolescent fashion. I started to be a little bit rude and a little bit independent and insouciant and whatever and cocky and didn't need anybody and that type of thing. But I was a little bit bitter about the experience, because I usually got the highest grade in the class, yet I never got the highest award. Each year the rabbi would come to me and say, "Zev, we're sorry, we know that you got the top grade, but we think that the award should go to . . ." One year it was Michael Stryor or somebody else, but it was somebody whose parents both happened to be Jewish or were influential in the community. So I got my little medal each year. I was really bitter about that.

Then there was Jewish camp. I could not have afforded to go, but I wanted the honor of being asked, of hearing, "We'd like to have you come." But I was never asked and I never went. That festered for a while to the point where I just became totally independent of it.

But then I think the biggest disappointment I had was, after going through Hebrew school for six years, almost seven years, counting when I started at six years old, I was told when I was thirteen that I could not be Bar Mitzvahed. The rabbi told me that unless either my mother converted or I went through a ceremony, which would involve me being put in a pool of holy water as such and a little ceremonial extraction of blood from a fairly existential place, I could not be Bar Mitzvahed. I went to my father with tears and said, "Dad, I'm not going to do that. Why didn't they tell me before? Why have I done seven years of double duty, public school and Hebrew school? They should have told me in the beginning. It's not fair." I was really angry about it. So it left some bitterness there. That's when the break came.

My dad is a baker. He still works eighteen hours a day. He owns a little tiny shop. He goes to work at nine-thirty at night now and comes home late in the afternoon. He bakes Jewish bread, rye bread and rolls. He himself is a very moral person. He doesn't smoke or drink. Occasionally he used to swear when he had an argument with his brother or sister in the bakery or something, but he leads a very good life with just sheer hard work and tries to kill everybody with kindness.

He's just a wonderful human being.

He really is committed to believing that the Jewish way of life is the best way of life, in terms of eating habits and culture and that sort of thing. He was not particularly religious. He would only go to shul on the High Holidays, but he nonetheless was intellectually very committed to the principles of being Jewish.

What did Jewishness and having a Jewish name mean to me? It changed again when I went to high school. I became a basketball player as a sophomore. It was a big deal in Bangor High School in those days. We used to get seventy-five hundred fans a game. They were big games. I got to be all-state in high school and college. It began to change because basketball was a very big thing in Bangor in those years and got tremendous coverage, which was excessive for a fifteen-year-old, to be on the sports pages with bold headlines. I recall one time I scored something like thirty-three points and they had a headline COYNE SCORES 33, and the Jewish community went wild. They called up and said it was deliberate that they'd misspelled Cohen. It was one of those things where "he's one of us."

I skipped over something. I recall I started to feel the real tension when I was twelve, where I was pitching in a baseball game. That was the beginning, too, where I used to be called Jew boy all the time, and taking all the insults. I had to say to myself — I never would release it to anybody else — "Wait a minute, why are you doing this to me? I'm not a Jew boy, because the Jews say I'm not a Jew boy." It was that kind of ambivalence. I had no place to really go. You're really out there alone. You're on a mound and they're throwing beer cans at you. That sort of made me go my own way. Then, when I was playing basketball, I would go to places like Old Town, which is just up the way. I'd drive up myself — I had a convertible — and find my top slashed, tires slashed, on account of the Jew boy business. It really used to get to me at that point, saying, "Here I'm taking all the grief, and I have none of the comfort." It was tough.

Locally, basketball was everything. I went on to Bowdoin College and Boston University, and then I returned and started practicing law. I was still kind of a home-town boy, and people remember athletes fondly. I started practicing law and ran for the city council, more as an attempt to get some business. We couldn't advertise, so you volunteered for public service. I was on the parks and recreation committee and the zoning board of appeals and then the city council and then they put me on the school board. Then I was mayor, and all those things designed to help raise my image as a local attorney, saying, "Hey, he's a nice young man; I think I'll give him my will." You know, that kind of thing.

In 1972 I decided to run for Congress. The conventional wisdom at that time was that you can't do this. It's okay, you're well known here, but someone named Cohen will never get elected. This is a very bigoted area. You get outside, in some of the rural areas, and they're not going to take too kindly to you.

I said I don't believe that. I said just the opposite. My name is so unusual for public office, maybe that'll be an attraction in itself. I said if they can

vote for a Muskie, they can vote for a Cohen. But there was great apprehension. I found that there were some remnants of bigotry out in some of
the more rural, really distant lands. Today it is not a factor at all.

Am I ever approached by Jewish organizations that think I'm Jewish or
should be Jewish? Well, maybe, until they look at me. I used to have this
problem all the time. I was teaching one summer at a camp in Maine and
I met a friend named Peter Chester and he took me to New York and we
went to visit a friend of his. I walked through the door and she said, "You're
not Jewish; the map of Ireland is written all over your face." And I said,
"No, I really am." And she said, "No, you're not." And I said, "Okay, I'm
half." I would go through that all the time. If I'd go to a Jewish family,
they'd know immediately. If I'd go to a goyisha family, they would say,
"You're a Jew." So it's been traditional. Now, as far as the Jewish community, I think that nationally they still take a measure of pride that the
last name is Jewish, and therefore they assume that you are at least quasi,
part of the family.

Then came AWACS. That was very tough, because I am a very strong
supporter of Israel and still feel a strong attachment; at least half of my
mind is still there. Ironically enough, and this is not a matter of public record
as such, I was speaking out against the sale of AWACS for a long time,
saying it was a mistake, writing letters, and then about two weeks before
the vote I got a call from some friends tied back through Israeli politics.
Word came through to me, very cryptically, on the phone: "Bill, what you
hear is not necessarily what is going on. Call the ambassador." So I ended
up calling the ambassador, and he came up, and I said, "Look, I don't want
to hear the party line. Tell me, is there something else involved?"

He said, "Well, as a matter of fact . . ." and he went through a whole
list of things that were of far higher priority to the Israelis than this particular
thing. They were locked into this thing publicly, but they were really more
concerned about other items. So I again felt some bitterness about this:
"Why me? Why not call one of your boys? Why pick on me to disclose
this, to have the burden of responsibility of now trying to reconcile a vote,
saying that you really are after something quite different?" I anguished on
this for about two solid weeks and could not sleep at night, because I did
not really know how to handle it. Finally, I requested two meetings with
President Reagan. To his credit, he never once called me. Nor did anyone
in the administration call me, because I was so solid on the other side. So
I called them and I said that I wanted a meeting with the President and I
didn't want anybody there. I wanted to meet with him, one on one. I was
granted my request on two occasions — the last one being the night before
the vote, because I still was undecided. I still did not want to do it, and I
went down there and it was late afternoon or early evening or whatever,

and I said, "Look, I really have to be satisfied that you are not going to compromise their security, either qualitatively or quantitatively, and that's of paramount importance to me. I know that you can't cut a deal with me personally that you are going to guarantee me all these other things that I have been talking about, but you have to understand that these are of interest to me and I want access to you whenever these come up." He said to me, "I will guarantee you personally, I will never undercut qualitatively, quantitatively."

I said, "Okay." I walked out. I still wasn't persuaded. I still was not going to vote. This went on all night long, and my wife, Diane, who is a Zionist, said, "What are you going to do?" I said, "I really don't know. I haven't yet decided." This went on until the next day — noontime. I had lunch. I went off with John Tower, who is a good friend. I just talked to him. I told him I was still undecided. The phones were ringing. I had the Jewish group — they were really banging my door. They were a lot of friends. Then someone grabbed me as I tried to go through the doors of the Senate. They put their arm across me. And they said, "Bill, we want to talk to —" I said, "Excuse me, I am going into the chamber." They said, "No, you can't go," and they stood in my way. I said, "You get the hell out of my way." I pushed a guy out of my way — he was trying to block it so I couldn't get into the chamber. I went to see Howard Baker and I said, "Howard, how many votes do you have?" He said, "I've got forty-nine." I said, "What about Russell Long?" He said, "He ain't talking." I went through a list of other persons, and then he said, "Bill, why don't you do this? Why don't you wait until the vote is in and then you can see how it shakes down and then you can decide." I said, "No, I'm not going to do that." I said, "I'll tell you what. Give me a half hour and let me take a walk." I went out and I walked all the way down the Mall and back, deciding what I was going to do, and I finally walked up and I came through the chamber door and I said to Howard, "I need some time." He said, "You've got ten minutes." I said, "Uh-uh. I need at least twenty." The time was running out and he said, "Okay, you've got it." So I walked out onto the floor and I made this speech, which was a tough one for me to make, but I decided that I did not want Russell Long to be the deciding vote. I did not want an oil state to bail out Ronald Reagan so that he would be the one that would be deciding future decisions affecting Israeli security. I wanted him to be indebted to me, if anybody, so that the next time I was going to be able to at least say, "Wait a minute; no more sales on this and this and this and whatever, and you've got to help out on the following attitude we talked about." And that's why I did it.

The reaction of the Jewish community was just vicious. I mean, it was brutal. I got on a plane and went back to Portland and got a group of all the local Jewish people together, my biggest supporters. Back to Bangor the same way. I said, "Look, I'm not going to give you as much detail. Believe me, there is a reason for it, and it has to do with Israeli security. There are things that are far more important. This is symbolic, and what they're upset about is we're doing business with the Saudis, but the Israelis can take those five aircraft out on a moment's notice. There's something that's much more important to them." I didn't go into too much detail with them. But I said one vote, and that's it. But apparently it was so bitter because, number one, my name was Cohen, number two, it hurt them to think that a half Jew at least would "sell them out." And them not realizing that the fact of the matter is that I was doing more to protect Israeli security than these five planes.

But that was 1981. It's been a good five years of just rebuilding. In a way I felt fairly liberated, to tell you the truth, because I was so angry about it. They were so emotional and so passionate that they would not even listen to an intellectual argument. I said, "The hell with you; I'm going to continue to do what I'm doing."

I think most of the bridges have been repaired, though there's always an element of doubt in their minds now. But I'm getting the same treatment from the veterans. I cast a vote a while ago, so the veterans disinvited me to a convention. I flew all the way to Bangor and found they wouldn't let me speak.

Do I accept the fact that the old problem of "he is but he's not" will dog me for the rest of my life? No, not dog me, because I've become relatively immune to it. I've been away from it so long, it's just part of me; that's all. But my kids have not had that. In my mind, I did not want them to have the same experiences, even though times have changed. There was a time when I was twelve years old I went to a place called Lucerne Beach. It had a sign: NO DOGS, NO JEWS ALLOWED. But that's long since past, and they have never experienced the same kind of conflict. I have a Kevin and a Christopher, and that's sort of to offset the name as such, because immediately everyone knows they're not Jewish. So they don't have to deal with that.

Joan Benny, Beverly Hills, California

I do some teaching and some lecturing; most of the time I'm just enjoying my freedom. I don't do much of anything.

I think there was a Jewish component in Hollywood, but it was something I didn't realize until I was an adult. I certainly wasn't aware of it as a child, or if I was, it rolled off my back. It wasn't quite as important to me as my activities in school and my friends and playing jacks and skipping rope or whatever it was I was doing. Yes, it was there, but it didn't seem to affect me. It's only looking back on it that I really can see the almost cliques. I was not raised Jewish by religion. I think my parents at one time sent me to temple Sunday school. I had a very strange upbringing, really, as far as religion was concerned. I think my parents' religion — certainly my father's — was show business. You were a good person if you were doing well. It didn't really matter what church you went to or what color your skin was or anything else. If you were a headliner, you were fine. That was the religion.

My parents' best friends, as I think most people were aware, were the George Burnses. My father and George Burns really were joined at the hip, just the way the columns said they were.

My dad never worked the Catskills. He didn't think of himself, and he wasn't obviously — as anybody who remembers his act and his radio show and whatever — a Jewish comic. I would say Milton Berle, who did work the Catskills, I guess, was a semi-Jewish comic. There are those such as Shecky Greene — they're Jewish comics. My father was not a Jewish comic. George Burns never did a Jewish act. He never told Jewish jokes. My father never told Jewish jokes.

The Burnses adopted a little girl the same year, the same time. I don't know who did it first or whether one followed the other or whether it became the thing to do. I'm not sure. We both were adopted at the same time and we were literally raised together. We went to different schools, but we spent weekend nights together. Sandy's mother, Gracie Allen, was an Irish Catholic. So Sandra was raised Catholic. She used to say that she was Catholic six days of the week and on Friday she was Jewish, because she hated fish. And every Friday they had to have fish — back in those days when you couldn't have meat on Friday.

Because I spent Saturday nights with her, frequently I simply went to church with her on Sunday or to Sunday school or whatever. So I think as far as religion was concerned I spent far more time in the Catholic church than I did in the temple. My parents didn't go to temple, not even on Yom Kippur. There was never any question about their Jewishness. They were Jewish, but they weren't religious.

I didn't really know my father's parents. His mother died long before I was born. His father died when I was six or seven. I hardly knew him, and he had retired and lived in Florida before his death. My mother's parents lived in Los Angeles near us, and I spent a lot of time with them. They were not religious the way you think of people's grandparents from the old country. I believe my grandfather, as I recall, read the Jewish paper, whatever that was called. They never spoke in Yiddish or anything. My grandfather came from Rumania, I believe, and he spoke with a bit of an accent. My grandmother was raised in Denver. I don't remember them going to temple. I remember that my grandmother cooked semi-Jewish meals. She used to make something that I loved, which was rendered chicken fat and gribiness. But I don't remember ever having gefilte fish or anything like that, and I don't remember the meals being Jewish meals. They never talked much about religion. I don't even know if they went to temple on Yom Kippur.

I think my first seder dinner was probably ten years ago. I mean I'd never been to a seder dinner. It simply wasn't a part of our lives. My parents decided I should have some religious training, which was sort of a laugh. It wasn't anything terribly serious, but it was like "Maybe she should go to temple." So I went to Sunday school. I think I went about three times, and thought it was boring. Any kid in school doesn't want to have to go back to school on Sunday. Sunday to me was sleeping late and playing around. So I didn't want to go, and I didn't like it, and I used to read comic books behind whatever I was supposed to be reading. I don't think I learned anything. I went three times, and that was the end of it. Nobody ever made a fuss about it. It was, like, I don't want to go anymore. Oh, okay, fine, and I never went again.

I'm embarrassed to say I've only been in a temple once in my entire life. I think I was eighteen years old and went to somebody's funeral, and I've never been in a temple since.

I have very strange feelings about being Jewish. I have a Jewish soul. I certainly think of myself as being Jewish. For some reason in my head, I separate the religion. I'm perfectly comfortable going to Catholic church. I'm a Zionist; I wouldn't drive a German car.

Looking back, I remember that when I think of my parents' close friends, they tended to be Jewish. I wasn't aware of it at the time, but I think there were the kind of cliques. I think the Gary Coopers and the Jimmy Stewarts and the John Waynes, which were the sort of Gentile group of people, had their group of friends. My parents' group of friends were the George Burnses and people who tended to be mostly Jewish. The kids I played with, who were my parents' friends' children when I was very young, were Barbara Warner, Jack Warner's daughter, Jules Stein's two daughters, Jean and Susan, Deedee Lemaire, whose father was Jewish in spite of the name, which had been changed. My closest friend was Barbara Goetz, who was Louis B. Mayer's granddaughter, Edie and Bill Goetz's daughter. My friends were for the most part Jewish. I don't think I was aware of it. Looking back, I remember when my public school had so many kids in the class that they divided it into two sections. It seems to me, and it's a vague recollection, they even divided the Jewish kids into one section and the Gentile kids into the other. I'm not sure that's true, but it seems to me.

Back then, Beverly Hills was not as it is today, ninety-five percent Jewish.

It was maybe fifty percent, maybe thirty-five percent, but not what it is today. At least half the kids in my class were not Jewish. The school did not close on Jewish holidays. Today the Beverly Hills public schools close on Jewish holidays, because there's nobody to go, including the teachers. As a matter of fact, I've had a few arguments with the principal when my kids were in school about what they laughingly called the "holiday program," because you couldn't use the word Christmas. When I went to school we sang Christmas carols and we had a Christmas program. Each of the classes sang two songs, and all the traditional carols were sung. Today, and when my kids were in school, each class still does two or three songs, but it's now a holiday program and supposedly they sing holiday songs from all over the world.

However, I find it fascinating that when the first grade gets up to sing, they sing a German song — you can't call it a carol — a German song, a French song, and a Jewish song. The second grade gets up and they sing an English song, a Swedish song, and a Jewish song. It's hysterical. Everyone has a Jewish song, a Chanukah song, somewhere in there. You go through the entire eight grades, and there isn't one traditional Christmas carol. The mention of Christ doesn't happen. The little school orchestra plays, very badly, "Silent Night," and finally the eighth grade sings "Adeste Fideles," but they don't sing it in English, which I just think is fascinating. I went to the school principal and really argued about that.

I was asking him to be fair. Would somebody object? It's okay to sing a Chanukah song, but how about "We Three Kings of Orient Are" or "O Little Town of Bethlehem." This is the Christmas season and there's a whole big world out there that celebrates Christmas.

We always had a Christmas tree, and I've always had a Christmas tree for my children. We never did Chanukah. But again, that's a kind of state-of-mind sort of thing. I realize there are a lot of Jewish people who think I'm nuts, or think what I do is terrible, or whatever. Because they don't have that kind of thing in the schools anymore, I sit at the piano and we play Christmas carols. I've taught my children Christmas carols, because they grew up not knowing any of those songs, and not knowing the lyrics. They're beautiful songs. You don't have to believe in it. It's a nice story. I read the New Testament — Saint Matthew, Saint Mark, and Saint Luke. We listen to *Messiah*, which is one of my great favorites. It isn't a matter of religion. It's a beautiful story. The birth of Christ is a lovely story. You don't have to be religious about that. Since most of the world believes in that, you should know it.

Were my parents members of the Hillcrest Country Club? Oh, yes, of course. I learned to play tennis there. I spent a lot of time there. I wasn't a golf player, but they had tennis courts. All of my little friends in school, whatever, we all played tennis there. Of course I knew it was a Jewish country club, and of course I knew that there were clubs we couldn't belong to because we were Jewish. I was aware of all that. It didn't affect my life.

Was it true that my dad couldn't belong to certain clubs? Absolutely. Of course, there's the famous L.A. Country Club. The L.A. Country Club is, interestingly enough, right in Beverly Hills. At least, part of the club is in Beverly Hills. Not only did they not take Jews; they don't take actors and never did. They had one actor in that club, who, I believe, was Randolph Scott. I believe this is still true today. It was for years and years. No actors and no Jews in the L.A. Country Club. The clubs were absolutely divided. Hillcrest and Brentwood were the two Jewish clubs, and all the rest were not.

Did my dad or mother ever talk about it? No, not really. I take that back. Yes, I suppose they did. Whether there was anti-Semitism; in looking back, I suppose there was. Being Jewish or Gentile was — I guess the best way to say it — just so unimportant in my life that I didn't dwell on it. I didn't think much about it. When I went to college, I was aware of being Jewish, but I didn't have a problem. I went to Stanford. Perhaps at another school I might have. But we had no sororities at Stanford, so there was never the problem of being in a Jewish or non-Jewish sorority. The boys I dated I don't think I ever asked. I had a mother-in-law who if you said you had lunch with So-and-so, would say, "Is she Jewish?" It was her first question. That's something that never occurred to me to even ask.

Were my children raised Jewish? No. I don't know whether that was good or bad, but since I had no religious convictions I . . . In a way, perhaps I'm a little bit sorry, because they don't have any identification. I suppose maybe they should have. But it doesn't seem to affect their lives either.

Was there ever any talk of Palestine or Israel at home? Or among the Jewish community? At home, no. Among the Jewish community, yes. But that all came much later.

I was not aware of any Jewish networking in Hollywood. I felt very much that if you were talented, you were okay, and if you weren't, you weren't invited anymore. You know how Hollywood works. There really isn't Hollywood today. Hollywood doesn't exist today the way it did at that time. It's all quite different. I think, if anything, there must be less feeling. I think today there's far more tolerance or less anti-Semitism or certainly more acceptance. And Beverly Hills is certainly a very Jewish community. Amazing how many Mercedes there are.

Do I feel a tug back now a little bit to Judaism? It's not a tug. It's something I've felt for a long time. For me it was a strange experience. I think William Shirer's book *The Rise and Fall of the Third Reich* was published when I was in my early to mid twenties. I read it, and it changed my life. That book was what changed my life, because I had always gone merrily on my way, living in a world with blinders like a horse, doing my thing, having a good time, getting married, having children, et cetera. I never really gave it much thought. Anything I had heard kind of rolled off my back. I was very young during the war. I had heard about the Holocaust, but it didn't really mean very much. It was sort of history and a long way away, and it didn't really affect me. It was reading that book that did it, the whole long chapter on the Holocaust. I read it with wide eyes, like, my God, this really happened. It not only really happened, but it happened to my people, and there but for the grace of God, that could have been me. It was so powerful, that book literally changed my life. That was when all of a sudden, my God, I am Jewish. These are my people.

I didn't discuss it with my parents. It was very personal. I went through many years of never wanting to hear about it again. It's too powerful. I remember there was a television show on a Leon Uris book, *QB VII*, I think, and it dealt with that. My husband said, "We're going to watch it." He wanted to see it. And I said, "I don't think I can watch this." He said, "You're being ridiculous. I know how you feel about it, but this was a long time ago. Sit down and watch it with me." And I did, and I couldn't watch it. I got hysterical and ran upstairs. I just can't deal with it. I'll never go to Germany. I don't want any part of it.

Did I ever ask my parents about being Jewish? What is it to be a Jew? No. My parents weren't people you could talk to about that; at least I never felt I could.

21

The Exclusionary Principle

THE SOCIOECONOMICS of prejudice proved to be a riveting repetition. I learned, for example, what some historians had learned well before me. In many a small town of America where the non-Jewish community could afford to build and to maintain a country club, Jews were excluded. Where the country club developers needed the financial help of Jewish townspeople, principally merchants, Jews were admitted.

Not surprisingly, a similar economic criterion was applied by German Jews, who were just as restrictive about keeping Eastern Europeans from their social and country clubs. Bernard Nordlinger, a lifelong native of Washington, D.C., recalled:

"The Woodmont Country Club is today a great civic institution; broad in its scope for Jews of all origins. I think that of the thirty-three or thirty-five Jewish congregations in this area, twenty-nine are represented in the club. At the time I came up, my father was a member. It didn't cost very much. It was modest. It wasn't anything compared to what it is today. It was way below the level of the Christian clubs in the area. They had maybe 100, 150 members, and it wasn't until a man named Morris Simon tried to help the club from going into bankruptcy in the early 1930s that non-German Jews were widely sought as members, and came in in great droves. Before then, it was almost totally a German Jewish group."

Dorothy Wershow, who was raised in Ocala in the north of Florida, has another view of the socioeconomics of prejudice. She said she "can remember going down to south Florida, and you could tell what kind of a season they had by the signs outside the hotels. CHRISTIANS ONLY meant it was a good season. If the sign wasn't there and they took anybody, it was a poor season. I'm talking about in the 1930s through World War II.

"There's also the story," she remarked, "told of Bernard Baruch [the

financial giant who was a confidant of Franklin Delano Roosevelt], who
went to Winter Park outside of Orlando. He went up to the hotel and when
they saw the name Baruch, they said, 'No.' It was only as he picked up his
bags to leave that they realized who he was. Then they said, oh, they'd
made a mistake; they had room. His answer was 'You didn't make the
mistake. I made the mistake.' "

Edward Elliott Elson, fifty-one, business executive, Atlanta, Georgia

I was at Andover from 1948 to 1952. I'll tell you an extraordinary story
about that. We were required to take a social problems course and a Bible
course — history of Bible. They were both taught by A. Graham Baldwin,
who was the school minister and a lovely man. Indeed, a very kind and
concerned and compassionate man. In my senior year I was taking social
problems and we were reading *Gentleman's Agreement*, which had recently
been published. I raised my hand, and said, "Mr. Baldwin, this book speaks
of quotas and discrimination. Why, we have quotas here at Andover." He
said, "That's absurd." I said, "I don't understand, sir, we have 720 boys
in 1948 and 72 Jewish students, 730 boys in 1949 and 73 Jewish students,
and 740 boys . . ." He vehemently denied any type of quota system existing
at Andover. Of course, being a senior and seventeen, eighteen years old, I
wasn't going to argue further.

He went into a great sermon one day about the importance of theological
background in any person's life. I raised my hand again and said, "Sir, I
don't understand something." He said, "What's that, Elson?" Of course, I
was then and now the gadfly of the class. If he knew tuppence, he would
have said, "Elson, that's where you're a pain." So I said, "Reverend Baldwin,
obviously you feel that a religious background is important in the development of any student here, and obviously you feel theology plays a great
role and a special role in the development of a person's personality and
character. Obviously the school feels that it's essential for us to take courses
in the Bible and to discover courses such as this, which involve social problems, so that we can be made aware of those issues of decency that exist
in the general community or should be addressed by graduates of this school
in the general community. Obviously you feel that it's important for this
to be further imbued in us through requiring us to go to chapel for five
days every week and requiring us to go to church on Sunday. Out of the
seven days of the week, you require us to be in attendance six days. The
only day that we aren't required to go is the one day my religion enjoins
me to go, and that's Saturday." I said, "Indeed, whereas I am told to observe
all the religious holidays of the school except be they Christmas or whatever,

I am not allowed to go to a seder for Passover, my religious holiday, nor am I allowed to be excused from school during Yom Kippur or Rosh Hashonah. I don't understand the application of your theory regarding religion and character."

He was shocked. He couldn't believe it. It was the first time since 1778, when the school was founded, that someone had bothered to ask a question about Jewish students. Well, twenty-some-odd years later I returned for a reunion. I'm with my wife, Susie, and I'm taking her around to show her the school and I walk into the chapel. It's a magnificent chapel, and way in the back is an elderly man, white-haired at this point. He turns around and sees me.

I have to tell you this: I went back to Andover and nobody remembered me. The only person who knew me was the fellow at the clothing store, because I spent so much time there. But no one else in the school knew me. By the way, an aside: subsequently I became extraordinarily active in the school — served on the alumni board for many years, headed up their campaign for the Addison Gallery of American Art, and still I'm now on their executive committee for the development of the school, and intimately involved. All of our sons went there; one of our sons taught there for three years. So we are partly family, so to speak.

However, at this particular point in history when I returned, no one knew who I was. I walked into the chapel and no one remembered me. And this elderly man way at the end of the chapel turns around and says, "Ed Elson," and he comes running up. I said, "Reverend Baldwin," and I said, "I'd like you to meet my —" and I started to say "my wife, Susie." He interrupted me and said, "I want to take you downstairs and show you where we have a chapel for the Jewish students to worship." That had been on his mind for twenty-five years or twenty, whatever. And he saw me after all of that time and remembered. They do have a synagogue in the chapel now. And they have a Jewish chaplain, full time, on the faculty. I don't think it occurred because of my conversation in 1951 in that social problems course, but I do think it had an effect on him, and he was the man who brought about the recognition that there were a lot of Jewish students and it was important that their religious needs be satisfied.

I have discovered that Jews are Jews, period. We use the word "goyim," which means other people. Gentiles in the South — indeed, everywhere I've found, but in the South, which I can speak of principally because it's been my home for my entire life except for a year or two — in the South, *we* are the "other people." No matter how well we are accepted individually, no matter how well we are liked, no matter how well we are integrated in the community, no matter how affluent we are or beneficent we are with our funds, no matter how cultivated or educated we are, no matter how ebullient or friendly we are, we are still "other people." I have never known any Jew at any time at any city in the South to be accepted, period. You can go back historically in Atlanta with Dick Rich. Dick Rich's family was one of the oldest families in Atlanta, early pioneer family, whose family owned one of the largest businesses; indeed, perhaps the largest business in Atlanta. He was the quintessential citizen. He was chairman of everything from the Metropolitan Transportation Authority to the Fine Arts Center. Whatever it was, Dick Rich was the head of, but he couldn't eat lunch downtown at a private club. He had to eat in the store.

And from Dick Rich to today, that pattern continues and persists. I had always felt that I or someone can change it. I don't believe it can be changed, because quite simply it's not bigotry any longer; it's habit. And no one is willing to challenge it, because we are quote "different" to them. We are Jews.

Some years ago, the American Jewish Committee was concerned as to how they should involve themselves in the early civil rights movement events here in Atlanta. I remember at one of those meetings — I was quite young then — saying that I think that this is going to be very beneficial to us as Jews, and I said this in a facetious way: "I think that the blacks will break down the barriers for us because of their confrontational tactics. It will then eventually yield to our benefit. Whereas we have never been able to eliminate barriers, they will, and we will ride their coattails, contrary to what most people felt: that they would ride our coattails." I said that our problems are social in nature; their problems are economic. Interestingly enough, that's what happened in the Junior League. They took in black women prior to taking in Jewish women, because the blacks confronted the issue, whereas the Jews were never really strong enough or willing enough to do it.

Have I thought why Jews would want to join the Junior League? I've thought of that quite a bit. Indeed, I've spent my entire adult life thinking about it, because I have done it in the context of social club discrimination, which is the same. You cannot live a complete life in a community, you cannot be a part of the total community, unless you take part in all activities in that community. That is to say, if I have a great friend who is a non-Jew who belongs to a club that excludes Jews, I can only be with him, perhaps, half the day, not the full day. In other words, if I didn't have a tennis court at home, which I do, and I wanted to play tennis with him, I couldn't go to the club for tennis. I couldn't have a drink at the club after tennis.

There was an incident where our son went up the street. Here's a son who's president of the Fly Club at Harvard, a graduate of Andover, a graduate of Eton, and he goes up the street to play tennis with a friend of his at a club that restricts itself in admitting Jews as members. One of the fellows turns to him and says, "How come you don't belong to this club, Lewis?" And another fellow says, "Well, hell, Lewis can't; he's a Jew." Now that camaraderie is broken by that little incident. The fact is that if I were to become chairman of the Citizens and Southern Bank, and I'm a director, or if I were to become president of Southern Bell Telephone Company, I couldn't be admitted into the most important business community, which is the Piedmont Driving Club or the Capital City Club or the P Street Golf Club, where more business is done than is done at any office.

Business as you know is not done across a desk at that level. It's done through personal communication and the accessibility and credibility that the union of affluency and being in the power circle gives you.

I've been quite involved with social club discrimination over the years. What I generally do is write a letter any time a civic event is held at a social club that systematically excludes Jews from membership. The letter generally ends up with the line: "I think the event should reflect those same civilized and civilizing values that the organization itself embodies, and therefore, it is inconsistent to hold it at a club that practices systematic exclusion." Usually these events are for the purpose of raising funds, and usually when you're raising funds you want to put people in the most comfortable setting in which they can be, and a Jew is always uncomfortable at a social club which deems him undesirable. Even more important, I go into the uncivilized aspect of the entire situation and how obscene it really is.

Susie and I move very freely in the general community. Susie is on the board and an officer of the High Museum; she's on the board and the executive committee of the symphony; she's secretary of the Metropolitan Opera of Atlanta, which never had Jews on their board until recent years; she was president of the Mental Health Association. You name the organization in Atlanta. Nationally, Susie is a trustee of Fiske University and of the American Craft Council. I've been nominated as a trustee of the American Federation of the Arts. We serve as co-chairmen of the Southeastern Center for Contemporary Arts in Winston-Salem, North Carolina, the museum started by the Haines family. There's a significant enough involvement in Atlanta — Susie's also a trustee of the Arts Council. I mention Susie specifically, because you mentioned the Junior League. So Susie is considered one of the leaders in this community as far as the arts and civic affairs go. Therefore, obviously, we move very easily with that group of people. You mentioned earlier the name of a very prominent Atlanta citizen. If she had to name her five or ten closest friends, we would be included. And I can say that for a dozen of the most respected community people in Atlanta, but we can't go to the same club.

Where do people go when you have a union of friends? You have a family; you do everything together. The incompleteness, the inability to belong to a club, suggests in itself an inferior-superior relationship, and a less desirable relationship. We are the undesirables. It has to affect our relationship. That's why it's important. If I sell my business, as most Jewish businesses are being sold these days, the great mercantile businesses, my sons would then have to go into general businesses, whether they be a bank, a utility, whatever type of manufacturing corporation. To rise to the top of that organization, they would have to participate in the total community. By being excluded from membership in clubs, systematically excluded, their chance to reach that top spot would be further limited. That's why it's important.

You can't feel the tension unless you involve yourself to the degree that suggests there can be a tension, a cutting edge. I'll give you an example. I'm going to give you my credentials so that you'll see the odd juxtaposition. I served as the vice-chairman of the Stadium Authority here for eight years, where we have professional athletics. I served as chairman of the Civil Rights Commission here for eight years, the Georgia advisory committee of the U.S. Athletic Commission. On and on and on as far as general activities. I was the first chairman and founded public radio in the United States. I also served as chairman of *Commentary* magazine; I'm treasurer of the American Jewish Committee; I'm a trustee of the Jewish Publication Society; I was vice-president and am a trustee of the Jewish Historical Society at this moment; and I'm very conscious of and involved in my Jewishness. I am not a religious Jew, but I'm a committed Jew. I am religious, but not in the traditional sense of religion.

I see no reason why I should be asked to change a historic peoplehood, an involvement with the people that has become intertwined with the religion itself. I accept that, and I feel very proud of it, satisfied with it. When I say pride, I'm not saying I'm better than they are. I'm saying that I'm satisfied. My own image of myself as a Jew gives me no reason to think that I should not be a Jew. I don't need an easy way out, because I'm satisfied. I've accomplished a lot within the general community. The only thing I'm saying is I can never be a total part of the general community as long as I'm a Jew, because the general community looks at Jews as a separate, almost a cocoon-like group of people who evolved within this . . .

What was the Vonnegut book about the fellow living in the glass jar? That's what we are to the general community. We could be great guys and nice people and generous and gracious. I'm on the board of this great British company, and I was at a meeting in England last week. The people involved could not have been nicer. I was at the University of Virginia; I'm on its board. This week they're meeting, and the people there could not have been more gracious. But I'm still always the Jewish representative to some degree. They always tell you their Jewish story. Always; you wait for it to come.

No matter how much you think you're one of the gang, you are, except you're set aside. Not unfriendly, not malevolently, but they're trying to be nice to say "Look, you're okay, don't let it worry you."

Do I find that true in business, or is it only in social affairs? Definitely in business. I have experienced very little overt anti-Semitism anywhere in my life. I had an incident at Andover when I was a kid. It was nothing. Business: I've had someone when they thought that the deal was too good; that it was because I was a Jew that I was able to pull off such a good deal. I've had that, but the strangeness is in business.

The story of Susie's family is rather an extraordinary story. I don't think it's unique, but it's unusual in the accomplishments that were made by her grandfather. Susie's family was without question *the* Jewish family at the turn of the century and beyond in Memphis. Her grandfather had the bank and most of the real estate and the big textile mills. He had three sons; one went to Washington and Lee and wasn't too successful as a student; another went to Dartmouth and Harvard; the other to Pennsylvania and to Harvard, Cambridge — all superbly educated, all given great dowries to begin, all having unusual accomplishments in the community. Susie's daddy was chairman of the black college board for thirty years. He was head of the United Way, the Community Chest, whatever. One of her uncles was one of the great men in American history. They're people of significance and affluence. But after more than a hundred years they still can't belong to a club in Memphis.

Susie's mother's family — one branch was from Kansas City and Saint Joe, Missouri; the other branch was from Opelika, Alabama, and West Point, Georgia. One of the West Point crowd was a sergeant in the Confederate Army and was captured and imprisoned in Baltimore. One of them was the founder of the temple here in Atlanta. On the other side, one of her cousins was Harry Truman's lawyer and signed his will. John Kander, who won a Tony as composer and lyricist of *Cabaret*, was her cousin. *The Settlement Cook Book* was written by her great-great-aunt, Mrs. Simon Kander. That's the great Jewish cookbook. Her family really is a microcosm of American Jewish history, of going back to that era, the Civil War.

You ask why I'm a Jew? That's why I'm a Jew. It's all in everything is why I'm a Jew.

When I was at the University of Virginia, the yearbook listed all the fraternities — a page was devoted to each individual fraternity. The fraternities were listed in Greek letter order, from *alpha* through *zeta*, except for the three Jewish fraternities. There were Jewish fraternities, of course, because the Jews did not belong to any other fraternities at the university. The three Jewish fraternities — one was Alpha Epsilon Pi, another was Phi Epsilon Pi, and the third was Zeta Beta Tau — were listed together. In this great block from *alpha* to *zeta* of fraternities, the three Jewish fraternities were listed right together, smack in the middle of all the other fraternities. It was always something that I not only found to be offensive, but it dominated my existence and my career at the university — that being set apart. I was taken into one of the secret societies at the university. I went back to their records. There were four other names I could identify as being Jewish for a hundred years back. There were numerous other secret societies, and only a handful, a literal handful — I mean five students or less — could ever have been counted as having been members of these organizations. The reason you couldn't be a member of the organization was that generally the fraternity system proposed you, since the fraternity system dominated the university life. If you weren't a member of the "in" fraternity, you weren't available for proposal unless you had achieved significant accomplishments — so significant that it was impossible to deny you the recognition. The problem with being a Jewish student in those days was that you had to do twice as much as anyone else in order to be so recognized. And that, too, truly was a part of our everyday being.

Susan Goodman Elson, forty-seven, business executive, Atlanta, Georgia

I go by the name of Susie. I am vice-president of marketing of Elson's, which is our family-owned company, and I'm also involved in a number of philanthropic and cultural activities.

I grew up in Memphis, Tennessee. My family was a very prominent Jewish family in the city. My grandfather had made one of the great real estate fortunes. He had owned a bank. He was a fascinating man, actually. His name was Abe Goodman. He came from Mississippi, and before that I think his family had come from Pennsylvania. I don't know exactly how he got from Pennsylvania to Mississippi, but the story as I know it begins in Mississippi, where he was an overseer on a strawberry plantation. He came to Memphis selling strawberries.

He had several brothers, and together they founded a tremendous fortune in Memphis. He started by being a liquor distiller and distributor. He knew all the telegraphers in each of the little towns in Mississippi, and they became his distributors. Then Prohibition came, and of course he closed his liquor business, and became a banker. He was in the real estate business and various other enterprises. After the Crash came in 1929, he inherited several other major businesses in Memphis, of which my father eventually became the chairman. They were independent manufacturers. They owned the American Finishing Company, which manufactured ninety percent of all the khaki in World War II. It was an interesting family.

My grandfather was a rugged individualist who in his mid thirties, I guess, developed diabetes. They told him he had one year to live. So he said, "If I have only one year to live, I'm going to live." He took his three sons, his wife, and the black chauffeur around the world for a year. By the time they got home they had discovered insulin, and he became one of the oldest users of insulin in the United States. He lived to be eighty-five years old. He was an amazing man.

My father's grandfather, Colonel Wolf, was involved in the war on the southern side. I think he was in the Battle of Atlanta. He was wounded at Kennesaw Mountain and then captured.

On my mother's side, her family was from Kansas City, although her grandmother grew up in Atlanta and moved to Kansas City when she was married. My mother's father was one of the early graduates of the University of Michigan Law School, and went into the family business in Kansas City. They were tobacco distributors, and they were the largest tobacco distributors west of the Mississippi for many years. My mother's great-aunt Lizzi Kander wrote *The Settlement Cook Book*. She grew up in Milwaukee and the story goes she lived with her three bachelor brothers, each of whom weighed 350 pounds because she tried all of her recipes on them before she published them. She would have pancake month, and they would live on pancakes, and the next month they would go to waffles. She was a great character. That family — John Kander, the songwriter, is a direct descendant of the *Settlement Cook Book* lady. That's on my mother's side of the family. Both had German roots.

My father had two brothers. His older brother was quite a prominent lawyer in Memphis and was active in World War II; he was liaison with all of the European air forces. He moved to Washington during the war. His name was Colonel William Goodman. He enlisted as a colonel, which was rather a bizarre thing. He had polio and he was in the hospital in Washington and met Eleanor Roosevelt. She took a liking to him. I think that's what helped his career. He had a fascinating life there. He met many of the important people who he followed all through his life.

One of the stories about him that was so interesting was that he decided to go to Russia. He was a great traveler. This was during the Iron Curtain years — in 1957, when no one was going to Russia as a tourist. He decided that he wanted to go and take his wife. He gets a letter back to come as a guest of the government. Marshal Zhukov was in power at that time, and Marshal Zhukov had been his friend during World War II. So he went as a guest of the government and they had a perfectly marvelous time with a bugged room and a wonderful guide and all the other things that one expects. One night they went to the ballet, and there's an empty seat next to them. In the middle of the ballet someone comes in and introduces himself and says, "Are you Colonel Goodman?" He says, "Yes, I am." The other man says, "I'm Guy Burgess." He was the first person to see Guy Burgess after he defected. His life was full of fascinating stories like that.

I went to Randolph-Macon in Virginia, which was a typical southern girl's college of that era — 1955. I went there because my mother's best friend at Wellesley was the dean of Randolph-Macon. So she encouraged me to go there. It was a very fine school intellectually. I think it was an excellent education, not particularly liberal, just straightforward, lots of Latin and that sort of thing. But being the only Jewish student — there was another girl there who was half Jewish, and she really didn't identify. There must have been between eight hundred and a thousand students then. There were sororities on campus, not important particularly, but they were sort of social clubs where you could go and take a date and that kind of thing. I was immediately rushed by various sororities. Of course, it reached a point where they had to say to me, "Well, we're very sorry, but we wouldn't want to embarrass you by asking you to take the Christian oath." It was a very southern, genteel way of putting it. I made some wonderful lifelong friends there and everyone knew that I was Jewish, and I made a point of letting them know. I did not date Gentile boys. I only dated Jewish boys. I had a marvelous time, because there were all these wonderful Jewish fraternities at Washington and Lee and at Virginia, and there were no girls. So I had a delightful time. It was very pleasant.

Epilogue

THE WORST MOMENT in the preparation of this book was when I came to the realization that I would have to stop interviewing. In all my years as a newsman, I never had had quite as much sustained fun, been as consumed, enjoyed as many people, and listened to such moving accounts of history, struggle, joy, anguish, delight, apprehension, achievement, loss, and love.

Many times during this odyssey I tried to imagine myself in some far-off land, saying good-bye to my daughters, Anna, Isabel, Julie, and Rebecca, and sending them off to America, singly or together, perhaps never to see them again; or saying good-bye to Tod, my wife, as I embarked alone on a journey to the other side of the world, to arrive, if at all, illiterate in the language of the new land and penniless. When I thought of either experience, I was seized with terror, because both seemed overwhelming and impossible, and yet millions and millions of immigrants — Jew and non-Jew — have lived through them.

I wanted to begin this book with a quote from Shirley Povich, the one with which he began his narrative about growing up Jewish in Bar Harbor, Maine:

"I knew my grandfather as a one-eyed man. He had one eye deliberately put out by his friends in Lithuania, a common custom of Jewish boys being voluntarily maimed to escape service in the Czar's army."

And I wanted to end it with a quote from Minnie Schreiber, who grew up in Brunswick, Georgia, and whose father left Poland, like Povich's grandfather, to escape the Russian army and who settled initially in Little Green, Georgia. She told me that the only time she saw her father cry "was the time I went to Washington and took him with me to sightsee and we walked through the Capitol chambers and we stopped in the Senate. Congress was not in session. And he started to cry, because he had never lived in a country where he could walk around as a free citizen."

But I decided, rather, to let Leonard Garment's voice give penultimate expression to the American Jewish experience for our generation, and then add my own voice. Garment characterized growing up Jewish fifty years ago in New York City as being derivative of "the nature of our parents' experience and all of the excitement and the difficulty and the promise of this wonderful land because the gates were open to endless opportunity." He added: "Some from that generation, spurred on by the immediacy of the immigrant experience visited upon them morning, noon, and night by their parents, moved in the direction of all these vast openings — into schools, into worlds of poetry, literature, law, business, making it. And very much the core experience was that of making it. I mean making it either in a financial way or making it in terms of security; making it into the larger American world; half making it into the great experience of assimilation. The melting pot melted a lot of people, but it didn't melt that generation of Jews."

Rather, said Garment, that generation was made "crankier and more ambivalent about all of their experiences as they shed some of the immigrant culture of their parents and inherited some of the new experiences of the American world and were caught between tradition and experimentation with all the amazing riches of the new land."

In the case of my generation, the past is epilogue, a rich and robust past. Today's American Jewish generation and the generations to follow face the prospect of far fewer Jews in America's future, not more; of a loss — if it has not already taken place — of Yiddishkeit, that self-sealing religious and cultural membrane that swaddled Jewish communities; a loss, too, of a good deal of the societal cement that kept the family together, the divorce rate low, and value of religious fervor high; and a further loss of the richness of the bubbe mayses, the grandmothers' tales that sprang from Yiddishkeit and the ghetto and the feeling of feeling different. If assimilation is success, it also can mean failure — a failure of identity.

As for anti-Semitism, it is here to stay, now dormant, now activated, now dormant again. The pardon of Leo Frank, given grudgingly after seventy years and clear evidence of his innocence, is symbolic.

But Jews are here to stay, too. And their experience over two hundred years ought serve as a paradigm for new immigrants who make their way to America and then make their way in America. Jewish times are not always good times or bad times, but they are always telling times.

ACKNOWLEDGMENTS

GLOSSARY

Acknowledgments

This book, like everything else I accomplish, would not have been possible without the love, help, and support of Tod Simons, who does not suffer fools gladly save this one. I want to thank Marc Jaffe, my editor, who from concept to conclusion has been enthusiastic, a joy to work with and to work for. I also want to thank Frances Apt for her rigorous and caring editing, without which this book could not have gone to press, and Carol Melamed for her wise counsel. I also owe a profound debt of gratitude to the scores of people I interviewed whose voices are not heard in this volume, victims of that painful institutional limitation called "space."

Finally, the following people responded unhesitatingly to my call for help and I thank them: Commander Steve Becker, Charles Berlin, Abraham S. Chanin, Sarah Flynn, Eugene Friend, Michael Gartner, Tom Gibboney, Ben Goldberg, Will Gross, Ed Guthman, Art Harris, Laurie Kahn-Leavitt, Myer Kessler, Jonathan Kleinbard, Paul Kulick, Pearl A. Laufer, Ben and Magda Leuchter, David Lipman, Jean Meltzer, Dot and Marvin Miller, Gerry Morse, Ed Muller, Hermine Newman, George Solomon, Gary C. Stein, Bea and Norman Teitle, Stan Tiner, Joe and Etta Weisman, George White, Fred Wiseman.

Glossary

The English transliteration and pronunciation of certain Hebrew and Yiddish words is hardly an exact science. These entries are presented informally and may not follow strict lexicographic rules.

aleeyah: the honor of being called up to recite a blessing over the Torah
aliyah: the term for going to live in Israel; literally, a moving up
apikoros, apikorsim (pl.): an atheist
Arbeiter Ring: Workmen's Circle
Bar Mitzvah: the ceremony at which a thirteen-year-old boy becomes a member of the congregation; the boy himself. Often used as a verb.
baruch: blessed
barucha: a blessing
Bas Mitzvah, Bat Mitzvah: the ceremony at which a thirteen-year-old girl becomes a member of the congregation. This ceremony is not observed by Orthodox Jews.
bema: the dais in the synagogue
bench: to say blessings
bench licht: to bless the candles, usually said of the Sabbath candles
beys midrash: a house of study
bris: the circumcision ceremony, performed eight days after the male is born
bubbe mayses: grandmothers' tales
chachem: a wise person
chachma: wisdom
chai: the Hebrew word for life, often inscribed on a charm
L'chayim: the toast "To life"
challah: the braided bread eaten on the Sabbath and at other celebrations
Chanukah: the Festival of Lights, celebration of the victory by the Maccabees
Chasid, Chasidim (pl.): a member of a pious, mystic Jewish sect begun in the eighteenth century
chaya: a wild animal

chazan: a cantor

cheder: Hebrew school

chevra kedisha: a burial society

cholent: a meat and vegetable dish, cooked overnight and often eaten on Saturday

chumish: the five books of Moses; the Torah

chutzpah: gall, nerve

cochaleyn: a bungalow in the Catskills with cooking facilities

cutlettin: lean meat chopped and made into patties

daven: to pray

din: justice

dinst: a housemaid

emes, emet: the truth

eppis: something; perhaps; debatable; a little

ferd ganovim: horse thieves

fleyshik: pertaining to meat and dishes prepared with meat. Fleyshik foods cannot be eaten with milchik foods.

Galitzianer: a Jew from Galicia, a province controlled alternately by Poland and Austria

galut: the Diaspora; exile

glat kosher: extraordinarily kosher. Glat is smooth, unblemished.

goy, goyim (pl.), goyisha (adj.): Gentile

gribiness: fried pieces of chicken skin or meat left after fat is rendered

Haftarah: the chapter from the Prophets read by the Bar Mitzvah

Haggadah: the book containing the story of the exodus from Egypt and the rituals of Passover, read at the seder

hakoras ha-tov: the acknowledgment of good

Halacha, Halachot (pl.): Jewish law

hamantashen: pastries, shaped like Haman's hat, eaten at Purim

helzel: stuffed intestine, a delicacy

heymish, heymisher: unpretentious, warm, friendly, homelike

Kaddish: the mourner's prayer

kalyeka: an inept, awkward person; literally, a cripple

karpas: a green vegetable, one of the symbolic foods eaten at the seder

kasha varnishkes: groats with noodles

kashrut, kashruth: ritual dietary laws; the observance of the laws

kavalat: the Friday evening services ushering in the Sabbath

kibbutz: a collective farm or settlement in Israel

Kiddush: the blessing over the wine

kipah: Hebrew for skullcap

kishka: a sausage of intestine casing stuffed with seasoned matzo meal

kishkes: the gut

k'nach: a blow, a smack

knobel: dumplings

koloel: an institution where adults study Torah and Talmud

kop: the head

kreplach: dumplings

kugel: a pudding, usually made of noodles, sometimes of potatoes

kumsitz: an informal get-together

kurva: a prostitute

landsman, landsleit (pl.): a fellow countryman

Litvak (n. and adj.): a Lithuanian Jew. Litvaks and Galitzianers were often at odds.

Litvish, Litvisher: Lithuanian

luftmensh, luftmenshen (pl.): an impractical man, a dreamer

lungen und miltz: a stew made of beef lungs and pancreas

mada: secular knowledge; literally, science

mamaligge: cornmeal gruel

mandelin: soup nuts

matzobrei: matzos soaked in eggs and fried in butter

mayrev: the evening prayer service

mechitzah: the partition or screen separating women from men in an Orthodox synagogue

melamed: a teacher

menorah: a candelabra; often denotes the candelabra lighted at Chanukah

meshuga: crazy

mezuzah: a container holding parchment bearing passages from Deuteronomy. It is affixed to the doorpost of a Jewish house.

mikvah: the ritual bath for Jewish women

milchik: pertaining to dairy products

mincha: the afternoon prayer service

minyan, minyanim (pl.): quorum of ten men needed to recite certain prayers

mishegoss: madness

misholoch: a traveling pushka collector

mishpoche: the family

misnagid, misnagdim (pl.), misnagdish (adj.): one who scorned the Chasidim

mitzvah: a commandment; a good deed

mizonos: small cakes eaten at Passover; literally, sustenance

mohel: the man who performs the circumcision

moshav: a cooperative settlement in Israel, with some private ownership

nafka: a prostitute

nisht gedugedocht: something that shouldn't happen; something to be avoided

ohav shalom: May he rest in peace, a phrase said after the name of a dead relative or friend

Oneg Shabbat: a small party following the Friday evening service

oysvorf: a rascal

pareve: food prepared without milk or meat that can be eaten with meat or dairy meals

paskudnyak: a contemptible person

perenah: a featherbed

Pesach: Passover

petcha: jelled broth

peyot (Hebrew); peyes (Yiddish): long earlocks

pilpul: complicated reasoning or analysis; literally, pepper

puch: down; the soft feathers used to stuff a perenah

pushka: a box for collecting charitable contributions

rebbe: a yeshiva teacher; a rabbi; a Chasidic rabbi

Rosh Hashonah: the New Year

schnapps: strong liquor

schnappsel: a little serving of schnapps

Schvayg!: Be quiet!

seder: the Passover feast; literally, prescribed order

Shabbat (Hebrew); Shabbes (Yiddish): the Sabbath

Shabbes goy: a Gentile who did tasks a Jew was forbidden to do on the Sabbath, like lighting a fire or turning on the lights

shachrith: the morning prayer service

shadchen: a matchmaker

shamus: a janitor

shayla: a question about kashrut

sheker: a lie

Shema: opening word, and name of, the prayer that is the Jewish declaration of faith

Shemona Esray: the eighteen benedictions of daily prayer

sheytel: a wig, worn by Orthodox women from the day they marry

shicker: a drunkard

shiksa: a Gentile girl

shiur: a class, a study

shiva: the seven-day mourning period for the dead

shlep: to drag

shmaltz: chicken or goose fat

shmuck: a dope; a son of a bitch

shochet: a ritual slaughterer

shofar: ram's horn. It is blown during Rosh Hashonah services and at the end of Yom Kippur.

sholesh sudos: the three feasts eaten on the Sabbath; colloquially, any of the three

shomer Shabbat (Hebrew); shomer Shabbes (Yiddish): an observer of the Sabbath. Colloquially, the singular form is also used for the plural.

shpatzir: a leisurely walk, a stroll

shtarker: a tough guy; a strong man

shtetl: a small village in Eastern Europe

shtick: a prank; a mode of conduct; a piece of show business

shtraymel: a broad-brimmed black hat, trimmed with velvet or fur, worn by some Orthodox men

shul: a house of worship

shvitz: a steam bath

siddur: a prayer book

Simchas Torah: the holiday, falling on the ninth and last day of Succoth, that honors the Torah

stchav: sour-grass soup

Succoth: the harvest celebration. Celebrants eat in a succah, a shelter made of boughs and decorated with fruits and vegetables

taka: indeed; really

tallis, tallit: a prayer shawl

Talmud: the Mishnah and the Gemara, rabbinic interpretation of biblical law and ethics, and the commentary on them

Talmud Torah: a Hebrew school

tashlich: the symbolic casting away of sins into flowing water, a ceremony performed on Rosh Hashonah

tatela: little father; an affectionate diminutive for a boy

tfillin: the phylacteries

Tisha b'Ab: the ninth day of the month of Ab, a day of fasting in commemoration of the destruction of the Temple in Jerusalem

Torah: the books of Moses; the first five books of the Bible

treyf: unkosher; unclean

tsedaka: charity. Every Jew is enjoined to perform charitable deeds.

tsibila kuchen: an onion roll

tsimmes: a stew of carrots, prunes, raisins, and other fruits and vegetables; colloquially, a big fuss

tsitsis (Yiddish); tsitsit (Hebrew): the fringed undergarment worn by Orthodox men; literally, fringes

tummler: a jokester, the life of the party

ulpan: a live-in, intensive Hebrew-teaching program

verein: a social organization

vilda: a wild one

volkshul: a secular Yiddish school

yahrzeit: the anniversary of a person's death

yarmulka: Yiddish for skullcap

yenta: an old woman; a gossip; a shrew

yeshiva: a school for Talmudic studies; an institution of higher education, both religious and secular

yeshiva bocher: a yeshiva student; a studious young man

yichus: prestige; good lineage

Yiddishkeit: Yiddish lore, culture, custom, and ethos

yingel: a boy; colloquially, a kid

Yizkor: memorial service for the dead

yold: a fool

Yom Kippur: the Day of Atonement

yontif, yom tovim (pl.): a holiday

zetz: a blow; a punch

zeyde: a grandfather

z'mires (Yiddish); z'mirot (Hebrew): songs sung after the Sabbath meal